THE OTHER SIKHS

A View from Eastern India

The Sikhs are universally respectful and proud of their Gurus' intimate contact with eastern India, representing the territories of Assam, Bengal and Orissa under British rule. It may be debated, however, whether the Gurus' disciples are generally aware of how the Panthic message has been transmitted and perceived over the centuries in this part of the country. Their comparative lack of enthusiasm may be partly due to the bulky nature of these sources as well as the difficulty of having them together in a public library or any single private collection. These materials are in regional languages and carry a distinct local flavour, differing significantly from those of the *manjha-malwa-doaba* watershed. They suggest not only the spirit of plurality in Indian cultural traditions, but also Sikhism's intimate link with it. Their identification and appreciation is likely to enrich our understanding of Sikhism in the wider context of the Indian unity and diversity.

The present study seeks to deal with some of these interesting issues recorded in three eastern Indian languages, namely, Assamese, Bengali and Oriya published over a century between the First Sikh War (1845) and the Partition of India (1947). In the process it outlines the history of the Sikhs and reveals how the message of Sikhism has been perceived in the context of different local issues by numerous eastern Indian authors.

Himadri Banerjee holds the Chair of Guru Nanak Professor of Indian History, Department of History, Jadavpur University, Kolkata. His published work includes *Agrarian Society of the Punjab: 1849-1901* (1982). He has also edited a volume for the Indian History Congress entitled *The Khalsa and the Punjab: Studies in Sikh History, to the 19th Century* (2002). He is currently working on a two-volume history of the Sikhs and Sikhism in eastern India.

THE OTHER SIKHS

A View from Eastern India

VOLUME I

Himadri Banerjee

MANOHAR
2007

First published 2003
First paperback edition 2007

ISBN 81-7304-736-7

Published by
Ajay Kumar Jain for
Manohar Publishers & Distributors
4753/23 Ansari Road, Daryaganj
New Delhi 110 002

Typeset at
Digigrafics
New Delhi 110 049

Printed at
Print Perfect
New Delhi 110 064

Distributed in South Asia by
FOUNDATION BOOKS
4381/4, Ansari Road
Daryaganj, New Delhi 110 002
and its branches at Mumbai, Hyderabad,
Bangalore, Chennai, Kolkata

Contents

Preface

THE SIKHS ARE universally respectful and proud of their Gurus' intimate contact with eastern India, representing the territories of Assam, Bengal and Orissa under British rule till 1947. It may be debated, however, whether the Gurus' disciples are generally aware of how the Panthic message has been transmitted and perceived over the centuries in this part of the country. Their comparative lack of enthusiam may be partly due to the bulky nature of these sources as well as the difficulty of having them together in a public library or any single private collection. These materials are in regional languages and carry a distinct local flavour, differing significantly from those of the *manjha-malwa-doaba* watershed. They suggest not only the spirit of plurality in Indian cultural traditions, but also Sikhism's intimate link with it. Their identification and appreciation is likely to enrich our understanding of Sikhism in the wider context of the Indian unity and diversity.

The present study seeks to deal with some of these interesting issues recorded in three eastern Indian languages, namely, Assamese, Bengali and Oriya published over a century between the First Sikh War (1845) and the Partition of India (1947). In the process it outlines the history of the Sikhs and reveals how the message of Sikhism has been perceived in the context of different local issues by numerous eastern Indian authors.

My association with these sources has also made me aware of other categories of indigenous raw materials often lying beyond the reach of the print medium. These represent an arena that has not been dealt with in the present study indicating another level of lively interactions between Sikhism and the local milieu. It may provide interesting insights into the complex transformations and re-adjustments that Sikhism had to make in a predominantly non-Sikh world since its first contact in the medieval days. There is the need, therefore, of an additional volume outlining the history of the local Sikh world engaged in a long dialogue with the wider non-Sikh milieu faraway from its place of birth. This is expected to follow the present study as a companion volume and may offer a refreshing view of how, when and by whom the message of Sikhism was transmitted in eastern India.

Here we are, thus, concerned with two broad levels of response towards the Sikh Panth. The first one mainly revolves round the print world of the intelligentsia of the region. The present work, when taken together with the companion volume, is likely to offer a meaningful and integrated profile of Sikh history and religion within a regional profile of our national polity.

HIMADRI BANERJEE

Acknowledgements

I GREW UP IN A Bengali middle class family during the post-Independence years. Like many of my schoolmates, I was brought up on some of those poems of Rabindranath Tagore highlighting the Sikh tradition of martyrdom and their reverence for the Gurus. We also inherited a part of our parents' faith in Sikh 'prowess'. The Calcutta taxi driver was an embodiment of care, responsibility and civility. It was perhaps a legacy of the Partition holocaust when the Sikhs were 'seen as soldiers in the service of the community'. Except for a brief interlude of tension in the mid-1960s, we have had very little difficulty in our interactions with the Sikhs. The number of Sikh taxi drivers might be going down, but there is a larger number of lorries run and managed by the Sikhs. Many of them have come to regard Calcutta their second home after Punjab, have shared Bengali homes, built gurdwaras and become an integral part of our urban experience. They have also brought with them *palak-paneer*, *maki di roti*, *sarson da saag*, and *dhaba* culture. Bengali culinary habits has by now come to accommodate all these. Sikh sardars have no doubt figured in occasional Bengali jokes, often imported into the Calcutta lifeline through Bengali tourists visiting northern Indian cities, particularly New Delhi. Days have thus rolled on during the early decades of the Nehruvian era after the Partition.

Our days of reckoning with the Sikhs soon followed. In the subsequent decades, our understanding of Sikhism has passed through many trajectories and by-lanes and evoked sharp reactions. These were perhaps a part of our larger political experiences of the 1970s, when many of our religious minorities were increasingly made to feel that they should come closer to what we call today the mainstream culture of the Indian nation. As many of us were marching towards an *Akhand Bharat* from Kashmir to Kanya-kumari, we managed to abandon a large part of our liberal, tolerant, and plural traditions respected and nurtured from our younger days. Whatever little autonomy and the public space the Sikhs were still enjoying for their *chardikala* experiences were increasingly narrowed down in the process. They could feel that these were being steadily brought within the ambit of the state political scanner. Perhaps there was a growing feeling of uncertainty and restlessness among a section of those Sikhs who tried to grapple with the implications of the State's interventions in their community life and politics. It was widely believed by many of them that Punjab tragedy (1980s) owes much of its unfortunate political implications and bloodshed to the equations worked out by the power-brokers of New Delhi in late 1970s.

Our perceptions of the Sikh world also underwent a significant change during these years. The Sikhs, so long projected as archetypes of national heroism and sacrifice in our fight against colonial rule, were increasingly viewed as dangerous forces threatening our national life and security. It stimulated a general hate campaign in many of the northern Indian cities against turbaned youths with the five Ks. The Sikhs were also made to feel that they were viewed as threats to public order and hence to be kept under close observation. Even in Calcutta, those who had still some sympathy and support for the sufferings and humiliations of the Sikhs of distant Punjab were decried as agents of secessionist forces. Sometimes their mails were intercepted so that these may not create any problem in the maintenance of peace and security in this part of India.

With these experiences in the background, I entered the arena of Sikh studies. Those were days when saying anything good about the Sikhs and showing interest about their history and culture were often regarded as unhealthy academic gestures. My problems were compounded owing to the scattered state of the sources of my enquiry. These lay dispersed in different public libraries and private collections as far as Dibrugarh in Assam to Berhampur in Orissa. Later on I would find invaluable materials preserved in other parts of India and even beyond. How could I bring them together without the support and cooperation of others?

It is my great privilege that I could gradually collect a sizable part of these materials over a period of nearly two decades. This was made possible only by the support of many of my friends and others from different academic institutions and research organizations. I could even procure valuable materials from private collections not visited by me through the courtesy of people whom I had not met earlier in my life. In course of these years, a few of my friends from Assam and Orissa steadily kept me in touch with a still larger number of good people scattered in different urban centres and mufassil towns over a thousand miles from the plains of the Brahmaputra valley to the shores of Orissa. They did make me aware of many similar men who did not necessarily belong to my discipline and interest. They offered me food, provided shelter, accompanied me to different public libraries and introduced me to people who in their turn sometimes extended help without expecting any return. Subsequently, I wrote back to many of them seeking clarifications on certain relevant issues of my enquiry and they generally responded providing necessary details with encouraging words. I regard it my privilege to have known many of them all these years through different stages of my research. Many of them are no more, but their memories remain my priceless possessions.

It is difficult to remember all of my friends and well-wishers. I must record my deep debt to many of them because it would not have been possible to complete the present work without their encouragement and support. They belong to conflicting shades of political opinions, coming from different parts of the country, speaking dissimilar languages, and representing various cultural traditions. Their love and warmth made me aware of the plural traditions of our country. On certain points, these traditions are so close to one another and yet so distinct and different, that their accommodations have generally been possible only through mutual self-respect and toleration. I would be failing in my duty if I do not remember these experiences after years of mutual give and take with many of them.

It is perhaps convenient that I should start from my friends and senior colleagues of Punjab, Haryana and Delhi who still respond to the numerous demands I have to make. Perhaps this has been going on since my initiation to Punjab studies more than three decades ago. It is likely to be a long list and may conveniently begin from my Patiala friends of the last three decades. Then I would come round to Delhi via Amritsar, Chandigarh, Shimla and Kurukshetra. I remember with deep love and appreciation the help of Devinder Kumar Verma, Parm Bakhshish Singh, Dalbir Singh Dhillon, Dharam Singh, Shiv Kumar Gupta (Punjabi University, Patiala), Radha and Harish Sharma, Joginder Singh, Sulakhan Singh, Madanjit Kaur, Sabinderjit Singh Sagar, Balwant Singh Dhillon, Harish Puri (Guru Nanak Dev University, Amritsar), Kharak Singh, Kirpal Singh, Gurdarshan Singh Dhillon (Institute of Sikh Studies, Chandigarh), Indu Banga, Kamlesh Mohan (Panjab University, Chandigarh), Ahsan R. Khan (Himachal Pradesh University, Shimla), Kundanlal Tuteja, Gianeswar Khurana (Kurukshetra

University, Kurukshetra), Mohinder Singh (Bhai Vir Singh Sahitya Sadan, New Delhi) and above all, Sisir Kumar Das (Delhi University, Delhi).

Since my major work primarily revolves round the different eastern Indian sources, I would be only too happy to record the inputs of my friends, contemporaries, senior academicians, teachers and colleagues nearer to my home in Assam, Bangladesh, Bihar, Orissa and West Bengal. They have extended all possible help during these years. Here I may conveniently start from the furthest point from Calcutta, i.e. Dibrugarh and close on my own metropolis. Compared to Punjab, it is perhaps not a long journey, but requires frequent halts at different places. Here I remember with a deep sense of gratitude the support of Nagen Saikia, Swarnalata Baruah, Sheila Bora, Sruti Deb Goswami, Dambarudhar Nath (Dibrugarh University, Dibrugarh), Prasenjit Choudhury (Chabua College, Chabua), Prafulla Chandra Bezbarua (Sibsagar), Ramesh Chandra Kalita (Tezpur), Prafulladatta Goswami, Hiren Gohain, Sailen Bharali, Parikshit Hazarika, Jogendra Narayan Phukan, Sudhashu Tunga, Birinchi Kumar Medhi (Gauhati University, Guwahati), Dudulmani Sharma (Anneshwa, Guwahati), Dhyan Singh (Assamese Sikh Association, Guwahati), Bhrigu Bharali (Directorate of Historical and Antiquarian Studies, Guwahati), Muffakarul M. Islam, Nurur Rahman Khan (Dhaka University, Dhaka), N.H.M. Abu Bakar (Chittagong University, Chittagong), Surendra Gopal, Sumanta Niyogi (Patna University, Patna), Ved Prakash (Guru Gobind Singh College, Patna), Brajanath Rath (Balasore), Sanatan Mohanty, Apurba Roy, Ratnakar Barik (Bhadrakh), Natabar Samantaray (Bhubaneswar), Manmath Nath Das, Atul Chandra Pradhan, Ashoke Patnaik, Baishab Charan Samal, Basanta Kumar Mallick (Utkal University, Bhubaneswar), Manmath Kumar Samal (Orissa State Museum, Bhubaneswar), Pathani Patnaik, Ratnakar Chaini, Shyamsundar Mishra, Lakshmikanata Mishra (Cuttack), Gaganendranath Dash, Bauri Bandhu Kar, Amiya Pattanayak, Sishir Kumar Panda, Lakshmi Narayan Raut (Berhampur University, Berhampur), Neeladri Bhusan Harichandan, Suchibrata Sen, Sandip Basu Sarbadhikari (Visva-Bharati, Santiniketan), Anuradha Roy, Mihir Roy, Somnath Roy (Burdwan University, Bardhaman), Swapan Mazumdar (Jadavpur University, Calcutta), Balai Chandra Barui, Nikhiles Guha, Smriti Kumar Sarkar (Kalyani University, Kalyani), Binay Bhusan Chaudhuri, Barun De, Ranajit Sen, Basudeb Chatterjee, Bhaskar Chakrabarty, Suranjan Das, Ramkrishna

Chatterjee (Calcutta University, Calcutta), Pradyumna Bhattacharya, Samik Bandyopadhyay, Pratap Kumar Mukherjee, Ashoke Upadhyay, Shyamal Sau (Calcutta), Tripti Chaudhuri, Chidananda Bhattacharya, Subir Dhar, Binode Kumar Das, Ranjit Kumar Roy, Sujata Mukherjee, Rajsekhar Basu, Sanjukta DasGupta, Sumana Ghosh (Rabindra Bharati University). Many of the respected Sikhs of Calcutta like Saran Singh, Narinder Pal Singh, Dimphy Gurvinder Singh (The Sikh Review), Bhupinder S. Sarna (Desh Darpan), Khazan Singh, Narinder Singh (Sikh Gurmat Society), Sohan Singh (Guru Tegh Bahadur Hospital), Mohinder Singh Gill, Man Singh Grewal (Badi Sikh Sangat Gurdwara), Jagmohan Singh Gill (Dum Dum Gurdwara), Ramavatar Singh, Manmouji Singh (Chhoti Sikh Sangat) always remained kind towards me and never hesitated to offer as much support as possible in my research.

Three of my esteemed friends beyond India offered valuable comments on my draft. They are Hew McLeod (University of Otago, New Zealand), Joe O'Connell (University of Toronto, Canada) and Karen Leonard (University of California, Irvine). I am thankful to all of them. Finally, I must record my debt to two organizations. One is the European Institute of Sikh Studies, London. It offered me an opportunity for a brief period of work in the India Office Library and Records, London. During my stay in Harpenden, Baljit S. Bagga and his family tried to make my stay all comfortable. Later on, the Indian Council of Historical Research, New Delhi, awarded me a two-year fellowship. It enabled to complete my draft. I am also deeply thankful to Manohar Publishers & Distributors for bringing out the book.

This long list of acknowledgement only confirms my conviction that the present work should be dedicated to all of them in recognition of my deep debt towards them.

HIMADRI BANERJEE

CHAPTER I

Introduction

IT IS DIFFICULT to assess the extent of the impact left on the Indian subcontinent by the Sikh ethno-nationalism in the past two decades. Controversy continues on the nature and depth of the relations between the Sikhs and other communities in the country. Some are sceptical about whether the Sikhs would remain a part of the Indian polity in the twenty-first century. A few have come forward to reassess the old fabric of Hindu-Sikh relations. Political analysts, who locate the root cause of the problem in the centralization provided for in the Indian constitution, suggest pluralism, regionalism and decentralization of power as the solution.[1] Some have been scathing about contemporary religious intolerance alleging that this has led to the blood-letting in Punjab.[2] The critics have been highly censorious about the assimilationist rhetoric of the majority community and have pleaded for a change in their aggressive attitude towards the Sikhs. Even the more recent Hindu-Sikh political honeymoon in Punjab has been projected as a marriage of convenience that could yield temporary electoral success, but could hardly offer any permanent 'healing touch' to the Sikhs' scars.

I

The bloodbath in Punjab and the search for its causes are bound to agitate students and researchers in the field. It is now generally

[1] Paul Brass has drawn our attention to the 'persistent centralization and concentration of power in New Delhi' in the post-Nehruvian era. Cf. *Ethnicity and Nationalism: Theory and Comparison*, New Delhi reprint, 1996, p. 317.

[2] According to one recent estimate, nearly twenty-five thousand people died in this violence. Shinder Purewal, *Sikh Ethnonationalism and the Political Economy of Punjab*, New Delhi 2000, p. 19. For a detailed discussion of the various aspects of Punjab violence, see Abida Samiuddin (ed.), *The Punjab Violence: Challenge & Response*, New Delhi 1989.

admitted that Operation Blue Star (1984) had only further complicated the Punjab problem. Perhaps the Sikhs have not yet recovered from the wound that it inflicted on their psyche. I had the opportunity of visiting the Golden Temple a few months after the anti-Sikh riots of November 1984. I met some young Sikh students of Guru Nanak Dev University near its *parikarma*. We talked about the Sikh insurgency and the activities of the Indian security forces. In the course of the discussions, one of them said in anguish, 'You [Hindus] have never bothered to appreciate our difficulties and tried to find out the causes of our [Sikhs] grievances. You will never understand what a disgrace it was for us to have the Indian army entering the Golden Temple complex. Do not expect any cooperation from us in future.' I had not much difficulty in sensing his grief and understanding the Sikh mind. The repeated use of the words 'you' and 'us' revealed the yawning gap that had opened up between Sikhs and non-Sikhs. The majority community was anxious to put down militancy but it did not care to appreciate the depth of their misery. To many, 'Sikhs' had become synonymous with terrorists and fundamentalists, hell-bent on fragmenting India.[3] Perhaps they would have been happy to read in the face of every Sikh youth the state-sponsored 'satanic' image of Jarnail Singh Bhindranwale. The impression of the Sikhs' 'otherness' from the rest of the Indians has over the years deepened misunderstanding and botched efforts to get to the bottom of the Punjab problem. Exchanging views with a cross-section of Sikhs at home and abroad, I have had the impression that many of them were losing faith in the bona fide of the majority community. A few of them even talked of a separate and distinct Sikh ethnicity in Punjab.[4]

Since then much water has flown down the Yamuna-Ravi watershed. It is time to unravel the social and political background that has led to the frequent blood-letting in Punjab in the last two decades of the twentieth century. How did this change surface so suddenly? Hindus and Sikhs fought the British shoulder to shoulder in the national movement and Sikhs saved so many Hindu lives in the bloody days of Partition (1947). Why have they suddenly grown hostile to Hindus? Theories of relative deprivation or uneven

[3] Saran Singh, 'The Sikh Image', *The Statesman*, 9 November 1997.

[4] Dipankar Gupta's recent study has reviewed some of the causes leading to the development of 'a single ethnic identity' among the Sikhs in the 1980s. Cf. *The Context of Ethnicity: Sikh Identity in a Comparative Perspective*, Delhi 1996, pp. 69-91.

development have not been of much help in understanding the Sikh mindset. But how would one explain the rise of Sikh militancy in a state like Punjab, which has had links with the rest of the Indian subcontinent and which contributed in no small measure to the country's national movement?[5] Sociologists, anthropologists, political analysts and others are working on the mystery. Historians need to study past evidence in search of possible seeds of antagonism. The Singh Sabha reformers, claiming and analysing a distinct Sikh identity towards the end of the nineteenth century, could represent one of these points in the history of Hindu-Sikh tensions. A section of them went beyond their initial 'We are not Hindus' to reject almost all social relations with the Hindus and were emphatic about their separateness, evoking in its turn a bitter Hindu reaction.

On the all-India level, the period was generally marked by assertions of communal separateness. On several political issues, Hindus and Muslims were almost at daggers drawn. Sikhs were not the only victims of the virus. Sanatani Hindus and the Arya Samajists were making communal assertions. They also fought the Sikhs. Litigation throve. The communal award in the twentieth century electoral exercise, the enforcement of *Anand Karaj* legislation, the institution of *suddhi*, the bitter controversy over the choice of Punjabi or Hindi as medium of instruction, the recognition of a separate legal status for Sikhs, the demand for an independent homeland for the Panth—all these added up to exacerbate Hindu-Sikh relations in Punjab.

II

There have been several works of research documenting and analysing the bitter-sweet relations between Hindus and Sikhs in pre-Independence India.[6] Scholars have studied Sikh separatism in the

[5] According to the Census of 1991 roughly one out of every four Indian Sikhs live outside Punjab. M.S. Gill, 'Distribution of the Sikh Population in India', *The Sikh Review*, February 1999, pp. 68-71.

[6] Kenneth W. Jones, *Arya Dharam: Hindu Consciousness in 19th-Century Punjab*, New Delhi 1976; Mohinder Singh, *The Akali Movement*, New Delhi 1978; K.L. Tuteja, *Sikh Politics, 1920-40*, Kurukshetra 1984; Richard G. Fox, *Lions of the Punjab: Culture in the Making*, Berkeley 1985; Rajiv A. Kapur, *Sikh Separatism: The Politics of Faith*, London 1986; Joseph T. O'Connell, et al. (eds.), *Sikh History and Religion in the Twentieth Century*,Toronto 1988; Harjot Oberoi, *The Construction of Religious Boundaries: Culture, Identity and Diversity in the Sikh Tradition*, New Delhi 1994.

historical context, the struggle for gurdwara reform, which ran parallel to Gandhi's Non-cooperation Movement, the alliance and break-up of alliance between the Shiromani Akali Dal and the other political parties contingent on circumstances, etc. Generally speaking, they provide a critical perspective of the Sikh point of view of the situation. But these works have little to offer on the thought and outlook of the non-Sikhs residing beyond Punjab. In any case, the Sikh point of view and the non-Sikh point of view would be different. Given the multilingual, multiracial and multi-religious character of Indian society, perceptions and reactions would vary from time to time and from region to region. The geographical distance of an area from Punjab, its specific religious experience, political outlook and cultural ambience are only too likely to provide yet another perspective to the study of Sikh history. Not enough importance has been attached to those factors.

On the other hand, Sikhism and Sikh history have interested people of different regions outside Punjab. Researches on the Sikh Panth often show a Punjab orientation. Undoubtedly, Punjab is the home and cradle of Sikh history. But one cannot wish away its past contact and present interaction with areas outside Punjab. A sizeable section of Sikhs came to be scattered in different parts of India before Independence. This goes back to the days of Guru Nanak. His *udasi* stands for spreading religion while travelling in different corners of India. Writings in Persian and Assamese record the visit of the ninth Guru Tegh Bahadur to eastern India.[7] The tenth Guru Gobind Singh spent his early years and his last days outside Punjab. Three of the five Sikh *takhats* are in Punjab, but two of them are outside. Sikh religious texts claim that most of the first *panjpiare* in Sikh history came from different parts of India. Again the importance of the numerous non-Punjab gurdwaras has generally been highlighted in various discussions about the proposed All India Sikh Gurdwaras Bill.[8]

It will be easier to understand the distinctiveness and importance of the regional perceptions of the Sikh experience, if one concentrates on a particular region at a time. Pluralism is gaining ground in the

[7] Ved Prakash, *The Sikhs in Bihar,* Patna 1981, pp. 39-76; Trilochan Singh, *Guru Tegh Bahadur: Prophet and Martyr,* Delhi 1967, pp. 189-256; Surya Kumar Bhuyan, *Lachit Barphukan,* Gauhati 1947, pp. 108-10.

[8] Harbans Singh, 'All India Sikh Gurdwaras Bill—Its Background and the Main Features', *The Sikh Review*, September 1998, pp. 32-7.

evaluation of the cultures and traditions of different regions in India. The present politico-cultural ethos sustains such pluralism. A survey of regional views of Sikhism therefore should be quite in order. But we are not altogether unaware of the various limitations of the study of regional history as pointed out by Bernard Cohn nearly three decades ago.[9] Here we may go for it without rigidly restricting our study to any definitive territorial limit. On the contrary, we would prefer to review cultural interactions among different linguistic groups beyond narrow regional boundaries. A close study of texts produced outside Punjab, responding to Sikh history, can facilitate an analysis of the cause, nature and level of interaction between Sikhs and non-Sikhs. Thus a study of regional responses to Sikh history and religion may provide an interesting alternative to the kind of Sikh studies generally pursued in some of the universities of Indian Punjab or in the West.

III

Thirty years ago, Ganda Singh, the doyen of Sikh historical research in post-Independence India, highlighted the regional angle in the study of the Sikh Panth. In his valuable bibliography on the history of Punjab, he listed many books on Sikhism written in other regional languages, opening the possibilities of a comparative assessment that he does not attempt.[10] Later, Gerald N. Barrier studied the history, philosophy and religion of the Singh Sabha period (1873-1918), referring in the course of his analysis to several biographies of the Sikh Gurus and translations of their religious preachings in Hindi and Urdu.[11] But as his study was centred on Punjab, there is virtually no light on the perspectives outside the state. Of late, some universities in the West have been seeking information about the Sikh diaspora and making a close study of the phenomenon. Several works published in the United Kingdom, the United States of America and Canada testify to significant research on the Sikh diaspora.[12] But these sources say little about regional outlooks within India.

[9] Bernard S. Cohn, *An Anthropologist Among the Historians and Other Essays*, Delhi 1994, pp. 100-35.

[10] Ganda Singh, *A Bibliography of the Panjab*, Patiala 1966, pp. 212-17.

[11] N. Gerald Barrier, *The Sikhs and their Literature*, Delhi 1971.

[12] For further discussion, see John Stratton Hawley and Gurinder Singh Mann (eds.), *Studying the Sikhs: Issues for North America*, New York 1993; W.H. McLeod, *Historical Dictionary of Sikhism*, Lanham 1995, pp. 313-18.

It will, however, be untrue to say that materials in Indian regional languages have not been discussed before. At least two scholars have made significant beginnings in the last few years. The first is Kulwant Singh Grewal, who brought out in 1967 a booklet citing the sources in Bengali on Guru Gobind Singh.[13] Like Ganda Singh, Grewal also cited only a few books. But while Ganda Singh had provided a glimpse of a comparative study of Sikh history in regional languages, Grewal confined himself to Bengali. Of course, Grewal mentioned more Bengali books than Ganda Singh on Guru Gobind Singh.

The researchers mentioned so far kept their enquiry more or less confined to the study of bibliographies; with the exception of R.K. DasGupta, who referred to the features, trends and importance of Sikh studies in Bengali.[14] He dealt with quite a few Bengali writers, referring in some detail to their content and backdrop. But his discussion was restricted only to some very familiar Bengali works on Sikhism. In order to present a large canvas of Sikh history in a limited space, he had to leave out many writers of note. He was perhaps acquainted with perceptions in other Indian languages but did not attempt any comparative review.

IV

It was the 1980s. Punjab was a battlefield. In some quarters of Punjab there was talk of severing ties with the Indian Union. On the other hand, during the period, there were also people who wrote about the past ties between Hindus and Sikhs. But nobody recalled Sikh studies in the regional languages, a field opened up by Ganda Singh, Kulwant Singh Grewal or R.K. DasGupta. In the changed context, any reference to them may have been considered an 'academic backlash'.[15] These materials could have provided an insight into the attitude of non-Sikhs to Sikh history and religion, which in its turn could have offered a better understanding of the embittered Hindu-Sikh relations of those days. These materials

[13] Kulwant Singh Grewal, *A Bibliography of References in Bengali to Guru Gobind Singh*, Patiala 1967.

[14] R.K. DasGupta, 'Influence of Sikhism in Bengal', in Gurmukh Nihal Singh (ed.), *Guru Nanak: His Life, Time and Teachings*, New Delhi 1988, pp. 207-16.

[15] I have borrowed the phrase from Bruce LaBrack. For its significance, see his 'Sikhs Real and Ideal: Discussion of Text and Context in the Description of Overseas Sikh Communities', in Mark Juergensmyer and N. Gerald Barrier (eds.), *Sikh Studies: Comparative Perspectives on a Changing Tradition*, Berkeley 1979, p. 132.

record the perceptions of non-Sikhs and offer a mosaic of the Sikh profile constructed over a century in different parts of India. Surprisingly enough, they did not interest modern scholars. Perhaps these writings were not recognized as a part of our larger historical tradition. It is true that some of these authors were engaged in popular writing not based on cast-iron evidence. Imagination played an interesting role in their reconstruction of the past.

There is more to the materials than what we have discussed so far. These regional writings beginning in the first half of the nineteenth century did not immediately manifest themselves 'in a consciously constructed alternate historiography, but as an integral part of the modernizing social movements' of the period.[16] In the second half of the century, when they sought to convey the spirit of nationalism, their agenda was 'an Indian historiography of India'—it 'was an agenda for self-representation, for setting out to claim for the nation a past that was not distorted by foreign interpreters'.[17] But not all these writers were historians—they were poets, playwrights, littérateurs and others. Their imagination was not circumscribed by archives. Folk culture contributes a lot to such writings. Their importance in the development of regional attitudinal trends cannot be underrated. They sometimes take the reader to a world of fancy not fettered by any strict academic syllabus or professional training.[18] Growing bitterness against British rule as well as the development of an Indian national consciousness played a pivotal role in the perspectives on the history of India offered by these writings. The reconstruction of India's past was motivated by the understandable pride in the glory and legacy of a very ancient civilization. Many of them felt that a few foreign authors had done a caricature of India's past and it required a rectification for the defence of higher national interests. This encouraged the invention of a new tradition and led to the use of 'history as a legitimator of action and cement of group cohesion'. While projecting the reconstructed past, they also talked about the nature of British rule, Indian nationhood, the fighting

[16] K.N. Pannikar, *Culture, Ideology and Hegemony: Intellectual and Social Consciousness in Colonial India,* New Delhi 1995, p. 112.

[17] Partha Chatterjee, *The Nation and its Fragments: Colonial and Postcolonial Histories,* Delhi 1994, p. 74. See also Ranajit Guha, *An Indian Historiography of India: A Nineteenth Century Agenda and its Implications,* Calcutta 1988.

[18] In this regard I would be drawing attention to the serial *The Sword of Tipu Sultan* telecast through Doordarshan in recent times. It belongs to the category of imaginary history.

tradition of the Sikhs under the Gurus and the 'brutal punishments' meted out to them by 'Muslim rulers of medieval days'.

It is hardly necessary to say that the storehouse of materials in regional languages did not grow in a day. They represent the experiences of different linguistic groups evolving over centuries. These continue to grow, perhaps with modifications. A large part of these writings became a natural vehicle for the contemporary political aspirations of the community and drew momentum from them. They also reflect a process of cultural mobilization often pronounced in political phrases or religious idioms. They trace their roots to diverse issues at the local level. Other factors like caste, class, gender, ethnicity and region added diversity to them. Biography, short stories, poetry, novels, plays, essays and travel accounts constituted the bulk of these writings. The authors differed in age and occupation. Some of them went to Punjab and took up studies after associating with the Sikhs. They presented to their readers the tales of the Sikhs of distant Punjab in their respective mother tongues. Some of them were path-makers. It is also relevant to consider what social and political environs produced them, and what kind of material they chose in Sikh studies. Today Sikh studies have broken many barriers and expanded to new frontiers, but are we to reject the regional Sikh studies for a century as unsophisticated dross?

V

The present discussion is based on those materials concerning Sikh history and religion that are available in three distinct and separate regional languages—Assamese, Bengali and Oriya spoken over more than 1,000 km of territories from the shores of Orissa to the foothills of the Himalayas in Assam. These three languages traced their common origin from Sanskrit and continued to remain one and almost indistinguishable till the middle of the twelfth century. Later on they assumed distinct forms in the sixteenth century. Geographical proximity facilitated their mutual give and take throughout medieval days. Both thematic and stylistic aspects helped to establish their closeness. 'These are not just superficial features: they point to deeper, underlying, complex aesthetic preferences and prejudices.' They also underline 'local ethos and image' and offer 'sub-regional affinities and affiliations'.[19]

[19] K. Ayyappa Paniker (ed.), *Medieval Indian Literature: An Anthology*, vol. I, *Survey and Selections*, New Delhi 1997, pp. xxxiii-iv.

Spoken by a population of more than 100 million now spread over India and Bangladesh, they are all closely related to each other and with Bihari (Hindi) constitute the eastern group of the Indo-Aryan language-family. Since they originated from the same source, these three languages share several common features in morphology and vocabulary. Likewise, people speaking these languages have several common cultural characteristics. Obviously, one can expect certain similarities in the attitude of the authors writing in these languages. Recent researches have thrown interesting light on the variety and nature of exchanges among different regional languages. Valuable theories have been expounded. Many old beliefs are being re-examined. We may question the validity of the statement—'Indian literature is one, though written in different languages'—uttered in the context of the Indian nation-building in the post-Independence years. The theory tends to ignore the distinctiveness of the different regional languages. While studying the pursuit of Sikhism in the east, one cannot deny the separate identity of these three languages. Bengali had the 'pride of place'[20] and that perhaps partly explains why the two other languages, namely, Assamese and Oriya, sometimes tried to stay apart a bit. Clashes took place, too. Initiation in Sikh studies did not happen simultaneously. As a result, there were divergent trends.

The role of Hindi no doubt has to be recognized. Colonial rule in Calcutta in the nineteenth century brought forth new impulses in the three eastern languages and that touched Hindi as well.[21] Sikh studies in Hindi began in the medieval days, later on in the nineteenth century it got a new direction. But the study of Sikhism in Hindi was increasingly linked with the Hindi heartland beyond eastern India and so we have generally kept it out. Only references have been made to explain the ongoing process in the three eastern regional languages.

VI

The period covered in the study stretches from the First Sikh War (1845) to the emergence of an independent India (1947). Sometimes,

[20] Sisir Kumar Das, *A History of Indian Literature 1911-56: Struggle for Freedom: Triumph and Tragedy*, New Delhi 1995, p. xiv.

[21] R.S. McGregor, 'Bengal and the Development of Hindi, 1850-1900', *South Asia Review*, January 1972, pp. 137-46; Krishnabehari Mishra and Ram Vyas Pande (eds.), *Hindi Sahitya: Bangiya Bhumika*, Calcutta 1983.

to do justice to the evolution of events in the eastern region, departures have been made from the time frame. The two extremities are landmarks in the study of Sikh history. The First Sikh War precipitated the dissolution of the independent Sikh State. The travails of Partition confronted the Sikhs with another trial. During these years, Sikh society changed. Likewise, political changes occurred in eastern India. How Sikh studies were enriched in the process calls for attention.

During the period, British rule contributed to the steady erosion and gradual breakdown of the old political framework, social understanding and economic relationships. It led to many changes, like the introduction of railways, development of markets and spread of Western education. All this strengthened the colonial grip over the Indian subcontinent. Urbanization came while the new educational system spawned new ideas and new social groups drawn from professionals, merchants, small entrepreneurs and service persons. Their aspirations and ideals no doubt remained varied and complex. Many of them became increasingly conscious of the colonial domination and felt the 'urge of having a sense of national self-respect in relation to their colonial masters'. They sought to express their hopes and frustrations as well as new-found self-respect and confidence through their mother tongues. By this time the British Raj had also brought in the benefits of 'print-capitalism'.[22] Books, newspapers, magazines, etc., were printed cheap and in large numbers and reached faster to countless people. Regional languages were 'standardized' and a bridge was built between town and country. Writers expressed views in their own language, created literature in their mother tongue providing an insight into the local mind. The process was also an exercise in ventilating their patriotism and a sort of anti-British feeling. A search for an Indian ethos began and the roots of the nation were sought in past heritage. Historical studies were adapted to the needs of the time and a great literary movement had its origin in this trend. Eastern regional languages received a new radiance and range and the readers in the vernaculars were exposed to a new experience.

Calcutta was the nodal point. The Calcutta middle class 'played a pre-eminent role' 'in creating the dominant forms of nationalist culture' and mediated 'at least some of the new ideas and influences

[22] For its long term impact, see Benedict Anderson, *Imagined Communities: Reflections on the Origin and Spread of Nationalism,* London 1991, pp. 18-45.

which shaped modern Indian life'.[23] The dawn of a new awareness in the city soon sent its message east to Dhaka, Chittagong, Sibsagar, Jorhat and Guwahati and south-west to Balasore, Baripada, Cuttack, Puri, etc. It is not always clear when and how the writers in their mother tongues started their quest for nationhood and Indianness. Their own opinions differed in this regard. But it was in the second half of the nineteenth century that the corpus of their work multiplied and their writing gave a new dimension to historically oriented writing. Sikh studies in the east were an outcome.

VII

There can be no two opinions about the fact that during the period the Brahmos in Bengal and Orissa were the first to make enquiries about Sikhism. They were against idolatry, they believed in one God and fulminated against the complicated and costly rituals of Hinduism. In doing so, they often recalled the religion, philosophy and protestantism of Guru Nanak. But the Brahmo enthusiasm about Guru Nanak did not apply to the next nine Gurus. Here lie the characteristics and limitations of the Brahmo writers.

Sikh studies in eastern India that primarily started with Guru Nanak as the focal point later started expanding. The lives of the other Sikh Gurus were added, and the eighteenth century Sikh struggle, the Khalsa Raj of Ranjit Singh and even the narrative of the non-violent Akali *satyagrahis* were incorporated. The copious and diverse materials of these Sikh studies were assembled by a number of well known and unknown writers hailing from places as far apart as Lahore and Chittagong. The question may naturally arise as to why these writers got interested in Sikh history and religion and wrote on the Sikh Panth for over a century. What strata of society and professions did they represent? And how many of them entered the arena with primary source materials at their command? Did they record all praise for the Sikh Gurus and hail the followers of Sikh Panth as heroes or did they have any serious reservation about these reconstructed personalities? In their pursuit of Sikhism, they also wrote a lot of things about contemporary

[23] Tapan Raychaudhuri, *Europe Reconsidered: Perceptions of the West in Nineteenth Century Bengal,* New Delhi 1988, pp. ix-x; Sumit Sarkar, *Writing Social History*, New Delhi 1997, p. 170.

Indian politics and society, which they could not express in any other way. The symbolic nature of the quest in the eastern region for the Sikhs was somewhat different from the pursuit of Punjab-based Sikh studies dominated by Sikh scholars. This difference merits our attention.

Another characteristic of the eastern Indian Sikh studies is the diversity of outlooks displayed by the writers. Some of them are engaged in research on the life of the Sikh Gurus and their history with the logical, factual approach of a thoughtful historian. Some others have relied on religious faith or poetic imagination. That is why considerable differences mark these writings as regards the definition of history, its methodology, coverage and purpose. It is necessary to consider how such diversity of viewpoints affected the history of the period beginning with the role of religious reformer, played by Guru Nanak, to the establishment of the Khalsa by Guru Gobind Singh and the ensuing conflict of the eighteenth century. One cannot dismiss the fact that Guru Nanak and Guru Gobind Singh have been presented differently by different writers. Sikh Gurus as depicted in eastern languages sometimes may differ from the delineation by Punjabi historians not merely in lifestyle but also in their language, dress, political philosophy and religious understanding. The many strands of the movement for religious reform in the nineteenth century, the ever-changing perception of the national identity, the increasing importance of the anti-British movement, the noxious vapours generated by the forces of communalism—all this endowed the diversity with a special richness.[24]

In the process, politicians and nationalist writers often conjured up a vision of Hindu unity and sought to invent a militant medieval tradition as a source of inspiration for their resistance against the British. Rajputs and Marathas along with Sikhs constituted the source. A section of the nationalists was inspired by the thought of a 'Hindu reawakening' and began a search for a 'glorious' Hindu past. The Sikhs had fought the Mughals, Pathans and Afghans in the medieval period to 'protect their religion and their community'. Towards the end of the nineteenth century, that was generally held up as a model to suit the spirit of the time and formed the subject-

[24] Pashaura Singh's recent study also draws our attention to the 'plurality of interpretations' of the *Adi Granth*. Cf. *The Guru Granth Sahib: Canon, Meaning and Authority*, New Delhi 2000, pp. 25, 261, 287.

matter of historical writings.[25] Historical research was enveloped by a religious atmosphere and patriotism often compromised with communalism.[26] Not merely Hindus, Muslims also wrote in the same vein. Many of these authors were encountering the 'oppressive present'[27] of the colonial hegemony and sought to negotiate it in the discovery of 'a glorious Indian past'. The past was dim. They could light it up their own way. Sikh history was given a new interpretation. Guru Gobind Singh and Maharaja Ranjit Singh were turned into patriots. Their numbers increased as the anti-British movement grew. They incorporated 'a range of diverse and discordant emotions' while reconstructing the Sikh past in eastern India. Surprisingly, these issues have so far remained virtually unnoticed in Sikh studies.

The diversity in Sikh projections in eastern Indian vernaculars is again likely to confront us with a few major issues debated in recent researches on Sikh history and religion. It may be argued whether this vast amount of vernaular material may be brought within the parameters of Sikh studies or better considered as streotypes in wide use in the print world of the period. As we would be reviewing these phrases and idioms in the following pages, we also need to negotiate with their complex and often conflicting connotations and nuances used in various contexts by the eastern Indian writers over the centuries. In the absence of any other convenient form of expression, we would continue to use the omnibus term 'Sikh studies' to represent these vernacular texts. Another related issue would be our response to the question of a 'separate and definite Sikh identity'. For quite some time, it has been generating heat in the realm of almost all serious enquiries related to Sikhism. This had always been a self-evident truth to faithful Sikhs. But some Western scholars have expressed grave doubts about it. They regard it as a recent addition to Sikh history. Superficially viewed, the problem may seem a narrow gap between Western historians and Sikh studies in Punjab, but the significance of the issue actually lies deeper. In the last three decades of the nineteenth century, the Singh Sabha movement which was

[25] R.C. Majumdar, 'Nationalist Historians', in C.H. Philips (ed.), *Historians of India, Pakistan and Ceylon,* London 1961, p. 423.

[26] R. Guha, *An Indian Historiography of India,* pp. 62-3; Anuradha Roy, 'Foreign Tyrants or Foster Brothers? Muslims in the eyes of Hindu Nationalists in Nineteenth Century Bengal', *The Calcutta Historical Journal*, January-June 1995, pp. 123-59.

[27] Sudhir Chandra, *The Oppressive Present: Literature and Social Consciousness in Colonial India,* New Delhi 1992.

committed to a new identity and the slogan *Ham Hindu Nahi* indicate a feeling of separateness. Many Hindus in Punjab often reacted by clamouring that *Sikh Hindu Hain*. It would be relevant to discuss whether there was any resonance in eastern India of the clash of slogans in Sikh studies. This may also add a new dimension to the field of historical enquiry and help us fathom what ailed that young Sikh friend I met from Guru Nanak Dev University in 1984.

CHAPTER II

Assamese

AT THE THRESHOLD of the twenty-first century, political unrest in the Indian subcontinent keeps on mounting. The polity is assailed by fundamentalism, terrorism and other forces. In addition to Jammu and Kashmir, the two states which have been and are likely to remain major storm-centres are Punjab and Assam. Strangely enough, there is very little resemblance between them. They are separated by barriers of history, culture, economy and anthropology. These two regions are sometimes mentioned together in some ancient texts but in the history of India before British rule, they are hardly ever juxtaposed.[1]

Some may argue that the problems arising from the difficulties in holding these two states in the Indian Union are due to the lack of shared sufferings in the past. They may even add that the effort to keep them together is a negation of history. Such coercive exercise has led to conflict and discontent. From the foregoing, it may seem that the Indian political structure today is a rejection of past tradition. The unreal identity, however, will be difficult to sustain for long. There is no point in condemning the *khadkus* of Punjab or the guerrillas of Assam for not speaking in unison with the rest of

[1] During pre-British times, the Mughals set up the largest all-India empire. In Punjab their rule was first established in the early sixteenth century and it continued till the middle of the eighteenth century. On the other hand, Assam was under the Ahoms for a longer period, almost six hundred years till the first quarter of the nineteenth century. For a short spell some parts of Assam came to be ruled by the Mughals. But they failed 'to integrate these peripheral zones within the state structure'. Thus Assam had not been under Mughal yoke for a long time. There is also a feeling in some quarters that 'historical events' of Assam are 'very little known' in the rest of India due to their lack of 'dissemination'. Cf. H.K. Barpujari, 'Lacunae in the Study of the History of Assam', *Proceedings of the Indian History Congress*, Twenty-fifth Session, Allahabad 1965, pp. 169-70; Gautam Bhadra, 'Two Frontier Uprisings in Mughal India', in Ranajit Guha (ed.), *Subaltern Studies II , Writings on South Asian History and Society,* New Delhi 1986, p. 59; Amalendu Guha, *Medieval and Early Colonial Assam: Society, Polity and Economy,* Calcutta 1991, p. xiii.

India. It is not unlikely that they may again attempt to change the political contours of India in the near future.

All this is not the desired domain of a historian. A historian is expected to delve into the past, not to make projections about the future. Of course, he is concerned with the present but how much he should be involved in it is debatable. However, current political problems can be analysed in the light of history. What was the nature of the problem in the past and how logically valid is its correlation to the present? This perhaps is the historian's domain, however limited. The question then arises: were Assam and Punjab unknown to each other in the past? If not, where is the historical evidence of contact? Who will provide the historical evidence? Which past is to be brought into focus—the dim past, or the colonial past? No historian can answer all these complex questions at once. The materials for the answers lie scattered and collation will take time. The historian has to mull over the method he is to adopt. And he has to be aware of the limitations of his craft.

Since the central point of our discussion is Assam, let us begin with the basics of Assamese literary sources. The development of modern Assamese literature may be traced to the middle of the nineteenth century. In fact, historical studies here began much earlier. Of all the eastern Indian languages only Assamese can boast of a tradition of historical writing. This is reflected in its *Buranji* literature which was fostered by the encouragement given by the Ahom kings to the writing and preservation of their history. The different *Buranjis* bear testimony to that tradition. Grierson commented: 'The Assamese are justly proud of their national literature. In no department have they been more successful than in a branch of study in which India, as a rule, is curiously deficient. The historical works or the *Buranjis* as they are styled by the Assamese, are numerous and voluminous.'[2] However, Punjab and Sikh history merited only a few references in the *Buranjis*. The silence on Sikhs is mystifying considering the extent and richness of the *Buranjis*. It may be partly due to the physical distance between Assam and Punjab. But no satisfactory answer has yet been offered by any Assamese historian or literary critic. The answer perhaps lies in the nature of the *Buranji* literature. Its main thrust was entwined with Ahom politics and so distant Punjab or even the rural Sikhs settled

[2] Grierson's view quoted in Lila Gogoi, *The Buranjis: Historical Literature of Assam*, New Delhi 1986, p. ix.

for long in Assam are of no consequence.[3] In the initial stages of our study, it is therefore quite in order to leave out the *Buranji* sources. Instead, we will concentrate where poets and writers have focused directly on Sikh history.

I

Any consideration of Sikh history in Assamese may conveniently start with the life and mission of Guru Nanak. In this regard one may look to the *Janamsakhis*.[4] Generally speaking, Sikhs regard them as the most important source on the life and message of the first Sikh Guru. It has been claimed in different traditions of the *Janamsakhi* literature that on his first *udasi,* Guru Nanak came to Kamrup in around 1508. He came with a disciple, Bhai Mardana, to the female-dominated land. At first, they were made to go through great difficulties. The magic and charms of the area were well

[3] According to the Census of 1971, the Sikh population in Assam totals a little over 11 thousand (approximately less than 1 per cent of the total provincial population). It includes four thousand Assamese-Sikhs. These Sikhs of Assam are inextricably linked with Assamese society, literature and culture. The political history of the state bears the stamp of their presence. They are mostly cultivators. There is a lot of controversy about how and when the Sikhs came to Assam. Perhaps they started coming there from Bihar at the time of the ninth Sikh Guru. Later on their successors settled down in villages like Barkola, Chaparmukh and Lanka in Nagaon district and mingled with the local Assamese people. These men cannot generally speak or write Punjabi but they are more or less conscious of the significance of the five Ks. The Assamese-Sikhs regard Assam as their own state. Birinchi Kumar Medhi has done a detailed study of the Assamese-Sikhs in his 'The Assamese-Sikhs: A Study of their Social Relations in a Rural Setting', Gauhati University unpublished Ph.D. thesis, 1989. Also see W. Robinson, *A Descriptive Account of Assam,* New Delhi reprint, 1975, p. 313; B.C. Allen, *Assam District Gazetteers: Goalpara,* Calcutta 1905, p. 79; Jiban Singh, 'Sikh aru Sikh Prabrajan', Naren Kalita (ed.), *Rahar Rahadai,* Jorhat 1980, p. 86; Kartar Singh et al., 'Asamiya Sikh Gaon Barkola: Ketor Samashya', *Ajir Batari*, 13 November 1993.

[4] Biographical literature on Guru Nanak written in Punjabi from the viewpoint of Sikh faithfuls in medieval days is called *Janamsakhi.* Almost as a rule, Sikhs accept most of the incidents related there as historical facts. Cf. Kirpal Singh, *Janamsakhi Parampara,* Patiala reprint, 1990, pp. i, iv. For a critical discussion of the significance of the *Janamsakhi* sources, see W.H. McLeod, *Guru Nanak and the Sikh Religion,* New Delhi 1978, pp. 8, 33. But Niharranjan Ray finds McLeod somewhat 'hyper-critical' towards the *Janamsakhi* sources. Cf. *The Sikh Gurus and the Sikh Society,* New Delhi 1975, p. xi.

known.[5] It is said that queen Nur Shah cast her spell and turned Mardana into a sheep. But Sakhi literature reveals that the hostility did not last long. She eventually recognized Guru Nanak's greatness and became his disciple. The Guru also brought Mardana back to human form.[6]

There is no echo of the Punjabi sources in contemporary Assamese history or literature. At the end of the nineteenth century Hunter brought out his *Statistical Accounts of Assam* which briefly mentioned the ninth Guru and his association with the Dhubri Sahib gurdwara.[7] But there was no reference to Guru Nanak's Kamrup visit in any Assamese sources of the nineteenth century.[8] It was Banikanta Kakati (1894-1950) who first gave the matter serious thought in 1919. He wrote that the Sikh Guru came to Assam for a short time in around 1517 to preach his religion and revealed his miraculous powers at one or two places. He tried to give a lyrical reorientation to the dialogue between Guru Nanak and Nur Shah. Kakati gleaned his information from the writings of British administrator-historian Macauliffe and he attempted to link his study with the philosophic message implicit in the *Janamsakhi* literature. It was written when Kakati was young and busy with his research on the religious tradition of Kamrup. He never questioned if Guru Nanak had actually visited Assam. The importance of his

[5] Sashibhusan DasGupta, *Obscure Religious Cults as Background of Bengali Literature,* Calcutta 1969, pp. 201-2, 244. Anil Chandra Banerjee has also spoken of it in *Guru Nanak and His Times,* Patiala 1984, p. 129.

[6] For this incident, see Kirpal Singh, *Janamsakhi Parampara*, pp. 20-1; W.H. McLeod (ed.), *The B-40 Janam-sakhi*, Amritsar 1980, pp. 89-91. McLeod writes that *Janamsakhis* like *Puratan Janamsakhi and Bala Janamsakhi*, have mentioned Guru Nanak's visit to Kamrup, the female-dominated land. According to him, the popularity of this episode confirms the prevalence of the Nath religious practices in Punjab. W.H. McLeod, *Early Sikh Tradition: A Study of the Janam-sakhis,* Oxford 1980, p. 70.

[7] The early history of the Dhubri Sahib gurdwara goes back to the medieval times but it is difficult to tell when a written account of it in Assamese appeared for the first time. Bhuyan points out that when Guru Tegh Bahadur came with the Mughal general Raja Ram Singh, he built the gurdwara on his own initiative with the help of his troops in 1669. Cf. Bhuyan, *Lachit Barphukan*, p.109.

[8] We, however, come across a sketch of Guru Nanak's life in the well known Assamese literary monthly *Jonaki* of the period. The essay is silent on the point. Cf. Tarinicharan Bora, 'Nanak', *Jonaki,* Magh 1812 Saka, pp. 129-31. Add 78/79 to Saka dates for Christian Era equivalents.

writing largely lies in the fact that he was the first Assamese writer to refer to the incident.[9]

A few years earlier, Lakshminath Bezbarua (1868-1938), the legendary Assamese littérateur, had made a brief reference to Guru Nanak. His article appeared in his own monthly *Banhi.* He referred to the Guru in the context of the reform movements in Hinduism from the ancient period to the middle ages. The Guru was among a galaxy of religious reformers from Buddha to Kabir. The piece appeared in four instalments. A whole page is devoted to the Sikh Guru in the third section. He is described as a revolutionary religious reformer like Buddha. His revolt was against the meaningless rituals and the caste hierarchy of Brahmanism. Bezbarua detected many points of resemblance between Nanak and Kabir in their religious beliefs. According to him, the two had met and Nanak even adopted from Kabir some of his anti-idolatry ideas and monotheism.[10] The writer also argued that the Sikh Guru was not merely a learned man, philosopher and religious preacher. He was more interested in the

[9] Banikanta Kakati, 'SikhGuru Nanak aru Tegh Bahadurar Kamrup Bhraman', *Chetana,* Puh 1841 Saka, pp. 223-8. The article appeared without any change in Kakati's *Purani Kamrupar Dharmar Dhara,* Gauhati 1955. The source of the article is M.A. Macauliffe, *The Sikh Religion,* vol. I, New Delhi reprint, 1978, pp. 73-8. Banikanta Kakati, an authority on Assamese language and literature, was associated with teaching and research at Gauhati University since its inception.

[10] Many historians have noticed a resemblance in the religious outlooks of Guru Nanak and Kabir. Even Guru Nanak was regarded a disciple of Kabir. According to Archer, 'The "Kabir portions" of the Sikh Granth Sahib are in themselves sufficient evidence that Sikhism is . . . intimately connected also with Kabir's reformation. . . . There is even the linguistic connection between Kabir and Nanak . . . they shared something of a common vernacular.' J.C. Archer, *The Sikhs in relation to Hindus, Moslems, Christians, and Ahmadiyyas: A Study in Comparative Religion,* Princeton 1946, p. 56. Hess has also emphasized that 'devotional element' which constitutes an important aspect in Guru Nanak's thought is 'at the top' in the two Western collections of Kabir's writings, one of which is *Adi Granth.* Linda Hess, 'Three Kabir Collections', in Karine Schomer and W.H. McLeod (eds.), *The Sants: Studies in a Devotional Tradition of India,* New Delhi 1987, pp. 121-2. There may have been a similarity but it will be taking away from Guru Nanak's originality if one says he borrowed ideas from Kabir. Monotheism, the cult of *bhakti,* the religious experience of the Nath tradition—these are the broad meeting points between Kabir and Guru Nanak. McLeod is also of the opinion that the Sikh Guru articulated his thoughts on godhead more clearly and logically than Kabir. Kabir's feelings about God were more personal and transcendental. Words cannot express them adequately. For further discussion on the similarity and dissimilarity between Guru Nanak and Kabir in their religious thought, see McLeod, *Guru Nanak and the Sikh Religion,* pp. 149-57.

practice of religion in everyday life. Bezbarua concluded his discussion by saying that Guru Nanak built a bridge between Hinduism and Islam.[11]

Though relatively short, Bezbarua's piece has three salient features. He discusses the religious views of Guru Nanak which virtually remain outside the scope of Kakati's article. But his comments are mainly restricted to the broader functional aspects of religion and miss some of the basic formulations associated with the Sikh Guru's concept of godhead. Secondly, he has described Guru Nanak as a Hindu revolutionary reformer and not as the initiator of a new religion outside Hinduism. Here he sharply differed from the early Brahmo reformers of the nineteenth century.[12] Thirdly, no light was thrown on the Guru's life. This was done later by Harichandra Bhattacharya.

Harichandra Bhattacharya (1909-92) had just completed his graduation when he wrote the life of the Sikh Guru in 1932.[13] The essay is factually quite limited in range and is of little significance at an all-India level. But it was of great importance from the Assamese point of view for he was the first writer to present to his readers in their mother tongue the genealogy of Guru Nanak, his boyhood, the places where he spread his message, his religious views, the controversy over the last rites when he died and how Sikh leadership passed on to his successor. The biography is precise and easy to read, but is nevertheless inadequate for the post-Guru Nanak developments. Readers are left in the dark about what happened to the disciples after the death of Guru Angad. Nor does he mention if the first Sikh Guru came to Assam to spread his religion. And there is nothing to indicate the importance of Guru Nanak's contributions in the vast Sikh religious literature.

In the pre-Independence period, these were the texts written about Guru Nanak in Assam. Compared to the literature of the two other

[11] Lakshminath Bezbarua, 'Bidrohat Hindudharmar Unnati (3)', *Banhi*, Saon 1838 Saka, pp. 455-74. The article was perhaps written at the time of the Lucknow pact (1916).

[12] Infra, pp. 80-5, 120-32.

[13] Harichandra Bhattacharya, 'Nanak', *Banhi*, Ahar 1854 Saka, pp. 138-40. Bhattacharya in later life taught Assamese language and literature at Handique Girls' College in Guwahati. His *Asamiya Natya Sahityar Jilingani*, Guwahati 1968, is regarded as an important source volume for studying the history of Assamese drama. I am thankful to Manjumala Das of the same college for necessary details of Harichandra Bhattacharya's life.

eastern regions, Bengal and Orissa, Assamese literature paid little attention to Guru Nanak and related matters and was less varied and rich. The Guru's visit to Puri as well as Kamrup may also be taken into consideration in this connection. After Kamrup, according to Sikh tradition, the Guru went to Puri through Cuttack. Two historical gurdwaras bear testimony to the visit—the one at Dhubri in Goalpara in Assam and the Dantan Sahib gurdwara in Cuttack skirting the Mahanadi. Local Sikhs in Cuttack made special efforts to ensure proper worship and maintenance of the gurdwara in the first half of the twentieth century. But the Oriya enthusiasm about the Sikhs in Cuttack was often missing in Dhubri Sahib (1928-30).

This was largely due to the different conditions in which the reconstruction of the historic gurdwaras was carried out in Assam and Orissa almost during the same period. The earthquake of 1930 seriously damaged the Dhubri Sahib gurdwara. Reconstruction began and the *mahant* of the gurdwara, Bachittar Singh, appealed to the Sikhs of Assam for funds. But there was little response. Even the Assam government seized a part of the gurdwara land and planned to build a circuit house there. Bachittar Singh protested against the move and was sent to jail. The government project ultimately came to naught. During the same period, the Assamese-Sikhs got entangled in a debate with the local administration on the issue of the influx of 'outsiders' in Assam, raising political tensions at the provincial level.[14] To 'compete for local government jobs, scholarships and contracts', the Sikhs of Assam had to obtain a domicile certificate stating that they were 'not aliens but permanent residents of Assam'. Such certificates were, however, 'a rare commodity'. Around 1920, the Assam government also sought to impose certain stringent restrictions on the residence of the immigrant population by imposing the 'Line System' legislation. The law was expected to restrict all forms of permanent entry and settlement within the area brought under the 'Line System'. It was likely to affect the position of the Assamese-Sikhs who had long Assamized themselves. Local Sikhs protested under the leadership of Rup Singh Sandhu. In the end, the Assam government apparently agreed to listen to the appeal of the local Sikhs.[15]

[14] Infra, pp. 52-4.

[15] I had the privilege of hearing all about the incident from Rup Singh Sandhu in Guwahati, 25 April 1994. See also Bharatchandra Das, *Byakti Parichay*, Part II, Barpeta 1979, pp. 159-64; A.S. Mann, *Guru Tegh Bahadur and Assam Pradesh*, New Delhi n.d., pp. 182-5; *Index to the Debates of the Assam Legislative Assembly*,

But the Sikhs of Orissa did not have to face any such difficulty. They were generally well received there. The message of Guru Nanak was also quite well known among the Oriya Brahmos, many of whom then came forward and provided a decisive leadership in restoring the Dantan Sahib gurdwara to its past glory. Local administration was perhaps sympathetic to the cause.[16] It was particularly evident when Bawa Kartar Singh, Professor of Chemistry at Ravenshaw College in Cuttack, took the initiative in this regard. In Cuttack he was widely respected and many Oriya intellectuals and leaders even helped Bawa in raising funds. After the reconstruction of the Dantan Sahib gurdwara, a large meeting was held there. Many Oriyas participated in the meeting. However, one must again bear in mind the sensitive political atmosphere then prevailing in Assam. Political developments of the 1940s, particularly the issue of influx of 'outsiders' made many Assamese feel an uncertainty about their future political status within the Indian constitutional framework. This dominated the Assamese psyche of the period. It also made the position of the Assamese-Sikhs equally difficult and uncomfortable. It is thus significant that despite such odds, there was considerable thinking on the Sikhs in Assamese writing of the period.

II

One important theme in the study of post-Guru Nanak Sikh history in Assamese is the evolution of the Sikh Panth under the remaining nine Gurus (1539-1708). The second Guru Angad, the fifth Guru Arjan and the sixth Guru Hargobind are mentioned a couple of times. But there is complete silence on the third Guru Amardas, the seventh Guru Har Rai and the eighth Guru Harkishen. It is also to be noted that while the Punjabi literary sources focus on the bitterness in the Sikh Panth over Prithichand and Ram Rai's bid for the *Guru-gaddi*, this had no impact on Assamese writing. To the Assamese, the history of the Sikhs during the period may seem free from turmoil but Sikh sources tell us a different story. The period from Guru Angad to the ninth Guru was one of continuity as well as

---

No. I, Shillong 1938, pp. 232-72, 662-3, 706-17, 1749-51, 1779-80; *Report of the Line System Committee*, vol. I, Shillong 1938, pp. 1-4; Amalendu Guha, *Planter-Raj to Swaraj—Freedom Movement and Electoral Politics in Assam, 1826-1947*, New Delhi 1979, pp. 206-8.

[16] Infra, pp. 89-90.

conflict. That is missing in the Assamese accounts. There are a number of acts in the succession drama which are also difficult to comprehend from Assamese sources.

The history of about 170 years of the Sikh Panth has been dealt with mainly in four pieces of writing. These appeared in three literary magazines between 1910 and 1932. To follow historical chronology, we have ignored the dates of the publications. First, we should mention 'Gurur Karane' by Sashikanta Gogoi (1916-89). It was the last to be published but it deals with the ninth Guru's sacrifice and its impact. It appeared in *Milon*, the organ of the student movement in 1932. Incidentally, it was one of the two articles in Assamese highlighting the tradition of Sikh martyrdom and resistance. Already a significant number of Assamese students were active in provincial politics. They had carried the Gandhian message of *satyagraha* to different parts of Assam under the aegis of the Assam Chatra Sanmilan. The writer was closely associated with the movement. He was born in Sibsagar but courted imprisonment for his involvement in the student movement in Guwahati.[17] Young Sashikanta had a fluent style and his emotional exuberance moved the readers. The piece deals with the ninth Guru's discussion on self-immolation with his son and successor Guru Gobind Singh.[18] The vocabulary of the father and son dialogue was significant in the context of the national movement in Assam. The strident tone of the dramatic dialogue proves that the writer had some idea about the mindset of his readers.

The theme of the piece is available in different Punjabi sources. But it is unlikely that young Gogoi got his materials directly from them, as the story was extant in various regional languages for a long time.[19] Gogoi probably gathered his facts from these sources

[17] Sashikanta Gogoi, 'Gurur Karane', *Milon*, Chat 1856 Saka, pp. 15-18. Cf. Sibnath Burman, *Asamiya Jibani Abhidhan,* Guwahati 1992, p. 280. For contemporary student movements in Assam, see Shila Bora, 'The Assam Chatra Sanmilan and Nation Building (1916-30)', in Udyan Misra (ed.), *Nation Building and Development in North East India,* Guwahati 1991, pp. 24-53. Also see Shila Bora's 'A Study of the Student Movement in Assam since 1916 (1916-1947)', Gauhati University unpublished Ph.D. thesis, 1984.

[18] For an interesting discussion on the ninth Guru's martyrdom, see Trilochan Singh, *Guru Tegh Bahadur: Prophet and Martyr*, pp. 310-29.

[19] In 1928 the Hindi monthly *Chand* had a discussion on Tegh Bahadur's martyrdom. *Hindupanch-Balidan Anka* of 1930 includes the ninth Guru's martyrdom in the section 'Madhyakalin Bharatke Balidan'. The Bengali monograph *Sikher Atmahuti,* Calcutta n.d. by Dineshchandra Burman was banned in 1932. Here also

and collated them in the form of a dialogue to make it attractive. He not only presented the last two Sikh Gurus but also the 'bigot' emperor Aurangzeb. At the end of the account were mentioned two other *gurmukh* Sikhs.[20] These two were prepared at any cost to take the executed Guru's body from Delhi to Anandpur. One of them—the father—gave his life so that the Guru's body could be spirited away from Delhi to Punjab. The story ends on a dramatic note with the self-immolation of the *gurmukh* Sikh.

Gogoi's writings conveyed a sense of drama, not to be found in Dhaniram Datta's 'Guru Gobinda Singha'. The writer was not a front ranker among Assamese authors and he wrote a simple biographical piece.[21] It appeared in the literary magazine *Alochani* published from Dibrugarh.[22] The protagonist is the tenth Guru. But his family tree takes up a lot of space before he puts in an appearance. The writer uses this backdrop to narrate the preliminary phase of Mughal-Sikh animosity which led to the creation of the Khalsa. A large part of the writing deals with military confrontations between Mughals and the tenth Guru. But there is no indication of the fierceness and self-sacrifice which Sikh authors generally speak of while describing the battles of Anandpur and Chamkaur (1700-5). The Khalsa no doubt fights the Mughals but nowhere in the article has the causes of its complaint against the imperial army been clearly elaborated. Similarly, one would hardly encounter a nationalist model-hero fighting for the country's independence in the Sikh Guru,

---

Tegh Bahadur's martyrdom is discussed. Basudeb Mahapatra raised the issue in his Oriya essay 'Atmabali' (*Satyabadi*, Mithun 1326 Masiha. Add 593/594 to Masiha dates for Christian Era equivalents). Later on it was reprinted in *Beera Bharata,* Cuttack reprint, 1950. I have mentioned to a few essays on Guru Tegh Bahadur's martyrdom which were either banned or written by well known authorities in these languages.

[20] Sikh religious interpretation refers to two kinds of men—*manmukh* or those who think only about themselves and *gurmukh* or those who think of Guru or God alone. See McLeod, *Historical Dictionary of Sikhism*, pp. 95, 135. Also see H.S. Dilgeer, *The Sikh Reference Book,* Amritsar 1997, pp. 50, 58; S.S. Kohli, *A Conceptual Encyclopaedia of Guru Granth Sahib,* New Delhi 1992, pp. 126-7, 188-9.

[21] Dhaniram Datta, 'Guru Gobinda Singha', *Alochani*, Ashar 1832 Saka, pp. 257-60. We do not know much about the literary activities of Dhaniram Datta. Pona Mahanta of Dibrugarh University informed me that Datta lived in Rangiya (then in undivided Kamrup District). Datta also wrote a mythological play *Urbashi Uddhar* (1920).

[22] *Alochani* was first published in Kati 1831 Saka (1910). This literary magazine was closed down in 1917.

a popular theme in the writings of many nationalist authors of the early twentieth century. Historical expertise which could do justice to the complexity and military significance of these battles was also lacking. Dhaniram Datta's contribution is more or less on the level of an ordinary school textbook.

'Guru Gobinda Singha' therefore had no militant political appeal for its readers. The same can be said about the next article, but its language is defensive. Towards the end of the nineteenth century one or two writers found signs of Hinduism in the creation of the Khalsa. Some designated it as a medieval precursor of the armed insurrection against British rule. These writers tried to serve some sort of religious or political end. In their eyes the birth of the Khalsa in 1699 carried a message of change.[23] On the other hand, the article 'Amaratwa Labh' published in *Assam Bandhav* merely conveyed a message of *status quo* in the contemporary social order.[24] The writer remained anonymous. The reason for this anonimity is difficult to understand for there is nothing objectionable in the article. On the contrary, there is rather a cautious streak. Unlike other biographers of Guru Gobind Singh, he has not detected any assertive martial tradition created by the Khalsa. Instead, he assumes a conservative position reminiscent of *Guru Gobinda Singha* in Bengali by Tinkari Banerjee.[25] The Khalṣa to him was a social bulwark to protect the Sikhs from Mughal power. It carried the message of immortality. It would enable people to meditate on God and lead good lives through disciplined thinking and purification by work. The organizational method of work of the Khalsa made social life in contemporary India harmonious and cohesive and helped men take a positive route to a definite goal that demanded self-sacrifice. The object was not to destroy the social fabric, but to maintain and preserve it. The author

[23] Detailed study is necessary for an evaluation of the problem from an all-India perspective. For a review of the issue based on Bengali sources, see the author's 'Guru Gobind Singh in Bengali Writings', *The Panjab Past and Present*, October 1985, pp. 354-62. Guru Gobind Singh has been described by many Hindi and Oriya authors as a saviour of Hinduism. Mention can be made of Beni Prasad, *Guru Gobind Singh*, Banaras 1977 Bikrami (deduct 57/58 from Bikrami dates for Christian Era equivalents), and Jiban Lal Prem, *Guru Gobind Singh*, Lahore reprint, 1942 in Hindi. For a similar view in Oriya, see Sivaprasad Das, *Guru Gobinda Singha*, Baripada 1929, and Lingaraj Mishra, *Guru Gobinda Singha*, Cuttack 1935.

[24] Anonymous, 'Amaratwa Labh', *Assam Bandhav*, Phagun 1320 BS (BS suggests Bangla Sal. Add 593/594 to BS for Christian Era equivalents), pp. 25-6. Many old numbers of *Assam Bandhav* are in the private collection of the late Benudhar Sharma, seen by courtesy of his son Ajit Sharma.

[25] Infra, pp. 156-8.

eschews conflict, unlike other writers who depicted the Khalsa as confrontationist. The Khalsa is given the role of putting society together in bonds of discipline.

A unique piece of work was the one by Phula Singh Chhetri (1890-1986). In *Alochani* he projects the sacrifice and death of Guru Gobind Singh's two sons—Fateh Singh and Jorabar Singh.[26] It conveys the message of martyrdom which remains a recurrent theme in the Sikh history of our times. Phula Singh Chhetri was an Assamese-Sikh in a true sense.[27] He was born, brought up and educated in village Chaparmukh in Nagaon district. But, unlike contemporary Assamese-Sikhs, he had not severed ties with Punjab. He had deep respect for Sikh religious literature. His writing is steeped in the Sikh historical works and religious tradition which gives it a new dimension.

The author begins with the famous battle of Anandpur. Guru Gobind Singh was then negotiating a critical phase of the battle. Students of Sikh history are well aware of how he gradually got out of the crisis. But a little later, his two sons—Fateh and Jorabar Singh—fell prey to a cruel betrayal. Although they were young, they could cope with the blandishments and torture of Wazir Khan, the ruler of Sirhind and in defence of their religion, they lay down their lives. It is such a painful and memorable episode in the Panthic tradition that the Sikhs recall it every day in their prayers to God.[28] The vigorously plaintive spirit of religious Sikhs which resonates in

[26] Phula Singh Chhetri, 'Fateh Singha aru Joyabar Singha', *Alochani*, Ahin 1836 Saka, pp. 442-9. The subject has assumed importance in Bengali, Hindi and Oriya in almost equal measure. There is, for instance, a poem 'Bir Balak' in Hindi by Jayasankar Prasad, *Prasad Granthabali*, Part I, Allahabad 1985, pp. 223-5. Also see Nandkumardev Sharma, 'Bachhonka Atmotsargya', *Balbir Charitabali,* Calcutta 1924, pp. 69-80. In Oriya, see Chintamani Acharya, 'Fateh Singha o Jerebar Singha', *Itihas Prasanga*, Part I, Cuttack 1916, pp. 141-53.

[27] A number of people have told me about Phula Singh Chhetri. He was born in village Chaparmukh in Nagaon district. He had his primary education in Assam. But he was in close touch with Punjab and Punjabi language till his death. He was the Head Master of a school at Nankana Sahib (now in Pakistan) for a long time. He died at Patiala at an advanced age. My informants include Dhyan Singh, President, Assam Sikh Association of Guwahati, Niranjan Singh of Dibrugarh, Jog Singh Chhetri of Nagaon and Raghbir Singh of Patiala.

[28] Here I draw attention to the sequel of the Sikh daily-prayer referring to the martyrdom of the two sons of the tenth Guru. For the content of the Sikh daily-prayer, see J.S. Neki, 'Ardas', Harbans Singh (ed.), *Encyclopaedia of Sikhism,* Patiala 1992, vol. I, pp. 184-8.

Phula Singh Chhetri's writing is matched by the author's own personality. The use of Assamese proverbs in his brief writing shows his intimate association with Assamese language. To that was added his knowledge of Sikh religious literature. The combination gives us a glimpse of the inner world of Sikhism in Assam. Besides, he depicts the trials and tribulations of the battle of Anandpur, the heroism and self-abnegation of the Sikhs. Together with them, the self-immolation of the two young men to save their religion and community is presented as an inspiration to build up a resistance. In this Chhetri had a lot in common with Sashikanta Gogoi and he differed vastly from the anonymous writer of 'Amaratwa Labh'.

The study of the history of the post-Nanak Gurus leaves a section partly unilluminated, namely, the visit of the ninth Guru Tegh Bahadur to Assam along with the Mughal general Raja Ram Singh. Historians agree on the authenticity of the incident but they disagree about the cause of the Guru's visit. The Assamese historian Surya Kumar Bhuyan tried to analyse *Buranji* literature in the light of historical perspective (1947). He says in his account of the Assamese hero Lachit Barphukan that the Guru came to Assam for three reasons: as a friend of Ram Singh, as a religious preacher (to spread Sikhism), and as a peace-maker (to stop the bloody war between Mughals and Ahoms). Bhuyan's views are not beyond controversy. It has been debated in Assam and in Punjab. An Assamese essayist argued that if the Sikh Guru came with the above three objectives, he failed in one, i.e. in ending hostilities between Ahoms and Mughals. This line of argument hardly evokes any enthusiasm among the local Sikhs of Assam. According to one of them, the Guru came to Assam as a friend of Raja Ram Singh. He maintains that the Guru also visited Assam to spread Sikhism there and it is therefore pointless looking for a political or military motive in it. He refers to an old document that was kept with the priest of Kamakhya (Kamrup) in defence of his argument. It deals with the Sikh Guru's visit to Assam. The same source has also been mentioned by others. But we are not certain whether the writers have actually consulted this document.[29]

On the other hand, we come across a somewhat different version

[29] For Bhuyan's view, see *Lachit Barphukan*, p. 108. For a critique of Bhuyan's view, see Goswami Jayashri Mahanta (ed.), *Smritigrantha: Gurudwara Mataji*, Guwahati 1990, p. 17. Also see Bhupen Singh, *Guru Teghbahadur*, Guwahati 1985, pp. 9-10; Rajmohan Nath, 'Kamakhyat SikhGuru Teghbahadur', *Asam Sahitya Sabha Patrika*, Bahag-Saon 1879 Saka, p. 11.

of the episode in non-Assamese sources. In Punjab, Trilochan Singh for example suggests that the ninth Guru played a very significant role in bringing about peace in Assam. Amolak Singh in one of his recent paintings points to something almost similar. In the picture the Guru is seen sitting on a raised platform while Raja Ram Singh and the Ahom King shake hands standing at a lower level. The exalted position of the Sikh Guru is clearly indicated.[30] But it is widely believed in Assam that the Ahoms were victorious in their fight with the Mughals at Saraighat (1671) and the defeated Mughal army left Assam in disgrace and humiliation. Assamese textbooks underline the point.[31] These issues thus clearly indicate how regional sentiments continue to play an important part in the reconstruction of medieval Sikh history.

With this we may conclude our review of the Assamese perceptions of the Guru period of Sikh history since the death of Guru Nanak. The period had been dealt with perfunctorily and haphazardly. Writers and historians often showed no definite sense of continuity in their choice of subjects. Besides, a dearth of materials may explain the lacklustre descriptions and presentation of wrong information. These flaws were most glaring in the biographical account of Guru Gobind Singh and the study of Khalsa.[32] The faults notwithstanding, it is appropriate to recall the name of Phula Singh Chhetri. So long Assamese-Sikhs had been conspicuous by their absence in Sikh studies. Phula Singh built a bridge with this broad stream of historical enquiry. As a result, interest in Sikh history and religion in Assam surged forward. As far as the wealth of materials is concerned, Oriya and Bengali Sikh studies are richer but Phula Singh Chhetri provided a distinct regional dimension to Assamese studies on Sikh history.

[30] Trilochan Singh even claims that a platoon of the Khalsa army was posted in Assam for the defence of the Ahom kingdom because the Ahoms remained extremely friendly to the Sikh faith. But he does not refer to any definite source in defence of his argument. For Trilochan Singh's views, see 'Social Philosophy of Guru Gobind Singh', in Niharranjan Ray (ed.), *Sikhism and Indian Society,* Simla 1967, p. 192. About Amolak Singh's paintings, see Makhan Singh (ed.), *Sikh Heritage in Paintings,* New Delhi 1995, p. 66. For the traditional Sikh view, see Macauliffe, *The Sikh Religion*, vol. V, New Delhi reprint, 1978, p. 4.

[31] Dambarudhar Nath, *Asam Buranji,* Guwahati 1996, pp. 187-8.

[32] In Dhaniram Datta's essay Chamkaur appears as Champakgarh and Tegh Bahadur as Tyag Singh. We are also told in 'Amaratwa Labh' that on the day the Khalsa was born, Guru Gobind Singh initially demanded the lives of one hundred Sikhs. Later the figure came down to five due to unknown reasons.

Subsequently, creative writers brought in variety. Their works will be discussed later.

III

With the death of Guru Gobind Singh, the age of the Gurus in Sikh history came to an end. Thereafter the Khalsa had to fight for self-assertion on a much wider front. First, they had to fight the Mughals and then the Afghans. That is why the greater part of the eighteenth century in Punjab is generally called the period of Sikh struggle. History in this age is crowded with the annals of heroism and martyrdom. These are reflected in Punjabi literary sources of the subsequent period. As nationalism burgeoned in the last days of the nineteenth century, the ideal of struggle and martyrdom fuelled the imagination of poets and writers.[33] Many historians of the period discovered in that age a prelude to the freedom struggle.[34] But Assamese literature makes no reference to the eighteenth century Sikh history. One does not know why. Incidents of martyrdom and

[33] The history of Sikh martyrdom has long remained a significant area of enquiry among Sikh scholars. Ratan Singh Bhangu's description of the eighteenth century Sikh martyrdom has almost become a classic. Cf. Bhai Vir Singh (ed.), *Bhangu Ratan Singh Sahid Krit Prachin Panth Prakash*, New Delhi reprint, 1998, p. 228. For an early twentieth century interpretation, see Bhagat Lakshman Singh, *Sikh Martyrs*, Ludhiana reprint, n.d. It remains an interesting part of the contemporary community memory. Also see Clarence O. McMullen, *Religious Beliefs and Practices of the Sikhs in Rural Punjab*, New Delhi 1989, pp. 53-4. Surjit Hans has attempted to reconstruct its philosophical background. According to him, Sikh martyrs thought that there was divine sanction behind their resistance. The Mughal rulers were oppressors and by their assault on the religion and everyday life of their subjects, they had forfeited the divine right to rule. As the persecution of the Mughals intensified, the resistance of the Sikhs mounted. Cf. Surjit Hans, *A Reconstruction of Sikh History from Sikh Literature*, Jalandhar 1988, pp. 234-5. It seems that Hans has been influenced by the revolutionary political philosophy of social contract of Europe of the sixteenth and seventeenth centuries. But it is doubtful whether such an ideology played any effective role in this regard. Recently Louis E. Fenech raised a few interesting points about the early tradition of Sikh martyrdom. For a detailed discussion, see his 'Martyrdom and the Sikh Tradition', *Journal of the American Oriental Society*, October-December 1997, pp. 623-42.

[34] For an early twentieth century nationalist discourse on the subject, see Brajasundar Sanyal, 'Sikh Swadhinata', which appeared in three instalments (Sraban, Agrahayan and Chaitra) in *Bharati* in 1313 BS. Narendra Krishna Sinha's *Rise of the Sikh Power*, Calcutta reprint, 1960, reflects the same outlook.

self-immolation in Sikh history were not altogether unknown to Assamese writers. But there was only a partial reflection of it in their works.

A close look at the regional scene may provide an answer to the Assamese 'silence' or 'indifference'. There was perhaps a deep underlying cause and the late nineteenth century political climate of Assam may provide some indications of it. Assam had then passed under the rule of the East India Company (1826).The British generally appointed educated Bengalis for running the administration at the local level, indirectly paving the way for the gradual introduction of Bengali language in Assam. This was destined to give rise to complex reactions in the Assamese psyche. During these years many Assamese authors noted with alarm the 'growing domination' of the Bengali educated middle class in the Brahmaputra valley, which, they feared, would lead to the 'increasing marginalization' of the Assamese cultural identity in their homeland. They were 'consequently obsessed with the thought of the defence and advancement of the Assamese language and literature as a principal means of progress in Assam'. On the other hand, the Assamese psyche did not always remain oblivious of the contemporary Congress-led Indian nationalist politics. While turning to the nationalism at the all-India level, it increasingly looked at the regeneration of Assamese literature and culture as another aspect of the great national movement. In this way the Assamese people not only appreciated the message of all-India nationalism, but supported the cause of Assamese resurgence at the linguistic-regional level. 'It was through these twin processes, more often complementary than conflicting, that nationalism in India' 'did project itself' in Assam. Later in the second decade of the twentieth century, as political ferment and national awakening increasingly took hold of the Assamese mind, they continued to find inspiration nearer home in the annals of Assamese heroes and martyrs like Lachit Barphukan, Chilarai, Queen Joymati Konwari and others.[35]

However, Sikh history of the eighteenth century did not remain unrecorded. The accession of Maharaja Ranjit Singh at the end of the century and his building up of a vast empire in the first half of the nineteenth were recorded briefly in Assamese writings. On the first death centenary of the Sikh monarch in 1939, the progressive literary magazine *Jayanti* evaluated him as a nationalist hero. The

[35] See Guha, *Planter-Raj to Swaraj*, p. 69; Bora, 'A Study of the Student Movement in Assam since 1916', pp. 7-8.

World War II had started and the Indian political scenario was changing. Even the permanence of British rule was in question. In that context, a brief analysis appeared concerning the character and achievements of Ranjit Singh, his importance in Sikh politics, his relations with the British, his administration and role as a general. In the preface, the writer has stressed the 'need of objectivity'. He has cautioned against hyperbolic praise or exaggerated criticism.[36] No other Assamese writer on Sikh studies had sounded the warning before. It shows that Sikh studies in Assam were coming of age.

The centenary article is generally free from the lavish statements characteristic of the occasion. The lack of discipline and flaws in the maharaja's character were highlighted. At the same time his many-splendoured qualities have been enumerated with respect. The writer was perhaps familiar with one or two definitive biographies on the subject. His style betrayed the influence of Griffin and Sinha's *Ranjit Singh*.[37] Towards the end, the article throws some light on Ranjit Singh's responsibility for the fall of the Sikh empire. But a more detailed analysis of the decline can be seen in *Assam Bandhav* published some years earlier. The anonymous author makes a trenchant attack on Ranjit Singh and holds him responsible for the fall of the empire. His faults included corruption, polygamy, excessive greed, among others. The article is quite one-sided.[38] The

[36] Samarbijayi Gupta, 'Maharaj Ranjit Singha', *Jayanti*, Magh 1861 Saka, p.12. For further information regarding the publication, *Jayanti*, see Hariprasad Neog, 'Bingsha Satabdir Asamiya Sahityar Patabhumi: Sambadpatra', Homen Bargohain (ed.), *Bingsha Satabdir Asamiya Sahitya*, Dibrugarh 1987, p. 134.

[37] Here I intend to draw attention to one comment by Gupta which resembles Sinha's. As a result of the treaty of 1809, Gupta writes, Ranjit Singh 'became horse and the British rider' (*ghora aru British tar achhoar*), *Jayanti*, Magh 1861 Saka, p. 15. Sinha also wrote, 'British Government was the rider and Ranjit was the horse'. Cf. *Ranjit Singh*, Calcutta reprint, 1975, p. 191. Lepel Griffin remains Gupta's main source of information on the maharaja's darbar and character. He has even borrowed Griffin's comments on Raja Dina Nath. See Gupta, p. 17 and Lepel Griffin, *Ranjit Singh*, New Delhi reprint, 1967, p. 127.

[38] The writer has referred to a few other things while talking of the downfall of the Sikhs. For instance, during the period of Ranjit Singh, Sikhs drew away from Guru Nanak's anti-idolatry and formless monotheistic concepts, and introduced several complexities in their religious practices. 'That was the beginning of the end.' The author is anonymous, 'Prabasir Toka : Sikhar Patan', *Assam Bandhav*, Phagun-Chat 1316 BS, pp. 129-34. He says that he got his materials from a lecture he heard in Calcutta. Earlier Brahmos like Krishnakumar Mitra held similar views. Even Rabindranath flayed the Sikhism of Guru Gobind Singh in *Prabasi* (Chaitra 1316 BS). It is difficult to tell which speaker or writer of Calcutta had actually inspired our author.

centenary article on the other hand was free from that bias. Thus one Assamese writer at least had dealt with Ranjit Singh with an analytical mind and it underlined a new trend in Sikh studies in Assam.

IV

Another trend could be seen in the journalistic pieces produced in the period on Sikh matters. Published about 150 years ago, they had little in common with modern journalism. Let us take *Orunodoi* (1846), the harbinger of a new era in Assamese language and literature. The contents, language and political views of the journal have been critically examined in Assam over a long time. Published from Sibsagar, it was run by the American Baptist Mission. It carried news on science, religion, etc., from different countries and played a significant role in the struggle for Assam's self-assertion in the mid-nineteenth century.[39]

The link between *Orunodoi* and Sikh studies dated back to its inception and it was quite accidental. It was first published in January 1846, shortly after the First Sikh War (1845) began. The excitement speeded up the heartbeat of a poet like Iswarchandra Gupta and a historian like Rajnarayan Bhattacharya in faraway Calcutta.[40] Beyond Calcutta, *Orunodoi* served as a channel of communication between the front and the different parts of Assam at the end of every month. Month-old news has no practical value now. But in those days, Assam had no rail link, no telegraph lines. No wonder a few educated people read the news with interest and sometimes wrote letters to the editor on the subject. In the columns of *Orunodoi*, missionaries like Father Bronson often carried news of the Sikh wars, of how the Sikhs crossed the Sutlej, the declaration of war by the East India Company, the casualties on either side during the hostilities, and the eventual defeat of the Sikhs. The brutality of

[39] Birinchi Kumar Barua, *History of Assamese Literature*, New Delhi 1978, pp. 105-6, 167, 175; Nanda Talukdar, *Sambad Patrar Raud-Kachalit Asamiya Sahitya*, Gauhati 1975, pp. 37-96. Recently the Publication Board, Assam has brought out the old issues of *Orunodoi* (1846-54) edited by Maheswar Neog in a single volume. I have used this edition of *Orunodoi*, Guwahati 1983.

[40] Rajnarayan Bhattacharya, *Panjabetihas*, Calcutta 1846, pp. 119-93; Iswarchandra Gupta, *Iswarchandra Gupter Rachanabali*, vol. II, Calcutta 1327 BS, pp. 142-6. For a further discussion of their writings on the Sikhs, Infra, pp. 216-7, 220-2.

the Sikh soldiers, British bravery against heavy odds, the role of a few Sikh leaders in further complicating the nature of the war were also recorded. The loyalist stance of *Orunodoi* was clearly in evidence when the Company won the war and annexed Punjab.

Orunodoi added another dimension to Sikh studies in Assam. So long these had been concerned only with the past. It introduced contemporary history as well. Secondly, the advent of the missionaries opened a new door as far as Assamese language and literature were concerned. Besides, pictures of the appearance of Sikh sardars, the characteristics of common Sikh soldiers, the outlook of the surroundings when the fort of Multan was besieged, etc., were published by the American missionaries. It added to the attractiveness of news presentation, something not thought of in contemporary newspapers in other eastern Indian languages. The poet Iswarchandra Gupta's *Sambad Prabhakar* published many satirical poems on the Sikh wars, but he was not keen on veracity. *Orunodoi* on the other hand showed factual fidelity and played a distinct role in Sikh studies.

It is, however, surprising that the enthusiasm with which *Orunodoi* presented the contemporary Sikh world was not matched later by anyone studying Sikhs of nineteenth century Punjab. Periodicals like *Mau* or *Assam Bandhu* perhaps found nothing to write about. But the bitterness between Duleep Singh and the British (after 1890) caused quite a stir in Oriya, Bengali and Hindi publications. Assam's reticence on the subject is surprising.[41] This situation continued until the third decade of the twentieth century when the Akali-led movement for reforms in gurdwaras convulsed the Golden Temple complex (1920-5). It generated widespread enthusiasm among the Indian nationalists, including those from Assam.

Under the Akali leadership the Sikhs once again hit the headlines of the Indian newspapers during the Non-cooperation Movement. The Akalis sought to spread their influence and power through

[41] The Calcutta papers had then carried the news of Maharaja Duleep Singh's confrontation with the British. I had also the opportunity of consulting some of the Oriya newspapers and weeklies while working in the Utkal Sahitya Samaj Library at Cuttack. *Nabasambad*, *Sevak*, *Sanskarak*, etc., published a variety of news on Duleep Singh. Their sympathy was generally with the Sikh monarch. Soon after Duleep Singh's death, *Sikhjuddher Itihas o Maharaja Duleep Singha*, Calcutta 1893, by Barodakanta Mitra was published. Duleep Singh did not receive such serious treatment from any other Bengali writer. Infra, pp. 217-18. Since the educated middle class opinion in Assam had not yet become directly critical of the British, the news perhaps did not get any major coverage in Assamese newspapers.

reforms of the gurdwaras. They took up the cudgels against the *mahants* who were then accused of using the gurdwaras in their own interest, with the support of the colonial rulers. The Akalis exerted pressure on the government to grant their religious demands. The non-violent Akalis also looked for support from the Indian National Congress. They gradually built up a mass movement in Punjab which ran parallel to the non-violent Congress agitation in other parts of India. The Akalis received serious attention of the non-Sikhs beyond Punjab.[42]

News of the Akali movement did not take long to reach eastern India. Assam at that time was also witnessing the tumultuous happenings of the Non-cooperation Movement. The message of the Akalis thus fell on receptive ears. The Assamese weekly *Sadiniya Asamiya* bore evidence of the warmth with which the news was received in the papers of Calcutta, Cuttack, Puri and Patna. The periodical covered Akali events from September 1922 to December 1925 and made frequent favourable comments. Editorials and discussions appeared on a number of topics—the causes of the clash between the Akalis and the British administration, corruption of the priests, idealism of the *satyagrahis*, police atrocities on peaceful demonstrators in different areas, importance of the Nankana Sahib gurdwara in Sikh history, the resignation of the Nabha ruler Ripudaman Singh, the Congress support to the Akalis, the causes and consequences of official intransigence and so on. *Sadiniya Asamiya* tried hard to satisfy its nationalist readers' curiosity about the Akalis.[43] This phase lasted only till 1925. The reason is not difficult

[42] At this point of time there appeared over a large part of north India a frame of mind that was sympathetic to the Sikhs and looked forward to a reunion with the Sikhs. A number of Hindi poets, journalists and playwrights saw it as a family reunion after long separation. Mention may be made in this context of Sampurnanand's *Akalion ka Adarsh Satyagrah*, Banaras 1922, and *Akali Darshan* edited by Sibnarayan Mishra, Kanpur n.d. One may also refer to Suryakant Tripathi Nirala's 'Jago Phir Ekbar', *Nirala Rachanabali*, New Delhi 1983, pp. 136-8 and Maithilisaran Gupta's *Gurukul*, Chirgaon 1985 Bikrami.

[43] This newspaper published from Dibrugarh was an important vehicle of nationalism in Assam. The famous poet Chandrakumar Agarwala and the well known nationalist leader Omeo Kumar Das were associated with it. The paper first came out in 1918, was a weekly from 1928 to1930 and later became biweekly. It suffered a lot for being an organ of the Indian National Congress. Cf. Prafulla Chandra Barua, *Asamar Batari Kakat Eti Ruparekha, 1846-1947*, Guwahati 1993, pp. 84, 94, 280. Probably the largest collection of copies of *Sadiniya Asamiya* is in the library of the Directorate of Historical and Antiquarian Studies (DHAS) Guwahati. I am indebted to Bhrigu Bharali, Librarian, DHAS, for his help in accessing the relevant files of *Sadiniya Asamiya*.

to locate. After 1926, the early Sikh enthusiasm about gurdwara reform subsided. Interest in Assamese nationalist papers about the contemporary Sikh politics thus waned. During the intervening period however the Sikhs had received a recognition which they had never attained before. Curiosity about the religion and politics of the Sikhs grew among the non-Sikhs.[44] The credit for it largely goes to *Sadiniya Asamiya*.

V

Instances of Sikh studies in Assamese also lie scattered in poetry, drama and fiction. These include *Padumkuari* (1895), *Manomati* (1900), *Dandua Droha* (1919), *Pashan Pratima* (1930), *Chandrakanta Singha* (1931) and *Haradatta* (1935). These were authored by well known writers who did not leaf through Sikh history to get their material. They found it in local anecdotes, narrative songs like *Padmakuarir malita*, *Barphukanar geet* and other folklore products. The background of their writings is entirely Assamese, the main and minor characters are also Assamese and their aspirations arose from contemporary and regional factors. The one or two Sikh characters who appear as dramatis personae in the chain of incidents can be divided into two broad groups. Some of them are described as aliens who betrayed the local political cause and are subjected to much vilification. On the other hand, there are a few Sikhs ready to die to protect the integrity of Assam. They were hailed as patriots in Assamese writings. Such a mixture of opposites can hardly be found in the literature of other regional languages. How could these Sikhs be linked up with Assam? The search for explanation would take us into past history of the region.

[44] At least five such incidents occurred in the 1930s. First, Bairam Singh, an Assamese Sikh of Dibrugarh, was imprisoned and fined for taking part in the Civil Disobedience Movement in 1930. He was released three months later. The news of his arrest and release appeared in *Sadiniya Asamiya* (17August and 28 December 1930). Secondly, Banamali Bhattacharya, an assistant teacher of Golagata High School, joined the Boys' Scouts movement and on his way to Australia spent a few days in Lahore and Amritsar. *Avahan* carried his travelogue in serialized instalments, parts of them describing the Golden Temple. Cf. *Avahan*, Bhada 1857 Saka, pp. 1251-3. Third, Jog Singh Chhetri, President of the Reception Committee for the Asam Sanrakhshani Sabha, Nagaon, featured in *Bardaichila*, 5th Part, 1858 Saka, pp. 216, 218. Fourth, Chitradas (Atulchandra Hazarika) wrote a short poem about the bravery of an unknown Sikh woman in *Banhi*, Kati 1856 Saka, p. 391. Fifth, Harichandra Bhattacharya's biographical sketch of Guru Nanak came out in *Banhi*, Ahar 1854 Saka, pp. 138-40. Supra, p. 34.

Our inquiry begins with the last two decades of the eighteenth century, marked by the waning power and glory of the Ahom kings.[45] Taking advantage of the internal and frontier problems, a mixed horde of mercenaries entered the province and went on a rampage. Among those were a few Sikh soldiers. They were mostly active in Guwahati, Darrang and Kamrup districts of Assam. It is very likely that the East India Company's frequent military operations against the marauders and others of the late eighteenth century compelled them to leave the frontiers of Bengal for Assam where they found a happy hunting ground of their own. They were known as *barkandaz*[46] in official and non-official writings. These men were given to looting which made the internal instability of Assam even more critical and fomented feudal unrest and palace revolutions. The financial structure of the Ahom kingdom weakened and the

[45] The political history of the period is recorded in many definitive works. Here are two: S.K. Bhuyan, *Anglo-Assamese Relations, 1771-1826,* Gauhati 1947 and S.L. Baruah, *Last Days of Ahom Monarchy: A History of Assam from 1769-1826,* New Delhi 1993. Amalendu Guha, 'Neo-Vaishnavism to Insurgency: Peasant Uprisings and the Crisis of Feudalism in Late-Eighteenth-Century Assam', in Asoke Mitra (ed.), *The Truth Unites: Essays in Tribute to Samar Sen,* Calcutta 1986, pp. 26-69 provides a socio-economic background of the Assamese scene. Also see Maheswar Neog, *Socio-Political Events in Assam Leading to the Militancy of the Mayamariya Vaisnavas*, Calcutta 1982; Amalendu Guha, *The Decline of the Ahom Kingdom, 1765-1826,* Calcutta 1986.

[46] Contemporary official documents describe the *barkandaz* as 'a matchlock-man but commonly applied to an Indian armed with a sword and shield, who acts as door-keeper, watchman, guard or escort'. Cf. A.I. Timirzi (ed.), *Calendar of Persian Correspondence, 1794-1795*, vol. XI, New Delhi 1969, p. viii. Five letters of 1794-5 show that they marauded the districts Guwahati, Darrang and Kamrup. In his *Sannyasi and Fakir Raiders in Bengal,* Calcutta 1930, Jamini Mohan Ghosh wrote that they played the same role in Bengal and Bihar. Taking advantage of Assam's political weakness these *barkandazes* entered lower Assam, having taken a beating from the English in Bengal and Bihar. They established their sway in Goalpara, Dhubri, the surroundings of Guwahati and the areas north of the lower Brahmaputra valley. There was a sprinkling of Sikh soldiers among them. Surendranath Sen mentioned a Sikh soldier called Dhir Singh in his *Prachin Bangla Patra Sankalan*, Calcutta 1942, p. 58. In her *Last Days of Ahom Monarchy,* Baruah offers a detailed account of Sikh *barkandazes* in different stages of the civil war. See also A.J. Moffatt Mills, *Report on the Province of Assam,* Guwahati reprint, 1987, p. 57. I am indebted to J.N. Phukan of Gauhati University for drawing attention to the report. But all *barkandazes* were perhaps not complete outsiders in Assam. A significant section of these mercenaries came from the Dhubri Sahib gurdwara region in lower Assam. Many of them had close contact with the Sikhs of Bihar and participated in the struggle for succession to the throne of Cooch Bihar which 'flared up periodically

royalty lost much of its prestige. Added to it were the indiscretions of the Ahom kings which encouraged the Burmese to invade Assam in the early nineteenth century and hastened the downfall of the kingdom around 1817-26.[47] On the contrary, rumour has it that a Sikh battalion courted death fighting for the Ahom king, Raja Chandrakanta Singha (1811-18), to defend the freedom of Assam. Many Assamese-Sikhs of Lanka, Barkola, Hathipara and other villages in Nagaon district even today worship these men as their forefathers and remember them through different cultural ceremonies and rituals.

We thus find two categories of Sikh soldiers—the mercenaries from outside, devoid of loyalty and driven by nothing but personal greed: and those who came to treat Assam as their own land, speak Assamese and were ready to die for it. Assamese writers made their choice according to their purpose and leavened the account with the spirit of the age.[48] In depicting these two types of Sikhs, two parallel trends in Assam's national consciousness were strengthened.

These two trends were: first, thoughts centred on Assamese language and culture which attached greater importance to localties than to the all-India vision; and secondly, thoughts in identification with the Indian subcontinent and the need to make the Assamese ethos part of the all-India psyche. The first trend was more

---

between 1765 and 1790'. Later on they remained around the Dhubri Sahib gurdwara and came forward during the revolt of Haradatta (early 1790s). It seems likely that during the pre-civil war period and after it, they gradually learned Assamese and became aware of the physical geography of the lower Assam. This might have facilitated their employment in the ranks of the Ahom army in the late eighteenth and early nineteenth centuries.

[47] The Burmese defeated the Ahoms and captured Assam in 1817. They ruled till 1826 when the British conquered the province. The Burmese killed, looted and pillaged to an unprecedented degree. The Assamese describe those days of anarchy as *Manar Din*. In Assamese, the Burmese are called *Man*. The Assamese did not forget their depredations even a hundred years after the introduction of British rule in the region. Poets, playwrights and others offered graphic descriptions of these days.

[48] Assamese literary resurgence since the last quarter of the nineteenth century did not fail to highlight the experiences of these days. To understand the cultural milieu, see Tilottoma Misra, *Literature and Society in Assam: A Study of Assamese Renaissance, 1826-1926,* Delhi 1986, and Nagen Saikia, *Background of Modern Assamese Literature,* Delhi 1988.

prominent in the concluding part of the nineteenth century while the second trend influenced Assam particularly after the 1920s. But the first trend was not altogether forgotten even in the latter period. As mentioned earlier, the influx of the educated Bengali middle class since the middle of the nineteenth century at different levels of the provincial social framework placed the Assamese on the defensive.[49] The Assamese middle class could scarcely hope to defend its interests in competition with these 'outsiders', i.e. the Bengalis, who were not only 'well-trained', but sometimes enjoyed 'favouritism' and support from certain British officials of the region. The reaction to it 'assumed the form of acute xenophobia'.[50] Xenophobia existed even under the Ahom kings.[51] Its mainfestation can be detected in the word *Bangal* which was frequently used in essays, novels, plays,

[49] This mentality was not peculiar to Assam. Comparison can be made with Orissa. A large-scale migration of the Bengali middle class, their domination in the local job market, the imposition of Bengali instead of the local language as medium of instruction and a few other factors caused deep reaction. Debates have been going on in both the provinces about the role of the Bengali middle class during the colonial rule. Strong criticism has been made of it by Jogendranarayan Bhuyan, *Unabingsa Satikar Asam-Sambad,* Dibrugarh 1990 and Natabar Samantaray, *Adhunik Oriya Sahityar Bhittibhumi (1803-1920),* Bhubaneswar 1981. A different view of Bengalis has been taken by Prasenjit Choudhury in Assam (see his *Itihas Charcha,*Guwahati 1995) and Gaganendra Nath Dash in Orissa (see his *Oriya Bhasa-Suraksha Andolan,* Cuttack 1993).

[50] Hiren Gohain, 'Origins of the Assamese Middle Class', *Social Scientist*, August 1973, pp. 11-26. But the contemporary educated Assamese also did not hesitate to welcome the advances in sciences and education attained by Bengalis in Calcutta. Mention may be made of Gunabhiram Barua, *Anandaram Dhekiyal Phukanar Jiban Charitra*, Guwahati reprint, 1972. See also Amalendu Guha, 'Impact of Bengal Renaissance on Assam: 1825-75', in Barun De (ed.), *Essays in Honour of Prof. S.C. Sarkar,* New Delhi 1971, pp. 462-76; Prafullakumar Mahanta, *Asamiya Madhyabitta Srenir Itihas,* Guwahati 1991, pp. 62-9; H.K. Barpujari (ed.), *The Comprehensive History of Assam* , vol. IV, Guwahati 1994, pp. 368-9 and vol. V, Guwahati 1993, pp. 218-21; Rajen Saikia, *The Social and Economic History of Assam: 1853-1920,* New Delhi 2000, p. 173. The self-divided nature of the Assamese mind is noticeable. A similar feeling also prevailed among the Oriya Brahmos. Infra, pp. 84-5.

[51] Xenophobia existed even in medieval Assam. Maharaja Rudra Singha (1694-1714) was the first Ahom king who wished to establish contact with the outside world. But his attempt 'to give a new colour to Assam's life by importing customs and manners from Hindusthan' failed because his nobles 'bluntly' opposed this move. Amalendu Guha has also spoken of Assam's limited contact with the external world which led to a *pyke*-based military feudalism and restricted use of currency as

short stories, etc.[52] It is indicative of an urge to preserve regional tradition and identity and generated deep contempt and caution about the influx of 'outsiders'.

There were other reasons as well for educated Assamese middle classes to vent their spleen on 'foreigners'. The British policy of replacement of Assamese in the law courts and schools by Bengali (1836) 'left a permanent scar on the linguistic life of these two communities in Assam'.[53] This was deepened by the educated Hindu Bengalis grabbing the lion's share of the local jobs; many of them were expressing scepticism about the distinctiveness of the Assamese language. Further, hard-working and enterprising Bengali peasants (mostly Muslims) started pouring into the less populated areas of Assam from the congested and populous districts of northern Bengal. Immigration of these enterprising cultivators was 'no doubt a welcome phenomenon for labour-short, land-abundant Assam from the economic point of view'.[54] It stimulated cultivation over marshy waste land. But this led to a serious political debate in the contemporary Assamese press and it assumed a communal character in the 1930s. Grave anxiety was thus expressed about the infiltration of Bengali Muslims in the Census of 1931. Nearly all of them came from Mymensingh district which had a common boundary with the

---

a medium of exchange. So long as such military feudalism and economy existed, the Ahom dynasty had its power and glory. In the eighteenth century the need for the use of currency was increasingly felt (especially in the lower Assam) and the Ahoms showed cracks. It may be argued that Assamese xenophobia partly derived from the odds against external trade.

[52] *Hema Kosha*, Guwahati reprint, 1992, by Hemchandra Barua describes *Bangal* as the inferior people of Bengal. *Chandrakanta Abhidhan,* Gauhati 1857 Saka, however, points out that the word *Bangal* stands for foreigners and *Bangalar Din* were considered synonymous with British days. The British were also called *Baga* (white) *Bangal. Bangal* was a term of contempt as Assamese literature shows. For a similar view, see Profulla Chandra Borua, *Assamese Proverbs,* Gauhati 1962, p. 27.

[53] Sisir Kumar Das, *A History of Indian Literature 1810-1910: Western Impact and Indian Response,* New Delhi 1991, p. 138.

[54] Guha, *Planter-Raj to Swaraj*, p. 206. For other economic changes brought about by these enterprising peasantry, see *Report on the Line System Committee*, vol. I, p. 7; Sajal Nag, *Roots of Ethnic Conflict: Nationality Question in North-East India,* New Delhi 1990, pp. 101-7, 127-8; Udayon Misra, *The Periphery Strikes Back: Challenges to the Nation-State in Assam and Nagaland*, Shimla 2000, pp. 126-9.

province of Assam.[55] The Assamese middle class feared that it would rob them of their majority and 'instigated a hate campaign against the immigrants'. It was also debated whether the Assamese language would be able to defend itself against a new powerful invader in the shape of Bengali which, with the coming of the Eastern Bengal settlers, had established itself firmly, in nearly all the districts of lower and central Assam.

Plays and novels bore evidence of this fear, sense of foreboding and contempt. Despicable characters who had come to Assam with an eye to the main chance were portrayed and these included the Sikhs. Their purpose was to harm the Assamese. Lakshminath Bezbarua had written about such Sikhs and after him came the famous playwright, Daibachandra Talukdar (1901-68) who dealt with contemporary events.

VI

Around the middle of the last decade of the eighteenth century, during the reign of the Ahom king Kamaleswar Singha (1795-1810), Choudhury Haradatta and his brother Biradatta of Jikeri (Kamrup) revolted against the persecution of the ruler of Guwahati, Badan Barphukan.[56] The rebels received mass support for quite some time and were able to extend their military might temporarily to northern Kamrup. Even the Koch king of Cooch Behar is said to have been sympathetic to Haradatta. This was perhaps because negotiations for his marriage to Haradatta's daughter, Padumkuari, were on. This is known as the *Dundia Droha* or *Dumdumiya* revolt (beginning in

[55] The following table shows how the immigrants from Mymensing district brought about a change in the demographic scenario in six Assam valley districts during 1911-31 (Ms = Mymensingh district and 000's omitted).

Year	Goalpara	Kamrup	Darrang	Nagaon	Sibsagar	Lakhimpur
1 2	3	4	5	6	7	
1911	77(Ms.34)	4(Ms.1)	7(Ms.1)	4(Ms.1)	14(Ms. Nil)	14(Ms. Nil)
1921	151(Ms.78)	44(Ms.30)	20(Ms.12)	58(Ms.52)	14(Ms. Nil)	14(Ms. Nil)
1931	170(Ms.80)	134 (Ms.91)	41(Ms.30)	120(Ms.108)	12(Ms. Nil)	19(Ms.2)

Source: *Census of India 1931*, Assam, Report, vol. III, Part I, Calcutta 1932, p. 50.

[56] There were many reasons for Haradatta's revolt. For a detailed discussion, see Gunabhiram Barua, *Asam Buranji*, Guwahati reprint, 1972, pp. 124-5. Barua was a pioneer in Assamese literature. He left a deep mark in the late nineteenth century as a liberal thinker.

late 1791). The rebel army had a large Punjabi-Sikh and Hindustani contingent.[57] A few of them were probably descendants of those Sikhs who came with Guru Tegh Bahadur (or might have come subsequently) from Bihar or other parts of India and resided around the Dhubri Sahib gurdwara. The Sikh shrine is also called the Damdama Sahib and its local corrupted form is *Dumduma*. It perhaps served as a military *akhara* to many of these rebels. Initial success notwithstanding, the rebels had to surrender to the ruler of Guwahati, Badan Barphukan.

The history of the revolt inspired many playwrights and novelists in Assam. Folklore apart, the writings of Gunabhiram Barua (1837-95) present a picture of the revolt and the movement of Sikh soldiers.[58] Lakshminath Bezbarua was, however, the first novelist to use the canvas in his *Padumkuari*, serialized in the famous periodical *Jonaki* for a year or so.[59] He was not too cautious in the use of historical material and gave a free rein to his imagination. His prose had a remarkable resonance with the contemporary national narrative of the Assamese. Historical events revolving round Haradatta, Biradatta, Padumkuari and Badan Barphukan were mentioned. There is also a reference to a Sikh soldier, Kumedan Singh, who makes a brief appearance towards the end of the novel as Badan Barphukan's general.[60] He is portrayed as a villain and a traitor, apart from being a 'foreigner'. His covetous eyes fall on the defenceless beauty, Padumkuari who had just lost her father (Haradatta), perhaps a veiled hint at foreign eyes on beauteous Assam. The Assamese of the period seeking the annihilation of 'foreigners', may have found a kind of wish-fulfilment in Kumedan Singh's death.[61]

[57] Edward Gait, *A History of Assam,* Guwahati reprint, 1981, p. 218; H.K. Barpujari (ed.), *The Comprehensive History of Assam,* vol. II, Guwahati 1992, p. 335.

[58] Barua, *Asam Buranji*, pp.125-6; idem, *Jibancharitra*, pp. 5-11.

[59] The novel was serialized in *Jonaki* from Magh 1812 to Aghan-Puh 1813 Saka.

[60] Kumedan Singh appears to be a historical character. Prafulladatta Goswami's collection of folk songs includes *Padumkuarir malita* which confirms it. Goswami thinks Kumedan is a corruption of the word commandant and acknowledged his historicity. Cf. Prafulladatta Goswami, *Bara Mahar Tera Git,* New Delhi 1970, p. 179. For a similar view, see Bhai Kahn Singh Nabha, *Mahan Kosh,* Patiala reprint, 1990, p. 1163.

[61] The word 'foreigners' here does not mean the British. Assamese thinking had not by then turned anti-British. Bezbarua was also not anti-British. On the other hand, the word *Bangal* seems to have been used against those Bengalis who were challenging the Assamese linguistic and cultural identity as well as seeking to

Bezbarua drafted the novel in Calcutta where the first batch of modern Assamese intellectuals were getting ready to participate in the ongoing cultural reawakening process in Assam. In Calcutta, they were in a minority, if not foreigners by culture, while the city itself was busy with the different politico-cultural experiments of the time. While admiring these developments, many of them were often critical about Bengali Hindus in the Assam valley following the bandwagon of the imperial masters. Living in the land of Bengalis, Bezbarua's love for Assam induced him to empathize with the pangs of Assamese intellectuals there. In the midst of all these conflicting developments, he could not but sympathize with Haradatta's fight in the previous century. Thus, Bezbarua's pen turned the local chief into a national hero of Assam. He could also make his voice felt in the Brahmaputra valley—it was a voice of protest against the cultural aggression of the 'foreigners' with a distinct linguistic identity. It was an appeal on behalf of Assam seeking to maintain her cultural hegemony within her own geographical limits. Lakshminath was not content with portraying Kumedan Singh in an unfavourable light in his novel. Maharaja Ranjit Singh was not spared either. During the *Dundia* revolt, Biradatta once suggested to his brother Haradatta that they should seek military assistance from the 'large-hearted and kind Lion of the Punjab'. But Haradatta in a long speech upbraided his brother and dismissed the suggestion. Ranjit Singh was to him a foreign king. Seeking his help would mean betraying Assam. Ranjit Singh was an enemy. To Haradatta it was a better fate to die at the hands of the local governor Badan Barphukan. Bezbarua thus expressed his hatred of 'foreigners' in no uncertain terms.

A question arises here. Poets and novelists in the regional languages generally describe the reign of Ranjit Singh as a glorious period in Indian history.[62] Bezbarua expressed high regard for Guru Nanak.

---

dominate the local job market. Here lies an important root of the regional nationalism of Assam. In this sense also, one may regard Bezbarua as the mentor of early Assamese nationalism.

[62] When Lakshminath Bezbarua was contributing to *Jonaki*, Manomohan Bose wrote his novel *Duleen Athaba Ranjit Singha Sankranta Aitihasik Nabanyas*, Calcutta 1813 Saka, in Bengali. Manomohan wrote that when the 'British were about to swallow up the whole of India', Ranjit Singh was the 'last independent Indian sovereign' whose 'powerful and radiant personality' gave lustre to the country. *Duleen* largely revolved round his reign. For further details, see the author's 'Maharaja Ranjit Singh in Bengali Literature', *Journal of Sikh Studies*, February 1985, pp. 55-64. Infra, pp. 201-3.

Why was he then so critical of Ranjit Singh? Bezbarua was not the only one in Assam to criticize Ranjit Singh. But the others did not call him a foreigner. At the time when Bezbarua wrote, Assamese nationalism was somewhat divorced from the aspirations of the Indian National Congress, but the national outlook was not underrated. There was therefore no contradiction between the two strands in Assamese thought in the eyes of Assamese writers. Bezbarua saw in Guru Nanak's message a syncretic effort. Here Assamese regional consciousness did not clash with the broader Indian nationalism, as the Assamese writers found the two complementary.

The same can be said about Daibachandra Talukdar who crossed many hurdles to attend the All India Students' Conference session at Nagpur (1920) and subsequently took an active part in the Non-cooperation Movement in Assam, but still spoke against the influx of 'foreigners' in Assamese politics.[63] He wrote a play entitled *Haradatta* in 1935. The dramatis personae remained the same—Kumedan Singh the Sikh villain, Haradatta the rebel, his devoted brother Biradatta, the cruel Ahom ruler Badan Barphukan. It is marked by the same contempt for outsiders. Through the interplay of the emotions of the characters, Talukdar introduced heated political debates. Without doubt, a lot of the material came from Bezbarua.[64] But Talukdar changed it a lot, especially in the portrayal of Kumedan Singh.

In Bezbarua's *Padumkuari*, Kumedan was the lone representative of Sikh mercenaries and had a brief presence in the whole novel. But Talukdar dwelt on his character more elaborately, providing him a larger role in the play and painting him with a deeper hatred. Besides, Kumedan is not alone in *Haradatta*. He appears as the leader of a large contingent of Sikh soldiers. They are all greedy and generally communicate in a mixed Hindi language. As outsiders they are universally guided by a profit-making motive. Talukdar has also made another change in the role of Sikh mercenaries. Bezbarua never talked of Sikhs deserting the cause of Haradatta. Talukdar, however, underlines that they shouted 'Victory be to Guruji' and infiltrated into Haradatta's army and then thought of nothing but betraying him. Finally, they did desert him in the expectation of getting a higher

[63] This information is from the late playwright's unpublished autobiography. I am grateful to his son Asoke Talukdar of Guwahati for this information.

[64] He also admitted having collected materials from the novel *Dandua Droha* by Rajanikanta Bardoloi.

pay from Badan Barphukan. In this way they prove themselves traitors in Assam. Their standard of morality was equally low. From the beginning, the playwright showed that Kumedan could stoop to anything for lust and lucre.

This is not the case in the novel *Padumkuari*. The lurid colours in which Kumedan is presented by Talukdar diminishes realism. Taken as a whole, Talukdar seemed to be more bitter and vocal against these Sikhs in the 1930s. Contemporary political tension over the question of immigrants as well as the publication of the 1931 census figures might have deeply influenced Talukdar. Besides, the demand for the introduction of the 'Line System' and the issue of domicile certificate made Assam politics extremely tense. While working in the office of the Deputy Commissioner at Guwahati, he might have become intimately aware of the 'immigrant' issue, which was then being widely debated in Assam. Perhaps here he had also gone through the census statistics and the relevant report. Against this political backdrop, Talukdar's hypersensitivity towards Sikh mercenaries could have become so pronounced. It must have reached out to the Assamese mind. But in his attempt to relate his subject to the heated contemporary realities, the playwright often sacrificed facts and got lost in his own imaginary ambience.

Studied against the broader perspective of Sikh studies, the treatment of Kumedan and his Sikh soldiers by Bezbarua and Talukdar raises a few questions. Are these harsh comments about the Sikhs altogether new or can these also be traced in other regional languages? Secondly, can Bezbarua and Talukdar's interpretations of Sikh *barkandaz* divisions be regarded as the last word of Assamese writers on the subject? As to the first question, it may be said that such uncharitable comments about the Sikhs were nothing new. Tagore's concern about Sikh bellicosity at the beginning of the twentieth century is an important indicator in this regard.[65] Comments from the Hindi belt were even ruder, bad enough to exacerbate relations between Hindus and Sikhs. The latter were there described as 'bigots', 'foolish and lacking in foresight'. Some of the Hindi books which were stridently critical of the Sikhs had to be banned.[66] But at the time when Bezbarua and Talukdar wrote, there were one

[65] Infra, pp. 150-3.

[66] Medieval Persian chroniclers occasionally made offensive remarks about Sikh soldiers. Echoes were heard in the first part of the nineteenth century when Wahabi supporters fought against the armies of Ranjit Singh at Balakot (1831). Many Hindi

or two Assamese writers who took a different view. They argued that Kumedan and the Sikh division of *barkandazes* were not representative specimens. They perhaps invented Chaitanya Singh out of oral traditions popular among the Assamese-Sikhs of the region and threw Kumedan Singh into a shed. Thus, Sikh studies in Assam acquired a new dimension which makes the quest still more intriguing and challenging.

VII

The novelist Rajanikanta Bardoloi (1863-1939) looked at the Sikh *barkandazes* in Assam from a diametrically opposite point of view. He threw new light on the role of Sikh soldiers in Assam separately in two novels—*Manomati* and *Dandua Droha*. Bezbarua and Talukdar had given history a back seat in their writings. Bardoloi, on the other hand, brought in history in such an extensive manner that none before and after him could match it in pre-Independence Assamese literature. He blended history with regional oral tradition, legend, folk language and the like. These sources enabled Bardoloi to draw the period under study in vivid colours. Some literary critics have alleged that his historicity sometimes impaired the literary values, but he provided future historians with source materials and made Sikh studies a little more colourful and popular. We should begin with his *Manomati* which is perhaps one of the finest historical novels in Assamese. Here he deals with Sikh mercenaries in a different light.

The novel was published at the beginning of the twentieth century. By that time the Assamese reader had formed some idea about Kumedan Singh and the Sikh *barkandazes*. But Bardoloi had a historical awareness of his own that made him different from his

---

writers also abused the Sikhs in the pre-Independence period. Nandkumardev Sharma (1882-1926), for example, expressed annoyance, petulance and concern about the Sikhs. See the author's 'Nandkumardev Sharma's writings on the Sikhs', *Sikhs: Past and Present*, December 1991, pp. 16-24. In the beginning of the twentieth century, Niranjanlal Gupta even accused the Sikhs of colluding with the Muslims against the Hindus in medieval days. He used extremely strong and harsh language in his book denouncing the Sikhs. The British government had to ban the book *Bhram Nibaran Arthat kya Sikh Hinduon ke Rakshak Hai?*, Delhi 1918. Contemporary Hindu authors of Punjab and the United Provinces abused the Sikhs in Urdu as well. The *Annual Native Newspapers Reports* of these two regions provide a glimpse of the situation. This attack on the Sikhs perhaps came mainly from the Sanatani Hindus and Arya Samajis.

predecessors. His reconstruction of the unfortunate days of Burmese invasions placed his historical perspective in the first quarter of the nineteenth century. He chose a period when the old Assamese royalty, society, economy and value-system seemed to be crumbling all at once. Against this environment enveloped with darkness, Bardoloi reconstructed a glowing picture of Assamese defence. The characters of his novel were projected as patriots resisting the process of disintegration and fighting for their hearth and altar. While providing a new dimension to the Assamese past, Bardoloi sought to absolve the Ahom crown of its medieval tyranny. It was given a refreshing look so that the royal power could give the Assamese an inspiring leadership in times of national crisis. The novelist could successfully convey a new sense of Assamese unity which we had often missed before Bardoloi.

Patriotic love for Assam represents an important aspect of Bardoloi's writings. With his intimate knowledge of the course of events of these years, he provided a nationalistic touch to the scene. His Ahom king gave a clarion call to all his subjects. The Assamese had thus prepared themselves to repulse the Burmese invaders at the battlefield of Hadirachaki (1821) situated in western Assam. The Sikhs were roped in. Their leader Chaitanya Singh was a *subedar.* He had come from distant Punjab along with five hundred fellow Sikh warriors. They were ready to fight for the defence of the freedom of Assam. The Ahom general welcomed Chaitanya Singh in the traditional Assamese fashion, by offering him *tamol-pan* with his own hand.[67] Chaitanya Singh did not come to Assam for plunder in 1821 as Kumedan Singh had done during 1792-5. These Sikhs shouted, 'Victory be to the Maharaja of Assam'. In Bardoloi's narrative these Sikhs fought with the patriotic Assamese against the Burmese invaders and shared their sufferings.

The treatment of Chaitanya Singh was definitely emotional but it pointed to a new direction in Assamese Sikh studies. Bardoloi's *Manomati* was distinctly different from Bezbarua's *Padumkuari.* He had changed the old-fashioned definition of 'foreigners' and had built a bridge between Assam and pan-Indian thinking. Both novelists,

[67] Chapter XVI of Part II of the novel *Manomati* refers to the battle of Hadirachaki. The description is reproduced from there. For the significance of *tamol-pan* in Assamese social life, see S.N. Sarma, *The Neo-Vaisnavite Movement and the Sattra Institution of Assam,* Guwahati reprint, 1999, p. 199. For the Sikh presence in the battle, see B.C. Allen, *Assam District Gazetteers: Nowgong,* Calcutta 1905, p. 95.

however, drew inspiration from their love of Assam. Kumedan was criticized for his rapacity, Chaitanya Singh praised for his determination to defend Assam. While Kumedan Singh had been created out of the unfortunate experiences of the civil war days, questions remain about Chaitanya Singh's historicity. Recalling Bardoloi's total view of history, it may be said that Sikh soldiers were present at Hadirachaki in large numbers. But how many were they? Was their leader called Chaitanya Singh and had all these Sikhs come from Punjab? It is doubtful if that were the case. Actually there was considerable difficulty for five hundred Sikh soldiers to come to Assam at that time. First, following the Amritsar treaty of 1809, there were certain restrictions on Ranjit Singh's movement of troops in the east of the Sutlej. Besides, how could five hundred soldiers traverse the territory from the Sutlej to the western border of Assam without being detected? Moreover till 1814, Ranjit Singh's relations with Burma was known to be good. We learn from the East India Company's records that in 1823 a band of Sikh soldiers even went to Burma.[68]

It seems improbable that five hundred soldiers had been brought from Punjab. This part of the story was incorporated perhaps to underline the importance of the battle. It is also debatable whether the bravery of Sikh soldiers was already known in eastern India in the first quarter of the nineteenth century when the battle of Hadirachaki took place. The military fame of the Sikhs came to be increasingly underlined only in the late nineteenth and early twentieth centuries when it became an integral part of Indian nationalist discourse. Besides, it owed much to the British theory of 'martial races'. Ranjit Singh's sending of five hundred soldiers for the defence of Assamese liberty therefore rests more on popular imagination than on actual historical facts. On the other hand, recent research suggests that most soldiers who fought for the Ahom king at Hadirachaki were locally recruited or brought from the Bengal Presidency.[69]

In Assamese Sikh studies, Bardoloi's second novel *Dandua Droha*, published in 1919, was yet another landmark. It also deals with the

[68] Tassaduk Amanul Hussain, 'The Burmese and the North-East (1750-1852)', Dibrugarh University unpublished Ph.D. thesis, 1999, pp. 127, 148.

[69] Anil Chandra Banerjee, *The Eastern Frontier of British India, 1784-1826*, Calcutta 1946, pp. 256-7; Baruah, *Last Days of Ahom Monarchy*, pp. 161, 224-5. For popular imagination regarding the presence of Ranjit Singh's army in eastern India, see Sukumar Sinha and Himadri Banerjee (eds.), *West Bengal District Records*, New Series, *Bankura District: Letters Issued, 1802-1869*, Calcutta n.d., p. 191.

revolt of Haradatta and Biradatta of Jikeri, their final defeat and death. Kumedan Singh and the Sikh *barkandaz* are once again part of the subject. In his autobiography, Bardoloi discussed the backdrop to the novel, Assam's past geographical distinctiveness, and the cultural ambience.[70] His closeness to all this makes us understand the time of the action narrated in the novel. In the preface, he writes that the venues of the events remained almost the same in his time. He goes sometimes into great detail about the Sikh *barkandaz,* something which no Assamese writer had done before.[71] According to him, Haradatta sent an emissary to Punjab to secure the service of five hundred Sikh soldiers. But he could not get more than three hundred, comprising two hundred swordsmen and one hundred totted guns. They were mercenaries and agreed to fight for Haradatta on a remuneration of three to four rupees per month. But it became difficult for Haradatta to afford the expense. Thereafter, Kumedan Singh and his associates started extorting money from the people of Kamrup. They also pillaged homes for provisions. Fighting started and the locals began looking upon the Sikhs as a contemptible people. The Sikhs were looking for fresh pastures and in the end came under the banner of Badan Barphukan, the ruler of Guwahati. They then defeated Haradatta in a battle fighting for Badan Barphukan and started oppressing the people of Kamrup. Haradatta and Biradatta were put to death and Padum died out of grief. It brought about Kumedan's change of heart and he took to *sannyas*. His one hundred and fifty comrades-in-arms, however, married Assamese girls and settled down there.

In *Dandua Droha*, Bardoloi attempts to answer many questions, including the role of the Sikh soldiery in Kamrup, why they lost the people's support, why they left Haradatta's camp, their relations with Badan Barphukan, etc. Unlike Bezbarua, he did not dismiss them as mere 'foreigners'. He went a step forward and pointed to how these mercenaries were gradually incorporated within the Assamese social fabric. According to him, they were initially despised for their

[70] Rajanikanta Bardoloi, 'Mor Sowarani', *Avahan*, Puh 1857 Saka, p. 321. In a letter to Tirthanath Sharma (5 December 1938), Bardoloi wrote about *Dandua Droha*: 'Historical-traditional imaginaton all used'. Cf. Upendrachandra Lekharu, *Asamiya Sahitya Sebak Rajanikanta Bardoloi,* Guwahati 1953, p. 18.

[71] Rajanikanta Bardoloi, 'Patani', *Dandua Droha,* Guwahati reprint, 1954, pp. iii-v. Bardoloi himself indicated how many sources he had consulted and other sources also confirm him. See 'Samarani' and 'Patani' in *Dandua Droha*. Also see Sailen Bharali, *Asamiya Sahityar Aitihasik Upanyas,* Guwahati 1895 Saka, pp. 42-3.

plundering spree in Kamrup. The writer has also tried to trace the cause. In his opinion their plunder of the Kamrup peasantry and going over to Badan Barphukan's camp were all dictated by the laws of necessity. The Sikh *barkandaz* had therefore something to do with the fall of Haradatta. But he points out that after the revolt, Kumedan's Sikh following did not return to Punjab but made Assam their home. The Ahoms helped them with land titles. Modern research refers to the persistence of this Sikh stream which began to settle down in Assam from the last decade of the eighteenth century. It echoes the view of Rajanikanta. They married Assamese women. Gradually their descendants became the sons of the soil. Later on a section of them perhaps fought in the battle of Hadirachaki of *Manomati* and laid down their lives for the defence of Assam. *Dandua Droha* thus presented Sikh soldiers in a different hue.

VIII

The Sikhs of *Dandua Droha* did not belong to Assam. But the Sikhs of *Manomati* were not foreigners. They were neither traitors nor were they out for loot. They had ties of blood with the local populace.[72] This interesting issue finds corroboration from contem-

[72] In this regard the unpublished research work of Medhi enriches our understanding. See his 'Assamese-Sikhs', p. 66. Recent studies of Lorenzen, Gold and Kolff also point out how the late eighteenth century warrior-ascetics of other parts of India were steadily incorporated within the peasant society after they had abandoned their earlier mercenary habits. The story of the Assamization of the eighteenth century Sikh *barkandazes* more or less follows the model. Talish, a late seventeenth century Muslim observer referred to the Muslims whom he met in Assam as 'Assamese in their habits, and Muhammedan in their names'. He also felt that they 'liked the Assamese better than the Assamese visitors like himself'. In the first half of the twentieth century, Muslim peasants also embraced the Assamese ethos in Goalpara, Kamrup and Nagaon districts. They speak Assamese and regard it as their mother tongue. The Census Report of 1951 confirms this point. Assamese-Sikhs also claim this linguistic identity. Another important factor contributing to the Asssamization process of these Sikhs is their marriage with the Assamese women. This took them into the *boudoir* of Assamese culture. A.N.M. Irshad Ali and Birinchi K. Medhi, 'The Assamese-Sikhs: Profile of a Minuscule Community', in S.B. Roy and Asok K. Ghosh (eds.), *People of India: Bio-Cultural Dimensions—A Tribute to Dr. Kumar Suresh Singh,* Calcutta 1993, pp. 167-79; H.K. Barpujari, Presidential Address, Modern Section, *Proceedings, Punjab History Conference*, Fourteenth Session, Patiala 1979, pp. 146-54; David N. Lorenzen, 'Warrior Ascetics in Indian History', *Journal of the American Oriental Society*, January-March 1978, pp. 61-75; Dirk H.A. Kolff, *Naukar, Rajput and Sepoy: The Ethnohistory of the Military*

porary Assamese history. Towards the end of the eighteenth century, the growing political weakness of the Ahom monarchy, its repeated military failures and harsh economic exploitation resulted in great political discontent in the kingdom. It prompted Haradatta and Biradatta to raise the standard of revolt in Kamrup in western Assam. There was also peasant insurgency (for example, the revolt of the Mayamariyas) in some parts of upper Assam. It decimated the Assamese population. During these years, the old glory of the Assamese military organization based on the *pyke* system greatly suffered. In view of the surrounding uncertainty and military decline, the Ahoms perhaps hired a section of those Sikh soldiers who had earlier come from outside and participated in the *Dumdumiya* revolt. A few of them were granted lands to settle down in Assam. Earlier in the mid-seventeenth century, following the conflict between the Mughals and the Ahoms (1662-71), many Muslim artisans and others also stayed back in Assam to be gradually integrated into the Assamese cultural fabric.

In the closing decades of the eighteenth century, Sikh *barkandazes* possibly went through a similar process of Assamization. Later on a section of them took up cultivation and returned to their 'peaceful pursuits'. It is likely that the resemblance between the Assamese Vaishnavism of Sankardev and the message of Sikhism helped the Assamization of the Sikhs. Subsequent demographic rise of the Assamese-Sikhs through marriage and gradual development of their filial relationship made possible the incorporation of the Sikh *barkandazes* within Assamese society. They are no longer outsiders representing an alien profile in Assamese society. They have become Assamese-Sikhs, speaking the native language and adopting the local lifestyle, value system, dress, rituals and other parameters of indigenous culture. Their successors gradually evolved a distinct Assamese profile of Sikhism, which would be missing among the Sikhs of Punjab. Here in Assam, they 'made many adptations to live and farm' in rural world and represent the syncretic face of the local culture. Assamization, however, does not suggest a one way process. Assamese-Sikhs continued to retain many of their Sikh characteristics in social behaviour and religious experiences, thereby

---

Labour Market in Hindustan, 1450-1850, Cambridge 1990, pp. 71-8; Daniel Gold, 'The Instability of the King', in David N. Lorenzen (ed.), *Bhakti Religions in Northern India: Community, Identity and Political Action,* Albany 1995, pp. 122-3.

evolving a distinct category of 'hyphenated' Sikhs in this part of the country.[73] Generally speaking, they keep *kesh* and wear turban with some modifications. They are not, however, unaware of the other external symbols of Sikhism. These Sikhs have not also forsaken Sikhism. Being in the minority, they carry a few of the identifying marks of their religion. They hardly know Punjabi. But they celebrate one or two *gurpurabs* and simultaneously take part in different local ceremonies. Their dual identity thus represents an interesting phase of the evolution of Sikhism beyond the frontiers of Punjab.

What historians and anthropologists may suggest was hinted at by Bardoloi in *Dandua Droha*.[74] His novel *Manomati* presented a scenario where the Sikhs of Punjab shared the aspirations of the Assamese. In other words, the people of Assam were not alone while fighting against the foreigners. This suggests the Brahmaputra valley's closeness to Punjab, a region separated from Assam by more than a thousand miles. It no doubt brings Bardoloi nearer to the contemporary pan-Indian consciousness of which Assam and Punjab constitute an integral part. With a deep love for Assam, he perhaps expected that his Assamese neighbours should also look beyond the frontiers of Assam and provide a place of honour to the Assamese-Sikhs living there. His Assam was a land of plural ethnic and cultural traditions. He had therefore very little difficulty in accommodating these Sikhs there. It no doubt offered Bardoloi an opportunity of refurbishing the brutish image of the Sikh Kumedan Singh. He (Kumedan) might have originally come to Assam for loot and plunder. But the rapid development of events in Kamrup brought about a change of heart. He was no longer a villain but a religious mendicant. Bardoloi's Kumedan Singh was different from that of Bezbarua. He merits compassion and love. His reconstruction of the regional Sikh world situated somewhere between myth and history

[73] I have borrowed this concept from Karen Isaksen Leonard. Also see her *Making Ethnic Choices—California's Punjabi Mexican Americans*, Philadelphia 1992.

[74] Medhi has also drawn our attention to their process of interaction with Assamese culture. Apart from his 'Assamese-Sikhs', one may also see Medhi's 'Asamiya Sikhsakal—Punjabar Para Pragjyotishpuralai', *Natun Din*, Special Number, Autumn 1991, pp. 26, 28, 31. But the financially rich Punjabi-speaking Sikhs residing in the different urban centres of Assam who came to the region at a later period do not regard these Assamese-Sikhs as their social equals. They also do not hold a very high opinion about the cultural distinctiveness of the Assamese-Sikhs. A deep tension has long been going on between them regarding the question of Sikh identity in Assam.

partaking the character of both underlined an interesting transformation in the Assamese perception of Sikhism. In the process he welcomed the Assamese Sikh villages of Barkola, Chaparmukh, Hatipara and Lanka to a world of greater honour and respectability. It did not fail to give them a new dignity and self-confidence which they never had in the past.

IX

Bardoloi also inspired some other poets and writers to think on these lines about the Sikhs. One example is 'Chandrakanta Singha' (1931) by Nakulchandra Bhuyan (1895-1968).[75] They were hardly contemporaries and when Bhuyan started writing, Rajanikanta's fame had already reached its zenith. Besides, Bardoloi had dealt with the same period three decades before Bhuyan. However, he (Bhuyan) came close to Bardoloi unwittingly. And he wrote the drama to serve the needs of contemporary Assamese theatre.[76] Bhuyan had to depend on readily available books for his source materials. His play, therefore, beat a familiar track. Thus, in the fifth scene of the fifth act of the play, Chaiat (Chaitanya) Singh makes a brief appearance in the barracks of the Ahom king Chandrakanta Singha. He appears in one scene, assures full cooperation in the fight against the *Man* soldiers, expresses allegiance and departs. His role in the play is brief and so he makes little impact.

Yet another contemporary poet was Sailadhar Rajkhowa (1892-1962). Like Bardoloi, he was a senior government official and toured a lot within Assam. It helped him gather experience and identify the scenes of Assam's past glory. Towards the end of the 1920s official duties took him to *mauja* Bagrimari in Barpeta district on the northern bank of the Brahmaputra. There, on the western border, he saw the battlefield of Hadirachaki. He camped near the hills, Fullara and Chatala, which were in the vicinity. To others the hills would have meant nothing. But Rajkhowa had read *Manomati*. He

[75] Nakulchandra Bhuyan,'Chandrakanta Singha', Jatindranath Goswami (ed.), *Nakulchandra Bhuyan Rachana Samagra,* Guwahati 1996, pp. 64-113. Chandrakanta Singha was the last independent Ahom ruler of Assam. The play is based on Hiteshwar Barbarua's *Ahomar Din* and it was written at the request of Ban Rangamancha of Tezpur.

[76] Atulchandra Hazarika, *Manchalekha,*Guwahati 1967, p. 232. Also see Satyendranath Sarma, *Asamiya Natya-Sahitya,* Guwahati 1983, pp. 250-2.

discovered a new meaning in the hills connected with the memory of Hadirachaki and wrote the poem 'Pashan Pratima'.[77]

The poem marginally refers to Chaitanya Singh's valour. And there is the incomplete tale of the puppy love between two young people.[78] Past and present meet here with modern geography thrown in. In the poet's imagination, the two hills appear as two cursed daughters of the gods, and witnesses to the death of Assamese independence, with their slopes reverberating with the memory of the heroism of Hadirachaki. Chatala and Fullara are portrayed as two young girls who fell in love with Chaitanya Singh and his associate, the Assamese hero Krishnaram. The girls were ready to wait for the battle to end. But the two heroes were slain in battle, and the girls became victims of the lust of the Burmese soldiers, and they turned into stone.

The poet thus took Chaitanya Singh to the hearts of his Assamese readers. Even Bardoloi had not clearly written that a Sikh soldier could be loved by an Assamese girl for his valour. Bezbarua in the past had condemned Kumedan Singh for his lust and greed. Talukdar had for that reason called him a 'foreign dog'. Rajkhowa opened a new chapter of intimacy. He did something which is perhaps the most desired objective of a minority community. In places like Barkola and Chaparmukh in Nagaon district, the Sikhs had married Assamese girls, as the poet might have personally witnessed. Here Sikh studies perhaps acquired a perspective so far unknown in some other parts of the Indian subcontinent.

X

In Assamese Sikh studies we come across another Sikh soldier who did not belong to either of the categories mentioned earlier. He

[77] The above information is taken from the biography of Rajkhowa written by Bhubanmohan Das, *Nijara Kabi Sailadhar Rajkhowa,* Jorhat 1995, p. 60. It is not improbable that Rajkhowa had read *Manomati.* Rajkhowa also tells us in his memoirs that he was not generally well-received by the government for his patriotic views. He tried to suppress it for fear of harsh punishment. Perhaps his suppressed emotion prompted him to write 'Pashan Pratima' underlining the Assamese patriotic tradition. His closeness to contemporary pan-Indian consciousness might have encouraged him to select a Sikh hero fighting for Assam's independence. Sailadhar Rajkhowa, *Atitar Sowarani,* Dibrugarh 1969, pp. 122, 123, 132.

[78] Sailadhar Rajkhowa, 'Pashan Pratima', Manjumala Das (ed.), *Sailadhar Rajkhowa Rachanabali,* Guwahati 1992, pp. 31-3.

carried the message of armed revolt against British rule, something never suggested by any earlier Assamese writer. It was left to Jyotiprasad Agarwala (1903-51) to draw the Assamese psyche towards an all-India consciousness. Agarwala is an outstanding talent in modern Assamese literature. He was engaged in a whole host of creative activities—poetry, lyrics, drama, film direction, newspaper management, etc. He was not, by any means, less knowledgeable about the myriad problems of social life in contemporary Assam. He had for long been associated with the national movement under Gandhi and had courted imprisonment. Therefore his writings deal with social problems along with the national movement. His play 'Lovita' (1947), like 'Chandrakanta Singha' of Bhuyan, was also written for the Ban Rangamancha in Tezpur. Some important questions about the role of women in Assamese social life were posed in this play placed against the background of the Quit India Movement and the World War II. Here in passing, he dealt with the impact of the successes and failures of the national movement in Assamese political life.

In one section of the play, he portrays an anonymous Sikh commander belonging to Subhas Chandra Bose's Indian National Army (INA). No major social issue was, however, linked up with his role. His dialogue makes significant references to Indian politics. That is how he becomes a subject in Sikh studies in Assam. The character makes an appearance on stage only once.[79] That is why some people may notice a resemblance with Chaiyat Singh in the play 'Chandrakanta Singha' by Nakulchandra Bhuyan. But the anonymous Sikh commander in the play stays a bit longer on the stage and his long political discourse gives him importance. He speaks in favour of the INA and urges the Assam Rifles to rebel against British rule. He symbolizes the tradition of armed resistance in the Indian national movement. But as he knew no Assamese, his role is limited.

Jyotiprasad seems to have been influenced by both the march of the INA and the naval mutiny of 1946 in Bombay. The dramatist was a votary of Gandhi as a mass leader, but did not hesitate to recognize the significant role of the armed revolutionaries in the

[79] Jyotiprasad Agrawala, 'Lovita', Satyendranath Sarma et al. (eds.), *Jyotiprasad Rachanabali*, Guwahati 1981, pp. 222-3. I am grateful to Prasenjit Choudhury for drawing my attention to this play of Jyotiprasad Agarwala.

national movement.[80] He saw no serious contradiction in blending these two opposite forces in his drama, putting the nameless Sikh commander before the footlights. The commander also symbolizes an all-India psyche. It is amazing that no other Assamese writer has suggested any link between the Azad Hind Fauz and the Sikh martial spirit.

XI

Under British rule, Assamese Sikh studies showed a distinct variety. The journey began with *Orunodoi* (1846) and ended with *Lachit Barphukan* by Surya Kumar Bhuyan (1947). Discussions began with Guru Nanak. Other subjects reviewed were the rise and fall of the Khalsa Raj, the Sikh wars and finally the life and times of individual Sikh soldiers. The Sikh *barkandaz* who owed no loyalty came to give up his mercenary habit, took up peaceful life, put his sword away and turned to cultivation.[81] Poets, novelists, playwrights, historians and essayists of Assam have in different ways traced the evolution of Sikh life. Sikh sensibilities may have been hurt by their representation as 'bigots' and 'avaricious'. But later the bonds between the Sikhs and the Assamese people have strengthened through matrimony. Its entire credit does not go to the Assamese literati. A part of it is shared by the rural Sikhs of Assam. They learnt the Assamese language, accustomed themselves to Assamese food, and started looking upon Assam as their own land. Some of the Assamese ethos was imbibed by these Sikhs. They thus became an important part of Assamese socio-cultural life. Hindu gods and goddesses flanked Sikh Gurus on their walls. Gurdwaras have turned into *namghars*. Assamese Vaishnavism blended with their rituals. A cultural interaction therefore cannot be denied.

Another interesting aspect of the Assamization process of the recent days is the publication of numerous monographs by the Assamese-Sikhs.[82] They provide the local Sikhs with an opportunity

[80] Pralhadkumar Baruah, *Jyoti Manisha*, Dibrugarh 1993, pp. 118-19.

[81] I have borrowed the analogy from the writings of the British official H.H. Calvert's *Wealth and Welfare of the Punjab*, Lahore 1922, p. 322.

[82] These are mostly written by Rup Singh Sandhu, Bhupen Singh, Iqbal Kaur and Charan Kaur. Much valuable material can be gleaned from the annual commemorative volumes of the Assam Sikh Association, dating mostly from the 1980s. Dhyan Singh, President, Assamese Sikh Association, claims the lion's share of the credit. I could not have read these booklets without the help of Bhupen Singh and

of conveying the message of Sikhism in their mother tongue. A new Assamese-Sikh identity is also visible in the recent construction of a gurdwara commemorating the arrival of their first batch of settlers in the Sikh villages in Nagaon district.

True, Sikh studies in Assam started later than in other eastern regions.[83] Speaking statistically, fewer books on Sikhs have been published in Assam. In the past, there were no separate publication on any Sikh Guru, maharaja, the Sikh wars or the Akali movement. Nothing was written on Sikh religion, Sikh women, Sikh subgroups either. Writers in the other two regional languages (Bengali and Oriya) tried to explore these fields. Assamese writings abound in errors. Such errors can be seen even in Assamese school textbooks.[84] No one here raised questions on issues like the views of early Sikh dissenters, the composition of the *Adi Granth*, causes of the conflict between the Sikhs and Mughals, etc. These omissions seem odd as a Sikh community has been in existence in Nagaon district for nearly two hundred years, carrying with themselves some of their religious identity and communal distinctiveness. With the exception of Phula Singh Chhetri, no one had access to primary sources. Besides, no Assamese author ever went to Punjab to have direct access to Punjabi sources on Sikh history.

Niranjan Singh to whom I am deeply indebted. Also see Mathuranath Deka, *Nanak*, Guwahati n.d. and Mahendra Bora, 'Samurai', *Asamiya Kabita Chayan*, Dibrugarh 1987, pp. 99-102. The last two works, however, underline the continued interest of the non-Sikh Assamese writers in Sikh history and religion in the post-Independence years.

[83] At least one medieval *Buranji* briefly refers to the ninth Guru's visit to Assam. On the basis of this lone reference S.L. Baruah is of the view that the beginning of Sikh studies in Assam may be pushed back to medieval days. The opinion of Baruah requires deeper attention. In the first place, except the lone reference, medieval *Buranjis* maintain silence about the Sikhs. It would be risky to push back the beginning of Sikh studies in Assam to medieval times merely on the basis of this source material. Besides, the particular *Buranji* was edited by Bhuyan and his methodology has been seriously criticized by the younger Assamese scholars. See Dhrubajyoti Bora, 'Dr. Surya Kumar Bhuyanar Aitihasik Abadan', *Deuka*, October-November 1995, p.12. We may, therefore, defer our conclusion till the arrival of more source materials in this regard.

[84] Take for instance *Bharat-Buranji*, textbook for classes V and VI. I have seen its 22nd edition at the Sibsagar Zilla School Library. S.K. Barpujari (Surya Kanta Barpujari?) was associated with its revised edition. On p. 115 occurs: *Nanakar dharmamatak Nanakpanthi ba Gurumukhi dharma bale*. But Gurmukhi is the name of the script not of a religion. This is purveying wrong information.

All these objections are valid. But the bulk of the Assamese writings has a distinct local character and their sources also lie outside recorded history, in the local folk culture. Instances can be culled from *malita*, *sadhukatha*, etc. The common people of the lower Brahmaputra valley regard all of them an integral part of their wider cultural milieu. A section of these materials refer to the revolt of Haradatta Choudhury, the tragic end of his beautiful daughter Padum, the oppression of Sikh soldiers, the complex political role of Badan Barphukan of Guwahati, etc. Assamese poets, playwrights and others have drawn on these folk memories. Littérateurs like Bezbarua, Bardoloi, Bhuyan and Rajkhowa did not look to Punjab for reconstructing their Sikh characters, preferring to stay within the confines of Assam.[85] These characters are recreated out of the bedrock of folk tradition and are rooted in the geographical ambience of Assam. They represent an area of historical writings often 'uttering what history could not'. Here 'in the realm of artistic sovereignty they could legislate with impunity' in favour of re-creating a world of 'wish fulfilment'[86] about Assamese history. One may also experience how Sikh studies based on folk heritage often throw interesting light on the rural Sikh settlements in Assam. These authors gave Assamese studies on Sikhism a direction which is not likely to be seen in the other two eastern languages. Latecomers, they proceeded apace underlining various fissures within their ranks. The reconstruction of Sikh soldiers in different hues in turn reflects the heterogeneity of the Assamese middle class. Sikh studies in Assamese also got intertwined with a few other local issues and came to be enriched in the process. Many of these problems, e.g. the supremacy of the mother tongue, concern over the growing influx of 'foreigners' resulting in the 'minoritization of the local populace', the vigorous growth of regional nationalism and the nature of its link with pan-Indian consciousness, etc., are still debated in public

[85] Perhaps the only exception to the literary trend is a novelette entitled *Tej aru Dhulire Dhusarit Pristha*, Guwahati 1994. It provides an illuminating account of the Delhi Sikh earnage of 1984. Mamoni Raisom Goswami is a Delhi based Assamese littérateur and her narrative does not deal with the mainfold problems of the local Assamese-Sikh world. In this sense, she does not represent those writers so far reviewed here. On the other hand, she sets a new trend in Assamese writings dealing with the Sikhs residing outside Assam.

[86] Sudipta Kaviraj, *The Unhappy Consciousness: Bankimchandra Chattopadhyay and the Formation of Nationalist Discourse in India*, Delhi 1998, p. 123.

life and at different forums.[87] These issues have undeniably vitalized the Assamese search for Sikh history and religion in the past. Whenever these problems come up today, some notable writings related to Sikhs may spring to mind. Herein also lies the success and achievement of Sikh studies in Assamese.

[87] For the recent debate on the infiltration of 'foreigners' issue, see H.K. Barpujari,'North-East India: The Problems and Politics since 1947', General President's Address, *Indian History Congress*, Fifty-sixth Session, Calcutta 1995. Also see Jyotirindra DasGupta,'Ethnicity, Democracy and Development in India: Assam in a General Perspective', in Atul Kohli (ed.), *India's Democracy: An Analysis of Changing State-Centre Relations*, Calcutta 1988, pp. 156-61; Sanjib Baruah, *India Against Itself: Assam and the Politics of Nationality*, New Delhi 2000, pp. 86-9; Sanjoy Hazarika, *Rites of Passage: Border Crossings, Imagined Homelands, India's East and Bangladesh*, New Delhi 2000, pp. 28-74.

CHAPTER III

Oriya

A FEW YEARS AGO the Research Committee on Punjab held an international conference (1987).[1] One of the subjects discussed was the trends in modern research on Punjab. The senior American historian, Barrier, presented a paper, which dealt with researches on Punjab being carried on in different countries. Here he referred to advanced centres of learning in Calcutta which have for many years been concerned with studies on Sikh history. His assessment was fulsome. Bengalis may be pleased with the fact that Calcutta ranked high in his estimation of the quality of research done on the Sikhs, which was next to the work done in Punjab, Haryana and Delhi.[2] But some may see in it a partial departure from the truth. He accorded almost international recognition to the studies done at the universities of Calcutta but in doing so he ignored work on Sikh history undertaken at other centres in eastern India. What are the distinguishing features of these trends? Was there any institutional support behind the work? Who were the pioneers and how was it that a scholar like Barrier totally overlooked them? These questions need to be reviewed.

Those who are familiar with his researches will know that the error is unintentional. He probably steered clear of the subject because he did not have definite information on Sikh studies in the different Indian languages. If he had set his sights on Orissa, he would have succeeded in guessing to what extent the subject

[1] The Research Committee on Punjab (RCOP) is an informal study group and its members are chiefly drawn from Canada and the United States of America.

[2] N. Gerald Barrier, 'The Evolution of Punjab Studies, 1972-87', in Surjit Dulai and Arthur Helweg (eds.), *Punjab in Perspective*, East Lansing 1991, p. 2. Earlier Juergensmeyer also referred to a certain apathy among Indian researchers about Sikh studies till the late 1970s. He thought it intentional. It is debatable, however, to what extent his view may also be extended to Barrier's silence about Sikh studies in Oriya. For his view, see 'The Forgotten Tradition: Sikhism in the Study of World Religions', in Juergensmeyer and Barrier (eds.), *Sikh Studies*, pp. 17-20.

influenced the Oriya mind. Some idea can be gained from the essays, plays and biographical writings which appeared in well known and lesser known papers and periodicals published at Badipada, Balasore, Berhampore, Bhubaneswar, Cuttack, Puri and even Sambalpur. Very little of it has been considered by scholars outside Orissa. It is, therefore, not easy to make a proper evaluation abroad.

Despite Barrier's reticence it is not possible to ignore Sikh studies in Oriya. The accumulated writings represent the varied experience of people over periods of time. The authors belong to different parts of Orissa; representing predominantly the south-eastern districts from Balasore to Puri. Their intention was to convey in their vernacular, the history of a religious community of India, little known to the readers. This was an excursion beyond the geographical limits of Orissa leading to interaction with the history and tradition of one of their distant neighbours. It also provided the Oriya-speaking people a refreshing literary activity enriching their mother tongue as well as redrawing Sikh historical traditions from an Oriya cultural framework.

I

The *Janamsakhi* literature is one such domain. It points out that Guru Nanak in his eastern Indian *udasi* came to Puri.[3] It is also said that he composed there the famous *sabad—Gagan mai thal*—in the *rag Dhanasari.*[4] On the way he passed through Cuttack. It is generally believed that Dantan Sahib gurdwara on the bank of the Mahanadi at Cuttack is a testimony in stone to the visit.[5] There are others who refer to scattered pieces of evidence to suggest his visit to Bhadrak also. For instance the palm leaf manuscript of the *Japji Sahib* is one

[3] It is said that Guru Nanak met SriChaitanya at Puri. There is a debate on the point. For different views, see Ganda Singh, 'Guru Nanak at Puri with Sri Chaitanya and His Followers', *The Panjab Past and Present*, Annual Number, 1969, pp. 334-9; Banerjee, *Guru Nanak and His Times,* pp.130-1; Bimanbehari Majumdar, 'Guru Nanak and His Contemporaries', in *Guru Nanak,* New Delhi 1969, pp. 126-7.

[4] S.S. Sagar and R.S. Tak, 'Departmental Notes—Guru Nanak in Cuttack, Orissa', *Journal of Sikh Studies*, August 1974, pp. 127-44.

[5] Numerous Oriya writers have also discussed the folk tradition about the foundation of the Dantan Sahib gurdwara at Kaliaboda. See Lakshminarayan Sahu, *Guru Gobinda Singha,* Cuttack n.d., pp.1-5; Amar Singh, 'Guru Nanak in Orissa', in M.N. Das (ed.), *Sidelights on the History and Culture of Orissa,* Cuttack 1977, pp. 424-5.

such document supposedly confirming the event. The name of the village where it was found is Sangat. There is also a locality called Guru Nanak Dihi. It is claimed that a number of families attached to the Nanakpanthi/Udasi faith lived there. Three more popular literary sources have been mentioned in this connection: *Shahijatra* of Puri, *Ramakatha* of Cuttack and *Mogal Tamsa* of Bhadrak, which are in the nature of folk plays. They refer to a group of *fakirs* known as Nanak or Nanaksain who speak with a north Indian Hindi accent and project a syncretic cultural group behaviour.[6] But these popular Oriya sources do not view the founder of Sikhism against the backdrop of Punjab. Here we come across a Nanak, in the garb of a peripatetic saint. Such wandering saints, pilgrims and traders used to travel from Banaras to Burdwan via Patna, then to Balasore, Bhadrak, Cuttack and Puri long before the creation of modern Orissa. Nanakpanthis and Udasis were probably among them. They built *sangats* and *deras* and lived there, interacted with the local people and carried on trade in the region. In the process they perhaps enriched the image of Nanak in Oriya folk tradition. The Oriya Nanak also differs from the Guru Nanak of *Janamsakhis*. They speak different regional languages and represent different cultural traditions. This perhaps suggest that early Sikh tradition while coming into contact with the distant eastern Indian socio-cultural milieu underwent a significant transformation in the process. The Oriya Nanak may not satisfy the emotions of the Sikh faithfuls, but he is dear and near to the Oriyas of Puri, Bhadrak and Cuttack, because he has been recreated out of their folk memory and local experience.

The foregoing may give some idea of Guru Nanak's visit to Puri, the trips made by other Sikhs to the area in subsequent times and the echoes of Oriya reaction. They do not just suggest that Guru Nanak came here once but that Sikhs were possibly here for a long time.[7] In

[6] S.S. Sagar and R.S. Tak, 'Departmental Notes: Guru Nanak's visit to Bhadrak', *Journal of Sikh Studies*, February 1977, pp. 163-5; A. Dash, *Saint Nanak*, Bhubaneswar 1971, pp. 41-51; Shyamsundar Mishra, 'Jhanjirimangalar Ramleela: Ek Bismrita Lokanatyakala', *Ramacharit Kathamrita*,Cuttack 1993, p. 21; Siddeswar Mohapatra, *Puri Boli*, Bhubaneswar 1996, pp. 71-4; Sachidananda Mishra, 'Mogal Tamsar Rachanakal', *Jhankar*, January 1974, p. 945. The date of composition of this folk drama (*Mogal Tamsa*) is disputed.

[7] For Orissa, see Randhir Singh, *Udasi Sikhan di Vithia*, Amritsar 1959, p. 475; Bhai Kahn Sing Nabha, *Mahan Kosh*, p.1001. For Bihar, see Saratchandra Roy, *The Mundas and their Country*, Calcutta 1912, pp. 191, 201; Ved Prakash, *The Sikhs in Bihar*, pp. 151-70; M.L. Ahluwalia, 'Records relating to the Land Grants in Bihar to Nanak Shahi Maths and Priests', *Proceedings, Punjab History Conference*,

the pre-modern period, many Hindu pilgrims, traders and holy men went that way, so perhaps did some disciples of Guru Nanak. It is not unlikely that Sikh *dharamsalas* came up there. An analysis of the human element in Sikh religion in the pre-Khalsa period may clarify the issue. The writings of Bhai Gurdas indicate the presence of a sizeable group of Khatris in the Sikh community.[8] They were not agricultural people but engaged in administration and trade and commerce. In Punjab the Khatris are either Hindu or Sikh. The Sikh-Hindu dividing line among the Khatris was not always quite distinct in medieval times, as borne out by recent research.[9] A few Khatri merchants came with Akbar's commissariat when the Mughal army invaded Orissa.[10] From the early seventeenth century Patna was an important centre of trade for Punjabi Khatris who were mostly Sikhs. Later on it also become a place of pilgrimage as the birthplace of Guru Gobind Singh. The Harimandir there is one of the sacred *panj*

Seventeenth Session, Patiala 1982, pp. 103-8; V.H. Jackson (ed.), *Journals of Francis Buchanan (afterterwards Hamiton), Patna-Gaya in 1811-12*, Patna 1925, pp. 170-2; Irfan Habib, *An Atlas of Mughal India*, Delhi 1986, pp. 41, 48, 51.

[8] For Khatri dominance in the early Sikh tradition, see W.H. McLeod, *The Evolution of the Sikh Community*, Delhi 1975, p. 91.

[9] In this regard, see Oberoi, *The Construction of Religious Boundaries*, pp. 24-5, 56, 62-3. Also see William R. Pinch, *Peasants and Monks in British India*, New Delhi 1996, pp. 30-43. McLeod has also drawn our attention to a similar situation about the Khatris. See his *Who is a Sikh? The Problem of Sikh Identity*, Delhi 1989, pp. 46, 76, 82, 112.

[10] The eminent author, historian and statesman Harekrushna Mahatab (1899-1987) has briefly discussed the subject in his autobiography, *Sadhanar Pathe*, Part I, Cuttack 1949, p. 2. Many have talked of the coming of Khatri merchants to eastern India in the pre-modern age. The Khatris were engaged in trading in foodgrains, clothes, precious stones, *pashmina* shawls and the like. In the early sixteenth century, they were already active in the eastern Indian markets. Political instability in the late seventeenth century Punjab hampered its overland trade with Central Asia and Middle East. The lure of the east Indian markets continued to draw them to the east. As a result, a section of Punjabi traders got interested in eastern India. They flocked to Banaras, Patna, Dhaka and a few other places. Some of them were Nanakpanthis. For details, see Sharifuddin Ahmed, *Dacca: A Study in Urban History and Development*, London 1968, pp. 12, 20-1; C.A. Bayly, *Rulers, Townsmen and Bazaars: Northern Indian Society in the Age of British Expansion, 1770-1870*, Cambridge 1983, pp. 140, 155-6, 203-4; Archer, *The Sikhs in relation to Hindus, Moslems, Christians and Ahmadiyyas*, p. 6; Muzaffar Alam, *The Crisis of Empire in Mughal North India—Awadh and the Punjab, 1707-1748*, New Delhi 1986, pp. 143-53, 180-4; J.R. McLane, *Land and Local Kingship in Eighteenth Century Bengal*, Cambridge 1993, pp. 129-31; Balwant Singh Dhillon, *Pramukh Sikh te Sikh Panth*, Amritsar 1997, pp. 112-13, Appendix II.

takhats. The local Sikhs[11] whose ancestry goes back three hundred years did business in cotton piece goods and food grains in the different areas of the eastern region. A few of them may be going to Orissa both to trade and worship Lord Jagannath. It is a plausible theory. Orissa was consequently not *terra incognita* to the Sikhs. How close was the connection? Some references can be seen in Ishwardas' *SriChaitanya Bhagabata* written towards the end of the seventeenth century.[12] Does it not partly corroborate the hypothesis that Sikhs used to visit Puri, Cuttack, Bhadrak and Balasore in the pre-modern period?

II

Although the East India Company established its administration in Orissa in 1803, the modern age dawned there much later as did the study of Sikhism—about sixty to sixty-five years later.[13] The poetry and folk tales of Orissa in the pre-modern age bear evidence of the coming and going of the Sikhs. But there is no reference to Sikhs and

[11] It is generally assumed that the local Sikhs, who call themselves Agraharis, were converted by the ninth Guru Tegh Bahadur in the second half of the seventeeth century. These Agraharis, however, constitute a separate ethnic and linguistic group from the Sikhs of Punjab. Many of the Agrahari rituals differ from those of the Punjabi-speaking Sikhs. I am told that local Sikhs play an important role even today in the worship and other activities at the Harimandir in the Patna Sahib. For a general description of the Patna Sahib in the late eighteenth century, see Charles Wilkins, 'The Sikhs and their College at Patna', in Ganda Singh (ed.), *Early European Accounts of the Sikhs,* New Delhi reprint, 1974, pp. 207-11. See also *Census of India 1931*, Bihar and Orissa, Report, vol. VII, Part I, Patna 1933, p. 257 for their internal group divisions.

[12] S.S. Sagar and R.S. Tak, 'Departmental Notes: Guru Nanak's visit to Jagan Nath Puri', *Journal of Sikh Studies*, August 1976, pp. 168-71. Also see Bimanbehari Majumdar, *SriChaitanya Charitrer Upadan*, Calcutta 1959, pp. 496, 500.

[13] In 1803 the East India Company defeated the Marathas and established its rule in Orissa, which then hardly resembled modern Orissa. Orissa then virtually meant the Cuttack division. Later on factors like the spread of Western education, opposition to Bengali domination, territorial dismemberment and the apathy of the British officials generated a sense of unity among the Oriya-speaking people. Towards the end of the nineteenth century, they gradually came closer and asked for a better deal from the British. The unity move among the Oriya-speaking people appealed for an administrative amalgamation of the Oriya tracts lying under three different governments of Bengal, Madras and Central Provinces. Later on, it led to a demand for a separate province of their own. They achieved their goal only in 1936. Cf. Nivedita Mohanty, *Oriya Nationalism: Quest for a United Orissa,* New Delhi 1982.

Sikhism in the early nineteenth century Oriya writings.[14] How do we explain the silence? A review of the various problems related to the contemporary social and political framework may throw some light on it. The conditions, which favoured the promotion of Sikh studies in other areas in India under colonial rule, were not noticeable in Orissa. These factors include the penetration of the colonial administrative apparatus at local levels, the introduction of modern means of communication, the presence of a middle class spawned by the new educational system, their link with the printing press and keenness to reconstruct medieval Indian history in the regional language. A consideration of one or two factors in detail may reveal the hindrances to Sikh studies at the time.

Take for instance the boundaries of Orissa. Orissa at that time was pretty different from what it is today. In those days it chiefly meant Puri and other areas of *Mughalbandi* districts of Cuttack division.[15] The focal point Cuttack was redolent with history. The Lieutenant-Governor of Bengal virtually dictated the principles of administration from Calcutta at a distance of about 500 km. A sizeable number of Bengali clerks, lawyers and teachers at different levels played a dominant role. The Bengali language exercised a significant influence. But Sambalpur where Oriya is also spoken was outside the region though it is now included in it. It was then linked to the Central Provinces, where the Oriyas had to recognize the might of the Hindi-speaking population. To the south was Ganjam which was administratively joined with Madras Presidency and so there the Telugus ruled the roost. In none of these three regions did the Oriyas find a proper place for their mother tongue. And how could there be any thinking on Sikhism in areas where the regional language took the back seat?

While Orissa was being stifled by the administrative structure, which provided for three separate provincial set-ups, a famine, commonly referred to as *Na Anka,* claimed nearly one-third of the

[14] Sachidananda Mishra, however, points out that *Mogal Tamsa* was written in the early nineteenth century.

[15] The three coastal districts under direct Mughal rule (Jaleswar, Bhadrak and Cuttack) are referred to. The tributary *mahals* under a British agent during the East India Company's rule were also included in nineteenth century Orissa. See Kishori Mohan Patra, 'Growth of Social Consciousness in Orissa in the 19th Century', *Proceedings of Indian Historical Records Commission*, Fortieth Session, vol. XL, 1970, pp. 144-5.

population of the Cuttack division in 1866.[16] The tragedy exposed the weakness of the colonial administration in Orissa. Many British officials and the middle classes of Orissa could see for themselves that the famine became so deadly only because no effective administrative infrastructure was readily available in the countryside to tackle the famine.[17] The government's attention then gradually focused on modern means of communication like the railways and roadways and organizational shake-outs at different tiers to strengthen colonial rule.[18] The *Na Anka* famine occasioned a momentous change in the Oriya mental environs, as the famine brought into sharp focus the agony of a humiliated mother tongue. The educated middle class Oriya grew acutely conscious of his pitiable status as he experienced the woes of the famine. Inclusion in the Bengal Presidency no doubt enforced an 'exploitative core-periphery relationship'; they also realized their 'backwardness' compared to Bengal and came to know how the government as well as a section of the Bengalis had generally ignored them.[19] Historians are in agreement that at this stage the

[16] There is a graphic description of the famine in the autobiography *(Atmacharit)* of Fakirmohan Senapati, the father of modern Oriya literature. Also see P. Mukherjee, *History of Orissa in the 19th Century,* Bhubaneswar 1964, pp. 358-97.

[17] Kishori Mohan Patra, *Orissa State Legislature and Freedom Struggle 1912-47,* New Delhi 1979, pp. 2-3.

[18] Orissa built close links with the outside world in the last three decades of the nineteenth century. Rail links were then established with Calcutta and Madras. H. K. Mishra's study furnishes statistics about the expansion of rail and roadways, *Famines and Poverty in India,* New Delhi 1991, pp. 310-15. Also see Kishori Mohan Patra, 'Growth of National Consciousness and Freedom Movement in Orissa', *The Indian Historical Review,* July 1985-January 1986, p. 318.

[19] For a critical discussion of some of these issues, see Jayanta Sengupta, 'The Political Economy of Oriya Nationalism, 1900-1936: Problems of Backwardness and the Financing of Provincial Autonomy', *The Calcutta Historical Journal,* July-December 1995, pp. 87-94. Almost throughout the nineteenth century in Sambalpur district also, the government 'felt no political need to take cognizance of Uriya sentiments'. Cf. Richard P. Cronin, 'Language and Nationalism in Late Nineteenth and Early Twentieth Century India: The substitution of Hindi for Uriya as the court language of Sambalpur District, Central Provinces and its Consequences', in Robert I. Crane and Bradford Spangenberg (eds.), *Language and Society in Modern India: Essays in Honour of Professor Robert O. Swan,* New Delhi 1981, p. 27. A number of contemporary Oriya leaders blamed Orissa's backwardness on resident and non-resident Bengali officials and landlords. They were particularly bitter towards those Bengalis who had been dominating the 'local job market' in the late nineteenth century. Cf. P. Mukherjee, 'The Employment of the People of Orissa in the Government Service in the 19th Century', *The Orissa Historical Research Journal,* July 1959, pp. 110-17. But during the same period, a section of the Oriya middle

major concern of the leaders of the new awakening in Orissa was to earn the cooperation of the colonial administration for the defence and development of their mother tongue.[20]

Hence an important feature of Orissa's new awakening was the spread and recognition of Oriya at the local level.[21] For half a century the language had remained in the wilderness. In 1869 it received official recognition as the medium of instruction and vehicle of culture. The mother tongue became the weapon of the people and reached out to Sambalpur and Ganjam. An organization based on language called the Utkal Union Conference was born in 1903. The new leaders joined hands under its banner. The language they used in representing their demand for redemarcation of Orissa's borders was somewhat moderate. But a new spirit was about and it touched literature, religion, and different strata of social ideas. The need was felt to rediscover the past. A new history was scripted with new shades produced by the new spirit, appropriate for the age. The study of Sikhism constituted a small part of the new historiography.

III

The pioneers in Sikh studies in Orissa during British rule were mostly the leaders of the Oriya Brahmo Samaj in Puri, Cuttack and Balasore who were at the forefront of the new age. Some of them had come to Calcutta in early life and fallen under the influence of progressive Brahmo ideas. Many of them could find a resemblance between monotheism and worship of the formless in opposition to idolatry as enshrined in Brahmoism and Guru Nanak's Sikhism. Brahmo writers in Bengal in the nineteenth century acknowledged it time and again

---

class had great respect for the progress of Bengali education and culture. There is thus an ambivalence in the Oriya attitude to Bengalis. A study of contemporary Oriya literary sources shows affiliations with trends in Assam in the same period. Supra, pp. 52-4.

[20] John Boulton, 'Nationalism and Tradition in Orissa, with special reference to the Works of Phakirmohana Senapati', in R.J. Moore (ed.), *Tradition and Politics in South Asia,* New Delhi 1979, p. 259; Biswamoy Pati, *Resisting Domination: Peasants, Tribals and the National Movement in Orissa 1920-47,* New Delhi 1993, p. 45; Jagannathprasad Das, *Desha Kaal Patra,* Bhubaneswar 1997, p. 158.

[21] G.N. Dash,'Jagannatha and Oriya Nationalism', in Anncharlott Eschmann et al. (eds.), *The Cult of Jagannatha and the Regional Tradition of Orissa,* New Delhi 1978, pp. 359-74.

in their correspondence, essays and discussions.[22] In the past, Guru Nanak had protested against the dominance of the priestly hierarchy, idol worship, expensive religious functions, casteism and superstition. The Oriya Brahmos also proceeded on the same lines.

The prophets of the new spirit in Orissa included Parimohan Acharya (1852-81), Bhaktakabi Madhusudan Rao (1853-1912), Fakirmohan Senapati (1843-1918), Biswanath Kar (1864-1934), among others. Most of them had embraced Brahmoism or were influenced by it. This is not to say that the new group was a monolith; within its apparent homogeneity it had several subgroups holding different views on the sense of history, understanding of the past, idea of progress and many other relevant issues of the time. Almost all of them knew Bengali and were aware of the social changes taking place in and around the metropolis of Calcutta. Notable among them was Madhusudan Rao, who did not merely articulate a profound devotion to God in his corpus of works but expressed the same religious awareness at many Brahmo prayer meetings. He used to speak of Sikhism at these gatherings and never hesitated to point out the resemblances between the preachings of Guru Nanak and Brahmoism.[23]

The Oriya Brahmo reformers evinced deep interest in transmitting the message of social protest through their own print media. This led to a significant change in contemporary Oriya journalism and the publication of newspapers. Their 'vernacularizing thrust' was widely appreciated; their 'mass-produced commodity' (i.e. newspapers, periodicals, etc.) was widely read and steadily reached out to distant Oriya-speaking regions, stimulating a new sense of Oriya identity in the closing years of the nineteenth century. Among the weeklies and monthlies, there was *Sevak*, which published a detailed account of the life of Guru Nanak in three successive numbers.[24] Although translated from Bengali, it was more or less faithful to the original.[25]

[22] Himadri Banerjee, 'Bengali Perceptions of the Sikhs in the Nineteenth and Twentieth Centuries', in Joseph T.O' Connell et al. (eds.), *Sikh History and Religion in the Twentieth Century*, Toronto 1988, pp. 96-8.

[23] Samantaray, *Adhunik Oriya Sahityar Bhittibhumi*, pp. 327-8.

[24] *Sevak* was first published from Cuttack Mission Press in September 1883. Chaturbhuj Patnaik, its editor, was a Brahmo. The journal was an important organ of the Oriya Brahmo Samaj. Later *Sevak* merged with *Sanskarak*. Cf. Mrutyunjay Rath, *Mrutyunjay Granthabali*, vol. I, Cuttack 1971, p. 411.

[25] Anonymous, 'Guru Nanakar Sambandhare', *Sevak*, 15 July 1885, 22 July 1885 and 29 July 1885. The original in Bengali is 'Kajer Loke Ke'. This was written by Rabindranath Tagore and was first published in *Balak*, a Bengali children's monthly. Infra, pp. 135-6.

The major events of the life of the founder of Sikhism were narrated in the short space. Miracles were eschewed. Efforts were made to make everything convincing, buttressed with suitable arguments. One can easily identify the analytic Brahmo mind.[26] Unlike the Sikh Guru in the *Janamsakhi* literature, Guru Nanak here was not shown as endowed with divine attributes right from his birth. He was not gifted with miraculous powers. No black poisonous snake of the *Janamsakhis* reared its head to protect him from the sun nor did the *kaba* of Mecca go round him.[27] The article represents Guru Nanak as a magnanimous great man dedicated to truth. It was claimed that he had earned the grace and blessings of God by pursuing the path of moral rectitude.

His father—Kalu Bedi—on the other hand, had very ordinary earthly desires and aspirations like other common folk and he was worried about his son's future. Guru Nanak, however, never aimed to achieve worldly success. He had set his sights on the all-round salvation of mankind. The article in question deals with that ideal. But there was a difference between the Bengali original and the Oriya translation. At the end of the Bengali treatise, stress was laid on the ascetic, eternal and unworldly value-system in Sikhism. The translator did not mention that and terminated the piece with the fact that Guru Nanak died at the age of 70 and so on. The Oriya translation lacks the timeless quality of the Bengali message.

Another noteworthy Brahmo writing of the period is 'Guru Nanak o Duijana Brahman'. The author, Sadhucharan Roy (1861-98), was closely related to Madhusudan Rao and was a teacher at Cuttack Mission School.[28] Like Bhaktakabi, he voiced his protest against social superstition and facilely extravagant religious ceremonies. In this context, he drew attention to the significant role of Guru Nanak as a religious reformer. The article appeared in the Ashar issue of the

[26] Infra, pp. 124-6, 130-2.

[27] For a detailed description of these two incidents in Guru Nanak's life, see McLeod, *Guru Nanak and the Sikh Religion*, pp. 73-5.

[28] Sadhucharan Roy, 'Guru Nanak o Duijana Brahman', *Utkal Sahitya*, Ashar 1304 Masiha, pp. 135-7. Sadhucharan Roy was the son-in-law of Jagannath Rao, younger brother of Bhaktakabi Madhusudan Rao. He died young. Apart from editing *Asha*, he translated Debendranath Tagore's *Brahmo Dharma* into Oriya. Abanti Devi has talked of Sadhucharan's mental affiliations with Bengali Brahmos in her *Bhaktakabi Madhusudan Rao o Utkale Nabajug*, Calcutta 1370 BS, pp. 179-80. See also Kunjabehari Das, *Kabi o Kahani*, Cuttack 1984, pp. 154-8.

first year of *Utkal Sahitya*.[29] Guru Nanak was shown speaking against pointless religious rituals in the presence of two Brahmans sitting on the steps of the Ganga.

In criticizing the ritualistic Hindus of the medieval days, the writer expressed his own views. He did not mention any particular place as the scene of the event. But it would not be difficult to determine its location because the reference is to the Guru's irrigating of wheat fields in Punjab mentioned in the *Janamsakhis*.[30] Sadhucharan did not quote any source. He had probably gleaned the theme from a Bengali journal.[31] He divided the essay into two halves. In the first half, two Brahmans are seen absorbed in doing *tarpan* for their forefathers. In the second, the Guru is found repeating the same thing. But in both sections, the Sikh Guru appears to be a rational person with a strong personality. The two Brahmans are portrayed as representatives of the arrogant priestly class in a caste-based society. The contrast highlights the distinctiveness of Guru Nanak's message.

Fakirmohan Senapati, like other Brahmo converts, was a monotheist and a devotee of the formless. His thoughts on the Divine went through several mutations during his life, and the influence of Guru Nanak had something to do with it. Unlike others, however, he never wrote about Guru Nanak independently. At the same time he never denied Guru Nanak and the distinctiveness and identity of his religion. His discussion of the subject began in his school textbook, *Bharatbarshar Itihas* (vol. I), where he traced in a brief chapter the history of the Sikhs from Guru Nanak to Banda Bahadur, covering nearly 250 years.[32] The chapter does not do justice to Guru

[29] *Utkal Sahitya* was the brainchild of the famous writer and editor Biswanath Kar who was also a Brahmo leader. It was first published in 1897 and was perhaps the most prestigious literary monthly of the first three decades of the twentieth century. For a further discussion, see Samantaray, *Adhunik Oriya Sahityar Bhittibhumi*, pp. 497-8. Recently, Bauribandhu Kar has discussed *Utkal Sahitya* in his book *Nana Alochana*, Bhubaneswar 1994, pp. 109-23.

[30] McLeod, *The B-40 Janam-sakhi*, pp. 81-6. Also see Himadri Banerjee, 'Sikh History and Religion in Oriya Writings: *Utkal Sahitya*: A Case Study', in Dharam Singh (ed.), *Secularism and Sikhism: Essays in Honour of Professor Harbans Singh*, New Delhi 1994, pp. 164-80.

[31] The famous Bengali literary magazine *Bangadarshan* highlighted the episode of Guru Nanak's life. Cf. Anonymous,'Nanak', *Bangadarshan*, Ashar 1285 BS, p. 110. Sadhucharan might have used this essay as his source.

[32] Fakirmohan Senapati, *Bharatbarshar Itihas*, vol. I, Cuttack 1869. I have consulted its 2nd edition.

Nanak's life and philosophy, but offers a lucid statement of the principal characteristics of God as related by the Guru, giving Fakirmohan a unique place in Sikh studies in Orissa in the nineteenth century. 'God is unparalleled, detached, unfazed, pure, permanent, the truth embodied, self-created. . . . And beyond the ken of word and mind. He [Guru Nanak] has described God as infinite, pristine, ancient.'[33]

When in his early life, Fakirmohan had to struggle with adversity, he wielded his pen against idolatry, pilgrimage and similar pursuits of God without a shred of scepticism. The same message resonated in the twilight of his life. His personal sufferings had not destroyed his faith in God. In his poem 'Saptarshi', he equated Guru Nanak with many other religious leaders of the world.[34] Buddha, Sankar, Jesus, Muhammad, Chaitanya, Nanak and Rammohun—they all chose different paths to spread the light of tranquillity which was one and the same. Their religions had certain similarities but they had also their own uniqueness. He evinced a similar sentiment at Santikanan in Balasore.[35]

At the end of the nineteenth century, the Sikh studies formed an important part of Orissa's new awakening. Improvements in the means of communication, the spread of print-culture, the social impact of an aware, educated class committed to the cultivation and enrichment of the mother tongue, all contributed to the development of Sikh studies. Interest in Sikhism brought Oriya and Bengali Brahmos closer. The interaction revealed the self-divided nature of Oriya intellectuals. A section of middle class Bengalis then waged a war of words against the recognition of Oriya and its cultural autonomy. During the time Oriya Brahmos were pragmatic enough

[33] Senapati, ibid., p. 79. While describing the form of Nanak's God, Fakirmohan has used these words. It seems these are largely borrowed from the essay, 'Nanak-panthi' by Akshaykumar Datta, which appeared in *Tattwabodhini Patrika*, Chaitra 1772 Saka, pp. 177-8.

[34] Fakirmohan Senapati, *Abasarbasare*, Cuttack 1935, p. 292. In the preface of the *Abasarbasare*, Senapati has candidly admitted his mental conflict.

[35] Fakirmohan Senapati laid a beautiful garden in a part of his house at Balasore, it was called Santikanan. He also built a small temple there which was the seat of all religions. The names of Buddha, Muhammad, Christ, Rammohun and others were inscribed there. Considering his catholicity, it is no surprise that Chaitanya and Nanak were also mentioned. Quoting Adhirajmohan Senapati, John Boulton in his essay, 'Religion in Contemporary Indian Literature with special reference to Phakirmohana Senapati in Orissa' has discussed it in Anncharlott Eschmann (ed.), *South Asian Digest of Regional Writings*, vol. III, Heidelburg 1974, p. 80.

to carry on cultural exchanges with Bengali Brahmos. It betokened the birth of a new mindset in Orissa where Oriya regional nationalism did not hesitate to look to the history of its distant neighbour to enrich the mother tongue and thereby strengthen its separate linguistic identity.

Strangely, however, their preoccupation with Guru Nanak kept them away from many other trends in Sikh history. The Brahmos perhaps did not consider those to be closely related to the founder of the Sikh faith. Thus the message of the military resistance of the Khalsa hardly evoked their genuine interest. It shows the nature of their involvement with Sikhism and at the same time explains the limited parameters of their Sikh studies.[36] It may be said that their inquiry into the subject was dictated by the constraints of their regional groups and the *zeitgeist*. As long as the movement had its own momentum, Sikh studies centred on Guru Nanak also flourished. But from the close of the nineteenth century, militant nationalism gradually gained ground and it was generally in no mood to listen to the message of reform of the earlier decades. On the contrary, it increasingly underlined that the existing Indian social structure did not require any further dose of reform and looked to many Sanatani Hindu symbols and institutions for an all-India mobilization. All these factors ran counter to the ideology as well as the plan of action of the Oriya Brahmos.[37] Besides, the Oriya Brahmos generally kept themselves away from many important political questions of their time. They had long been shaking hands with those 'neighbouring ethnic groups' who were increasingly marginalized and excluded in the resurgent Oriya identity movement of the early twentieth century. With the steady rise in the tempo of the Oriya unity movement, they lost much of their early relevance and appeal. Their Sikh studies also ebbed away. The curtain was thus temporarily drawn on the Panthic discussions and no revival was on the cards until there was a renewal of interest in Sikhism at the local level in the subsequent decades of the nineteenth century.

[36] Himadri Banerjee, 'Sikh Identity Question: A View from Eastern India', in Pashaura Singh and N. Gerald Barrier (eds.), *Sikh Identity: Continuity and Change*, New Delhi 1999, pp. 196-216.

[37] In the last quarter of the nineteenth century, the Brahmos of Bengal also experienced frequent ideological conflicts and organizational problems. Cf. Kenneth W. Jones, *The New Cambridge History of India*, vol. III.1, *Social-Religious Reform Movements in British India*, Cambridge 1989, pp. 38-9.

IV

The deep interest and enthusiasm with which the Brahmos in Orissa reviewed the mission of Guru Nanak did not exercise any powerful influence on the lives of non-Brahmos there. Studies on Guru Nanak therefore suffered a temporary decline in the early years of the twentieth century. But later the movement against the British Raj engendered a pan-Indian feeling.[38] It gave rise to a new point of view in the study of Indian history. Delving into the past, littérateurs and historians rekindled interest in the struggle that the Sikhs had carried on against the Mughals and Pathans in medieval days. The new leadership of Orissa also indicated the changed political ambience of the nation. Among the Oriya leaders of the time, mention must be made of Utkalmani Gopabandhu Das (1877-1928). He had long been in intimate touch with the manifold problems of rural Orissa and was aware of the limitations of the Utkal Union Conference leadership. In the columns of his *Samaj*, he had also conveyed to his distant readers the news of the Oriya plight caused by famine, flood, drought and poverty in the region.[39] Besides, he could convince the Indian National Congress leadership that the demand for the unity of the Oriya-speaking population should receive its immediate attention. The Congress under Gandhi responded to the call and the Mahatma even agreed to visit Orissa to convey the message of non-cooperation there.[40] The administrative unity of the three Oriya tracts based on loyalty to the British thus gradually gave way to growing opposition to colonial rule and the question of Oriya unity graduated from the local to the all-India level through the Indian National Congress.

The new Oriya leadership also laid emphasis on the expansion of mass education. They knew that the massive illiteracy of the countryside stood in the way of growth of national consciousness.[41]

[38] For an understanding of the process of gradual change in the Oriya politics of the first two decades of the twentieth century, see Bishnu N. Mohapatra, 'Anti-Colonial Politics in Orissa, 1920-1936: The Power and Limits of Oriya Nationalism', *The Calcutta Historical Journal*, July-December 1975, pp. 141-9.

[39] 'Samaj', 24 January 1920, *Gopabandhu Rachanabali*, vol. II, Cuttack 1977, p. 40.

[40] On Gandhi's visit to Orissa (1921), see Atul Chandra Pradhan, *The Nationalist Movement in a Regional Setting, 1920-34: The Rise of Congress to Power in Orissa*, New Delhi n.d., pp. 43-6.

[41] Harekrushna Mahtab et al. (eds.), *History of Freedom Movement in Orissa (1857-1911)*, vol. II, Cuttack 1957, p. 113; Radhakanta Barik, 'Gopabandhu and the National Movement in Orissa', *Social Scientist*, May 1978, pp. 47-8.

Gopabandhu held the educational policy of the colonial administration responsible for it. Efforts were, therefore, made to isolate education from the colonial administrative control by setting up Satyabadi School (1909) near Puri. Here Gopabandhu with his celebrated colleagues like Pandit Nilakantha Das (1884-1967), Godavaris Mishra (1886-1956), Krupasindhu Mishra (1886-1926), Basudeb Mahapatra (1888-1977), Lingaraj Mishra (1894-1957) and others wrote 'histories, poems, plays and innumerable essays in their zeal to awaken in the hearts of their people a patriotic consciousness, the desire to live again as free men and revive the glories of their forebears'. It provided a new dimension to the evolution of the Oriya literary psyche. The literary journal *Satyabadi* published from Satyabadi School and the weekly newspaper *Samaj* mirrored the freedom-loving mind of the Oriyas.[42] In their editorial columns, Gopabandhu linked the sense of unity of the Oriya-speaking people with the national movement and referred to the recent struggle of the Sikhs for reforming their gurdwaras. Against this background, Gandhi came with the message of non-cooperation with the British in Orissa. Welcoming him, Utkalmani said: 'Friends . . . the great men born in India so far whose achievements have enriched the holy soil of this land have all visited Orissa. Buddha, Kabir, Ramanuj, Sankar, Nanak, Chaitanya—all these saints left their mark in Orissa.'[43]

This reference to Guru Nanak in the passage against the regional backdrop of the twentieth century Oriya nationalism was very brief but it partially echoes the thoughts in Fakirmohan's 'Saptarshi'. The Oriyas were perhaps then in no mood to check up whether these great men mentioned by Gopabandhu had actually visited this part of the country in the past. It, however, underlines the Oriya yearning for a closer interaction with the different all-India symbols and traditions. Gandhi's presence no doubt drew the nationalist Indians' attention to the shores of Orissa. Their sympathetic response to the Oriya linguistic aspiration paved the way for its all-India recog-

[42] J.K. Samal, *A History of Modern Orissa,* Calcutta 1984, pp. 172, 207; Mayadhar Mansinha, *History of Oriya Literature,* New Delhi 1962, pp. 235-43; Chandrasekhar Mishra, *Satyabadire Satabarsha,* Cuttack 1953; Janakiballav Mahanti (Bharadwaj), *Adhunik Oriya Sahitya,* Cuttack 1963, pp. 156-74; Shrinibas Mishra, *Adhunik Oriya Gadya Sahitya, 1811-1920,* Cuttack 1978, pp. 354-420; Chittaranjan Das, *A Glimpse into Oriya Literature,* Bhubaneswar 1984, pp. 196-208.

[43] Suryanarayan Das, *Utkalmani Gopabandhu Das,* Cuttack 1987, p. 372.

nition. In the meantime, the struggle of the non-violent Akalis (1920-5) had provided a new height to the ongoing Non-cooperation Movement. Their fight for reforming gurdwaras, many of which were associated with the memory of the founder of the Sikh Panth, generated a new sense of identity with the Oriya non-cooperators. News of contemporary political developments in Punjab created quite a stir in publications in Orissa,[44] stimulating fresh considerations of the life of Guru Nanak.

A notable piece of writing of the period was *Sadhucharit Mala* (1932), in which Guru Nanak figures among other Indian preachers and reformers whose lives are delineated in it.[45] The Sikh Guru is projected with his miraculous powers, which the Brahmo authors had sought to avoid in the late nineteenth century. He is said to have been singled out by God since boyhood. Familiar incidents of his life of the *Janamsakhi* tradition have been related: for instance, incidents like the teacher saying that his education was complete before he went to school, his refusal to take the sacred thread, his father's chiding at *khara sauda*, the miraculous role of the black snake, the nomination of his disciple Angad as heir, etc. But all this is presented respectfully and in a simple manner. He is not, however, represented as an apostle of a new religion as he was in the past by Brahmo writers. There are one or two factual errors but the essay received partial recognition from later writers.[46] The Oriya life-sketch of Guru Nanak published after a gap of nearly thirty years also underlines a change in the direction of Sikh studies in the region.

In the 1930s, discussions on Guru Nanak in Orissa did not remain confined to books. The Akali movement of the previous decade was directed towards the reform and control of the gurdwaras. It sent

[44] I had the privilege of going through some of the old files of *Utkal Dipika*, *Samaj*, *Sakti*, *Prajatantra*, *Puribasi* and *Lokamukha* at the Utkal Sahitya Samaj Library, Cuttack. They provide extensive coverage of the Akali movement from 1920-5. For Gopabandhu Das's comments on the Akalis, see 6 March 1921, *Gopabandhu Rachanabali*, vol.VI, Cuttack 1978, pp. 102-3; 7 March 1925 and 18 April 1925, ibid., vol. VIII, Cuttack 1978, pp. 168-9, 232-3.

[45] Bankanidhi Patnaik and Kunjabehari Mohanti, *Sadhucharit Mala*, Cuttack 1932, pp. 25-33. See also Labanya Nayak, *Oriya Charit-Sahitya*, Cuttack 1988, pp. 255-6. Infra, pp. 137-8.

[46] *Sadhucharit Mala* (p. 31) provides incorrect information about the origin of the city of Amritsar. The same is almost repeated in Chandramani Das's *Nanak* (p. 22). Both of them also agree that at the request of his family, Guru Nanak wore the sacred thread.

important signals to the people of Orissa. Already the Oriya non-cooperators had expressed all their sympathy for and solidarity with the Akali cause. Subsequently, a few Oriya loyalists headed by Rai Bahadur Chintamani Acharya (1891-1957)[47] of the Cuttack Bar and the essayist Rai Bahadur Gopalchandra Praharaj (1874-1945)[48] seem to have tried to exploit the situation to the best of their advantage. Perhaps they also enjoyed the blessings of the provincial administration in rallying the 'distractors' of the Civil Disobedience Movement and driving a subtle wedge in the Oriya nationalist camp over the support of the Sikh cause in the 1930s.[49]

They turned their attention to the dilapidated gurdwara of the Dantan Sahib on the bank of the Mahanadi. Bawa Kartar Singh and Niranjan Neogy joined hands.[50] A few other eminent citizens of the city were touched by their combined influence. Jointly they were instrumental in the reconstruction of the derelict gurdwara redolent with Guru Nanak's memory. On 10 November 1935, which was a Sunday, the birth anniversary of Guru Nanak was celebrated there with great fanfare. At least two Oriya newspapers gave coverage to the congregation.[51]

[47] Rai Bahadur Chintamani Acharya was connected with the moderate politics of the Utkal Union Conference. Many of his articles were published in the *Utkal Sahitya* and *Mukur*. His writings on the history of the Sikhs have been discussed later. See also Mishra, *Adhunik Oriya Gadya Sahitya*, pp. 347-52.

[48] Gopalchandra Praharaj was a well known littérateur. In 1931 the government honoured him for his alleged 'cooperation' during the Civil Disobedience Movement.

[49] The assumption is based on the following points. Both Acharya and Praharaj deliberately kept themselves away from the Oriya nationalist politics led by the Indian National Congress. They were very close to the loyalist movement of the Utkal Union Conference and the news of the celebration of Guru Nanak's birthday organized by them was very widely circulated in the *Satya Samachar*, which received regular official patronage for its survival. Further Bawa Kartar Singh and Niranjan Neogy served the Ravenshaw College run by the government. We do not have any information regarding their direct involvement in the contemporary Oriya politics. For a general description of the contemporary Oriya political scene, see Bijoykumar Pradhan, 'National Movement in Orissa (1920-1936 A.D.)', Rabindra Bharati University unpublished Ph.D. thesis, 1997, p. 196.

[50] I heard (5 July 1993) about Bawa Kartar Singh's close relationship with Niranjan Neogy from Bani Neogy, Niranjan Neogy's daughter. Niranjan Neogy taught English at Ravenshaw College and was a notable Brahmo author. See also Abanti Devi, *Bhaktakabi Madhusudan Rao o Utkale Nabajug*, pp.185-94; Hardev Singh Virk, 'Bawa Kartar Singh', *Encyclopaedia of Sikhism*, vol. I, pp. 450-1; Sahu, *Guru Gobinda Singha*, pp. 2-3.

[51] *Samaj*, 13 November 1935; *Satya Samachar*, 13 November 1935.

At the meeting Niranjan Neogy made a long speech on the monotheism of Guru Nanak and his influence but there was no mention in the newspapers. Gopalchandra Praharaj made many significant observations. The essay, which he read out at the congregation, came out in the Magh issue of *Utkal Sahitya* next year. In his paper, he drew a dark picture of the Indian religious scene in the pre-Nanak era. In his view, Guru Nanak preached Sikhism to 'protect the true religion and the religious people of the country'. Two features of the essay are to be noted. He stressed that Guru Nanak's Sikhism was based on one God and did not have any room for idol-worship or casteism. He mentioned as evidence Guru Nanak's *mulmantra* of the *Japji* and emphasized the spirit of synthesis of Hinduism and Islam in Sikhism. Praharaj had used Macauliffe as his source. But he did not attempt to interpret Sikhism from the standpoint of the Singh Sabha Movement. Nor did he make any comment on the distinctiveness and individuality of Sikhism. It is in this that he also differed from the Oriya Brahmos. In the last three paragraphs of the essay, he traced the evolution of Sikhism in the post-Guru Nanak phase. It is not based on cast-iron evidence. Some of the facts presented in explaining Guru Nanak's life seem distorted. By this time, he had also taken the initiative in publishing the famous Oriya encyclopaedia *Purnachandra Bhashakosha* in several volumes.[52] There he elaborated his position on the subject in three separate entries, viz., 'Nanak', 'Nanakpanthi' and 'Sikh'. His tribute to Guru Nanak on his anniversary in popular language from a public platform was outside the confines of his intellectual pursuits. Praharaj was, thus, one of those rare Oriya intellectuals who did not hesitate to respond to the call of the wider world, though not always directly related to his literary career.

It has to be borne in mind that although a lot of discussion had taken place on Guru Nanak in Orissa, no separate biography of him had yet been published. Reconstruction of the Dantan Sahib gurdwara and the commencement of regular prayer meetings there drew wide attention. It is likely to have encouraged Chandramani Das to bring out the book. The author was happy to detect divine greatness even in child Nanak. He was confident that God willed Guru Nanak's birth at an auspicious moment. It is likely that the writer

[52] Praharaj was the editor of the *Purnachandra Bhashakosha*. This was published in four volumes in the 1930s thanks to the munificence of Maharaja Purnachandra Bhanjadeo of Mayurbhanj and other big landlords of Orissa.

gleaned his information from very well known source materials but he kept reticent about it. He gave free rein to his imagination. So while some of the episodes in the life of the Sikh Guru as narrated in his book seem partly familiar to us, his imagination has sometimes given them a different dimension. It is hard to differentiate in places the historical Nanak from the imaginary one. Das relates the Sikh Guru's varied experiences during his *udasi* to a number of places. Other Oriya writers do not refer to it. According to Chandramani Das, Guru Nanak sought fulfilment through *hathyoga* but such practices had been severely criticized in the message of the *Adi Granth* as well as in the everyday life of a Sikh. Chandramani Das seems to be unaware of the metaphysical details of Sikhism. In the biography, the writer offers no rational explanation of the presence of the poisonous black snake. Similarly the absence in it of the village zamindar Rai Bullar (who is again present in an earlier Brahmo account of the Guru) makes the narrative all the more unconvincing. The writer's ignorance of historical dates is also quite incredible.[53] He had put in whatever details he could get hold of without checking them. And then he embroidered on them with his imagination. History frequently surrendered to fancy.

Chandramani Das's *Nanak* is the only biography of Guru Nanak in Oriya in book form at that time. Its significance also lies in its difference from nineteenth century Oriya Brahmo writing. They represent two different trends in Sikh studies in Orissa. The Brahmo writers generally resorted to logic and facts. Chandramani Das laid stress on faith and emotion. Das's Guru Nanak is virtually removed from the Brahmo historical tradition. Das may not be placed among the front-ranking Oriya writers, but one has to consider on what foundations of knowledge he pioneered this kind of writing. Nobody spoke of Sikh studies at the level of higher education in Orissa in those days. School texts bristled with discrepancies. Orthodox religious beliefs rooted in the writers' point of view ran through the pages. No wonder Chandramani Das mixed up the Guru Nanak as seen by the devout with the Guru Nanak of history. One should not forget, however, the debate over the historical Guru Nanak and the

[53] According to Chandramani Das, the first battle of Panipath took place in 1226 while Maharaja Ranjit Singh captured Amritsar in 1602. See *Nanak*, Cuttack 1940, pp. 23-5.

Guru Nanak of faith that goes on even today.[54] How could a writer of the 1940s enrich his account with the findings of recent research? That will be negating the evolution of historiography. Also relevant is the readership. Few publishers would have been interested in a thick tome written in a serious vein. One should keep in mind the parameters within which Oriya writers, readers and publishers functioned.

V

The study of the life of the founder of Sikhism formed a major part of Sikh studies in Orissa, but there was a wide Sikh world beyond him. Oriya writers showed considerable interest in the lives of historical figures in the Sikh community after Guru Nanak. These writings partly conveyed the message of Indian nationalism. The tenth Guru was portrayed as a leader ever ready for any sacrifice for the country or community. Separate biographical accounts came out in periodicals or in book form. Sometimes isolated incidents of his life were also presented to convey some definite message to readers.

The first of such works to be published was 'SikhGuru Gobinda Singha' by Madanmohan Patnaik (1890-1967). The article appeared in the Magh issue of *Utkal Sahitya* in 1912.[55] Madanmohan Patnaik was known as a poet and his lyrical style revealed his talent in more than one section. He has not acknowledged any source, but the choice of words and the structure of sentences remind one of the Bengali writers, Rajanikanta Gupta.[56] But the opening and concluding sentences were decidedly his own.

[54] Attention is drawn to the ongoing debate about the source materials for reconstructing Guru Nanak's biography. Perhaps Karam Singh first raised some serious doubts about them a long time ago, when he said that the contents of the *Janamsakhis* had to be critically analysed and evaluated. Recently McLeod has formulated a few other serious questions. He thinks that the historicity of the incidents in Guru Nanak's life as related in the *Janamsakhis* require rigorous scrutiny before they could be accepted for reconstructing the Sikh Guru's biography. Nearly sixty years ago, Indubhusan Banerjee also wrote about *Janamsakhi* sources: 'Our position is thus a desperate one. . . . We have hardly any material for a satisfactory biography [of Guru Nanak] on critical lines'. Cf. *Evolution of the Khalsa,* vol. I, Calcutta 1963, p. 63.

[55] Madanmohan Patnaik, 'SikhGuru Gobinda Singha', *Utkal Sahitya*, Magh 1319 Masiha, pp. 278-87. He was a village school teacher in Puri district and a brother of the poet Padmacharan Patnaik.

[56] Rajanikanta Gupta, *Sikh,* Calcutta 1883, pp. 9-20. He is again discussed in the following two chapters.

The biographer has shown Guru Gobind Singh as a defender of Hinduism like Chhatrapati Shivaji, Maharana Pratap Singh and Raj Singh. According to him, the only mission of the life of the tenth Guru was to 'serve the country and its people'. The writer claimed that the Guru awakened new hope and a sense of unity among Hindus long oppressed by 'Muslim tyranny' in the medieval days. Through the creation of the Khalsa, he abolished caste, struck at old religious superstition and called upon the people to lay down their lives to protect religion. The writer was distressed that the Guru's life was brief. He believed that had the Guru lived longer, he would have done a lot more for the people. At the end, he expressed his deep admiration and respect for the Guru.

Madanmohan repeatedly stressed that Guru Gobind Singh was a follower and defender of Hinduism. The battle between the Mughals and the Sikhs in the middle ages was but a precursor of the twentieth century Hindu-Muslim strife. From the orthodox Hindu point of view, it was an idealistic stand but many others could trace in it a narrow Hindu communalism, particularly obvious in his use of abusive adjectives about the Muslim rulers of medieval India. He found them all to be foreigners in the motherland (*matribhumi*) of the Hindus. Consequently, his Guru Gobind Singh's aggressive attitude tended to wipe out many of the distinct Sikh religious symbols and rituals that had been so minutely underlined by the Singh Sabha reformers since the late nineteenth century. The Sikh search for a separate communal identity in Punjab might have had repercussions in the Hindu-Hindi belt in north India but it evoked little interest among writers like Madanmohan in eastern India. Thus, the essay did not introduce readers to the arena of the twentieth century antagonism between Hindus and Sikhs in Punjab. On the contrary, Sikhs appear as members of a larger Hindu family.

Another well known biographer of the age is Brundabanchandra Patnaik. He, however, did not invest the tenth Guru with so much Hindu distinctiveness. Guru Gobind Singh not merely fought the Mughals to defend religion. His boyhood capers at Patna, domesticity on return to Punjab, call to arms, worship of *Sakti*, the *rahit maryada* of the Khalsa, list of battles fought, won and lost—all this has been given importance.[57] He also recalled the Guru as one of the great Indian poets and religious reformers of all time. There is a lot

[57] Brundabanchandra Patnaik, 'Guru Gobinda Singha', *Bharatgaurab*, Cuttack 1937, pp. 47-61. I have consulted its 2nd edition.

in Brundabanchandra's writing, which is missing in Madanmohan's. Madanmohan portrayed the Guru as single-minded. Brundabanchandra's serious literary style often failed to keep pace with facts. Madanmohan's poetic gift gave his style an easy flow. Guru Gobind Singh thus appears in two different manifestations in these two essays. One piles up facts and the reader finds the tenth master a distant personality, the other uses emotional language that brings the Sikh Guru closer to the heart of his readership.

The tenth Guru also figured in a poem by the poet Nabakishore Das published in *Utkal Sahitya* in 1939.[58] Here the Guru is a magnanimous character, averse to worldly possessions. There is a scene where, away from society, Guru Gobind Singh thinks of his future strategy after the death of his father Guru Tegh Bahadur. His disciple Raghunath had presented to him a pair of bracelets. One fell into the waters of the Yamuna. Raghunath jumped into the river and searched for it in vain. At day's end, he came back and found his Guru deep in study. He asked where the bracelet had gone. The Guru threw the other bracelet into the water to indicate where the first one was.

There is a reference to the bracelet-throwing episode in M'Gregor's *History of the Sikhs* (1846), where, however, it does not occupy any central place.[59] The disciple is not even named there. But the episode was destined to play an important role in the formulation of nationalist thought in eastern India. In Bengali, for example, Rabindranath projected a 'selfless', 'contemplative', 'other-worldly' and 'patriotic' image of the tenth Guru out of it. In the last decade of the nineteenth century, Tagore was fed up with the activities of the moderates in the Congress, and was looking for an ideal person like Guru Gobind Singh, i.e. someone who could be India's leader. This led him to dig into Sikh history and write three poems about Guru Gobind Singh, which threw light on different facets of his personality. 'Nishphal Upahar' is one of them.[60] The resemblance between Rabindranath's poem ('Nishphal Upahar') and Nabakishore's just cannot be missed—in their common theme, the time, the characters

[58] Nabakishore Das, 'Guru Gobinda', *Utkal Sahitya*, Magh 1346 Masiha, pp. 411-12. Nabakishore Das (1912 -?) is acknowledged as a nationalist Oriya poet. Among his other writings, the life of Madhusudan Das stands out.

[59] W. L. M'Gregor, *The History of the Sikhs*, vol. I, Patiala reprint, 1971, pp. 79-80.

[60] *Rabindra Rachanabali*, vol. I, Calcutta 1980, pp. 429-30, Infra, pp. 148-9.

and the choice of words. Furthermore, Nabakishore's poetic appeal also betrays Rabindranath's impact. In both poems, Guru Gobind Singh is projected as a soul of generosity. At the same time, the contrast with the disciple has also come through in both compositions. It is by highlighting the contrast that the two poets sought to present the Guru's role as something for all to emulate.

One can assume that Nabakishore, a young poet, paid a tribute to Guru Gobind Singh in his mother tongue with the same outlook as Rabindranath. When he wrote the poem, he was not totally unaware of his dependence on Rabindranath. He tried to prove his originality by introducing a variation in the description of nature. Rabindranath describes a dry, rough landscape. Nabakishore speaks of the earth verdant with crops. Besides, he draws a fuller picture of Guru Gobind Singh, which we do not get in Rabindranath's poem 'Nishphal Upahar'.

VI

But Rabindranath and Nabakishore did not claim Raghunath to be an ideal disciple of the tenth Guru. There is, however, no dearth of ideal disciples in Sikh history. A memorable incident occurred towards the end of Guru Gobind Singh's life. A band of his followers gave up their lives in battle. It is one of the supreme instances of sacrifice in Sikh history. Sikhs recall the incident every day in their prayer.[61] Chintamani Acharya gave a brief account of it in his essay 'Muktashwar'.[62]

The battles of Anandpur represented a momentous phase in the life of the tenth Guru (1700-5). Sikh authors aver that during those days of agony, forty disciples deserted the Guru, leaving him at the mercy of the enemy because they could no longer suffer the pangs of hunger. But they did not get any support from their relatives and friends. Pricked by their conscience, the deserters are said to have resolved to sacrifice their lives in a coming battle for their Guru. The opportunity came in the battle of Khidrana (1705), where they fought

[61] In Assamese, Phula Singh Chhetri's essay carries an emotional appeal, which suggests its close link with the Sikh *ardas*. Supra, pp. 40-1. But this we miss in the essay of Chintamani Acharya. It is likely that Acharya was not aware of the importance of the martyrdom tradition in the Sikh daily prayer.

[62] Acharya, 'Muktashwar', *Itihas Prasanga*, Part I, pp. 153-7. The author is mentioned again later on.

with great valour to pave the way for the Guru's victory. To perpetuate the memory of the forty disciples, who died, the Guru forgave all forty deserters and reinstated them as disciples (*Chali Mukte*).

The relationship between the Guru and his disciples thus occupies a significant place in the evolution of Sikh history. A Sikh believes that there is no alternative to the Guru and similarly the Guru's yearning for his disciples recurs in the community's psyche. British administrator-historians like Cunningham and Macauliffe discuss the theme with respect.[63] Macauliffe in particular went into it in detail. In fact, Macauliffe could have influenced Chintamani Acharya's five-page essay. But there is a 'but'. Macauliffe's book was first published in 1909 in London. Chintamani Acharya wrote in Cuttack in 1916. It is debatable if a successful lawyer like Acharya with his busy public life could have read the relevant volumes of Macauliffe's book and adapted it in his mother tongue in such a short time. Besides, he had written a number of articles on Sikh history earlier. Even there we do not come across any sign of Acharya's originality.[64] It is doubtful that he had obtained materials for them from Macauliffe's works.

Chintamani Acharya wrote another piece on the tenth Guru, concentrating on the Guru's last days.[65] He based his account on materials obtained chiefly from Syad Muhammad Latif's *History of the Panjab* (1889). Perhaps he made a few alterations in his original scheme. He must have realized that it was necessary to fill in the readers on details of the Guru's early life. These were added on and then the writer reverted to his original scheme. This hampered the movement of writing, but it made him more comprehensible to his readers.

The period is important according to many historians. Guru Gobind Singh was said to have declared two things: (1) after him the office of the individual Guru would come to an end, and (2) the *Adi Granth* was to be the Guru.[66] And he also asked his disciple Banda

[63] J.D. Cunningham, *A History of the Sikhs*, New Delhi reprint, 1985, p. 70; Macauliffe, *The Sikh Religion*, vol. V, pp. 181-4, 210-4.

[64] Infra, pp.112-13.

[65] Acharya,'Guru Gobindankar Sesh Dasha', *Itihas Prasanga*, Part I, pp.158-66. The essay first appeared in *Mukur*, in Ashar 1322 Masiha.

[66] For a confirmation of the above two observations, see Ganda Singh, 'Guru Gobind Singh Designates Sri Granth Sahib To be Guru', in Daljeet Singh and Kharak Singh (eds.), *Sikhism: Its Philosophy and History*, Chandigarh 1997, pp. 406-23. For a critique of the above view, J.S. Grewal, 'The Khalsa of Guru Gobind Singh', in

to complete his unfinished work in Punjab. Some years earlier, Aurangzeb had called him to the Deccan. The Guru did not go and sent a letter of protest in Persian known as *Zafarnama*. During the reign of Bahadur Shah (1707-12), there was some sort of political rapprochement between the Mughals and the Sikhs. As Acharya had accepted these facts presented by Syad Muhammad Latif, he is open to mild criticism. For instance, Banda was not the 'first Sikh king' as suggested by Acharya. It may make a section of Punjabi historians happy, but he had no evidence to substantiate his viewpoint. He had accepted Latif's account with some pain. There is even a streak of protest in his writing.[67] Chintamani Acharya was one of the leaders of the Utkal Union Conference, which was the nodal point of Oriya nationalism. But they were believers in constitutional protest and moderate politics. Perhaps that made Acharya's Guru Gobind Singh a moderate political negotiator of the early twentieth century.

VII

Another aspect of Guru Gobind Singh came into focus in Oriya writing. Two biographies were published from Cuttack and Baripada within a gap of six years (1929-35).[68] The authors belonged to two different parts of Orissa and were familiar with British administration in different ways. The portraits of the Guru they present have similarities but also differ in many respects from the different ways in which they reacted to the all-India political ambience.[69]

J.S. Grewal (ed.), *From Guru Nanak to Maharaja Ranjit Singh,* Amritsar 1982, pp. 82-8, 100, 106; W.H. McLeod, *Sikhism,* Harmondsworth 1997, pp. xxiii-iv, 58-61. But these critical observations of Grewal and McLeod have come in for strong criticism and denunciation from a section of Sikh scholars.

[67] 'Even today it remains a mystery why he [the Guru] did accept the overlordship of the Mughal Emperor.' Chintamani Acharya, 'Guru Gobindankar Sesh Dasha', *Itihas Prasanga*, Part I, p. 166.

[68] During these years, Oriya authors also brought out biographies of a number of Indian saints, military heroes and statesmen. In this regard the Utkal Sahitya Prachar Sangha's encouraging role merits special attention. Lakshminarayan Patnaik founded the Sangha, which contributed to the development of Oriya literature and went on till the third decade of the twentieth century, before it folded up in 1930. Cf. Pathani Patnaik, *Jibani-Sahitya: Ek Adhyayan,* Bhubaneswar 1977, pp. 106-8. See also Janakiballav Mahanti (Bharadwaj), 'Chalit Satabdire Oriya Jibani Sahitya', *Jhankar*, February 1971, p. 1061.

[69] After 1921, the spirit of militant protest and sacrifice for the national movement animated the public mind. Biographies of this sort were in great demand. The

Sivaprasad Das's (1900-76) *Guru Gobinda Singha* was published in 1929. The extent of matter, time of publication, style of writing and excellence in handling materials, conviction about the period dealt with, taken together give him precedence over Lingaraj Mishra.[70] In his life of the tenth Guru, Das spoke of thc praiseworthy role of the Sikhs in the national regeneration.[71] In his view, Guru Gobind Singh's leadership was destined to generate a new energy and confidence among his followers. The Sikh Guru was projected with all reverence for his attempt to secure for them a place of honour in their hour of crisis. The book is in eighteen chapters but the Guru does not appear in the first six. The next twelve trace his life, boyhood in Patna, his mobilization of strength in Punjab in the pre-Khalsa period, the establishment of the Khalsa, the struggle and suffering of the Sikhs, signs of change in Mughal-Sikh relations in the twilight of his life and his tragic end. The writer, however, does not offer any clue about his source materials. He taught history at school and wrote many valuable history textbooks. It is also quite possible that he was acquainted with Bengali writings as well as the works of a number of leading British administrator-historians on the Sikhs. But apart from a mention of *Suraj Prakash* in a footnote, he is totally reticent about it.[72]

Government of India Act of 1919 vested education at the provincial level in the hands of Indian ministers and it led to a change in the provincial administrative outlook. The governmental expenditure on education marginally went up and the merger of Bihar and Orissa caused a spurt in Oriya publicatons. Cf. Sridhar Mahapatra Sharma, *Oriya Prakashan o Prasaranar Itihas,* Cuttack 1986, pp. 48-9. See also Bandita Devi, *Some Aspects of British Administration in Orissa (1912-1936)*, New Delhi 1992, pp. 91-127.

[70] Earlier Sivaprasad Das had also written a biography of Shivaji in which he reminded the reader of the military greatness of Guru Gobind Singh. Cf. Sivaprasad Das, *Beerakesari Shivaji*, Cuttack 1929, p. 152. Sivaprasad belonged to the Baragarh region of the former Sambalpur district. Later on he also authored the history of Rajasthan and Sambalpur district.

[71] Das, *Guru Gobinda Singha*, p. 152. Balkrishna Kar printed the book from Cuttack. There is a surprising resemblance between this book and the *Beera Jibanimala* series published by Utkal Sahitya Prachar Sangha. In a sense, the Baripada Book Depot, which brought out *Guru Gobinda Singha* of Sivaprasad Das, may be called a worthy successor of Utkal Sahitya Prachar Sangha.

[72] He has mentioned *Suraj Prakash* in a footnote of the book but one wonders to what extent he had made use of it. Sivaprasad might have become aware of the significance of the *Suraj Prakash* from Tinkari Banerjee's *Guru Gobinda Singha.* In Bengali, Banerjee alone made an effective use of it in his biography of the tenth Guru. Perhaps this prompted our Oriya biographer to refer to *Suraj Prakash* in this form. Infra, pp. 156-8.

The preface and the conclusion reveal the stamp of Sivaprasad Das's own point of view. According to him, Sikh history in the age of the Gurus falls into two parts. In the first stream, Sikhs under Guru Nanak embraced a catholic, universal religious order. Religion was their pursuit and they were not interested in political freedom or annihilation of the enemy. In the second phase, Guru Gobind Singh gave Sikhism a new direction. He armed the Sikhs and directed the movement towards a defence of religion. The name, the dress, the language and the code of conduct became identified with a new awareness and organized the community.[73] Guru Nanak and Guru Gobind Singh, therefore, stood at the two extremities of the early Sikh tradition and they represented the two distinct stages of the Panthic evolution. According to Sivaprasad, the second or the last part does not consist in the first. This was a period when Guru Gobind Singh was at the helm. The combination of war with religion was not there when Guru Nanak had begun preaching Sikhism. On the other hand, Guru Gobind Singh realized that without this blending the Sikhs could not survive while fighting the Mughals. Sivaprasad suggests that this modification of the Sikh tradition during the Guru period was a historical necessity and it reminds us of the views of Tagore in the early twentieth century. The growing militarism of the Sikhs since the late seventeenth century under Guru Gobind Singh worried Tagore. He then wrote (1909):

> The disciples of Nanak can fight now. Nanak did not dedicate his life to a cause which would enable its adherents only to parade in the barracks. . . . Guru Gobinda Singha pressed the Sikhs into a particular service. . . . Sikh humanism was diverted from all other channels. . . . A river which had risen from the white peak of a mountain reaching up to the sky to meet the sea lost its direction in a desert of sands. . . . It is an inglorious failure. . . . Sikhs were developing into a stream of humanity [under Guru Nanak], then they turned into mere soldiers [under Guru Gobinda Singha] and that ended their history.[74]

But Sivaprasad could not agree fully with the above contention of Tagore.[75] We do not, however, definitely know whether Sivaprasad did read the particular essay of Tagore on Sikh history and explicitly

[73] Das, *Guru Gobinda Singha*, p. 90.

[74] Rabindranath Tagore, 'Bhumika' [Shivaji o Guru Gobinda Singha] in Saratkumar Roy's *SikhGuru o Sikhjati,* Calcutta 1909, pp. i-xiv. The essay is also included in the *Rabindra Rachanabali*, vol. XV, Calcutta 1994, pp. 523-8.

[75] Infra, pp. 150-2.

responded to it in the following paragraph. His possibility of reading it cannot also be ruled out because of the long and intimate association of a section of Oriya authors with Bengali sources on Sikhism. Perhaps Das accepted bits he considered relevant and then modified them. He thus observed:

> When Guru Nanak preached Sikhism, political freedom was not part of his vision. . . . It [Sikh religion] was very broad, universal. . . . The wide stream rushing to the ocean hit the rocky edifice of Mughal persecution and formed a small lake. In self-defence, the Sikhs took up arms. . . . Guru Gobinda Singha showed his genius and tenacity in disciplining the mission of spreading his religion, broke the fetters of the caste-system among the Sikhs and developed them into a powerful race of India. He gave them a spirit of national existence. The Sikhs combined religion with politics; the Guru added a name, a dress, a language, a code of conduct etc. and thus created a vast field of an opportunity of spiritual upliftment for them.[76]

The first few lines of the foregoing paragraph broadly follows Rabindranath. Thus, the Guru Nanak of Sivaprasad did not differ from that of Tagore. Both believed that the message of spiritual uplift dominated Sikhism under Guru Nanak. This was expected to carry mankind to a higher plane of humanity. But then Sivaprasad deviated. He did not think Guru Gobind Singh merited criticism. The Guru did not divert Sikhism from religious salvation to aridity. Martial life imparted a sense of sacrifice and devotion to duty that opened the way to a greater national life from day to day trivia. It did not repudiate the message of religious greatness of Guru Nanak. On the contrary, Guru Gobind Singh integrated it with everyday life. His religion engendered a soldierly philosophy of life, which showed the path to survival in the face of peril, to a calling, to honour and to symmetry with life. Rabindranath, however, criticized Guru Gobind Singh for the growing militarization among the Sikhs. But Sivaprasad held the aggressive policy of the Mughals responsible for it. Recent historical analysis has introduced more complexities into the evaluation of the post-Guru Nanak period of Sikh history.[77] One

[76] Das, *Guru Gobinda Singha*, pp. 89-90.

[77] In recent times there is a debate about the nature and extent of change in Sikhism during the days of Sikh Gurus. For the debate, see. McLeod, *The Evolution of the Sikh Community*, pp. 7-14. See also Nripinder Singh, *The Sikh Moral Tradition*, New Delhi 1990, pp. 42-3. Sivaprasad Das had not also denied the process of change in the early Sikh tradition, but he did not talk of a total change there.

cannot expect that vision from Sivaprasad Das 70 years earlier. He visualized Guru Gobind Singh as a saviour of the Sikhs. It required courage to take up the cudgels with Rabindranath at that time.

Although Sivaprasad praised Guru Gobind Singh for his militarism, he kept him away from the heat and dust of Indian politics of the 1920s. According to him, Sikhs took to arms to defend religion, not political freedom. It offers an opportunity of analysing the author's political viewpoint. On the question of resisting the Britishers he remained more or less silent. His writings, however, suggest that he generally favoured the British presence in India. He had very little doubt that its continuance was better than its forceful removal by the Indian nationalists. Here one may find some dichotomy in Sivaprasad's mental world. He praised the Guru for his fight to achieve political freedom for the Sikhs in medieval days. But the biographer seems to discourage a similar line of action in relation to the Britishers of his times. It is perhaps not hard to tell why. In his early life, Sivaprasad taught at a government school and was later promoted to the post of Inspector of Schools. Many of his textbooks had been prescribed in the school syllabus. He was understandably reluctant to talk about Indian political freedom even in the 1930s. On the contrary, Das was not pained by Sikh soldiers fighting in the British army in different theatres of war. He was not ashamed of glorifying the valour of Sikh soldiers under the British flag. Thus his Guru Gobind Singh also sharply differed from Lingaraj Mishra's.

Lingaraj Mishra, a freedom fighter, naturally took a different route. He was not merely a scholar but a patriot who gave up his government job during the Non-cooperation Movement and joined the Satyabadi School. Lingaraj was once jailed for his involvement in the national movement.[78] A good student of Sanskrit, he interpreted Indian history and literature to his students and then took up writing himself. His colleagues at the Satyabadi School inspired him. Lingaraj, on joining the institution, felt the need to convey to his people in their own language the lives and thoughts of those who were truly 'great sons of the country'. His *Guru Gobinda Singha* rolled out of the Satyabadi Press in 1935. It is smaller than Sivaprasad's book. Some factual errors may make the cognoscenti wince. But the book was written in a hurry because of pressing political

[78] *Utkal Sevak*, 15 December 1921; Mohanty, *Oriya Nationalism*, p. 92; Patra, *Orissa Legislature*, pp. 71-2.

needs. The intention was to make his readers aware of the country's past. His language was not academic and his facts would keep the historian at bay. Here are a few instances of inexactitude:

1. Guru Gobind Singh did not create the Khalsa. He got the blueprint of it from Guru Nanak.
2. Guru Nanak created the Sikh community to spread pure Vedic religion.
3. Through quaffing 'nectar' (*amrit*), the Dasam Guru created the Akalis.
4. Guru Gobind Singh did it in 1698.[79]

According to Mishra, Sikhism as preached by Guru Gobind Singh was Hinduism. At the other end was the 'anti-Hindu, dissolute, persecutor' emperor Aurangzeb. During his reign, 'no Hindu woman could preserve her chastity without difficulty'. For Lingaraj, Aurangzeb was nothing less than a brute, a monster that struck fear in the heart of his subjects. The Guru thus became the 'defender of Hinduism' and he took up arms to 'save the people and the country'. He smoothed over the dissensions in the Hindu society. He sent some celibate disciples to Banaras to study the Hindu scriptures. The Guru was unparalleled in his devotion to God and Brahmins. He taught his disciples the martial arts by telling them accounts of the bravery of Hindu mythological heroes like Rama, Vishwa, Drona, Arjuna, etc. He worshipped Goddess Durga on the battlefield and remained true to the Hindu faith till the end of his life.

In other words, Lingaraj Mishra's Indian nationalism excludes not only Muslims of the past, but the contemporary Muslims too. In the 1930s, he did not have much difficulty in projecting Guru Gobind Singh in a Hindu garb. Long before it, many Punjabi Hindus were articulating themselves in a similar vein against the Sikhs since the days of the Singh Sabha movement. But it evoked a strong response from the Singh Sabhaites, *Ham Hindu Nahin*. It led to some skirmishing on paper and even court cases.[80] Sometimes official restrictions were imposed.[81] But Orissa remained unaffected. What

[79] Mishra, *Guru Gobinda Singha*, pp. 1, 19, 22.

[80] Many writings of Bhai Ditt Singh led to such developments in Sikh public life. Cf. N.G. Barrier, 'Vernacular Publishing and Sikh Public Life in the Punjab, 1880-1910', in Kenneth W. Jones (ed.), *Religious Controversy in British India: Dialogues in South Asian Languages*, Albany 1992, pp. 213-14, 221-2.

[81] Supra, p. 59.

was the cause? First, the Singh Sabha movement had no real backing in Orissa and what Lingaraj Mishra wrote never got into the pages of *Khalsa Samachar* or *Khalsa Advocate.* [82] On the other hand, the Oriyas lapped up what he wrote about the new Hindu political identity couched in the language of history. Mishra was convinced that the people of Orissa were looking for a leader who had the qualities ascribed to Guru Gobind Singh. This was after the Non-cooperation and Civil Disobedience Movements. The leader in their imagination was expected to fight the Britishers and end their rule like Guru Gobind Singh who had made short work of the Mughals. What Mishra left unsaid was clear to his readers, who could put English in place of the Mughal.

Lingaraj's *Guru Gobinda Singha* helps us understand the changed scenario of the national movement in another way. After the death of Aurangzeb (1707), there was a struggle for the Mughal throne among his sons and successors. According to Sikh tradition, Bahadur Shah took Guru Gobind Singh's help and ascended the throne after his victory in the wars of succession. In Mishra's view: 'Bahadur Shah became victorious, but the laurels of victory decorated Guru Gobinda Singha's head. . . . Bahadur Shah was in his thrall.'[83]

But the reader could not have forgotten the agony and bewilderment of Chintamani Acharya in 1916 when he reviewed the changed relations between Sikhs and Mughals at the fag end of Aurangzeb's life. He was reluctant to accept Latif's view that the Guru had submitted to Mughal overlordship. The Indian political panorama had changed by the 1930s. Why should the Oriya biographer of the Guru accept that surrender at this period? The days of the politics of loyalty of the Utkal Union Conference were then almost over. Lingaraj Mishra's Guru Gobind Singh and Chintamani Acharya's Guru were poles apart. The tenth Guru was no longer a moderate leader. He was now the hero of Hindu nationalists who believed in direct action. He represented the mindset of the time. Orissa had undergone a transformation in political agitation.

[82] During the days of the Singh Sabha movement, these two English periodicals advocated the views of the young Sikh reformers. For a further discussion, see Satpal Kaur, 'Journalism in the Punjab and the *Khalsa Samachar* (1899-1919)', Guru Nanak Dev University unpublished M.Phil. thesis, 1985; Joginder Singh, 'Resurgence in Sikh Journalism: Early Decades of the 20th Century', *Journal of Regional History*, Annual Number 1982, pp. 99-116.

[83] Mishra, *Guru Gobinda Singha*, p. 50.

VIII

The study of Sikhism in Orissa was not confined to Guru Nanak and Guru Gobind Singh and the separate strands which they represented. The history of Sikhism and its evolution from the fifteenth century onwards has been told in many ways. The other eight Gurus, the birth of the Khalsa, Banda Bahadur, the *misls*, Ranjit Singh, the Sikh wars, etc., had all been focused. The Sikh sacred texts or the salient features of Sikh religion did not, however, draw the attention of Oriya writers. Towards the end of the 1920s, books on some of these subjects appeared. The Akali movement gave rise to a fresh interest in historical Sikh characters. The purpose was to present Sikh religion and history in a wider framework. There is less emotion here, more fidelity to facts and logic. Brahmo Oriya writers evinced this propensity in the past.

Among the three works published at this time,[84] the first chronologically was Niradbhushan Ghosal's *Sikh Abhyudaya*. The book is dedicated to Utkalmani Gopabandhu Das and does not always replicate the Hindu ideology of Lingaraj and Madanmohan. It was published by the Prajatantra Press in 1928, an important centre of nationalist activity at Balasore. The writer began with the birth of Guru Nanak in the fifteenth century and ended with a reference to the rule of Ranjit Singh in the nineteenth century. According to the author, the history of every nation has a lesson to teach. Some significant conclusions can be reached 'from the way the Sikhs marched towards freedom from a political morass'. The Sikhs, in the opinion of the writer, set an example for any nation with faith in their religion, readiness to lay down their lives to protect their home and a resolve to carry out the Guru's instructions. Doubtlessly, the book was inspired by contemporary events.

Ghosal spoke of the origins of Sikhism to establish the revolutionary role of Guru Nanak. The Guru emphasized a synthesis of different religions and believed in a philosophy which was opposed to *sannyas*. The second Guru strengthened the base but it was the third Guru, Amardas, who played an evangelist role. The fifth Guru, Arjan, has been represented as a devotee and an astute politician committed to freedom. The Mughal emperor Jahangir is said to have

[84] Two of the three are separately titled books, the third a periodical called *Sanskara*, one issue of which exclusively dealt with Sikh history. Whether the latter can be called a book is open to question. Liberty has been taken to facilitate discussion.

been responsible for his death but not for religious reasons. Rather it is alleged to have been caused by the personal antagonism between the Guru and the Mughal revenue minister, Chandulal (Chandu Shah?). Militarization during the tenure of the sixth Guru, Hargobind, was a natural consequence. The role of Kashmiri Brahmins in the death of the ninth Guru has been denied. Guru Tegh Bahadur is portrayed as a law-breaker; his killing drove Guru Gobind Singh to retaliation and encouraged him to build up an army to cope with Mughal harassment. His band of followers was ready to do anything in defence of religion. The writer spoke of Guru Gobind Singh as one who kindled the flame of patriotism in the Sikhs. He did not live to see Sikh independence. Banda had to fight for that. The author closes the book with a salute to the Sikh love of freedom and martyrdom. His account from Banda Bahadur to the age of the *misls* was more or less based on Cunningham's work.[85] His respect for Cunningham comes very close to Indian nationalist historiography on the study of the Sikh Panth of the period.[86] It is a mystery, however, why he put an end to his narrative with just a mention of the rise of young Ranjit Singh. Ghosal neither acclaimed the Sikh monarch as the harbinger of a new era nor did he suggest the emergence of the Maharaja as an answer to the infighting of the *misls*. He perhaps came to an abrupt termination so that the eighteenth century tradition of Sikh militarism and resistance could be in tune with India's fight for freedom from British rule.

Another publication of the period was an essay entitled 'Sikh Parichaya' which appeared in the periodical *Sanskara* (1928) edited by Jayamangal Rath (1894-1952). It covered an entire issue but the writer's name was not given. The editor perhaps wrote it himself. The chaptering and the style confirm the impression. It is shorter than the *Sikh Abhyudaya*, but the range of ideas, the variety of the contents and the logical presentation make it more valuable. The essay covered the period starting with the dawn of Sikhism (1469)

[85] On certain points Ghosal also differed from Cunningham. It persists even about the number of Sikh casualties during the *Vadda Ghalughara* (1762). Cf. Cunningham, p. 92 and Ghosal, p. 32.

[86] For the Indian nationalist authors' bias towards Cunningham, see Nandkumardev Sharma, *Punjab Haran aur Maharaja Duleep Singh*, Calcutta 1979 Bikrami, p. 7; Durgadas Lahiri (ed.), *Sikh-Itihas*, Calcutta 1905, pp. 225-8. See also the author's 'Sikh-Itihas: A Supplement to Cunningham's History of the Sikhs in Bengali', *The Panjab Past and Present*, April 1986, pp. 188-94 .

to the end of the Second Sikh War (1849). The emphasis is, however, on the history of the age of the ten Gurus (1469-1708).

Every Guru receives a short but separate treatment. Attention has been drawn to the changes in the Sikh Panth during the period. One or two miracles associated with the life of Guru Nanak have been mentioned but the writer did not fail to highlight the Sikh Guru's faith in the formless God. The writer praises Guru Angad's veneration of Guru Nanak and he projects him as 'a mere shadow' of Nanak. No criticism has been aired about Guru Arjan. He is portrayed as a great organizer, a farsighted politician, a talented poet and a favourite of God. Rath says that organizational talent peaked at the time of the tenth Guru. He realized the need for unity and that led to the creation of the Khalsa. But the circumstances, which the writer describes as the moving force behind the birth of the Khalsa, do not jibe with historical evidence.

The writer has dealt with subsequent Sikh political history (1708-1849) very sketchily. But he has not omitted to mention in the short space, albeit vaguely, that the success of the Sikh movement in the eighteenth century was due to its broader social base. 'Hordes of new people joined the Sikh community. Those deprived of social rights, those persecuted and despised in society, those tortured by the Muslims and those who were given to banditry and warlike pursuit embraced Sikhism.'

Jayamangal Rath was long associated with the protestant social reform movement in Ganjam district in south Orissa.[87] The experience had enriched his vision and enabled him to realize that the Sikh struggle in the past had mobilized countless people from the lower stratum of society.[88] He seems to have tried to locate the cause of the success of the Sikh movement in that factor. He thus sought to provide a broader social base to the Sikh upsurge, which many of his contemporaries in Orissa had often missed. It no doubt gives him a

[87] Anonymous, 'Sikh Parichaya', *Sanskara*, Nos. 7-8, 1928, pp. 1-41. The editor of *Sanskara*, Jayamangal Rath, was born in an orthodox Brahmin family at Ganjam but was later on converted to Brahmoism. Towards the end of his life, he dedicated himself to the cause of social reforms. His Patit Paban Sangha played a major role in removing untouchability in the Ganjam area.

[88] For the support of the lower castes to the Sikh movement under Banda Bahadur, see Muzaffar Alam, 'Sikh Uprisings under Banda Bahadur, 1708-15', *The Panjab Past and Present*, April 1982, pp. 95-107; Gurtej Singh, 'Image of the Sikh Panth in the work of an Early Nineteenth Century Sikh Historian', *Proceedings of the Indian History Congress*, Twenty-ninth Session, Patiala 1967, pp. 396-7.

distinct place in the development of Sikh studies in the region. But this socially conscious man again strikes a strange note while writing about the foundations of Guru Nanak's religion: 'Nanak was a monotheist. His instructions in many places convey the message of pure *Adwaita Vedanta*. . . . He also borrowed from the six philosophical systems.' All this is quite surprising. His proposition could hardly provide any elaborate exposition to the message of Guru Nanak, nor could it clarify the backdrop to Sikhism in fifteenth century Punjab. The ambience in which Guru Nanak spread his religion was also pervaded by a variety of popular religious beliefs and practices, the Nath message and so on. Islam was also triumphant there. It does not believe in idol worship either. A give and take of ideas was going on between Vaishnava *bhakti* and Sufism in Punjab.[89] The varied religious roots of Sikhism may also be traced in the message of Guru Nanak. But the essay under discussion is reticent about these significant issues. The author was a pioneer in excerpting from the writings of the Gurus, setting forth the salient features of the Sikh religious texts, detailing the subdivisions of the religious community and conveying all this to the reader in his mother tongue.

Another significant Oriya work on the Sikhs in the pre-Independence period is *Sikh Prakash* written by Sivaprasad Das.[90] He has been mentioned before. While writing a biographical account of Guru Gobind Singh, he became quite familiar with the sources on Sikh history. On the strength of that and adding a lot of fresh materials, he encompassed nearly four hundred years of Sikh history from Guru Nanak to the Second Sikh War. The book runs to over four hundred pages. So far no Oriya author had written on the history of the Sikhs so extensively. In fact, there is only a handful of such books in the whole of eastern India dealing with the history of the Sikhs. But the Cuttack publishers showed no interest in its publication for commercial reasons. He accordingly published it himself. The question is: why did a well known and worldly-wise man like him take the risk?

[89] Ray, *The Sikh Gurus and the Sikh Society*, pp. 12-15. McLeod called Guru Nanak a very important personality of the *Nirguna Sant* tradition of the medieval days. See his *Guru Nanak and the Sikh Religion*, pp. 149-57.

[90] Sivaprasad Das, *Sikh Prakash*, Sambalpur 1935. The book was printed under the name of his son, A.K. Das (Akshayakumar Das) from his own press. His other son Asutosh Das (from Bargarh) provided me with biographical materials on his father. I am grateful to him for this help.

It is difficult to answer the question straightaway. Perhaps his *Guru Gobinda Singha* (1929) raised some doubts about his political commitment towards British rule in India. That is why he wanted to clarify his political standpoint. Sivaprasad was concerned about the promotion, transfer, sale of his textbooks, his social status, etc. That partly explains the labour he put into *Sikh Prakash* and the money he spent. He marginally rearranged the basic structure of *Guru Gobinda Singha* published in 1929 when he took up his second work in the early 1930s. He added the history of the nine Gurus who preceded the tenth and gave an account of the next 140 years after Guru Gobind Singh's death. His cautious loyalty to the British came through more prominently this time. Macauliffe influenced Das. Macauliffe in his magnum opus on Sikh history and religion emphasized that the Sikhs were loyal to the British Raj and the militarization advocated in their religion was a great support to the British empire. Sivaprasad took up the same theme. He adapted Macauliffe's ideas and quoted from him extensively. The Oriya author also referred to the message of other Gurus and *bhagats* mentioned by Macauliffe; they do not find much space in other Oriya writings. Das stayed away as far as possible from Cunningham's works which inspired the nationalist Lingaraja Mishra and Nirad-bhushan Ghosal. But after the end of the age of the Gurus, Macauliffe was virtually of no help and Das had to turn once or twice to Cunningham. He was, however, very careful in selecting materials. He did scant justice to the sanguinary history of the Sikhs in the eighteenth century. The reader is not reminded of the tradition of martyrdom, the oppression of the Mughals or the resistance of the Sikh *jathas,* facts that Ghosal and Rath described in their respective monographs.[91]

Sivaprasad Das did not write about all this. His treatment of Ranjit Singh resembles that of another British administrator-historian, Lepel Griffin. The stress is on loyalty to the British. Writing about the Sikh wars, Das mentioned indiscipline among the Khalsa, their unprincipled politics and the aggressive policy of the Lahore darbar. He virtually ignored the warlike aggrandizing attitude of the East India Company and glossed over its failings. Cunningham put

[91] Almost during the same period, Narendra Krishna Sinha's *Rise of the Sikh Power* came out (1936). He differed significantly from Das in his understanding of the history of the Sikhs of the same period. According to Sinha, these years represented 'the most glorious period' of the eighteenth century Sikh history.

the blame for the First Sikh War on the East India Company. In spite of knowing all this, Das dealt with the two Sikh wars perfunctorily and briefly. The First Sikh War takes up more than fifty pages in Cunningham, Sivaprasad devoted only eight pages to the two Sikh wars. And he ended the book almost repeating two lines from his *Guru Gobinda Singha* (1929): 'A large number of Sikhs joined the army under the British. In recent times, they have given ample proof of their soldierly ethic and intrepidity.'[92] Sivaprasad had studied Macauliffe and Griffin for several years to corroborate his views. What he had thought to be true at the time of writing *Guru Gobinda Singha* was further buttressed in the monograph. Here he made no secret of his loyalty towards British rule as well as his decision to keep himself away from the heat of the contemporary nationalist politics. In other words, what he believed to be true in 1929, he continued to regard the same as the truth in 1935. He found no reason in six years to alter his views. He did not consider historical truth to be rapidly changeable. Why should he then also be departing from his notion of truth of history? So he did not hesitate to repeat his earlier statements. There also lies the significance of his *Sikh Prakash*. Many other historians of the period had the same attitude, which also makes Das typical of his age.[93]

IX

We have more or less come to the end of our Oriya journey. We still have not discussed certain aspects, which cannot be labelled. In this section, we will refer to stray pieces in various publications—these include sections of writings where Sikhs have been mentioned accidentally or some events concerning Sikhs which took place in

[92] Das, *Guru Gobinda Singha*, p. 3; idem, *Sikh Prakash*, p. 404.

[93] We come across almost a similar thing in the writings of Nandakumardev Sharma. In his three monographs dealing with three different periods of Sikh history in Hindi, published between 1914 and 1921, Sharma underlined: (1) the Sikhs were not separate from the Hindus; (2) since the Sikhs were then demanding a separate communal status, it would intensify the bitter conflict between the Hindus and the Sikhs affecting Indian unity, especially as relations with the Muslims had already been soured; (3) Hindus had been defeated by foreigners several times in the past because of their own disunity and infighting; (4) let the Sikhs learn lessons from Indian history and forsake the dangerous path (i.e. search for a separate communal identity). The Sikh reformers of Punjab of the first three decades of the twentieth century were in no mood to listen to Sharma's lament. But Sharma never shifted from the conclusion that he had reached in 1914.

Punjab and were discussed in Oriya newspapers for some time or found place in school textbooks in Oriya. These materials are numerous and the space is limited. Hence we limit ourselves to some salient features.

We begin with an essay titled 'Dwitiya Sikh Yuddha' published in 1878. It appeared in a prestigious periodical called *Utkal Madhup*. The article seems to have been carried serially in two issues.[94] The writer remained anonymous and it is not clear what prompted him to write.[95] It can be said on the basis of available facts that the essay pertains to the state of the Lahore darbar on the eve of the Second Sikh War. It analyses the causes of the war, the composition of the people who stoked the fires of war, etc. According to the writer, 'only an ignorant historian will look for deeper causes'. In his scheme of history, one person was responsible and he was the Governor-General Lord Dalhousie. That combined with the incompetence of Frederic Currie, the British resident in Lahore. Otherwise, there would have been no war. Lord Hardinge had taken the necessary steps to ensure that no conflict occurred in Punjab and there was perfect peace even in the initial stage of the administration of Lord Dalhousie. But the latter's aggressive policy generated bitterness in parts of Punjab—Multan and Hazara for instance. Currie delayed in taking necessary action and the local uprising in Multan spread all over Punjab. The Second Sikh War thus began. It is surprising that an anonymous writer could be so anti-British, especially at a time when Oriya politics was primarily based on loyalty. Such a message of protest is also generally missing in Sikh studies in other Indian languages. Only Amritalal Chakrabarty was equally strident in

[94] These two issues of *Utkal Madhup* came out in Bhadra and Ashwin of 1800 Saka. In the Ashwin issue of the publication, the discussion ended as 'to be continued'. I do not know whether the article was actually published in the subsequent issues of *Utkal Madhup* or any other journal. I could not trace any other issue of the periodical in the Orissa State Museum (Bhubaneswar). Samantaray, an authority on the late nineteenth century Oriya publications, also failed to shed any light on it in his *Adhunik Oriya Sahityar Bhittibhumi*. I made several enquiries at the Orissa State Archives Library (Bhubaneswar), Utkal Sahitya Samaj Library (Cuttack) and Maharaja Purnachandra Library (Baripada), but with no results. At this stage, it is not possible to form any definite conclusion.

[95] A senior Oriya scholar said in this context: '*Madhup* is very sensitive in publishing the names of its authors. In the contents or the annual index, names of authors were not given'. Gokulchandra Adhikari, 'Utkal Madhup', *Bhanja Pradeep*, Paush 1348 Masiha, p. 11.

Hindi,[96] but his works appeared sixteen years later. All other writings advocated loyalty and made a feeble constitutional protest. Who wrote the vitriolic article in *Utkal Madhup*? So far, we are in the dark.

Protest in Orissa might have been unnatural in 1878, but the time and the country were ripe for it in 1919. This outlook was partially focused by the Satyabadi School and its literary organ *Satyabadi*. Basudeb Mahapatra, a teacher at Satyabadi and a close associate of Utkalmani Gopabandhu, wrote the article.[97] The article is mainly about the martyrdom of Guru Tegh Bahadur. The tenth Guru also makes a brief appearance. The Mughal emperor, Babar, is shown touching Guru Nanak's feet with his head. The authenticity of the incident is, however, open to doubt. The central point of the article is the last days of Guru Tegh Bahadur. No other Oriya author has written with so much enthusiasm about the ninth Guru's martyrdom. Here also the conventional theory that Aurangzeb caused his death has been propounded. The Guru's name has been deliberately or unwittingly changed to 'Tej Bahadur'. But unlike the author of *Sikh Abhyudaya*, Mahapatra has not portrayed him as a man deserving criticism for breach of local peace and discipline. Kashmiri Brahmins are present in the scene, driving him to self-immolation. The writer describes the ninth Guru as one believing in *Vedic Siddhantabad*. Mahapatra's writing could not be pleasing to the Khalsa in Punjab or the Sikh faithful. On the contrary, he was likely to give satisfaction to their Sanatani opponents. Mahapatra was of the opinion that the death of the ninth Guru led to Sikh militarization, which weakened the foundations of the Mughal empire. The article about Tegh Bahadur's self-immolation was meant to stimulate the political climate in Orissa.[98]

[96] Anonymous (Amritalal Chakrabarty), *Sikh-Juddha*, Calcutta 1894. The name of the author is not there for obvious reasons. Amritalal perhaps provided the first nationalist interpretation of the Sikh wars in Hindi. Bharatendu Harishchandra is said to have made fun of his Hindi as 'Bengali Hindi'.

[97] Basudeb Mahapatra, 'Atmabali', *Satyabadi*, Mithun 1326 Masiha, pp. 87-95. Later the article was included in *Beera Bharata*. I have checked its 3rd reprint (1950) and found no change in its text. For Mahapatra's literary career, see Kunjabehari Das, 'Pandit Basudeb Mahapatra', *Nabarabi*, October 1972, pp. 102-10.

[98] For an almost similar account of the martyrdom of the sons of Guru Gobind Singh, see Chintamani Acharya, 'Fateh Singha o Jerebar Singha', *Mukur*, Baisakh 1322 Masiha, pp. 17-21 (later included in his *Itihas Prasanga*, pp. 141-53), and 'Ajit Singha o Jhujhar Singha', *Utkal Sahitya*, Sraban 1322 Masiha, pp. 146-50. Perhaps

Militarization under Guru Gobind Singh constitutes an interesting theme in Sikh studies in Oriya. Oriya writers were not generally concerned about the 'glorious role' of the Sikhs in defending the British empire in the nineteenth and twentieth centuries. Ramchandra Acharya (1895-1934),[99] an active member of the Utkal Union Conference, alone reviewed the question in a part of his long essay in the periodical *Mukur*. It was entitled 'Bharatar Samarpriya Jatisakal'.[100] Acharya wrote about the Marathas, Gorkhas, Rajputs and Sikhs. He briefly referred to the militarization of the Sikhs under Guru Gobind Singh. But he then proceeded to their role in the British-Indian army in the defence of the empire. He quoted a few British administrator-historians and generals to underline the point. He wrote about the valour of the Sikhs in action on different fronts in World War I. The writer did not miss the fact that their heroism in the Sikh wars and later their keeping out of the Sepoy Mutiny had brought them close to the British. Jobs were reserved for Sikh soldiers. From Turkey to Mesopotemia, the Sikhs fought under the British flag. But the writer kept quiet about the recent rift caused by the Akalis in the early 1920s. Perhaps Acharya's loyalism did not approve of the Akali confrontation with the Punjab government. However, he is the only essayist who concentrated on Sikh militarism during British rule and bypassed its medieval heritage.

We have already mentioned Chintamani Acharya. He published in *Mukur* another long article captioned 'Sikhjatir Sadhana'[101] in three successive numbers. There he discussed developments from the accession of Farrukhsiyar (1713) to the capture of Lahore and the establishment of Sikh domination there (1765). The footnotes contain references to Malcolm, M'Gregor and Latif. The essayist has narrated the trials and tribulations faced by the Sikhs in the second half of the

---

these were borrowed from two of Basantakumar Banerjee's essays published in *Aitihasik Chitra* in Sraban 1315 BS, pp. 159-74 and Agrahayan 1315 BS, pp. 337-55. Supra, pp. 40-1.

[99] Ramchandra Acharya hailed from Ganjam district. He died early and had written a novel entitled *Beera Orissa*. Also see Binayak Mishra, *Adhunik Oriya Sahityar Itihas,* Aska 1968, pp. 295-6.

[100] Ramchandra Acharya, 'Bharatar Samarpriya Jatisakal', *Mukur*, Magh 1330 Masiha, pp. 38-9.

[101] Chintamani Acharya, 'Sikhjatir Sadhana', *Mukur*, Agrahayan 1320 Masiha, pp. 248-52; Baisakh 1321 Masiha, pp. 6-11; Ashar 1321 Masiha, pp. 159-63. Cf. Basantakumar Banerjee, 'Sikh-Sadhana', *Aitihasik Chitra,* Bhadra-Ashwin 1315 BS, pp. 234-41; Kartik 1315 BS, pp. 306-18; Chaitra 1315 BS, pp. 540-50.

eighteenth century in achieving political independence. But this is not what makes the article stand out. It was not an original work of Chintamani Acharya of Telengabazar in Cuttack. The credit should go to Basantakumar Banerjee of Chandannagar (Bengal),[102] a prolific writer on Sikh history, literature and philosophy. Chintamani Acharya translated Banerjee's Bengali article verbatim, footnotes and all. Earlier, Madanmohan Patnaik had adapted the writing of Rajanikanta Gupta in his 'SikhGuru Gobinda Singha'. But Patnaik altered the beginning and the end to give it a stamp of originality. Chintamani Acharya had not done even that. It was an exact reproduction. He did not make any acknowledgement to Basantakumar Banerjee. Perhaps he took the risk to enrich his mother tongue.

It is said that as he lay dying, Maharaja Ranjit Singh gave orders that the Kohinoor should be placed in the Jagannath temple in Puri. But it was not sent there because of objections from the Khalsa chiefs. Later the East India Company annexed Punjab and sent the diamond to England. Some Oriya writers expressed regret over the incident. Apart from that, not much was written about Ranjit Singh in Oriya.[103] Ranjit Singh's rule (1799-1839) features prominently in Hindi and Bengali. Plays, biographies, essays and fiction had been written about him. It makes the Oriya reticence surprising. Perhaps the Oriya authors did not find anything interesting in this period of Sikh history. The only exception is Kunjabihari Das (1914-94), who wrote a poem entitled 'Mahabir Ranjit Singha'.[104]

The poem was published on the occasion of the maharaja's death centenary in 1939. It is full of customary enthusiasm about the Sikh monarch. The old valour of Punjab was recalled to renew the spirit of resistance. There is also a reference to the Jallianwala Bagh massacre (1919) and the popular discontent against it. The proverbial quote *sab lal ho jayega* is also repeated. The English have been identified as the offenders. At the same time, the poem presents a panoramic view of the rivers and fields of Punjab and calls for emotional identification.

Kunjabihari Das wrote the poem when he was very young. Perhaps

[102] Infra, pp. 158-60.

[103] We come across two more brief references to the reign of Ranjit Singh in the writings of Fakirmohan Senapati and Sivaprasad Das. Both of them, however, very briefly reviewed it in the context of four hundred years of Sikh history.

[104] Kunjabehari Das, 'Mahabir Ranjit Singha', *Sahakar*, Sraban 1346 Masiha, pp. 304-5.

this is why history often took a backseat and emotion prevailed. Here there is nothing definite about Ranjit Singh's administration and his conquests. But it shows how a young heart was moved by the maharaja's achievements in faraway Punjab. Thus, the Oriya writer not merely lamented that the Kohinoor did not come to Orissa, but conveyed Ranjit Singh's greatness to his readership.

Comparatively speaking, the religion and philosophy of Sikhism are poorly lit areas in Sikh studies in Oriya. Considering the long interaction between Sikhism and Orissa over a few centuries it seems quite disappointing. We have so far come across a few conflicting versions of Guru Nanak's philosophy. The small piece by Padmacharan Patnaik (1885-1956) entitled 'Sikh Dharmer Sar Katha'[105] tries to provide an introduction to Sikhism. Padmacharan was essentially a poet. He strung together passages from the *sabads* of the Gurus and drew a picture of Sikhism from a humanist point of view. While projecting the distinctive features of the Sikh religion, he drew attention to the social significance of the message of the Gurus. The Gurus took a special interest in the welfare of the downtrodden people with two goals: to save them from torture by the Muslim political power and to show them how to escape from the oppressive Hindu social structure. Guru Nanak was quite distressed by the humiliation and indignity of man. His religion, therefore, laid emphasis on the natural and inborn dignity of humanity. Like Guru Nanak, his successors also set their sights on developing the inner mind of individuals. Patnaik, however, did not fail to point out that dignity of labour (*kirat karna*) represents another important area of Sikh philosophy. 'Earn your bread by the sweat of your brow', they said and urged the followers to dedicate themselves to the welfare of man regardless of geographical limits. The Sikhs, Patnaik pointed out, tried to achieve social integration in the way recommended by the Gurus. Sikhism could thus ensure the support of the socially downtrodden. Here Padmacharan came very close to Jayamangal Rath. But he said nothing about Sikhism's relationship with the different branches of Vedic philosophy earlier

[105] Padmacharan Patnaik, 'Sikh Dharmar Sar Katha', *Utkal Sahitya*, Baisakh 1342 Masiha, pp. 30-4. It was later included in his book, *Parijat Kusum*, Cuttack 1940. I am indebted to Bauribandhu Kar of Berhampur University for drawing attention to this essay. For a short life-sketch of the writer, see *Encyclopaedia of Indian Literature*, vol. IV, New Delhi 1993, p. 3168.

underlined by many Oriya writers in the 1920s and 1930s of the twentieth century.

Oriya interest in contemporary Sikh affairs grew in the late nineteenth century. There was little enthusiasm about the post-annexation socio-economic developments of Punjab. Even the Sikh wars passed almost unnoticed because there was virtually no modern Oriya press till the end of the famine of 1866. But the tragic death of Maharaja Duleep Singh in France caused quite a reaction in Oriya newspapers. Loyalist landlords generally ran the contemporary local papers and they did not regard favourably the anti-British activities of Duleep Singh. But his premature and unfortunate death caused them to highlight the raw deal that Ranjit Singh's descendant had received from the British. While underscoring their deep loyalty to British rule, these reports often made no secret of their anguish over the young maharaja's tragic end faraway from Punjab.[106] Perhaps their deep faith in British imperial greatness expected a better deal from that end. A subtle note of disillusionment could thus be detected in some of the brief reportings on Maharaja Duleep Singh.

The subservient sentiment, however, started melting away in the 1920s when anti-British politics surfaced. Oriya newspapers took notice of the gurdwara reform struggle, which coincided with the Non-cooperation Movement. The Punjab government turned the heat on the Akali agitators in the form of arrest, imprisonment, fine, deportation, physical torture, etc. But it only intensified public support for the Akalis and the struggle for reform of the Sikh shrines took a bloody turn at Nankana Sahib, Guru-ka-Bagh, Jaito and such other places. *Samaj* and *Utkal Dipika* from Cuttack, *Prajatantra* from Balasore, *Puribasi* and *Sakti* from Puri, *Lokamukha* from Banpur and *Utkal Sevak* from Sambalpur spread the news about Punjab. The official policy of repression was criticized and sympathies were expressed for the Akalis. Readers wrote letters to the editor, which helped build up support in Orissa for the Akali movement.

A comparison between the quantum of publications in Assamese and Oriya would indicate that Orissa reacted more firmly against the British suppression of the Akali movement. *Sadinia Asamiya* was

[106] Maharaja Duleep Singh's death was generally highlighted in the contemporary Oriya press. But long before it, even in 1887 *Nabasambad* made no secret of its dissatisfaction about British policy towards him. Cf. *Nabasambad*, 27 July and 10 October 1887.

the most important nationalist organ in Assam, which published such news. But the nationalist press in Orissa was more considerable and so the Akali struggle for gurdwara reform drew wider support there. Frontline writers like Gopabandhu Das and Godavaris Mishra were involved in contemporary Oriya journalism. They took their readers back to the old history of Punjab, the significance of the gurdwaras in the evolution of the Sikh Panth and the long tradition of martyrdom while commenting on current events. In Oriya, the movement in Punjab was located against a broader backdrop. *Sadinia Asamiya* could not do it single-handed in Assamese. In some of their editorials, the *Samaj* (edited by Gopabandhu Das) and *Lokamukha* (edited by Godavaris Mishra) could link the Akali struggle to the Non-cooperation Movement in Orissa. Both Gopabandhu and Godavaris were active non-cooperators. They had therefore a feeling that the Akalis were fighting for a similar cause in Punjab. Their editorial comments and observations could perhaps establish an invisible tie between the aspirations of the Akali *satyagrahis* and the Oriya non-cooperators.

X

It is hard to resist the temptation to compare Sikh studies in Oriya with those in other eastern Indian languages. During colonial rule the Oriyas had many shared experiences with writers in other parts of eastern India. Hence the similarities and dissimilarities.

The search for the Sikhs in Orissa began before the British takeover, but in Assam and Bengal it started much later. Quantitatively, Oriya writings on Sikhism are more copious than in Assamese but did not number as much as in Bengali and Hindi. Again the direct contact that Sikh studies in Oriya had with the Bengali stream was often missing in Assamese.[107] On the other hand, Sikh studies in Assam were often propelled by the forces of regional nationalism and gradually assumed a distinct Assamese label by the end of the nineteenth century. In many of these works, like the Sikhs, the Bengalis were sometimes denounced as foreigners. The situation is partially different in Orissa. Like Assam, here bitterness and

[107] This kind of give and take has been going on for a long time on the all-India level. Cf. Das, *A History of Indian Literature 1911-1956*, p. 399. Also see Esha Dey, 'Neither a Borrower nor a Lender Be: A Note on Oriya Reception of Bengali Influence', in Subha Chakrabarty DasGupta (ed.), *Regionality and Comparative Literature*, Calcutta 1998, pp. 93-108.

animosity against their Bengali neighbours remained an important ingredient in the Oriya identity fomation of the period. But this never reached the peak it had attained in Assam. Even those who were vigorously propagating the cause of Oriya linguistic identity in the twentieth century did not envisage any confrontational attitude towards pan-Indian nationalism. Neither did they ever focus Bengalis as 'foreginers'. Besides, in Orissa the politics of conciliation left behind a significant impact on the evolution of Sikh studies. It began with the Oriya Brahmos of the late nineteenth century and was continued by the members of the Utkal Union Conference in the 1930s. The loyalists even enjoyed the blessings of the colonial authority in the reconstruction of the Dantan Sahib gurdwara (1933) which the Sikhs of Assam often missed during the same period. In Assam the forces of regional nationalism, however, continued to be rallied in favour of or against the local Sikhs almost till the end of our period. But in the Oriya-speaking tracts they lost much of their appeal before the rising tides of the pan-Indian politics of the Satyabadi school. Regional naionalism, therefore, played a complex but major role in shaping Sikh studies in both the areas. Writers in both provinces presented that trend to readers from their own local positions and differing points of view. Thus, Sikh studies in Orissa and Assam went ahead with a touch of variety and distinctiveness of their own.

An important aspect of Sikh studies in Oriya was the tendency to spread over a large area. In the concluding part of the nineteenth century, Cuttack was the nerve-centre of modern Oriya culture. Initially, all writings on the Sikhs were published here.[108] But new centres sprang up as the twentieth century wore on. Baripada, Balasore, Berhampore and Sambalpore started bringing out new publications and spawned new ideas. With the expansion of publishing in Orissa, Sikh studies also spread.

Another feature as mentioned earlier is its closeness to Bengali studies on the Sikhs. The Oriya Brahmo writers were the pioneers. They tried to overcome the prevailing bitterness with the Bengalis in the local job market from their commitment to the enrichment of their mother tongue. In the subsequent years, Madanmohan Patnaik, Nabakishore Das, Chintamani Acharya, Sivaprasad Das and others

[108] It continued to maintain its dominant position in the next century. Pati's recent study confirms the point. Biswamoy Pati, *Situating Social History: Orissa (1800-1997)*, New Delhi 2000, pp. 28-32.

continued the trend. Again their pattern of interaction often varied in accordance with their individual needs and requirements. Thus, Chintamani Acharya might have occasionally copied from a few Bengali sources, but Sivaprasad Das had a distinct methodology of his own. He was quite knowledgeable about the different trends in Sikh studies in Bengal. It might have prompted him to review Rabindranath's view and thereby add a new perspective to the Oriya Sikh quest of his times. If Chintamani Acharya represented one end of it, Sivaprasad Das perhaps stood for the opposite.

It is, of course, necessary to mention a few of their shortcomings. While dealing with the Sikhs of history, the Oriya writers could not make any effective use of their local source materials which the Assamese authors had achieved almost during the same period.[109] Contemporary Oriya Sikh World perhaps missed much of its medieval folk cultural heritage owing to the lack of political unity of the Oriya-speaking tracts. It may be also because of the absence of a sizeable number of indigenous Sikh population in Orissa. Perhaps that is why, with the exception of a few interesting folk images of Nanak, here regional materials did not play any important role in Sikh studies. These invaluable ingredients of Oriya popular culture might have occasionally nourished the folk theatres of Puri, Bhadrak and Cuttack. But no great Oriya author ever thought of bringing them within the parameters of the modern print-world which their counterparts could achieve in Assam. Further, no interesting analytical book review on the subject came out in any of the Oriya newspapers and periodicals of the period. It might have stimulated newer areas of enquiry. Critics turned a blind eye even on the mistakes in the textbooks.[110] There was an obvious reluctance among the Oriya authors to go for the primary sources. They relied predominantly on books written either by British administrator-historians or by authors in Bengali.

All these flaws notwithstanding, Sikh studies in Orissa are unique.

[109] Supra, p. 71.

[110] Here I will refer to three Oriya school textbooks which ran into several editions: (1) Niranjan Mahapatra and Baidyanath Tripathi, *Am Itihas Gap*, vol. II, Cuttack 1951. On p. 51, they wrote: 'It was the aim of Guru Gobinda to establish Hindu empire in India'. (2) Kedarnath Mahapatra, *Uchcha Prathamika Nutan Bharat Itihas,* Cuttack reprint, 1950. On p. 110, Mahapatra wrote: 'Seeing Tegh Bahadur's valour, Aurangzeb had him beheaded'. (3) Sivaprasad Das, *Uchcha Prathamika Bharat Itihas,* Cuttack 1951. On p. 96, he wrote: 'Ranjit Singha is a Sikh by race'.

A book like *Sikh Prakash* came out here, the likes of which one will not get in any other eastern Indian language. None of the books used primary sources or stimulated a debate at the national level. But as soon as Orissa got involved in the Non-cooperation Movement of the twentieth century, the rush of reports on the Akali agitation which came out in the Oriya press cannot be underrated. The Utkal Sahitya Samaj Library at Cuttack has a collection, which gives a fair idea about the keen interest with which Oriyas looked at the Akalis. Editorials written by Gopabandhu Das at Cuttack or Godabaris Mishra at Banpur still invite attention. They can be considered a part of the larger Oriya literary heritage. The seeds of Sikh studies lurk in these pieces. Hence the post-Independence period has witnessed the publication of the lives of different Gurus or of maharajas.[111]

[111] Sivaprasad Das, *Am Deshar Bir*, Cuttack 1957; Gokulchandra Kar, *Guru Gobinda Singha*, Cuttack 1981; Saratchandra Panigrahi, *Guru Nanak: Jiban o Darshan*, Cuttack 1994. I am indebted to Pathani Patnaik of Cuttack and Gaganendra Nath Dash of Berhampur University for drawing attention to these sources.

CHAPTER IV

Bengali 1

THE PUNJAB tragedy of the 1980s generated a sort of contempt and bitterness in some of the Hindi-speaking states of northern India. Many zealous Hindus of that region had often regarded the Sikhs as *khadkus*. The old refrain was heard once again: *Pagri, Kirpan, Pakistan.*[1] After having lived for a long span in a situation of daily give and take, the two communities suddenly started looking upon one another as enemies and rivals. The mud-slinging among Hindus and Sikhs in northern India did not affect the distant Bengalis so much. The Bengalis had not designated the Sikhs in the past as a religious community, which violated peace. When Delhi plunged into the mass slaughter of Sikhs in 1984, Calcutta caught the malaise to some extent but it never reached the proportion of a genocide in the city. People in Calcutta had no hesitation in registering their protest against Operation Blue Star. Here they had no serious apprehensions about the Sikhs of the region.[2] It may be partly due to the fact that West Bengal and Punjab constitute two distant frontier provinces of India separated by more than a thousand miles. Thus, the people here are, unlike their counterparts in northern India, not sullied by everyday contact.

I

Bengali interest in understanding Sikh history and religion is reflected in different works of the nineteenth century, and continues to the

[1] For a modified form of the slogan, see Sangat Singh, *The Sikhs in History*, New Delhi 1996, p. 380. For other slogans of the period, Khuswant Singh, *A History of the Sikhs*, vol. II, New Delhi reprint, 1997, p. 298.

[2] Talking to the Sikhs of Calcutta, one gathers the impression that they lived in greater peace in West Bengal than in many other urban centres of northern India. An instance will reveal the measure of security enjoyed by them in Calcutta. For the last 50 years, an English monthly called *The Sikh Review* has been coming out regularly. In 1992 Captain Bhag Singh, the editor of the monthly, died and there was talk of

present. Many Bengali writers were associated with the endeavour and numerous factors brought them together on a common platform. A few of them even spent long years in Punjab, where they had gone following the British annexation of the province (1849) in response to the growing administrative needs of the colonial government.[3] The development of Sikh studies was closely associated with the Brahmo search in the nineteenth century for a religious identity separate from that of orthodox Hinduism. A few Hindu nationalist and Sanatanist authors who added distinctiveness to the Bengali understanding of the Sikhs subsequently reinforced the Brahmo inquiry into the Panth. They were deeply impressed by Bankimchandra Chatterjee's Hindu revivalist sentiment and wanted to glorify the medieval Indian Hindu fighting tradition. Many of them drew their inspiration from the contemporary militant politics of Bengal and wanted to support the spirit of resistance against British rule. In their eyes the birth of Sikhism, the martyrdom of the Gurus, the military success of Maharaja Ranjit Singh carried the message of patriotism. These authors reconstructed the past and reinterpreted it to satisfy their contemporary needs.

The volume of materials is so extensive that the present study may be confined to the first 250 out of the 500 years of Sikh history—the Guru period (1469-1708). The stream of literature began with Guru Nanak. It has already been mentioned that the work was pioneered by Bengali Brahmo writers.[4] They are credited

---

shifting its editorial office to Chandigarh. In view of the press-censorship and political uncertainty of Punjab, the idea was dropped. *The Sikh Review* is still being published from Calcutta.

[3] After the annexation of Punjab in 1849, a large number of educated Bengalis went over to Punjab to serve the British administration. Some related information can be had in Kenneth W. Jones, 'The Bengali Elite in Post-Annexation Punjab: An Example of Inter-Regional Influence in Nineteenth-Century Punjab, 1851-1871', in Norman G. Barrier and Harbans Singh (eds.), *Essays in Honour of Dr. Ganda Singh*, Patiala 1976, pp. 234-51. Before Jones, Jnanendramohan Das provided some significant information in his *Banger Bahire Bangali—Uttar Bharat,* Calcutta 1322 BS, pp. 404-39. The autobiography of Nagendranath Gupta who served *The Tribune* (Lahore) for some time is also valuable. Cf. *Reflections and Reminiscences,* Bombay 1946. See also Jeffrey Perrill, 'Punjab Orientalism: The Anjuman-i-Punjab and Punjab University', University of Missourie-Columbia unpublished Ph.D. thesis, 1976; Madan Gopal, *Dayal Singh Majithia,* New Delhi 1994, pp. 32-50.

[4] Supra, pp. 25, 80-5. Some researchers are convinced that interest about Sikhism in Bengali began as early as the twelfth century. They mention two *sabads* from poet Jayadeva in the *Adi Granth*. One of them is in *rag Gujri* and the other in *rag Maru.* But the two *sabads* are not in the standard twelfth century Bengali. Here is a quote

with the writing of one or two significant biographies of Guru Nanak in the second half of the nineteenth century. But Sikh studies in Bengali had then already taken a few strides. It was during the first part of that century that Raja Rammohun Roy (1772-1833) had pointed out the many similarities between Brahmoism and Guru Nanak's Sikh Panth.[5] It was in Calcutta that the British administrator-historian Malcolm read some Sikh religious texts with the help of a Nirmala Sikh and drafted his famous book, *Sketch of the Sikhs* (1812). Later Wilson, while reviewing the different sects among the followers of Guru Nanak, came to know the Nirmala Sikh scholar but we do not know to what extent the British expert received his

---

from Anil Chandra Banerjee, 'In the *Bhagatbanis* of the *AdiGranth* two *sabads* of Jayadeva of Bengal occur. Perhaps these were not written by Jayadeva, the immortal author of the *Gitagovinda*, who was a courtier of Lakshman Sen. They are by some other Jayadeva.' Cf. 'AdiGrantha', *Prabasi*, Agrahayan 1352 BS, p. 141. Banerjee, however, revised his opinion in *The Sikh Gurus and the Sikh Religion*, New Delhi 1983, p. 191. Suniti Kumar Chatterji also argued that the language of the *Gitagovinda* 'is professedly Sanskrit' and there is no 'absolute certainty whether the author (or authors?) of these two poems [i.e. two *sabads* in the *Adi Granth*] and Jayadeva of the *Gitagovinda* are the same person.' Cf. Suniti Kumar Chatterji, *The Origin and Development of the Bengali Language*, vol. I, London reprint, 1970, p. 125; *Jayadeva*, New Delhi 1973, p. 34. We are also not sure whether Jayadeva, the author of the *Gitagovinda*, was from the village Kendubilla in Birbhum district. Some Oriya critics have adduced evidence to prove that Jayadeva wrote in medieval Oriya and was born near Puri. Cf. B. Rath, 'Orissa, the Land of Jayadeva', *Orissa Historical Research Journal*, vol. XXII, October 1974-January 1975, pp. 1-18. So there is likely to be difference of opinion about the Jayadeva of the *Adi Granth*. But we cannot altogether rule out the possibility of two versions of Jayadeva's compositions prevailing in different parts of India following the argument of Linda Hess about Kabir. Supra, p. 33.

[5] Rammohun Roy perhaps got acquainted with the Sikh religion while he stayed at Patna and Banaras. Both Wilkins (*Asiatic Researches*, 1788) and Wilson (*Asiatic Researches*, 1826) mentioned the Sikh *sangats* of Patna and Banaras. In his booklets, *Vedantasar* (1815) and *Prarthanapatra* (1823), Rammohun referred to the Nanakpanthis. Cf. Ajit Kumar Ghosh (ed.), *Rammohun Rachanabali*, Calcutta 1973, pp. 8, 260. The interface between Sikhism and the Brahmo movement survived throughout the nineteenth century. Examples are scattered through Sikh studies in Bengali. The following comment may be taken into consideration in this context: 'The spiritualism in Sikhism is as appealing as that in Brahmoism. Among all the religions in India, greater feeling and enthusiasm can be seen nowadays in Sikhism and it has much in common with Brahmoism. Brahmo devotees should be acquainted with the essence of the religion'. Cf. *Dharmatattwa*, Chaitra 1, 1793 Saka, p. 619. Also see Satikumar Chatterjee, 'Response of the Brahmo Samaj to the Message of Guru Nanak', in K.R. Srinivas Iyengar (ed.), *Guru Nanak—A Homage*, New Delhi 1971, pp. 103-10.

help. Sikh settlement in Calcutta had existed even before the nineteenth century. There had been the Gurdwara Badi Sikh Sangat on Mahatma Gandhi Road[6] and a settlement of Agrahari Sikhs had grown up in Bara Bazaar[7] (a trading centre in Calcutta) and its surroundings where the visits of the upcountry Khatri merchants had been common.[8] We also have firm evidence that the Sikh *vakils* and some politicians of Ranjit Singh's court used to visit Calcutta from time to time as the city was the capital of the East India Company.[9] It is, however, not possible to make an estimate of the extent of the impact of these visits on Bengali society with any precision.

On the other hand, contemporary Brahmo materials exhibit an influence of Sikh religion and culture. Rammohun's fondness of the Nanakpanthi salutation, *Alakh Niranjan,* would be an instance. The same sources tell us that a few melodious Sikh *sabads* were recited at

[6] According to Sikh tradition, this is a historical Sikh shrine. Among the old papers of the gurdwara, I came across a document (civil case No. 91 of 1870, Calcutta High Court) which claimed that it had been built at least two hundred years earlier. I am thankful to Man Singh Grewal, General Secretary, Badi Sikh Sangat, Bara Bazaar, Calcutta, for furnishing a copy of the document (10 July 1996).

[7] For the Agraharis in Bihar, see L.S.S. O'Malley, 'The Agraharis of Sasaram', *Journal of Asiatic Society of Bengal,* vol. LXXIII, Part III, 1904, pp. 35-43. Ved Prakash has also mentioned the Agraharis of Bihar in his *Sikhs in Bihar.* But no serious research has so far been undertaken about the Agraharis of Bara Bazaar-Tulapatti, Calcutta. They are different from the Punjabi-speaking Sikhs in various respects. Talking to these people, I got the impression that their ancestors generally came from Sasaram, Gaya and other places of Bihar towards the end of the eighteenth or the early years of the nineteenth century either on foot or by boat down the Ganga. They speak in Hindi and Bengali and have separate gurdwaras of their own. Many told me that they do not have any social relationship with the Punjabi-speaking Sikhs of Calcutta. They also represent a distinct category of 'hyphenated' Sikhs in this part of India. For their early history in the city of Calcutta, see Ramavtar Singh, 'Purva Bharat mei Sikh-Parivar: Punarvas ki Adi-Katha', *SriGuru Gobind Singh Traya Satabdi Mahotsav,* Calcutta 1967, p. 54. Also see Karen Leonard, *Making Ethnic Choises,* pp. 206-19.

[8] It is hard to tell when the movement of Khatri merchants began in the Bara Bazar area. It is generally believed that they came here even in the late eighteenth century. Anonymous, 'Khatris', *Indian Antiquary,* vol. II, 1873, p. 26.

[9] For information on how Bengalis of the period assessed Ranjit Singh, see 'Maharaja Ranjeet Singh', 27 March 1834, Sureshchandra Maitra (ed.), *Selections from Jnanannweshan,* Calcutta 1979, pp. 155-8; Haripada Bhoumik (ed.), *Sekaler Sambadpatre Kolkata,* vol. II, Calcutta 1988, pp. 5-6; Lepel H. Griffin, *The Panjab Chiefs: Historical and Biographical Notices of the Principal Families in the Lahore Kingdom,* Lahore 1866, pp. 82, 86-8.

prayer meetings of the Brahmo Samaj.[10] Discussions at the end of the prayer meetings sometimes drew on Guru Nanak's views against idolatry and casteism. From the beginning, Debendranath Tagore (1817-1905) called his religious assemblies *Sangat Sabha*.[11] He appears to have borrowed the name from the Sikhs. Those members of the Samaj who went to Punjab from time to time never missed the opportunity to pay a visit to the Harimandir of Amritsar. These exchanges culminated in the writing of Guru Nanak's biographies, which were said to be of an excellent quality.

The first notable piece of writing in Bengali on the Sikhs was by Akshaykumar Datta (1820-86),[12] editor of *Tattwabodhini Patrika*. He was a well known rationalist. His long essay titled 'Nanakpanthi' was serialized in *Tattwabodhini Patrika*. The author was acquainted with Punjabi sources and the writings of British authorities like Forster, Malcolm, Wilson and Cunningham. His essay does not portray Guru Nanak as one having miraculous powers. Instead, he appears as an honest religious preacher and a Sikh Guru, stripped of *Janamsakhi* trappings. He was born in Samvat 1526, son of Kalu Bedi and was in his early years engaged in trade. His subsequent life was devoted to religious reflections and instructions. That took him to different places in India on *udasi*. He believed that there was but one formless, immortal God and he was not opposed to family life. Datta put almost every material in the *Janamsakhis* to the test of reason while writing on the Sikh Guru's life. More than once, he warned against the 'anecdotes', which had grown around Guru Nanak. According to him, disciples concocted these 'tales' to enhance the Guru's 'greatness'. So he did not hesitate to exclude

[10] Satishchandra Chakrabarty (ed.), *Brahmasangeet*, Calcutta 1931, pp. 1053-7. It may also be mentioned that Guru Nanak's *sabad*, *Gagan mai thal* in *rag Dhanasari* was sung at the Brahmo Samaj in *rag Jayajayanti*. Rabindranath translated the *sabad* into Bengali.

[11] Sibnath Sastri, *History of the Brahmo Samaj*, Calcutta reprint, 1974, p. 81; Jogananda Das, 'The Brahmo Samaj', in Jagannath Chakrabarty (ed.), *Studies in Bengal Renaissance*, Calcutta 1977, pp. 488-9.

[12] For his biography, see Mahendranath Roy, *Babu Akshaykumar Dattar Jiban-Brittanta*, Calcutta 1292 BS; David Kopf, *The Brahmo Samaj and the Shaping of Modern Mind*, Princeton 1979, pp. 49-54. Datta's writings on the history of the Sikhs were published from Chaitra 1772 Saka to Phalgun 1773 Saka in *Tattwabodhini Patrika*.

them from his writing. His system of logic was different from that of the faithfuls and at times it may have appeared shocking to many of them. But these are useful pointers in modern Sikh studies in Indian languages.

Akshaykumar Datta's essay was printed the year after the British annexation of Punjab. A little earlier the *Journal of the Royal Asiatic Society* had carried Wilson's essay.[13] On certain issues there are remarkable resemblances between the two. It is surprising that a rationalist like Datta accepted Wilson's controversial subdivisions of the Sikhs without scepticism, while setting his face against the legends in the medieval *Janamsakhi* literature. One feels that these materials should have been handled with greater discernment. Had he applied his critical mind to Wilson's article, he could have avoided the errors and omissions about Sikh sects in his own writing.

Another important biographer of Guru Nanak was Bhai Mahendranath Bose (1838-1915).[14] He was close to the nineteenth century Brahmo reformer Keshabchandra Sen (1832-84). At Sen's instance, he went to Punjab as a preacher. There he learned Punjabi and after his return started writing the biography of Guru Nanak. A significant portion of the work was first published in the Brahmo organ *Dharmatattwa* (1794-6 Saka). Later he expanded his writing and published it in two volumes (1885 and 1893). Mahendranath's *Nanak Prakash* is the longest biography of Guru Nanak in Bengali and the best among those based on the *Janamsakhis*. He presented the founder of Sikhism in the light of *Bala Janamsakhi*. So there is extensive information about his family tree both on the paternal and maternal sides.

The first part deals with the phase before Guru Nanak set out on his travels. This was the time when he was staying mainly at Talvandi, Sultanpur and Kartarpur and he is not seen in the variety

[13] H.H. Wilson's article was brought out in 1848. See also his *Essays and Lectures on the Religious Sects of the Hindus*, London 1868. Wilson was invited to give a talk on civil and religious institutions of the Sikhs at the Royal Asiatic Society before the beginning of the Second Sikh War. There he briefly spoke about the differences between Hindus and Sikhs. Grewal recently referred to Wilson's talk on Sikhism in his *Guru Nanak in Western Scholarship*, Shimla 1992, pp. 8-10.

[14] For his biographical sketch, see Saurindrakumar Ghosh, *Sahitya Sevak Manjusha*, vol. II, Calcutta 1985, p. 445.

of costumes of the *udasi* days. But in the next phase, Guru Nanak is seen busy communicating with the world outside Punjab. The writer did not attach equal importance to the four *udasis*, which the Sikh faithfuls talk about. His discussions of these fall into two halves. He has made a detailed comparative study of the travels in Kashmir, Kabul, Sind, Singhal (Sri Lanka), the hilly region of Himachal, Kamrup and Mecca. Visits to Kurukshetra, Gaya, Banaras, Ayodhya, Mathura, Vrindavan, etc., receive a short notice. But the writer claims that the Guru won the hearts of people wherever he went. The epilogue of the book also takes a look at the great changes, which overtook the Sikh Panth in the post-Guru Nanak period.

An important feature of Mahendranath's work is that he relied too much on *Janamsakhi* literature. He was not unaware of its shortcomings, though Mahendranath claimed that he 'used materials avoiding miracles and everything that was unsuitable for the modern age' and proceeded on the basis of credible events and the spiritual as well as moral aspects of the Guru's work. But unlike his predecessor Datta, he did not reject all supernatural legends as 'imaginary' and 'unbelievable'. Those 'stories', which had 'a kernel of spiritual truth' in them, were retained as he tried to evaluate them to some extent. He deserves praise for combining 'religious tolerance' with 'historical caution' in using materials collected from *Janamsakhi* sources.

The Brahmo biographer was generally sympathetic to *Janamsakhi* literature, but he was not unacquainted with the contemporary Sikh studies in Europe. He started writing Guru Nanak's biography basing it on *Bala Janamsakhi* at a time when modern analysis of *Janamsakhi* literature had begun in the West. So far Sikhs had regarded the *Janamsakhis* as a part of their sacred text and offered it veneration and worship. But the German linguist, Trumpp, questioned its historical value, standard of scholarship, date of writing and the like and raised some pressing but bitter queries (1877). This made the leaders of the contemporary Singh Sabha movement angry and critical of him. Perhaps Mahendranath came to know about it while on his evangelical mission in Punjab and in his preface to *Nanak Prakash* he also made no secret of his dissatisfaction about Trumpp's uncharitable comments. This put Mahendranath in the camp of Trumpp-bashers.

But his critical vein can hardly be equated with the hostile stance against British rule which was to dominate Sikh studies from the early years of the twentieth century. Like many contemporary

Brahmos, Bose believed in the blessings of British rule and attainment of progress through existing political institutions. This in no way prevented him from criticizing Trumpp on his harsh and unsympathetic comments on the mission of Guru Nanak. His attempt to evaluate Trumpp, however, indicates a change in the Bengali outlook on the contemporary Sikh studies in Europe. The rationalist, Datta, had posited some criticial queries about the writings of Cunningham but his criticism was in a low key.[15] Maybe the protestant point of view of the Singh Sabha leadership of Punjab influenced the strident tone of the Brahmo biographer's critique.

Why was Mahendranath overly sympathetic to *Bala Janamsakhi*? That calls for critical analysis. When the biographer went to Punjab (1871), he saw 'a variety of *Janamsakhis* there'. Later Trumpp (1877) in his translation recognized the authenticity of the *Colebrooke Janamsakhi* as his material for the study of Guru Nanak's life.[16] What makes one wonder is why in spite of that, Mahendranath used *Bala Janamsakhi* as his source though in comparison, it is considered 'puerile' and 'full of inconsistencies'. It seems that in criticizing Trumpp's translation, Sikh scholars of the late nineteenth century refused to credit the German linguist with an attempt to open the door to a modern scientific treatment of a piece of old religious literature. As a result, few in Punjab then recognized the superiority of the *Puratan Janamsakhi.* And the Singh Sabha leaders generally put their trust in the *Bala* version.

There were other reasons for the great popularity of the *Bala* version. The main reason was the current belief and the lack of inclination to dissect and analyse the text. According to the common people and even many scholars of the time, the incidents relating to Guru Nanak which are in the *Bala Janamsakhi* were actually narrated by Bhai Bala in the presence of Guru Angad. This belief led to the popularity of the *Bala Janamsakhi.* Besides, its language and presentation are captivating.[17] Contemporary Sikh scholars regarded it

[15] Akshaykumar Datta, 'Nanakpanthi', *Tattwabodhini Patrika*, Chaitra 1772 Saka, p. 177.

[16] Ernest Trumpp, *The Adi Granth,* New Delhi reprint, 1989, pp. ii-v. For a general discussion of the subject, see S.S. Sagar, 'A Study of Janamsakhi Scholarship', *Journal of Sikh Studies*, August 1987, pp. 47-8. Many Sikh historians and essayists have written about Ernest Trumpp. For a general discusion, see Fauja Singh (ed.), *Historians and Historiography of the Sikhs,* New Delhi 1978. There are two interesting discussions on Trumpp in the volume by N.G. Barrier and A.C. Aurora.

[17] Gurpreet Kaur, 'An Attempt to Account for the Popularity of Bhai Bala Janamsakhi', Guru Nanak Dev University unpublished M.Phil. thesis, 1982, pp. 63-84.

as the only trustworthy source for the study of Guru Nanak's life. Mahendranath learned Punjabi from some Sikh scholars and perhaps it was they who led him to the world of Bhai Bala. Taking the cue from them Mahendranath then proceeded to write the Guru's biography in an unquestioning spirit.

Modern research has brought about considerable change in the attitude of historians to the *Bala Janamsakhi*. Many now look askance at it.[18] But when Mahendranath wrote, only Trumpp had raised some serious doubts about its textual content, authorship and date of composition. That was a hundred years ago, when a Sikh resurgence under the Singh Sabha movement was reconstructing their old tradition and faith. It largely explains their enthusiasm in favour of the popular *Bala Janamsakhi*.

Nanak Prakash by Mahendranath based on the *Bala Janamsakhi*, however, introduced Bengali readers to the wider arena of Punjabi literature of the medieval days. Earlier Datta had briefly surveyed the *Adi Granth* (1849). In this direction Mahendranath's endeavour was a step forward. Meanwhile, broadening of the provincial administrative machinery following the British annexation of Punjab had encouraged many Bengalis to migrate there. The flow later increased for various reasons. Sikh studies by Mahendranath strengthened these ties. We will now talk of a few others who also reviewed *Janamsakhi* sources to reconstruct the life story of Guru Nanak.

Following in the footsteps of Mahendranath, Debendranath's grandson, Ritendranath Tagore (1870-1936), also came to study the life of Guru Nanak. As editor of *Tattwabodhini Patrika* and secretary of the Adi Brahmo Samaj, he generally had a knowledge of Sikh studies. *Punya* was an important literary publication of the Tagore family. For almost five years (1307-12 BS) he published scattered writings in it on Guru Nanak's life. Ritendranath wrote seven essays of varying length and a sonnet on Guru Nanak.[19] In his poem, he referred to

[18] McLeod has done the most trenchant criticism of *Bala Janamsakhi* in recent times. For his view, see *Guru Nanak and the Sikh Religion*, pp. 22-3.

[19] Ritendranath Tagore, 'Saisabe Guru Nanak', *Punya*, Ashwin-Kartik 1307 BS, pp. 90-6; 'Jagannath Tirthe Guru Nanak o Jagannather Arati', Phalgun 1307 BS, pp. 271-8; 'Guru Nanak o Makkeswar Siva', Kartik 1310 BS, pp. 82-7; Agrahayan-Paush 1310 BS, pp. 169-78; Phalgun 1310 BS, pp. 278-86; Chaitra 1310 BS, pp. 363-8; Baisakh-Jyaistha 1311 BS, pp. 472-5; 'Guru Nanak Abatar', Sraban 1311 BS, pp. 492-5; 'Guru Nanak', Bhadra-Ashwin 1311 BS, p. 197; 'Guru Nanaker

Guru Nanak as a 'very great man'. The essays also reflect the same kind of veneration. Four of them were about the Guru's childhood and boyhood. Two are based on his *udasis*. One represents him as an illustrious Indian *avatar*. His style is indicative of his deferential attitude. Some of the episodes in the *Janamsakhis* appear in his writing completely unaltered. Occasionally it is just a rendering of Punjabi into Bengali. There is no attempt to check their veracity. His adoration of his subject puts the Guru above all doubt, debate and discussion.

The attitude of veneration apparently brought Ritendranath close to Mahendranath but there were differences in methodology. Mahendranath based his work on *Bala Janamsakhi* and at times he weighed his material. As a result, one notices an occasional clash between the writer's adherence to logic and received Sikh ideas. Ritendranath, however, made no effort to evaluate the material he got from the *Janamsakhi* sources in the light of reason. He does not project the Guru Nanak of history. The Sikh Guru is wrapped in the mysticism of religious faith. Secondly, Mahendranath does not refer to the Hindu pantheon, but Ritendranath makes Guru Nanak look like a defender and saviour of Hinduism in medieval times. Here an unbelievable similarity with the Sanatani Hindu outlook is discernible. The reason is that the two writers represent the two different schools of Brahmo thought.[20] Ritendranath did not attempt to conceal his bias in favour of the Hindu pantheon. He also made no serious effort to review the Sikh sources critically. On the other hand, Mahendranath never used the language and divine messages of the *Janamsakhi* verbatim. Why did Ritendranath rely so heavily on the *Janamsakhi* sources? As a contemporary, he must have read Mahendranath's work and perhaps tried to surpass him. He

---

Vyabasaik Buddhi', Kartik 1311 BS, pp. 216-20; 'Guru Nanak o Vaidya Haridas', Magh 1311 BS, pp. 327-30; 'Guru Nanaker Upanayan', Paush 1312 BS, pp. 441-6. Some of the issues of the *Punya* (1311-12 BS) are preserved in the Rabindra Bharati University Museum and Bangiya Sahitya Parisad, Calcutta. These are so torn that the months of publication and the issue numbers cannot be correctly traced.

[20] It may be partly due to their allegiance to two different groups within the Brahmo Samaj. Bhai Mahendranath Bose belonged to the Bharatbarshiya Brahmo Samaj headed by Keshabchandra Sen while Ritendranath, a grandson of Debendranath Tagore, was in the Adi Brahmo Samaj. There was the second split or schism in the Bramho Samaj in 1878 as a result of which the Sadharan Brahmo Samaj came into formal existence. Krishnakumar Mitra, another Brahmo biographer, came from the group.

attempted to look at the Sikh Guru from a different angle so that he was not called an imitator. Mahendranath sought to project the Guru on a broader plane in two volumes while Ritendranath in his scattered pieces presented fragmentary pictures. By sticking to the original style of the *Janamsakhis* he added a new piquancy to his style.

The last notable Brahmo biographer of Guru Nanak was Krishnakumar Mitra (1852-1936) of the Sadharan Brahmo Samaj. Like Mahendranath, he went to Punjab in the second half of the nineteenth century. But unlike his predecessor, he was a sharp critic of British rule and the main reason of his visit was political.[21] In some of his speeches to the Brahmo Samaj, Mitra spoke of his painful experiences in the environs of the Golden Temple at Amritsar.[22] The predominance of Hindu icons and rituals there hurt him. He was influenced by the Brahmo system of values and he naturally expected the prevalence of monotheistic beliefs and anti-idolatry practices in the *parikarma* there. With this disappointment he embarked on writing Guru Nanak's biography from a Brahmo point of view. He, however, soon got embroiled in the anti-Partition agitation (1905-11) and was incarcerated for his extremist views. He therefore could not complete the biography.[23] But Sikh studies continued unabated in his family circle and so his sense of compulsion remained.[24] He was then acquainted with the writings of Trumpp and Macauliffe. At the same time he also read *Bala Janamsakhi* with the help of a Sikh interpreter and got on with his work with speed. In spite of police interference, arrest, imprisonment, loss of manuscript and so on, he could complete his work.

[21] Krishnakumar Mitra, *Atmacharit,* Calcutta reprint, 1381 BS, p. 105.

[22] *Tattwakaumudi*, 16 Ashar 1800 Saka, p. 28 and 3 Kartik 1800 Saka, pp. 93-4.

[23] For a further discussion of the point, see the author's 'Satabdir Sikh Sandhan (Guru Parba)', *Rabindra Bharati Patrika*, Chaitra 1401 BS to Jyaistha 1402 BS, pp. 52-3.

[24] There was a continuous trend of Sikh studies in Krishnakumar Mitra's family. His daughter, Kumudini Bose (Mitra), wrote a collection of popular biographies entitled *Sikher Balidan,* Calcutta 1905. It discussed the sacrifices of Sikh Gurus and Sikh martyrs. Five editions of the book were sold out within twenty years of its publication. Besides, it was translated into more than one Indian language. Krishnakumar Mitra decidedly had a role to play in inspiring his daughter Kumudini to write it. For further information on the writer, see Basanti Chakrabarty, *Kumudini Bose Amader Ratandidi,* Calcutta 1351 BS, p. 25. Infra, pp. 184-6.

'Nanak-Charit' by Krishnakumar is largely based on the *Bala Janamsakhi* but his individuality shows in different ways. Like some other writers, while describing the childhood and boyhood of Nanak, he mentioned his initiation in studies, the presence of the physician, *khara sauda*, and appearance of the black serpent, and other miraculous incidents. His marriage, his services at a grocer's shop, his encounter with God, religious preaching and some of his *udasis* also come in. In presenting these familiar episodes, he did not confine himself to the spirit of the *Janamsakhi*. When necessary, he stepped out of its confines and described Guru Nanak's agonies, the conflict between his hopes and frustration, his yearning for God while bound by family ties with the sympathy of a common man. Sometimes, the world of the supernatural is effaced and Guru Nanak, a man of flesh and blood, appears before us.[25] In the process, he often seems far removed from the limits of Punjab and sometimes even practising the local customs and ways of Bengal.[26]

The people around the Guru move about like ordinary folk in Krishnakumar's writing. But that was in their day-to-day life. Each one had a distinctive character. While the Guru was a saintly person, Mitra juxtaposes his supernatural experience with the smallness and greatness of the common people around him.[27] It seems this has been done to prevent the Guru from being interpreted merely in the light of his extra-terrestrial activities. That has added to the appeal

[25] Mitra dealt with the mental oscillations of Guru Nanak at the time of his sacred thread ceremony, his bawls over his mother's mental agony, his anguish at the rudeness of his wife, his suffering caused by his yearning for God while being confined within the mundane world, even his going into business to please his father, etc. No other Brahmo biographer attached so much importance to the psychosomatic experiences of the Sikh Guru while he lived like a common man in Talvandi village.

[26] In *Nanak Prakash* we come across the process of initiation of children in studies in the *manjha* area of Punjab. Mahendranath thus wrote, 'According to the custom of the land, Kalu handed to his son a vessel filled with sugar and went to the teacher with five rupees. . . . Nanak was put in the teacher's care'. *Nanak Prakash*, vol. I, p. 4. On the other hand, Krishnakumar wrote, 'On an auspicious day Kalu went to the school with his son. Nanak made an offering of rice, betel-nut and two paise to the *Gurumahashay*'. 'Nanak-Charit', *Suprabhat*, Sraban 1316 BS, p. 44. In Bengal rice and betel-nut are considered auspicious things. It is likely that Krishnakumar was influenced by his local experience.

[27] In this context, the writer has spoken of the anger and contempt of Kalu as a father at the son's suffering. The biography also refers to Mardana's self-sacrifice and suffering of hardship for the Guru. At the same time Mardana's greed and moral lapses have been mentioned. Man cannot be all black and white, he represents complex and contradictory qualities—this is perhaps the writer's message.

of Krishnakumar's writing. Unlike some modern Western critics, he has not rejected his miracles. Not in toto. Instead, he looked for historical validity lurking in some of them. But he did not succeed in every instance.

In this effort, Krishnakumar was a follower of Mahendranath.[28] Unlike Datta he did not reject the beliefs of the Sikh faithfuls and look for a Nanak of history devoid of all the attributes of the *Janamsakhi*. Mitra did not restrict his Sikh Guru to a bare one-sided portrayal divorced from religion. On the other hand, he sought to underline the significance of the *Janamsakhi* sources in Sikh studies, straying from Mahendranath's path. But with all his religious orientation, he did not wish away history. To stress the time-factor, he sometimes mentioned historical dates and years and spoke of the occupant of the throne in Delhi. At the same time he portrayed the life and times of the *hoi polloi*. It was his intention to emphasize that the common man had his incompleteness, both good and bad sides and so expressed himself in a variety of ways. He began in the company of Mahendranath but sometimes excelled him. Perhaps there lies the importance of his biography of Guru Nanak.

II

The biographers discussed so far were not unacquainted with *Janamsakhi* literature. Here we will take up writers who did not base their work on such source materials. Generally speaking, they were not all directly associated with Brahmoism and their contributions appeared in different periodicals in the late nineteenth and early twentieth centuries. These are not long like the biographies mentioned earlier and are silent on many important events connected with the life of Guru Nanak. Some of the authors were not well known in literary circles. A few of them had also nothing positive to

[28] According to the *Janamsakhi* tradition, Guru Nanak once took Mardana to matriarchal Karudesh (Kamrup), an area associated with many stories about sleight-of-hand and black magic. It is rumoured that if an outsider goes there, the local beauties cast their spell over him and turn him into a sheep. Mardana also apparently was turned into a sheep. When Guru Nanak came to know about it, he took the necessary steps and Mardana became a man again. Mahendranath and Krishnakumar both narrated the episode in the light of their logic and understanding. See *Nanak Prakash*, vol. II, p. 38 and 'Nanak-Charit', *Suprabhat*, Phalgun 1316 BS, p. 87. Both writers say that Mardana did not actually turn into a sheep. One can note how close they come to each other.

say about their quest and the materials they used. So it is hard to tell what prompted them to take up Sikh studies and with what objectives.

Chronologically, the first text to deal with Nanak is an anonymous essay titled 'Nanak' that came out in the prestigious literary monthly *Bangadarshan* in Ashar 1285 BS. It was probably written by Rajanikanta Gupta (1849-1900).[29] In spite of his literary fame, why he wrote anonymously remains a mystery. To him the Sikh Guru was a monotheist and a man of saintly character. Nanak was also a shadow of Kabir in his religious system. As for the reconstruction of other episodes of the Guru's life, the author took the stubborn critical line of Datta. He confined his life-study only to incidents of whose veracity he was in no doubt.

Rajanikanta's writings constitute an interesting step in the evolution of Sikh studies. Generally speaking, he is characterized as a writer imbued with the Hindu nationalist pride and sense of history advocated by Bankimchandra.[30] That mindset is absent in the essay under discussion. Rajanikanta projects the Sikh Guru as one of the many social reformers of medieval India. Here he was, however, missing many of the key-markers of Hindu communal self-identification. But the attempt to transcend miracles, to look for the Nanak of history linked him to the contemporary critical historical tradition. Based on secondary sources in currency, the essay 'Nanak' may cause serious reaction in Sikh believers. It added a touch of modernity to Bengali Sikh studies of the period. Subsequently, his

[29] The article was subsequently incorporated in a collection of eassys titled *Prabandhakusum* (1879) without any significant change in language and content. Later the spirit of *Hindutva* was injected while incorporating the same essay in the book *Sikh* (1883). Rajanikanta Gupta published both books under his own name. The inference about the authorship of 'Nanak' of *Bangadarshan* (Ashar 1285 BS) can be drawn from a comparative study of the style and content of all these three works. About the life and literary pursuits of Rajanikanta Gupta, see Brajendranath Banerjee, 'Rajanikanta Gupta', *Sahitya-Sadhak Charitmala*, vol. VI, No.71, Calcutta 1355 BS, pp. 17-31; Nirmal Sinha, *Freedom Movement in Bengal, 1813-1904, Who's Who,* Calcutta 1968, pp. 384-8.

[30] Shyamali Sur, 'Bangalir Itihastattwer Bikash, 1870-1912', Jadavpur University unpublished Ph.D. thesis, 1980, pp. 132-5. See also T.W. Clark, 'Bengali Prose Fiction up to Bankimchandra', in T.W. Clark (ed.), *The Novel in India,* London 1970, pp. 64, 69; Rajat Kanta Ray, *Social Conflict and Political Unrest in Bengal, 1875-1927,* Delhi 1984, p. 120.

mind was coloured by the Sanatani Hindu attitude. He then revised the earlier essay and added a definite Hindu overtone and included it in the book *Sikh* in 1883. In this sense, 'Nanak' written in 1878 remains distinct from his other essays on Sikh history.

Mahendranath Roy (1854-1912) wrote the second article. *Aryadarshan*, a respected literary monthly published it in one of its issues (Chaitra 1287 BS).[31] It was 'to be continued' in the next but for some reason the sequel was never published. Since the complete piece is not available, a full discussion is not possible.

At the outset, the writer expressed his deep dissatisfaction at the fact that the life story of Guru Nanak was not known to the people of the country. But it does not appear that he himself purveyed the history of the Guru's life and times in its entirety and with critical methodology. Mahendranath considered the boyhood experiences of Guru Nanak to be 'illogical and hard to understand'. He, however, accepted the account of his entry into a forest in search of God and narrated the incident at the end of his essay in the belief that it was a historical fact. Punjabi source materials are more or less silent on the subject. Since Mahendranath worked rather perfunctorily with second-hand materials, there are quite a few errors about years and dates.[32] The publication of discussions on Sikh-related subjects in *Bangadarshan* perhaps encouraged the panel of writers of *Aryadarshan* to present the piece.[33] But as young Mahendranath did not fulfil the expectations of the editorial board, the second part of the writing was not published. The various shortcomings notwithstanding, he was the first to familiarize the Bengali readership with the different gurdwaras of Nanakana Sahib (Talvandi), which were redolent with the memory of Guru Nanak's birth and nonage. Bhai Mahendranath and Krishnakumar had first-hand knowledge of

[31] Mahendranath Roy, 'Guru Nanaker Jiban-Charit', *Aryadarshan*, Chaitra 1287 BS, pp. 555-63. Mahendranath also wrote the biography of Akshaykumar Datta. He was associated with the editing of several literary monthlies, which included *Aryadarshan* and *Janmabhumi*.

[32] At least five historical errors occur in a nine-page article. Here is one of them: 'Daulat Khan Lodi was a close relative of Babar, emperor of Delhi. . . . Babar was responsible for paying his salary.' It seems Mahendranath had not even reviewed his sources with adequate seriousness.

[33] Four articles on Sikhism and Punjab appeared in *Bangadarshan* between Ashwin 1284 BS and Magh 1285 BS.

Punjab and yet they were silent on the point. Mahendranath Roy's achievement in this field is undeniable.

The third piece was called 'Kajer Lok Ke' and the author was Rabindranath (1861-1941) himself.[34] Published in the children's magazine *Balak* (Baisakh 1292 BS), its form and content are both suited for children. It narrates some of the most familiar events of Guru Nanak's life and tries to convey an underlying message. The Guru is not depicted merely as an honest and religious person. Rabindranath shows how the Sikh Guru's sweet and yet magnanimous disposition attracted the common man. The sequence of events reveals the religiousness of Guru Nanak in contrast with the worldliness of his father Kalu Bedi. The clash between father and son is understandable. But Rabindranath's Kalu Bedi is not as ruthless and heartless as he is often depicted in Punjabi sources. Tagore, however, dismissed the tale of the appearance of a black serpent to shelter the Sikh Guru's head with its hood.

This is the first of the essays and poems that Rabindranath wrote about the Sikh Gurus. Familiarity with some Sikh-related articles in Brahmo periodicals may have prompted it. He speaks of the Sikh Guru's childhood days, his service at Sultanpur, and his search for God and his *udasis*, all in a very short span. The simplicity of the language makes the honest lifestyle of Guru Nanak palatable to children. That explains why the central episode of the article is *khara sauda*. Kalu Bedi gave his son some money to go into his paternal business. The Guru did not invest the money in commercial transactions but used it to feed hungry holy men. People like Kalu Bedi only think of pecuniary gain and so earn little respect from society at large. On the other hand, the Guru built the foundation of a 'great concept and spiritual power' as well as of a 'great nation' through his service to humanity. Tagore writes: 'The money that Kalu earned was spent to feed him. Nanak earned religious wealth which people have thriven on for four hundred years. Who did more work?' Rabindranath used a language that could convey the main content of Sikhism to children in a simple manner. The weight of detail or

[34] *Rabindra Rachanabali*, vol. XV, Calcutta 1994, pp. 503-5. He then said nothing about his source materials. But his subsequent writings suggest that he had read Cunningham and M'Gregor. Rabindranath's link with Sikhism went far back. Other issues involved in Rabindranath's Sikh studies have been taken up later in the chapter.

unnecessary rhetoric did not hamper the direct communication. He realized that Guru Nanak's disapproval of idolatry and monotheism stirred the elders of the Brahmo Samaj but that idealism would not touch children's hearts. They would respond to a more simple and straight account in informal language.[35] Tagore was the pioneer in introducing Bengali children to Sikh culture. He opened a new avenue, which remains loaded with traffic in ideas even today.

The fourth piece of writing in this category appeared nearly 16 years later, at the beginning of the twentieth century in *Nabyabharat*, a popular periodical like *Aryadarshan*. The essayist, Rajendralal Acharya, was a sub-deputy magistrate in the judicial department. While studying the life of the Sikh Guru, he had access to substantial materials on Sikh history as evident from the footnotes to his writings. In the footsteps of the British administrator-historian Elphinstone, he portrayed Guru Nanak as a Hindu monotheist, but he was not unfamiliar with his knowledge of Islamic philosophy and religion.[36] In fact, the writer expressed the view that it was the Sikh

[35] At that time many writers wanted to create an awareness in the minds of young people about the significance of a simple, unostentatious life which spurned luxury. Rabindranath also laid stress on ascetic ideals towards the end of the article. But in his lifestyle, Guru Nanak never showed an unworldly attitude. According to McLeod, this bias in favour of 'the ascetic values' is derived from *Janamsakhi* sources. See McLeod, *Guru Nanak and the Sikh Religion*, pp. 221-2. In a number of *Janamsakhi* episodes and paintings, the Sikh Guru has been described as a Hindu *sannyasi*. McLeod, *Early Sikh Tradition*, pp. iv, 81, 229. Also see S.S. Hans, *B-40 Janamsakhi: Guru Baba Nanak Paintings*, Amritsar 1987.

[36] Rajendralal Acharya, 'SikhGuru Nanak', *Nabyabharat*, Ashar 1308 BS, pp. 126-32. Subsequently, many other writers described Guru Nanak as a defender of Hinduism and God's incarnation on earth. It is not possible to cram the limited space with a discussion of all those biographies. A few names should suffice. (i) Akinchan, 'SriNanak-Charit', *Grihastha*, Ashar-Sraban 1318 BS, pp. 185-202. Here the Sikh Guru's horoscope has also been drawn up in accordance with Hindu astrology. (ii) Krishnabehari Datta, 'Guru Nanak', *Janmabhumi*, Agrahayan 1317 BS, pp. 324-6. It was reprinted without any change in *Anjali*, Jyaistha 1321 BS, pp. 34-7. The brief life sketch of the Sikh Guru contains nothing significant about his life and religious philosophy. It is also difficult to explain the reasons behind its reprint. (iii) Bipinbehari DasGupta, 'Guru Nanaksaheb', *Bangashri*, Kartik 1348 BS, pp. 657-63 and Agrahayan 1348 BS, pp. 822-8. The author has stretched his account on many minor-details of Guru Nanak's life. He has comparatively taken larger space to record the same. (iv) Rakhaldas Kavyananda, *Guru-Nanak*, Calcutta 1928. His discussion of Guru Nanak's concept of *bhakti* and the 'determination of differential' are very peculiar and intriguing. It is of course debatable to what extent

Guru's mission to bring about a synthesis between the two communities.

Like some of his predecessors, the Acharya dismissed most of the *Janamsakhi* accounts of the Sikh Guru during his boyhood as untrue. But he did not raise any questions about Guru Nanak's wearing the sacred thread and the *khara sauda*. Similarly, he discussed the many travels of the Guru. According to him, Guru Nanak went to Mecca through Persia. The author also briefly analysed the Guru's metaphysical thought. He said that the Guru did not give his disciples social or political advice. His instruction, in his view, was related to religion only. Needless to say, compared to the biographies by the Brahmo authors the work is of an average quality. It seems that the author wanted to produce an instant biography of Guru Nanak. So he quickly put together material from readily available sources and got trapped in factual errors. Besides, being close to the British administration, he might have had some difficulty in highlighting the protestant role of the Sikh Guru. His Guru Nanak therefore does not provide a glimpse of the pioneering social reformer.

The growing pan-Indian thinking of the twentieth century cast a noticeable influence on the study of Guru Nanak's life. These books discussed the lives of saints in different periods of Indian history in simple language. Guru Nanak was among the saints. The purpose of discussing these biographical accounts was to acquaint readers with an all-India history and religious vision. Some of these writers tended

---

the ideas of Kavyananda are in conformity with the approved Sikh religious belief. What he has presented as Guru Nanak's concept of *bhakti* is mostly sprung from the outlook of Gaudiya Vaishnavism. In his quest for solutions to complicated philosophical problems, the author follows curent belief in his biographical narrative. The sequence of events in the biographical sketch does not generally fit in with the framework based on the *Janamsakhi* tradition. In the last two pages of the book, the author speaks of Guru Nanak's visit to the temple of Jagannath. But it has been claimed that he had gone to Mecca earlier. Similarly, he has portrayed Guru Nanak as a rabid advocate of the caste system. It is possible to get confirmation from Kavyananda's description of Guru Nanak's reaction to the *tarpan* of the Brahmins. The stridency with which other Bengali writers, Hindu or Brahmo, proclaimed Guru Nanak's bitter reaction to the *tarpan* is strangely missing here. What is more, there are many details in the book, which are not confirmed by other sources. Here they are: Guru Nanak was born in 1496 (p. 55) and the Sikh Guru himself dug the tank at Amritsar (p. 147). There are also references to legends, which make one feel like characterizing Kavyananda as a Sanatani Hindu biographer. Such traditionalists have again been discussed later.

to define Indianness in terms of Hinduism. Others left the issue alone. Here we can mention two writers in connection with the probe into Guru Nanak's life.

Chronologically the first mention should go to *Bharater Sadhak* by Saratkumar Roy (1878-1935), a teacher at the Brahmacharyashram at Santiniketan during Rabindranath's lifetime. He put Guru Nanak on the same pedestal as Ramanand, Kabir, Ravidas, Rammohun and others. The author highlighted Guru Nanak's fight against superstition and idolatry in Hindu society and the bigotry and intolerance among the Muslims. A few years later was published *Bhaktacharitmala* by Sashibhushan Bose. Here Nanak appears as a devout saint, spawned by the message of *bhakti* of the medieval days. He is among those devoted saints of India graced by God, one of those who had dedicated themselves to the alleviation of the suffering of common men and promoted peace and toleration. The Sikh Guru is seen amid many supernatural situations and the writer pleases faithful readers by making Guru Nanak accept established manners and customs. In sharp contrast, Saratkumar takes the path of analysis and evaluation and presents a rebel Guru Nanak. The two viewpoints are utterly dissimilar.[37]

III

In the twentieth century poetry was chosen as the medium in some cases in the quest for Guru Nanak's life. In this section we may review three poems and books of poems where Guru Nanak has been viewed from different angles. We will follow the chronology of publication. The first of them was published in the well known literary monthly, *Bharatbarsha* in 1320 BS and the other two came out in book form in 1323 BS and 1328 BS.

The first one was modelled on the narrative poems of Rabindranath's *Katha o Kahini*.[38] There is a facade of historical past but it is

[37] Saratkumar Roy, 'Nanak', *Bharater Sadhak,* Calcutta 1914, pp. 34-47; Sashibhushan Bose, 'Nanak', *Bhaktacharitmala,* Calcutta 1918, pp. 310-27. Supra, pp. 87-8.

[38] Tagore's *Katha o Kahini* is a collection of poems dealing with the heroic deeds of the Rajputs and Marathas of the medieval days. It also includes a few poems drawn from the ancient history of the Buddhists, Jains and other religious orders. The metre and the poetic ambience created in the poem of Amodini Ghosh encourage me to view it in the category. Rabindranath has recalled with respect the principle of begging for a noble cause in *Katha o Kahini*. In the poem also Guru Nanak was found begging in the streets of an unknown city. All this was done for a great ideal.

just not easy to find in it the Guru Nanak of history. The poem is captioned 'Nanak' and was written by a lesser known poetess—Amodini Ghosh. Here the Guru is shown submitting to the oppression of royal power without protest. She has also related an incident about how his kindness and tolerance brought about a change in the life of a poor prostitute. But neither historical evidence nor the *Janamsakhi* sources refer to the episode. There is no mention in history of any king who evicted Guru Nanak from his homestead. Our Punjabi literary sources give us an account of his conversations with some women of evil repute in Singhal. But the Guru is not shown there going around with them for alms. Again the principle of begging is bitterly denounced in Sikhism.The poem also does not state the name of the king or where he ruled. The period is not mentioned either. Yet, the picture of the oppressed Guru Nanak fits in with the description of sufferings of *nirguna* saints who had experienced many 'unfair tests' at the hands of the 'arrogant representatives of "official" religious and political authority'. [39]

Amodini Ghosh presented a slight and fragmentary picture of the founder of Sikhism. A lawyer of Midnapore, Kshitishchandra Chakrabarty wrote a book of poems about the Guru's life and mission.[40] It runs over a hundred pages and is divided into thirteen chapters. As his source, he cites only Annie Besant's *Children of the Motherland* but one gets the impression that he had also read articles on the history of the Sikhs published in Bengali journals. He speaks of the Guru's birth, education at school, the feeling of his pulse by the physician, wearing of the sacred thread, marriage, and communion with God, spreading religion at home and abroad. The style does not achieve the excellence of Tagore's poems set in Sikh history but he showed a new direction in knowledge on Sikh studies.

It is necessary to mention some of the distinctive features of Guru Nanak as delineated by Chakrabarty. The greedy Kalu Bedi of the *Janamsakhis* is seen here too, but more stress is laid on the man's sufferings on broader worldly issues. Secondly, the agony of Nanak's

---

While reading about the prostitute in the poem, one is reminded of the courtesan in Tagore's poem 'Apamanbar' in *Katha o Kahini.*

[39] For the poem, see Amodini Ghosh, 'Nanak', *Bharatbarsha*, Ashwin 1320 BS, pp. 822-3. For similarity with the lives of other *nirguni* saints, see David N. Lorenzen, 'The Lives of *Nirguni* Saints', p. 159.

[40] Kshitishchandra Chakrabarty, *Nanak,* Calcutta 1323 BS.

mother Tripta and wife Sulakhana at the time of the Guru's renunciation of his family ties.reminds one of the same kind of anguish which Chaitanya's mother and wife felt when he took *sannyas*. Thirdly, no other Bengali writer has described the habitations, rivers, trees, birds and seasonal changes during Guru Nanak's period of *udasis*. Poet Kshitishchandra relates a long *udasi* that goes against the notions of Sikh faithfuls. Chakrabarty strayed from the course charted by the *Janamsakhi* sources so popular with the Sikhs and chose a new track often covered by Bengali Vaishnavas leading to faraway places or pilgrimages like Puri, Mathura and Vrindavan. He recreated the life of Guru Nanak on an edifice built with his regional experience, religious faith, education, geographical concepts and human values, all of which came into his poetry, perhaps unwittingly. His Talvandi reminds one of the green village-scape of riverine Bengal and not the arid *manjha* region of Punjab. The personae are also more Bengali than Punjabi. The manner in which the author transferred his religious experiences to Punjab, Kshitishchandra's *Nanak* has a place of its own in Bengali Sikh studies.

A slim volume entitled *Sri Sri SatGuru Nanakjir Agamani Gita ba JagatGuru Parichay* (1328 BS) by Nityananda Goswami expresses the same regional Bengali sensibility.[41] Introducing himself as a disciple of a Bengali saint (Brahmananda Roy) of the Nanakpanthi order, Goswami begins his study with a salutation to him. Then he reviews the teachings of Guru Nanak but remains silent on the Khalsa tradition of Guru Gobind Singh. A non-military Nanakpanthi tradition in the garb of Gaudiya Vaishnavism of Bengal occupies the central point of Goswami's study. The writing follows the pattern of a *panchali* and the metre is *payar*. Through it, he seeks to convey the greatness of God in the *Kaliyuga*. Guru Nanak's name occurs frequently. And the Sikh sacred text is described as Vishnu's revelation. According to Goswami, Guru Nanak meditated with great rigour, fought with providential and royal forces and then

[41] In the booklet the *BaheGuru* (i.e. *Wahe Guru*) salutation has been uttered frequently. Even today temples of *BaheGuru* of varying sizes run by the Nanakpanthis are seen in and around Calcutta. In some of these temples, the veneration of the *Adi Granth* goes side by side with the celebration of a few Hindu festivals. It seems that they are in cross-currents of Hinduism and Sikhism.

spread God's beatitude in the world. The poet cannot come to terms with the failure of the Bengalis to appreciate its worth. So he appealed to them to take Guru Nanak's route to salvation by calling on God with love and devotion.

The distinctiveness of the booklet does not end here. It represents an interesting articulation of the Nanakpanthis in Bengali, and contains evidence that there was a give and take between Hinduism and Nanakpanthi-Sikhism in this part of the country. The colour of the dress, rituals, lifestyle, etc., came closer to the Vaishnavas of Bengal. One also comes to know that even here the Sikh Panth is not a monolith and undifferentiated community. There is considerable diversity in dress, salutation, ritual, philosophy and belief system.

IV

Some Hindu and all Brahmo writers stress that Guru Nanak was against idolatry, and believed in one, formless God. But none of them said that he was a follower of Islam. Some found in his preachings a blending of Hinduism and Islam as practised in the medieval days. In some twentieth century Bengali Muslim journals, certain writers claimed that the Sikh Guru defended Islam and had been converted to that religion. Three articles deserve mention in this connection. These were published in periodicals edited by Bengali Muslims.

The first article in chronological order is 'Baba Nanak', appearing in the monthly, *Al-Eslam* in Baisakh 1325 BS. This publication was the organ of the Bengali *ulemas* known as Ulema-i-Bangla. The author was a littérateur and educationist, Mozammel Haq (1860-1936). He was well versed in Islamic theology and Arabic philosophy. Haq was also acquainted with the writings of Trumpp and Pincott, the two Western scholars who had detected some apparent points of similarity between Sikhism as preached by Guru Nanak and Islam. Taking their statements as gospel truth, Haq in his article tried to prove Guru Nanak a Muslim *fakir*. He accepted Pincott's ideas as infallible and drew his conclusions from that assumption. He pointed out that the Sikh Guru did not criticize the Koran anywhere in the *Adi Granth*, did *namaz* five times a day and did not hesitate to call himself a servant of Allah. He also pointed out that Guru Nanak spent a long time with the Sufi *fakir*, Baba Sheikh Farid; and many of the latter's sayings found place in the *Adi Granth*. Guru Nanak travelled in the country and abroad wearing clothes, which was nothing but the *choga* worn by Sufi *darvishes*. And there the *kalmah* was written proclaiming the uniqueness of God.[42] It was to discover the true identity of this God that he went to Mecca.

Quite a few Punjabi scholars and researchers are in agreement with Mozammel Haq in that Guru Nanak's religious thought had an affinity to Islamic religious ideas. In his *History of the Panjab* (1891), Syad Muhammad Latif had said almost the same thing two decades before Haq did.[43] Looking at it from that angle, one does not find anything new in Haq's article. Incidentally, even Frederick Pincott did not do away with Guru Nanak's Hinduism the way Haq did. Modern Sikh studies acknowledge that in Punjab in the medieval days, there was a great deal of interaction, however unstated, between Nanak's religion and Islam. The communal politics of the early decades of the twentieth century might have encouraged Mozammel Haq to represent Guru Nanak as a follower of Islam. He lifted excerpts from Pincott's writing to give his theory shape and coherence.[44] Since he started off with a preconceived notion, he had

[42] McLeod has expressed grave doubts about the influence of Sufism on Guru Nanak's religious thought. According to him, there are some apparent resemblances in certain areas and if these are overemphasized, the individuality of the Sikh Guru will be obscured. His research shows that in certain matters Guru Nanak was opposed to Sufism (about previous existence and the fruits of endeavour). Cf. McLeod, *Guru Nanak and the Sikh Religion*, pp. 158-9. On the other hand, Niharranjan Ray has written about the interaction between Sikhism and Islam, particularly Sufism. In his view, Sikhism was 'kind of a response' 'to the challenge of the uncompromising monotheism of Islam'. Cf. *The Sikh Gurus and the Sikh Society*, pp. 51, 108.

[43] According to Latif (1889), 'an idea generally prevailed among the Mahomedans that Nanak was a true follower of the Prophet'. Cf. *History of the Panjab*, p. 248. See also Abdul Majid Khan, 'The Impact of Islam on Sikhism', in Niharranjan Ray (ed.), *Sikhism and Indian Society*, pp. 219-29. Similarly, in 1885 Mirza Ghulam Ahmad, the Ahmadiya chief, claimed that the Sikh Guru was a Muslim proselytizer. For the Ahmadiya point of view, see Spencer Lavan, *Ahmadiya Movement: Past and Present*, Amritsar 1976, pp. 27-8; Barrier, *The Sikhs and their Literature*, pp. 26-7. Recently Dominique-Sila Khan draws attention to a similar area of interaction. *Conversions and Shifting Identities: Ramdev Pir and Ismailis in Rajasthan*, New Delhi 1997, p. 236.

[44] Grewal drew our attention to it. According to him, Pincott emphasized that Guru Nanak never openly seceded from the pale of Hinduism. 'In fact in some of the *sakhis* it is explicitly stated' that he was 'a Hindu'. Cf. *Guru Nanak in Western Scholarship*, p. 28.

no difficulty in tailoring Pincott's material to his need for substantiation.

Apart from Mozammel Haq, there were two other writers who did not wish to accord Sikhism a separate identity from Islam. One of them is S. Omed Ali. In his essay 'Baba Nanak o Sikh Dharma', he congratulated Guru Nanak for communicating the message of Islam through Sikhism. Similarly, Ali Ahmed Ali Eslambadi highlighted the fact that the founder of the Sikh Panth did *namaz* and was respectful to the Islamic religious tradition.[45]

The essays by Bengali Muslims on Guru Nanak were few in number but their salient points deserve notice. First, one can trace a sense of 'aggressive chauvinism centred on Islam and the Muslim identity' in the writings of these authors. Second, these essays were all brought out in the first part of the twentieth century. In this sense the Bengali Muslims participated comparatively later than the Bengali Hindus in the literary endeavour dealing with Guru Nanak. It may be partly due to the educational backwardness, inadequate development of the 'print-culture' and other channels of mass communications in the Bengali Muslim society.[46] Third, unlike many Bengali Hindu writers, they were not interested in studying the primary Punjabi sources relating to Guru Nanak's life and mission. Their sole objective was to prove that the Sikh Guru was a servant of Islam. They picked out relevant materials to suit their arguments. As the objective was limited, the discussion lacked wide range. Besides, they made no reference to the link between Sikhism and the medieval *bhakti* tradition. The essays are largely parochial and fail to satisfy the wider readership.

[45] S. Omed Ali, 'Baba Nanak o Sikh Dharma', *Tablig*, Ashar 1334 BS, pp. 40-5; Ali Ahmed Ali Eslambadi, 'Guru Nanaker Islam Priti', *Gulistan*, Ashwin 1340 BS, pp. 344-6. I am indebted to Ashoke Chakrabarty for drawing attention to these sources. *Tablig* was primarily devoted to the various Islamic religious issues but it was not silent on political questions. It was the mouthpiece of the *pirs* of Furfura. The periodical occasionally expressed rabid Islamic ideas. *Gulistan*, however, was mainly a literary magazine.

[46] It is generally believed that Muslims brought out periodicals to foster religious awareness at the community level. Cf. Mustafa Nurul Islam, *Samaikpatre Jiban o Janamat*, Dhaka 1977, p. 5. See also Rafiuddin Ahmed, *The Bengal Muslims 1871-1906: A Quest for Identity*, Delhi 1981, pp. 24-37; Tazeen M. Murshid, *The Sacred and the Secular: Bengal Muslim Discourses 1871-1977*, Calcutta 1995, p. 153.

V

Bengalis took equal interest in the lives of Guru Nanak and Guru Gobind Singh. While the two lines of inquiry ran parallel in the nineteenth century, the second gradually surpassed the first in the twentieth century as a direct consequence of the growing momentum of the Indian national movement. The tenth Guru loomed large in the nationalist discourses—sometimes in the writings of Sanatani Hindus, sometimes in the thoughts of militant leaders and sometimes in the conception of Rabindranath. It will be a mistake to say that Sikh studies in Bengal were all praise for him. A few authors criticized him in scathing terms.

The case of Bengali Brahmos is different. They were predominantly interested in Guru Nanak and regarded him as one of the forerunners in their search for a similar tradition. But the subsequent changes in the Sikh order underlining the growing militarization, the rise of the Khalsa at the time of Guru Gobind Singh, the conflict with the Mughals and the Afghans did not appeal to them. They found no spiritual affinity with the second trend. The discussion on Guru Gobind Singh was thus more or less confined to non-Brahmo writers, who tried to present him in Hindu garb. The author of *Panjabetihas* (1846) writing after the First Sikh War made a brief reference to the tenth Guru. Later, the trend continued in the *Bibidhartha Samgraha* (1851). The Bengali search for sources on Guru Gobind Singh widened with the increasing popularity of the militant politics drawing ideology and support from the resurgent Hinduism of the closing decades of the nineteenth century. By the 1880s, the social reform movement and Westernization had lost much of their early appeal. Many educated Bengalis often expressed grave doubts about the blessings of British rule. They drew considerable support from the bitter experiences of the Ilbert Bill agitation and the 'political mendicancy' of the moderate Congress leadership. To many of them Bankimchandra Chatterjee's (1838-94) series of novels and philosophical treatises relying on 'political and historical imagination as a tool for remaking society' envisaged the birth of a Hindu India. This not only made 'many anglicized Hindus proud of their Hindu past', 'but denied the Muslims any honourable place in it'. We may here consider three brief essays that appeared in different publications of the period.

Chronologically, the first and the third were by the aforementioned

Rajanikanta Gupta. The second author remained anonymous.[47] These essays were published between Magh 1285 and Sraban-Bhadra 1296 BS. A distinctive feature of these writings is the references to the tragic death of Tegh Bahadur while dealing with the changes in the Sikh community at the threshold of Guru Gobind Singh's career. They all maintain that the ninth Guru was a victim of Aurangzeb's 'bigotry'. Consequently the death of the ninth Guru united the Sikhs. The unity had a religious appeal. The reader may see the noxious vapours of communalism in it. The articles seek to highlight a concerted move by Guru Gobind Singh to unite his 'community' to liberate the 'country' and 'homeland' in an atmosphere reeking of retaliatory religious violence. But the biographers of this phase were not always very clear about what words like 'country', 'homeland' and 'community' meant.[48] There was also no definite indication of an anti-British stance in these essays. On the contrary, one writer even hinted that the British 'liberated' India from Muslim rule and persecution. Besides, when they spoke of an Indian national unity, it primarily suggested a pan-Hindu identity leaving the Muslim heritage of medieval India generally out of it. The rule of Aurangzeb in particular was projected as a period of relentless Muslim tyranny and Hindu resistance. In this context, the birth of the tenth Guru was considered well timed and many Hindus of the nineteenth century regarded him as a saviour of the Hindu nation. The essayists further emphasize that the tenth Guru made significant changes in Sikh social and religious life from what Guru Nanak had fashioned. Homage is paid to his lifelong sacrifice and struggle. The writers also recognize with a sense of gratitude that his defence of the Hindus paved the way for the future Sikh political greatness in the eighteenth and nineteenth centuries.

Guru Gobind Singh again figured on three different occasions in the brief lifespan of Swami Vivekananda (1863-1902). He did not write

[47] Anonymous (Rajanikanta Gupta), 'Guru Gobinda', *Bangadarshan*, Magh 1285 BS, pp. 433-43; Rajanikanta Gupta, 'Tegh Bahadur o Gobinda Singha', *Karnadhar*, Sraban-Bhadra 1296 BS, pp. 213-16; anonymous,'Guru Gobinda Singha', *Nalini*, Baisakh 1288 BS, pp.1-6; Jyaistha 1288 BS, pp. 33-9.

[48] Even Bankimchandra, who played a significant role in the formulation of the militant ideology of the period, had 'some ambiguity of this sort.' Attention is drawn to his use of the word *jati* in this regard. See Kaviraj, *The Unhappy Consciousness*, pp. 112-13, 128-9.

any separate biography of the Sikh Guru, but has left behind a few scattered comments and observations, each consisting of a few lines. They underline the Guru's greatness as a political leader and spiritual organizer of the Sikhs. Needless to add, he is portrayed as one of the Hindu 'race' 'shedding his own blood, and that of his dearest and nearest, for the cause of his religion'. Like Bankimchandra, Vivekananda had an important role in the formulation of a militant nationalist ideology in Bengal. A deep love for the country's past prompted him to refer to a few 'common' elements of Hinduism in his speeches and writings.[49] The politically subservient and economically backward Bengali Hindu *bhadralok* could find there a bold defence of his embryonic national consciousness. Guru Gobind Singh, however, did not meet his end like a tragic hero as Vivekananda makes us believe. Nor was the Sikh Guru 'deserted' 'by those for whose sake' he had 'earlier shed his blood and the blood of his dearest and nearest'. Vivekananda is silent about his sources on all these points. He might have collected relevant information from his informal discussions with the Punjabi Hindus of Lahore. There he delivered the speech (1897) briefly referring to the Sikh Guru's 'self-sacrifices' for his 'race' and 'community'. It might have again inspired Rabindranath to write poems on the Sikh Guru's 'self-sacrifices' almost within a year (1898-9).

VI

Rabindranath wrote quite a few significant poems and essays on the tenth Guru over a period of twenty-five years between 1886 and 1910. These writings show a gradual evolution in his evaluation of Guru Gobind Singh and at the same time mark a notable step forward in the study of Sikh history in Bengal. Except one essay, all of them show a respectful attitude.

In his early youth, Tagore wrote an essay entitled 'BirGuru'—the first he wrote about the tenth Guru—which was published in the

[49] For Swami Vivekananda's writings, see 'Hindudharmer Sadharan Bhitti', *Janma Satabarsha Smarane Swamijir Bani o Rachana*, vol. V, Calcutta 1369 BS, pp. 267-88. For the ideological background of militant Hindu nationalism, see Bimanbehari Majumdar, *Militant Nationalism in India and its Socio-Religious Background*, Calcutta 1966, pp. 1-35; Amales Tripathi, *The Extremist Challenge—India between 1890* and *1910*, Calcutta 1967, pp. 19-30.

children's magazine, *Balak* (Sraban 1292 BS). A youthful enthusiasm permeates both his language and his message. The tenth Guru's sacrifice, heroism, patriotism and attachment to his people have been so glorified that it can make a deep impression on young minds. Tagore seems to have had this purpose in mind when writing this piece. Guru Gobind Singh as presented in the essay was not a remote person. Rabindranath's style had given him the radiance of valour and for the young, the distance between faraway Punjab and Bengal was eliminated.

Between 1898 and 1899 Rabindranath wrote three poems about three phases of Guru Gobind Singh's life.[50] The first two are about the pre-Khalsa period when he meditated for years in the lower hills on either side of the Yamuna, studied different branches of the liberal arts, learnt the art of war and accumulated spiritual prowess. In the last poem, the poet writes about how the Guru gave up his life, a victim to a Pathan's knife. Chronologically, the first is 'Guru Gobinda' (1888) written a few years after the first session of the Indian National Congress. Disgusted with the politics of petition of the moderate Congressmen, Tagore longed for the leadership of some robust personality dedicated to idealism and abhorring publicity. To him the twenty years that the tenth Guru spent preparing himself appeared to be the gestation period of the saintly person's debut in the service of the nation. Days rolled by and then six or so disciples came to persuade Guru Gobind to come out of his seclusion and take up the leadership of the larger Sikh society.

The poet sought to project the Sikh Guru in such a situation at the beginning of the poem 'Guru Gobinda'. The Guru tries to dissuade

[50] These three poems by Rabindranath appear in the anthologies 'Manasi' and 'Katha', *Rabindra Rachanabali*, vol. I, Calcutta 1980, pp. 383-8, 429-30, 770-3. Echoes of Rabindranath's proposition can be heard in J.N. Farquhar, *Modern Religious Movements in India,* New Delhi reprint, 1977, pp. 337-8. As sources of these three poems, see (a) 'Guru Gobinda': Cunningham, *A History of the Sikhs*, p. 60, (b) 'Nishphal Upahar': M'Gregor, *The History of the Sikhs,* vol. I, pp. 79-80 and (c) 'Sesh Siksha': M'Gregor, pp. 99-100 and Cunningham, p. 73. Tagore himself referred to his association with Cunningham's book. On the other hand, we do not have any documented evidence for the poet's direct accesses to M'Gregor's writings. In this regard Ujjwalkumar Majumdar's *Kabir Adhyayan,* Calcutta 1994 and Prasantakumar Pal's *Rabijibani, 1292-1309*, vol. III, Calcutta 1394 BS do not add anything new.

the disciples by speaking of his incomplete tutelage. The poem, on the one hand, expresses the Guru's deep agony at his isolation from the 'mainstream of national life'. On the other hand, the Guru does not hesitate to admit that he needed additional training to make himself more eligible for the leadership of the country by going through trials and experiments away from the public eye.[51] Tagore's frustrating political experience at the time no doubt gave birth to the poem. The poet depicted the Sikh Guru after his own aspirations. In his attempt to add lustre to this obscure phase of the life-story of the Guru, can be seen the poet's own anticipation of the coming of a similar personage in Indian national politics. Tagore had to do a lot of brushwork to envision the Sikh leader of the medieval period in this light, which made it colourful and suitable for the age. Rabindranath's Guru Gobind hugged the past but the confines of petty religiosity could not imprison him. He was called upon to take the leadership at the national level. Others wrapped the Guru up in aggressive *Hindutva*. Rabindranath distanced himself from that narrow stance. There lies the significance of 'Guru Gobinda'—at least partly.

The second poem is called 'Nishphal Upahar', written about the same time as 'Guru Gobinda'. Here also one hears the same refrain. In the poem, the Guru has been described as a large-hearted person disinterested in worldly possessions. The incident described took place some time during the pre-Khalsa period. The Guru was deeply absorbed in his study on the bank of the Yamuna. At this moment, his disciple, Raghunath, presented him with a very expensive pair of

[51] Tagore firmly believed that this criterion held good for the Indian leadership of his times. He referred to the point in many of his writings of the period. The germination of 'Guru Gobinda' may even be traced to his earlier essay 'BirGuru'. Rabindranath then wrote: 'Those who want to be done with doing good to the country in a short space of time display speed and flamboyance which cast a spell over people. . . . But they are not great men. . . . Gobinda was not like them. For about twenty years he fixed his resolve among the hills on the banks of the Yamuna or in the wilderness. Having made his resolve, he bade his time for the critical moment.' Cf. 'BirGuru', *Rabindra Rachanabali*, vol. XV, p. 505. Rabindranath recalled with veneration the Sikh Guru's contribution in 1893 in another article, 'Ingraj o Bharatbasi', *Rabindra Rachanabali*, vol. XIII, Calcutta 1990, p. 403. For more instances of this respectful attitude of Rabindranath towards Guru Gobind Singh, see 'Chhinapatrabali', Letter No. 20, ibid., vol. XI, Calcutta 1989, p. 405; 'Samudrayatra', ibid., p. 372; 'Swami Sraddhananda', ibid., p. 712.

bangles. Unknown to the Guru, one bangle suddenly fell in the waters of the Yamuna. Raghunath jumped into the water and looked for the bangle for a long time. At the end of the day, he came out of the water and requested the Guru to tell him where the lost bangle was. The Guru was still immersed in studies. He did not lift his gaze from the book, threw carelessly the second bangle into the water to indicate where the first one was.

A partial reference to this episode occurs in M'Gregor's *History of the Sikhs*. There also the Guru has been portrayed as one averse to worldly belongings. But there the disciple has not been named and the Guru was not so lost in his own thoughts. Rabindranath's Guru Gobind Singh was engrossed with patriotic thoughts and that heightens his greatness beyond measure. Of course, it is hard to tell how historical the episode is.

The main theme of the last poem on the tenth Guru also occurs in Cunningham and M'Gregor's writings. The poem is called 'Sesh Siksha' and the narrative goes as follows: at one stage of his life, anger drove the Guru to slay a Pathan trader. Later, stung by repentance, he educated the son of the dead trader under his own supervision. When the boy came of age, the Guru urged him time and again to avenge his father's death. The young man was reluctant at first but in the end his passion was so fanned that he attacked his benefactor. The Guru was mortally wounded. But he smilingly accepted the sudden end.

In the poem, the poet has shown how the Guru invited death to pay for his 'own wrong doing' and it reminds us of the last Sikh Guru's prophetic assertion of the universal equality among man. It is again a recognition of the fact that those at the top of society are not outside the pale of law. The value of life of everybody is the same as that of anybody else and there should be the same penalty for the same offence, irrespective of who the culprit is. The tenth Guru was dedicated to the vindication of the principle. The poet's style gave an intimate human touch to his tragic end, lifting him out of the dry as dust system of law.

Some may find a trace of unreality in the philosophy of the tenth Guru as presented in 'Sesh Siksha'. Rabindranath may be accused of making him a figment of the imagination, a divine personality, and a man ready for every sacrifice in life. It would appear that Tagore did it on purpose. He presented to his readers his own desires and aspirations as the Guru's idealism with the objective of injecting it into contemporary national politics. His own times did not give him a role model, so he dug into the past. While reconstructing it, he added a significant dimension to the role of Guru Gobind Singh. The poem could not satisfy a section of the contemporary Sikh leadership.[52] But Tagore put the Guru at the apex so that he could hold the society together and rejuvenate its polity through his ethical lifestyle. His imagination added a new perspective to the mission of Guru Gobind Singh. Here the cementing force is once again not *Hindutva* but an awareness of an all-Indian unity based on the dignity of every human life. Many had by then learned to appreciate the spirit of liberal humanitarian nationalism. Rabindranath perhaps echoed their emotions.

But within a decade or so, Rabindranath had substantially revised his assessment of Guru Gobind Singh. He articulated his changed attitude in the preface he wrote to the book, *SikhGuru o Sikhjati* authored by Saratkumar Roy, a teacher at the Brahmacharyashram at Santiniketan. According to Tagore, the 'finale' of Sikh history was 'very tragic' and the tenth Guru bore the lion's share of the responsibility for that.[53]

One naturally asks why Rabindranath criticized Guru Gobind Singh so harshly. The answer lay in his revised assessment of the contemporary political situation. During the Swadeshi and Boycott Movements, Rabindranath's views on militant politics underwent a change. The widely spread communal riots and the bloodletting by terrorists worried the poet. He held the national leaders responsible for the gradual deterioration in Hindu-Muslim relations and slated

[52] Rabindranath's poem 'Sesh Siksha' created a sharp reaction among a section of the Sikhs. Drawing on Cunningham's account (*A History of the Sikhs*, p. 73), he wrote that Guru Gobind Singh met his tragic end at the knife of a Pathan assassin. But Sikh faithfuls could hardly support the view. They believe that the Guru had a natural end (Macauliffe, *The Sikh Religion*, vol. V, pp. 242-6). Tagore's view therefore came under severe criticism in a section of the Punjabi press. It persisted over three decades. The bitter relationship came to an amicable end when Tagore visited Lahore and was warmly received by a group of senior Sikh leaders there. After his meeting, Tagore issued a press statement and that made the Sikh leadership happy. Cf. *The Tribune*, 21 February 1935; *The Akali Patrika*, 20 February 1935; *Ananda Bazar Patrika*, 20 February 1935.

[53] Supra, pp. 99-101. See also Rabindranath Tagore, 'Shivaji o Guru Gobinda Singha', *Rabindra Rachanabali*, vol. XV, pp. 523-8.

them. He believed that during the anti-Partition agitation, the national movement had suffered an irreparable loss by losing the confidence of the Muslim community. So he set his face against political violence and the Boycott Movement, which threatened communal harmony in Bengal. He looked forward to the rise of a great tolerant nation beyond the petty confines of race, religion and communal feelings.[54] The poet's revised point of view naturally led him to make a fresh evaluation of the Indian history and culture of the past. In this context, Rabindranath raised a few questions about the contributions of Guru Gobind Singh and his Khalsa. He felt that the prolonged sanguinary warfare between the Sikhs and Mughals had rendered the serene, tender and broadminded humanistic idealism of Guru Nanak pointless. In order to gain military success, the Khalsa gradually abandoned the values of catholicity embedded in Sikhism. The wars of the seventeenth century exacerbated Hindu-Muslim relations. Even in the twentieth century, the tradition of bloody conflict created by the Sikh history of the medieval days raised obstacles in the path of the rise of 'a great nation', as visualized by the poet. So Rabindranath did not hesitate to point an accusing finger at Guru Gobind Singh. He was content to reassess the past history of his country in the light of contemporary political experience. But it is equally necessary to examine the strength of the historical evidence on which Tagore's critique of Guru Gobind Singh and the Khalsa was based and the extent to which this was justified.

Rabindranath's historical revaluation of the tenth Guru received powerful support from the celebrated historian Jadunath Sarkar.[55] Nevertheless, some questions regarding Rabindranath's reassessment linger on. It is not surprising that the poet lost sight of some complex

[54] This paragraph is based on Sumit Sarkar's *The Swadeshi Movement in Bengal: 1903-1908,* New Delhi 1973, pp. 82-5, 90-1, 326-49 and Hiren Chakrabarti's *Political Protest in Bengal: Boycott and Terrorism 1905-18,* Calcutta 1992, p. 63. During the period, the poet also wrote about the rise of 'a great nation' in his novel *Gora.* Cf. *Rabindra Rachanabali,* vol. VII, Calcutta 1985, pp. 923-5. The present essay, however, does not suggest that Tagore lost all faith and conviction in the message of Sikhism. Nowhere in the essay do we come across any such sentiment. On the contrary, during the same period Rabindranath composed a song (*Baje baje ramyabina baje*) based on a Sikh hymn. *Rabindra Rachanabali,* vol. III, p. 1261; Prabhatkumar Mukherjee, *Geetabitan: Kalanukramik Suchi,* Calcutta 1399 BS, p. 162.

[55] He translated Rabindranath's essay into English and it was published in *Modern Review,* April 1911, pp. 334-8. Sarkar almost repeated a part of these observations in his *History of Aurangzib,* vol. III, Calcutta 1928, pp. 320-1.

cause and effect factors behind the great upheaval in Sikh history before and after the advent of the tenth Guru. The message of radical social protest voiced by the Sikh Gurus led to many significant changes in the rural society of medieval Punjab. Even before the birth of the Khalsa, it gave the Punjab peasant a voice of protest against contemporary political oppression. Besides, the influx of militant Jats in the Sikh movement, the idealism of the recusants, the prevalence of the *Sakti* worship in the Sivaliks where the Guru spent his days of tutelage, the diffusion of armed politics surrounding the death of two Gurus, their own system of taxation, all these along with many other factors led to historical changes in the Sikh Panth. They contributed to the birth of the Khalsa by the close of the seventeenth century. It may also be recalled that the Punjab peasantry were then frequently in revolt over an extensive area against the oppressive taxation of the Mughals.[56] Actually the spirit of protest raised by the Sikh Gurus encouraged the peasantry of the *manjha-malwa* area to fight for their survival while the Mughal empire was breaking up. The Sikhs took arms under the tenth Guru to preserve their existence. So to criticize him for the communal discord in eastern India in the first decade of the twentieth century is perhaps an incorrect historical formulation.

It is surprising that Sarkar is the only historian who supported Rabindranath's interpretation. Of course, no one has ever averred that Sarkar's assessment of Sikh history was based on primary sources and above criticism. On the other hand, the poet came in for sharp criticism, as his study was not validated by historical evidence. Rabindranath's critical observations about the tenth Guru raised a mild protest in Calcutta. From Orissa, Sivaprasad Das perhaps responded and sought to provide a revised version of it in his book *Guru Gobinda Singha*.[57] Rabindranath's digs no doubt hurt a few Sikh intellectuals in distant Punjab.[58] Their protest did not betray

[56] Irfan Habib, *The Agrarian System of the Mughal India, 1556-1707*, Bombay 1963, pp. 317-25; Alam, *The Crisis of Empire in Mughal North India*, pp. 179-85.

[57] Binaykumar Sarkar, 'Itihase Sikh Jati', *Aitihasik Prabandha*, Calcutta 1914, pp. 42-6; Indubhusan Banerjee, *Evolution of the Khalsa*, vol. II, Calcutta 1962, pp. 122-5, 153-6; Das, *Guru Gobinda Singha*, pp. 89-90; Anil Chandra Banerjee, *Guru Nanak to Guru Gobind Singh*, New Delhi 1978, pp. 185-97.

[58] Bhagat Lakshman Singh, *The Sikh and His New Critics*, Lahore 1918; Puran Singh, 'The Sikh and His New Critics: Our Viewpoint', *Puran Singh Studies*, January-April 1981, pp. 26-39.

regret but pain. Never before had Bengali Sikh studies been so criticized and debated.

VII

During the anti-Partition agitation, the *jatras* played an interesting role in spreading radical political passions in the districts of Bengal. Their themes usually dwelt on the necessity of making 'sacrifices' for the 'motherland' and 'patriotic songs were often sung in course of acting'. The Calcutta theatres also staged plays with patriotic themes and conveyed inspiring messages to the audience. Sikh studies in Bengal reflected similar sentiments. In the early part of the twentieth century two historical plays were written about the tenth Guru. But they differed in their approach. The first one published was all praise for Guru Gobind Singh. The second one attacked him bitterly.

Guru Gobinda (1909) in five acts written by Haranath Bose appeared during the Swadeshi Movement in Bengal. It was marked by an ebullience of patriotism and an appeal for unity among Hindus and Muslims.[59] The playwright presents the tenth Guru primarily as a leader of the Sikh community. In the concluding part the Guru appears before readers as a symbol of communal harmony on the all-India level. At the two extremities in the plot of the play are the Mughal emperor, Aurangzeb and the Sikh Guru. To depict the conflict of the time, the dramatist had to create twenty odd other characters of varying stature. Seven of them are historical characters. Prominent among them are the ninth Guru Tegh Bahadur, Ram Rai who rebelled against the Gurus, the Mughal emperor Bahadur Shah, Jahanara, daughter of Shah Jahan, Gujri, mother of Guru Gobind Singh. The other fictional characters were either cogs in the Mughal administrative machinery or disciples and well-wishers of the tenth Guru. They included Hindus as well as Muslims.

The Guru has been called the defender and guardian of Hinduism and the playwright considers the two terms Hindu and Sikh to be synonymous. Some broad-minded Muslims are shown fighting for

[59] Haranath Bose, *Guru Gobinda,* Calcutta 1909. For the contemporary Calcutta cultural scene, see Jayanti Chattopadhyay, 'The Rise and Fall of Chandragupta', in Amiya Dev and Sisir Kumar Das (eds.), *Comparative Literature: Theory and Practice,* Shimla 1969, p. 222.

the Guru and getting killed. Some again bitterly criticized emperor Aurangzeb's 'religious intolerance'. It is needless to say that the incidents do not always stand the test of historical corroboration. But the Bengali middle class society of the period did not mind reading such pseudo-historical writing done within a semi-historical framework. The playwright tried to put his play on stage but did not succeed.[60]

Towards the end of the play, Haranath Bose sought to establish that virtue prevails and vice has to succumb. In order to do that, he kept Aurangzeb away from historical veracity, which few historians will support. It is impossible to find any historical evidence for the words that were put into the mouth of the 'repentant' Aurangzeb:

> I remember everything. I am old. . . . I am repentant for the mistakes I made in my life. . . . You, Guru of the Sikhs, do forgive me. I really did not understand the true meaning of Islam. . . . Gobind Singh is no longer my enemy. He has vanquished me. I ask him to come and punish me.[61]

This is not the end of the role that the 'repentant' Aurangzeb plays in the drama. On the eve of his death, he calls upon Hindus and Muslims to build a new India jointly. One cannot recognize him as the eighteenth century emperor Alamgir. Instead, here is an appeal for communal harmony emanating from the Bengali Hindu middle classes prompted by anguish at the absence of Muslims in the movement against the Partition of Bengal in the first decade of the twentieth century. It is from the last quarter of the nineteenth century that Sikh studies had often been influenced by contemporary political needs to go in for a revision in the assessment of Muslim rule in India. Instead of criticizing one and all, Bose points to the need of joining hands with 'good' and 'sympathetic' Muslims who were equally anxious to 'cooperate' with the 'majority community

[60] Haranath Bose called the play 'Punjab Gaurav' and made arrangements to stage it at Calcutta's Star Theatre. But the Sikhs of Calcutta, unhappy over the prospect of a common mortal playing the role of their Guru, tried to create many obstacles to the staging of the play. The playwright had to go to Patna Sahib to obtain the permission of the *mahant* of the *takhat*. For the bitter experience of the playwright in the matter, see 'Bhraman na Niryatan', *Natyamandir*, Paush 1317 BS, pp. 451-67. For contemporary reaction in Bengal and Punjab, see *The Khalsa Advocate*, 5 January 1907. I am thankful to Louis E. Fenech for drawing attention to the point.

[61] Bose, *Guru Gobinda*, p. 135. Bose wrote another drama *Maharashtra Gaurav Rajaram*, Calcutta 1909. Here also his Aurangzeb is different from the Aurangzeb of history.

of the country'. Haranath Bose's Guru Gobind Singh did understand the point and it made his mission great. Aurangzeb's death may carry a melodramatic message towards the end of the play, but it went a long way in cementing the ties of Hindu-Muslim cooperation on a solid foundation. The playwright was confident that it would keep India strong and united. Guru Gobind Singh has also been compared to a *karmayogi* devoid of desire as delineated in the *Gita*, in the emotionally charged atmosphere of death. The Sikh Guru of history is virtually lost in this description.

Jatindranath Samaddar wrote his five-act play *Sikher Katha* in 1911. It is a closet drama and covers the period from the martyrdom of Tegh Bahadur (1675) to the death of Guru Gobind Singh (1708). There are over thirty characters in the play but only five of them are historical figures, viz., the emperor Aurangzeb, Guru Tegh Bahadur, Guru Gobind Singh, his son Ajit Singh and the apostate Ram Rai. Samaddar, like Rabindranath, took a grim view of Sikh militarization (1909). But there is no evidence that he was influenced by Rabindranath's viewpoint. The play has for its source an anonymous and undated article in *The Statesman*. According to Samaddar, Guru Gobind Singh strayed from the religion of Guru Nanak by going for quick militarization of the Sikhs. He has complained that bellicosity became a kind of addiction with the Sikhs of Guru Gobind Singh, 'In the name of self-defence, the Sikhs have gradually become inclined to vengeance. Your neighbour has done you an injustice. . . . So you want revenge. No great work of worldwide significance can be performed with this attitude.'[62]

Consequently, in the opinion of the playwright, the life of the tenth Guru was a total failure.[63] In the twilight of his life, the Guru realized

[62] Jatindranath Samaddar, *Sikher Katha*, Calcutta 1317 BS, pp. 65, 133, 134, 143, 144, 148.

[63] The playwright has described Guru Gobind Singh as a hero who failed. Nor does he make any laudatory remarks about Sikh military power. On the other hand, an imaginary Bengali young man (Sudev) has been ascribed a glorious role. When the play was written, the gallantry of Bengali heroes was getting increasing attention in Bengali literature as a reaction to the cowardly, meek, conspiratorial and garrulous images of Bengali babus of the late nineteenth and early twentieth centuries Anglo-Indian writings. The creation of a Bengali hero by Samaddar may be a reflection of that trend. About such contrasting roles, see Das, *A History of Indian Literature, 1800-1910*, pp. iii, 8, 120. The need to 'duplicate the masculinity' of different

that his mission had no salutary effect because 'he did not use power with restraint'.

The narration of the events of the last days of the Guru by Samaddar does not fall in line with the facts derived from contemporary or near contemporary sources. *Sikher Katha* thus purports to be a historical analysis of the life of the tenth Guru but projects a Sikh Guru of the writer's imagination. That often slows down the pace of the play.[64] There is merely despair surrounding Guru Gobind Singh. It is hard to tell whether Samaddar had read Rabindranath's withering comments on Guru Gobind Singh but he certainly was much concerned and pained at the contemporary political terror and growing communal discord, which induced him to write the play.

VIII

The life of Guru Gobind Singh with a definite Hindu bias constitutes the subject matter of two different biographies. To Tinkari Banerjee goes the credit of writing the most detailed biography of the Guru in Bengali. Basantakumar Banerjee's study came out later. They, however, differed on many important issues like the projection of Guru Gobind Singh and his contemporary relevance.

Tinkari Banerjee presented the life of the Guru with suitable quotations in the original with Bengali translations from authoritative works like *Suraj Prakash* and *Dasam Granth*, besides the *Adi Granth*.[65] He was also acquainted with the writings of British administrator-historians like M'Gregor, Malcolm, Cave Brown and Cunningham. To sort out factual inconsistencies, he always turned to *Suraj Prakash* of Bhai Santokh Singh. He received unstinted help from the Gurdwara Badi Sikh Sangat (Calcutta) to accomplish this voluminous work. The writer also acknowledged his debt in no

---

'martial races' of India and the world also became an important part of the Bengali nationalist narrative of the period. Cf. Indira Chowdhury SenGupta, *The Frail Hero and Virile History,* New Delhi 1997, pp. 5, 22-3.

[64] The book also evoked bitter criticism in *Bharati,* Baisakh 1302 BS, p.122.

[65] Tinkari Banerjee was the nephew of the famous nineteenth century novelist and social thinker Bhudev Mukherjee. It is told that he was so overwhelmed by listening to the *Bhagavati* hymns at a gurdwara at Tundla (near Kanpur) that he embarked on the biography of the tenth Guru. Bhudev's conservatism had influenced him considerably. Anurupa Devi, *Bhudev Charit,* Calcutta 1330 BS, pp. 41-2, 53.

uncertain terms. But the first edition, which was published in 1896 after a decade's labour, was incomplete and crowded with inconsistencies. The biographer was sufficiently aware of the shortcomings. In a footnote he gave the assurance that these would be removed in the next edition. Fortunately, the second edition of the book (1918) fulfilled much of the author's promise. The first edition had sixty out of two hundred and fifty pages on the tenth Guru. The second edition devoted three hundred and fifty out of four hundred and sixty pages to him. Besides, the enlarged second edition had two notable characteristics. This is the first Bengali book with separate pictures of all ten Sikh Gurus. Secondly, a map plots the various Sikh places of pilgrimage of historical interest. The two editions of the book differ in size but the author's angle of vision does not vary.

The writer discusses the lives of the first nine Gurus as a preface and claims that all of them were defenders of the Hindu faith. He sketches the life of Guru Gobind Singh in five long chapters. The first section is 'Patna Parba' which details the Guru's boyhood deeds from his birth at Patna till his arrival in Punjab. This part is relatively short. The 'Anandapur Parba' describes his military conflict while in Anandapur, the invocation of Nainadevi, the establishment of the Khalsa, the writing of *Dasam Granth*, etc. It is the largest section of the book. Then comes 'Chhdavesh Parba' dealing with incidents following the Guru's battle at Chamkaur. The closing chapter features 'Nander Parba', describing the Guru's departure for the Deccan, his political negotiations with Bahadur Shah, the appointment of Banda Bahadur to the Sikh leadership, the assault of the Pathan assassin and his death.

Guru Gobinda Singha by Tinkari Banerjee is a landmark in Sikh studies in Bengali. The author spent more than thirty years on the entire corpus. It also merits attention for the richness of its Punjabi source materials.[66] He studied the Sikh Guru from the point of view of a Sanatani Hindu, missed the significance of the *rahits* and regarded the facts in *Suraj Prakash* as the most reliable.[67] But it did

[66] For a critical assessment of Tinkari Banerjee's work, see Suniti Kumar Chatterji, *Guru Gobind Singh (1666-1708)*, Chandigarh 1967, p. 38. The leading contemporary literary periodical, *Bharati* (Kartik 1325 BS) described the volume as an important addition to Bengali literature. Also see Anarupa Devi, *Bhudeb Charit*, p. 53.

[67] For Tinkari Banerjee's respectful attitude towards the Guru, see *Guru Gobinda Singha*, Calcutta 1918, pp. 91, 403, 412, 446-7, 462. For the Hindu bias of Bhai Santokh Singh, see Macauliffe, *The Sikh Religion*, vol. I, p. lxxvii. Recent researches also confirm the point. Cf. Sagar, *Historical Analysis of Nanak Prakash*, pp. 34-7, 91, 122; S.S. Hans, 'The *Gurbilas* in the Early Nineteenth Century', *Journal of*

not occur to him that it was necessary to cross-check the facts in *Suraj Prakash* with those in other sources. It may be mentioned here that he was the only author writing in Bengali who made extensive use of a huge tome like *Suraj Prakash*. Banerjee's unqualified dependence on medieval Punjabi sources reminds us of the writings of Bhai Mahendranath, although their points of view differed.

Another salient feature of the biography is that the author did not consider the Sikh community separate from the Hindu *parivar*. According to him, the Gurus never raised their voice against the caste system, the *sati*, the status of widows and other social customs. His conservative viewpoint might be pleasing to contemporary Sanatani Sikhs or Hindus but he failed to grasp the significance of the social and religious reforms introduced by Guru Gobind Singh in the Sikh community. In the eighteenth century there were so many changes—the bloody wars, the stream of martyrdoms, the formation of *misls* and the like. The reforms of Guru Gobind Singh played an important role in the revitalization of the Sikhs of the eighteenth century. Tinkari Banerjee handled a vast and varied amount of materials and these aspects should have drawn his attention. He chose not to look beyond the confines of the well demarcated orthodox sense of history and distanced himself from contemporary political complexities. When the enlarged second edition of the book was published, the Indian national movement was well on. Meanwhile, a large number of writers and thinkers had portrayed the tenth Guru as a militant patriot of the medieval days, but Tinkari kept himself away from the radical ideas of his own time. His Sikh Guru believed in the status quo and never put on an aggressive Hindu garb. Later on nearly half a dozen of Bengali monographs relating to different facets of Sikh history were published and they frequently quoted from Banerjee's *Guru Gobinda Singha*. This is a great tribute to his historian's craft.

Basantakumar Banerjee's (1886-1970) biography of the tenth Guru represents another notable area of Sikh studies in Bengali.[68] The

---

Regional History, Annual Number 1981, pp. 50-1. But the *rahits* found an important place in Jogendranath Gupta's *Guru Gobinda Singha*, Calcutta 1333 BS, pp. 21-3.

[68] Basantakumar Banerjee, *Guru Gobinda Singha*, Calcutta 1909. The writer was imprisoned for sometime because of his involvement in the Manicktala Conspiracy Case (1908). British official documents and his son's evidence indicate that he had links with the revolutionaries centred at Chandannagar (near Calcutta). Cf. James

author was associated with the militant nationalist movement of the period and so his Sikh Guru was an embodiment of the spirit of protest against the oppression of Mughal power. Needless to say, the book was inspired by the heated political atmosphere of the age. The writing also received appreciation when it came out.[69]

A shorter biography of Guru Gobind Singh by the same author was published in stray instalments in the periodical, *Aitihasik Chitra*. Later it was edited, expanded and published in book form (1909). It is divided in eighteen parts, sixteen of which revolve round the tenth Guru. Writing about the period from Guru Nanak to Guru Gobind Singh, Basantakumar spoke of the metamorphosis of the Sikh community and scathingly criticized the Mughal policy towards the Sikhs from the time of Jahangir. The author contends that the Sikhs rose against the continuing persecution under the leadership of the tenth Guru. The author slates Aurangzeb's bigotry but compliments Bahadur Shah's efforts to revive Hindu-Muslim amity. The last chapter attempts a historical evaluation of the Guru's role. According to him, the tenth Guru's 'spirit of sacrifice, magnanimity of character and love for his community' helped engender a 'new feeling' in India. 'He did not restrict himself to being a religious preacher. He set about creating a martial race imbued with a religious spirit. Such an effort was "unique" in history. The Guru showed in his life how a religious community could turn into a militia.' The above assessment of Basantakumar would appear to be oversimplistic in the light of other historical evidences. The inadequacy of the writing is evident in the reticence on the other causes of conflict, which brought about the transformation in the history of the Sikhs. Besides, there is no denying that the writer was also deeply influenced by the *Hindutva* rhetoric. He does not hesitate to say that the Sikh Guru represented

---

Campbell, *Political Trouble in India, 1907-17*, Calcutta reprint, 1973, p. 362; Bimalendu Mukherjee, *Biplabtirtha Chandannagar*, Chandannagar 1994, pp. 38-44. Basantakumar wrote a variety of essays in Bengali on the history of the Sikhs. Scattered evidence can be had in periodicals like *Swadeshi*, *Bharati*, *Aitihasik Chitra*, *Prabartak*, *Janhabi* and others. He also wrote a voluminous history of the Sikhs called 'Sikh Sampradaya', a part of which was later summarized to become the first four chapters of his *Guru Gobinda Singha* (1909). But it ('Sikh Sampradaya') was never published in the form of a book. A section of it dealt with the history of the Sikh Gurus. It came out in *Swadeshi* in the early years of the twentieth century.

[69] The book was reprinted three times between 1909 and 1926, and translated into Hindi in the 1920s and English in 1950. It received high praise in *Prabasi* (Ashwin 1316 BS) and from Jadunath Sarkar. Banerjee also wrote a short essay on the tenth Guru in *Prabartak*, Kartik 1330 BS, pp. 598-600.

Hinduism.[70] His *Guru Gobind Singha* is not typical of Hindu orthodoxy seeking a status quo; on the contrary, he stands for Hindu aggrandizement, and reminds us of Lingaraj Mishra's *Guru Gobinda Singha*, which came out in the 1930s. The *Hindutva* implicit in the national movement of the author's time also comes through.

IX

In the twentieth century Bengali Sikh studies came to be enriched with the appearance of a number of poetic narratives of Guru Gobind Singh's life. In this context, we will mention three works of varying length, which depict the life of the Sikh Guru in its totality or in fragments. There is an intimate touch of Bengali sensibility about them.

Chronologically, the long narrative poem, *Sikh* (1909) by Bipinbehari Nandi (1870-1937), is the first in the series.[71] The tide of nationalism generated by the Partition of Bengal gives the poem its fervour. In the blank verse and through long dialogues, the emperor Aurangzeb, the Mughal general Dilir (Diler?) Khan, the ninth Guru Tegh Bahadur, the last Guru Gobind Singh and Bahadur Shah make their appearance in different scenes. Aurangzeb and Dilir Khan discussing the religious policy of the Mughals bring in instances of their oppression in Sikh history. The death of the ninth Guru is depicted in a tragic spirit. Its far-reaching consequence was the militarization of the Sikhs under the leadership of the tenth Guru.

[70] For a similar view prevailing in contemporary Punjab about the Sikh Guru, see Gokul Chand Narang, *Transformation of Sikhism*, New Delhi 1960, p. 78. Narang's book was first published in 1912. Many Sikh scholars, however, have objected to the description of Guru Gobind Singh as a defender of Hinduism. In the recent years, Trilochan Singh's comments can be mentioned for they are the most trenchant. In his opinion, it will be entirely unjustified to call the Khalsa of the tenth Guru '*chowkidars* of the weak and timid Hindus'. See also his 'Social Philosophy of Guru Gobind Singh', in Ray (ed.), *Sikhism and Indian Society,* pp. 179-204. On the other hand, Basantakumar is silent on the opposition of the Hindu Rajput kings of the Himalayan Hill States to the Sikh Guru. This mindset of Hindu writers has been discussed by J.P.S. Oberoi, *Religion, Civil Society and the State,* New Delhi 1996, p. 87. For the early twentieth century Punjabi Hindu views on Guru Gobind Singh, see also Mahata Anand Kishore, *Jiwan Charitra Sri Guru Gobind Singhji*, Lahore 1971 Bikrami.

[71] Bipinbehari Nandi was a lawyer by profession and wrote a few books of poems. His descriptive poem *Sikh* was moderately praised in *Prabasi,* Paush 1316 BS.

The poet becomes a bit effusive in welcoming him. In the end, Guru Gobind Singh's series of military successes compelled a change in the continuing oppressive policy of the Mughals under Bahadur Shah who had a rapprochement with the Sikh Guru.

But the historian is led to wonder when he finds Bahadur Shah discussing an entente at Guru Gobind Singh's deathbed in a cordial climate. He has to surrender to the poet, as Bahadur Shah refers to the emperor Aurangzeb as a bigoted father. The Hindu-Muslim cooperation and the pan-Indian unity sought in the poem offer a picture of the Hindu-Muslim mindset in the freedom movement. To express the aspirations of his own time, Nandi has come a long way reconstructing the past. When the life story of the Sikh Guru is centred at the *zeitgeist* of Bengalis in the poet's lifetime, the Panthic hero of faraway Punjab turns into a repository of Bengali dreams and aspirations and perhaps ceases to be a Punjabi hero and turns into a leader of the Swadeshi Movement.

Jibendrakumar Datta (1883-1921) wrote the other two poems.[72] The second poem was published (1919) ten years after the first. The first one is relatively short and deals with the Guru's creation of the Khalsa at Anandpur on the day of Baisakhi (1699). The subject is a well known event in Sikh history and Datta presented its traditional version. Almost all biographers of the Guru have touched upon the episode. But Jibendrakumar Datta is the only one who put it in verse. The contents of the second poem are chiefly based on an episode from the *Dasam Granth* and Punjabi folklore. Here the poet talks of how a beautiful woman called Anupkumar (Kaur?) tried to put obstacles in the way of Guru Gobind Singh's endeavour to set up the Khalsa. The Guru guessed at the base motive of the woman and frustrated her efforts firmly. The doings of Anupkumar remind one of the temptations put in the way of saints in their meditation by the enchantresses from heaven as related in the epics and the Puranas. The poet has put Guru Gobind Singh in a realm of fancy.

[72] Jibendrakumar Datta wrote two poems on Guru Gobind Singh. They are 'Gurur Ahban', *Prabasi*, Agrahayan 1316 BS, pp. 655-6 and 'Wahe Guruji ki Fateh', *Nabyabharat*, Agrahayan 1328 BS, pp. 410-2. The poet probably borrwed the relevant information about Anup Kaur from J. Campbell Oman's *The Mystics, Ascetics and Saints of India,* London 1905, pp. 196-8.

X

Sikh studies in Bengali largely revolved round Guru Nanak and Guru Gobind Singh but the evolution of the Sikh community during the period of the ten Gurus as a whole did not entirely escape their attention. Sometimes the spirit of sacrifice of a particular Guru and the *sahibzadas* was elaborately reviewed while depicting the first 250 years of Sikh Panth. The martyrdom of Tegh Bahadur was as a rule dealt with as a preamble to the life of the tenth Guru.[73] Leaving aside these isolated pieces, we will discuss here some writings, which provide a key to the understanding of the evolution of the Sikh Panth in the age of the Gurus.

Rajnarayan Bhattacharya (1807–50) who wrote *Panjabetihas* (1846) was the first to cover all the ten Gurus briefly while writing the history of the First Sikh War. The ten Gurus figure but the continuity of Sikh history is not quite discernible all through. In this piece, the ten Gurus are limited by the bounds of fragmented and isolated slices of time. Almost during the same period, Akshaykumar Datta wrote about the other nine Gurus while focusing on the life and philosophy of Guru Nanak. But the nine Gurus appeared chiefly as complementary to the founder of Sikhism. Towards the end of the nineteenth century, Rajanikanta Gupta also wrote about the significance of the Guru period (1469-1708) in Sikh history. After the publication of his two essays on the first and the last Gurus in *Bangadarshan*, he was invited to give a talk on Sikhism at the City College in Calcutta. On that occasion he collected materials from different English sources and added his observations on six out of the remaining eight Gurus.[74] Later, he expanded his lecture to stretch it to the annexation of Punjab.

[73] The life of the fifth Guru Arjandev was separately published only once in two instalments during the long period. Pramathanath Sarkar, 'Guru Arjun Singha', *Abasar*, Ashwin-Kartik 1325 BS, pp. 77-82; Agrahayan 1315 BS, pp. 146-51. Similarly Kumudini Bose wrote an essay on the ninth Guru. See her 'Teghbahadur', *Sikher Balidan*, pp. 6-13. The martyrdom of Guru Gobind Singh's four sons has been briefly discussed in three essays—one by Kumudini Bose (Mitra) in *Sikher Balidan* and the two other by Basantakumar Banerjee, 'Singha-Sishu', *Aitihasik Chitra*, Sraban 1315 BS, pp. 159-74 and 'Ajit Singha o Jhujhar Singha', *Aitihasik Chitra*, Agrahayan 1315 BS, pp. 337-55.

[74] In the writings of Rajanikanta Gupta, the Gurus Angad, Amardas and Ramdas are mentioned only once. Guru Har Rai and Guru Harkishen do not find any place. Rajanikanta made no factual change in this part of his work. See his *Sikh*, Calcutta 1883 and *Aryakiriti*, Calcutta reprint, 1908.

His writing shows the continuity of Sikh history and offers some rationalization of its course. Rajanikanta combined Hindu devotion to religion with patriotism and his *Sikh* (1883), thus, became very topical.

A relatively clear and comprehensive history of the Guru period emerges from Saratkumar Roy's *SikhGuru o Sikhjati.*[75] Roy had a framework handy, in Cunningham's *A History of the Sikhs*. Besides, he consulted Macauliffe, Court and Griffin whenever necessary. Saratkumar lists ten Gurus, their terms of office, and details the expansion of Sikhism together with a profiling of each Guru's role in it and in promoting harmony. He also speaks of the change in the relationship between Mughal imperial power and young Sikhism, internal dissensions in the Sikh Panth over the succession to the Gurudom and the emergence of the dissenting groups.

Following a long discussion on the founder of Sikhism, the writer goes into the circumstances relating to the elevation of his favourite disciple for the Guru's post. In the first two cases, the Gurus succeeded in getting the most eligible candidates nominated. During the tenure of the fourth Guru, the office became hereditary which led to tension and rivalry. The writer of course presents all this along with other changes in Sikh history. He speaks of the development of Ramdaspur (later Amritsar) at the time of the fourth Guru, Ramdas. He also writes about the experience of political organization during the term of the fifth Guru Arjan. But the Guru was 'slain in a conspiracy', while giving the political organization necessary cohesion. The fifth Guru succeeded in investing his community with a definite character by compiling the *Adi Granth*—the sacred text of the Sikhs—and making Amritsar their principal place of pilgrimage. His tragic end led to the rapid militarization of the Sikhs at the time of the sixth Guru, Hargobind. The ninth Guru Tegh Bahadur once again became a victim of Mughal 'political machination' and it was during the period of the tenth Guru that the Sikhs emerged as a 'martial race'.

Saratkumar's main objective was to record the history of the Sikhs from the birth of the founder of the faith (1469) to the end of the Second Sikh War (1849). The book runs into 155 pages out of which only 50 pages are on the Guru period (1469-1708). The history of the Guru period does not receive the importance and gravity that it

[75] Supra, p. 150.

deserves. Also, in his attempt to condense the history of the period, he has fallen into making quite a few factual errors. But Saratkumar Roy has added weight to his book by referring to the communal separateness of the Sikhs.[76]

Sikher Atmahuti is a notable addition to the study of the Guru period.[77] The writer, Dineshchandra Burman fell foul of the British authorities because he compared the war between the Sikh Gurus and Mughal power with the struggle of Indian nationalists against British rule.The book under discussion praised the valiant fight of the Sikhs from the time of the fifth Guru to that of the tenth to defend their land, race, religion and freedom. The writer held up the Sikh struggle as an example to emulate in demolishing the shackles of colonial bondage. The death of the fifth Guru, Arjan (1606), is considered the auspicious beginning of the struggle. The war continued till the eighteenth century, until the Sikhs won independence. True, the author pared off a lot of details. He ended the book giving an indication of Guru Gobind's historic success in the battle of Muktsar (1705). There is hardly any doubt that Burman blessed the Sikh struggle with an eye to the future success of the Indian confrontation with the British.

Unlike other Bengali writers, Dineshchandra did not think that Sikh militarization began with the sixth Guru, Hargobind. He did not find any Guru apolitical since the fifth. The relentless offensive of the intolerant Mughals brought the Sikhs out of the religious

[76] A number of other Bengali writers have studied the evolution of the age of the Sikh Gurus. Special mention should be made of Basantakumar Banerjee's 'SikhGuru', *Swadeshi*, Agrahayan 1314 to Kartik 1315 BS, Kartikchandra Mitra's *SikhGuru,* Calcutta 1928 and Bimanbehari Majumdar's *Sikhjatir Itihas,* Calcutta 1929. Perhaps the first of them is a revised but an incomplete version of his 'Sikh Sampradaya' mentioned earlier, which, however, makes no reference to the tenth Guru. Supra, p. 159. Kartikchandra Mitra criticized the tenth Guru for the 'growing belligerence' of the Sikhs and their 'waning religiousness'. But he also acknowledged that contemporary historical necessity led to Sikh militarization. He injected a measure of complexity into his writing by trying to seek a linkage between religious ethic and historical compulsion. Bimanbehari Majumdar sought to encompass the entire evolution of the Sikh community though his discussion is extremely brief and sketchy. He claims to have explored history with a fidelity to facts but in reality he follows Macauliffe uncritically.

[77] Dineshchandra Burman, *Sikher Atmahuti,* Calcutta, n.d. The book was proscribed in 1932. See *List of Publications Proscribed in Bengal from 1920 to 1934*, Calcutta 1935.

bounds drawn at the time of Guru Nanak, till they came to choose war as a weapon of self-defence. Their struggle gave a language of protest to all scattered, small and persecuted groups of people in India in the medieval days. The Guru's Khalsa was the symbol of strength for the life-and-death struggle of the time. The repeated Sikh successes compelled the Mughals to pull out of Punjab.

Sikher Atmahuti tried to absorb the political and military language of protest of the age. Burman believed that every political battle is inspired by religious directive. It is not difficult for the reader to see that here Sikhism is not different from Hinduism. It is also evident that the Mughal empire had in it the shadow of British rule. History was reconstructed injecting the spirit of the time of writing and so past and the present merged into one.

XI

While studying the lives of the Gurus, Bengali authors show a fairly accurate knowledge of the different subdivisions and sects in the community as well as their places of worship. They represent two significant aspects of Bengali interest about the Sikh Panth, which do not figure prominently in the writings of Assamese and Oriya authors. Here we would first refer to the different Sikh subgroups as described by them.

The Bengali authors' closeness to Cunningham perhaps first gave them some vague indications that the Sikh Panth was not always a united phalanx in the Guru period. Of course they could not say what McLeod did later very distinctly—that not all Sikhs were members of the Khalsa with five Ks to their gear. Those who failed to make it to the office of the Guru sometimes cut themselves off the mainstream of Sikhism, i.e. from the tutelage of the ten acknowledged Gurus, and formed dissenting groups. Tinkari Banerjee, Saratkumar Roy and Basantakumar Banerjee recognized this aspect. They knew that some anti-Guru sects arose at different stages of Sikh history, viz., Niranjani (Handali), Ram Raiya and so on. To Akshaykumar Datta goes the credit of first identifying different Sikh sects *a la* Wilson. His writings mentioned the Udasis, Nirmalas, Akalis, etc. According to him, Nirmalas were sometimes seen almost naked. It is likely that Datta could not differentiate between the Nirmalas and 'the naked Udasis'. The Nirmala followers were, however, trained in Vedantic philosophy and Sanskrit and played an important role in propagating the message of the Gurus beyond Punjab. Bhai Mahendranath had considerable knowledge of the Sikh community but he mentioned only the Udasi group, founded by Sri Chand, son of Guru Nanak whose members 'renounced the world and activity and wore saffron clothes'. He added that both of them (the main Sikh body and the Udasis) recognized Nanak as the Guru despite their distinct rituals and philosophy. But others did not receive his attention. It is surprising that the diversity of groups within the Sikh community escaped the attention of prolific writers like Rajanikanta Gupta and Basantakumar Banerjee.

At the beginning of the twentieth century, a great deal of complexity bedevilled Punjab politics. In matters of employment, voting rights and management of the gurdwaras, it was often imperative to draw a dividing line between Sikhs and non-Sikhs. A debate raged about the Hindu-Sikh line of demarcation. The growing influence of the Tat Khalsas often stimulated tensions in Sikh politics. In this ambience, the anti-British Akalis also started a movement for reforming the gurdwaras and the Sikhs drew close to the Indian national movement, kindling in its turn a new interest about them among non-Sikhs. Who the Akalis were, whether they had a Guru of their own and what their role was in the history of the Sikh Panth—these questions came up for discussion. At this time, incidentally, other Sikh sects also came into focus.

A pioneer in these discussions was the famous writer Dinendrakumar Roy (1869-1943), contributing to *Bharatbarsha*.[78] He related two anecdotes to illustrate the role of Guru Gobind Singh in the formation of the Akalis and the Nirmalas. According to him, these two sects represented two opposing trends in Sikhism—the quietist Nirmalas continuing Sanskrit studies and the pursuit of Vedantic philosophy and the Akalis cultivating valour. The writer considered them complementary. Asutosh Tarafdar carried on the discussion in *Bharatbarsha*. He threw light on the Nanakpanthis and Akalis. Besides, he made clear the difference in religious practices between the Nanakpanthis and the Khalsa of Guru Gobind Singh. Tarafdar added that the Nanakpanthis do not wear the five Ks. But neither Dinendrakumar nor Tarafdar distinguished popular denominations like Keshdharis, Sehajdharis and Amritdharis, which were in wide currency in Punjab politics of the first quarter of the twentieth

[78] Dinendrakumar Roy, 'Nirmali o Akali,' *Bharatbarsha*, Ashwin 1324 BS, pp. 574-9.

century. They also remained silent about the Agrahari Sikhs who were widely seen in Bara Bazaar area of the city of Calcutta.[79]

Another feature of Sikh studies of the Guru period in Bengali is the reference to the gurdwaras, the places of Sikh worship. The holiest place for the Sikhs is the Golden Temple at Amritsar, a site enthusiastically celebrated by Bengali writers. After the annexation of Punjab, the British administration drew a large number of Bengali officials to Punjab. Many others went there to preach Brahmoism, to travel, to pursue journalistic and political ends. They looked at the Golden Temple from different angles, adding colour and variety to their writings.

The connection between the Tagores of Jorasanko and the Golden Temple goes a long way back. After his sacred thread ceremony, Rabindranath went there with his father Debendranath. It was in 1873. They were there for a month. We find in his autobiography the influence it had on the young mind:

> I remember the Gurudarbar of Amritsar like a dream. . . . Worship went on there all the time. My father used to sit amid the praying people and suddenly would join in their prayers tunefully. Such prayer from a non-Sikh much inspired them and they respected him for that.

The placid atmosphere of the Harimandir, the care that the Sikhs took of the visitors, the religious rites of the place—all this impressed others as much as Rabindranath, as a large body of writing bears out.[80] The number and style of these works influenced the Bengali

[79] Supra, p. 123. Also see Asutosh Tarafdar, 'Nanakpanthi–Nanakshahi', *Bharatbarsha*, Phalgun 1325 BS, pp. 334-5; 'Akali Nihang', *Bharatbarsha*, Chaitra 1325 BS, pp. 500-2; Matilal Roy, 'Akali', *Prabartak*, Kartik 1329 BS, pp. 625-9; Bimanbehari Majumdar, 'Akali Sikhdiger Itihas', *Bangabani*, Magh 1330 BS, pp. 756-63. The last two articles generally highlighted the history of the Akali movement of the 1920s. Debendranath Mitra followed Cunningham's group division in his *Sikh Parichay,* Chandannagar n.d.

[80] Rameshchandra Datta, 'Amritsar', *Mukul*, Ashar 1302 BS, pp.10-11; Sitalakanta Chatterjee, 'Punjab Bhraman', *Bharati o Balak*, Bhadra 1293 BS, pp. 274-6; anonymous, 'Brahmo Parjataker Patra', *Tattwakaumudi*, 16 Jyaistha 1816 Saka, pp. 43-4; anonymous, 'Amritsarer Subarnamandir', *Satsang*, Baisakh 1302 BS, pp. 21-5; anonymous, 'Amritsarer Gurudarbar', *Purnima*, Kartik 1307 BS, pp. 239-42; Anonymous, 'Kada Prasad', *Sahitya-Sevak*, Jyaistha 1303 BS, pp. 161-3; Jyotiprasad Singha, 'Sikhdiger Jatiya Kirti—Swarnamandir ba Gurudarbar', *Sudha*, Phalgun 1308 BS, pp. 134-8; Kunjalal Saha, 'Amritsar', *Nabyabharat*, Chaitra 1317 BS, pp.722-5; Amritalal Gupta, 'Patiala o Amritsar', *Bharat-Mahila*, Ashwin 1318 BS, pp. 166-70.

mind. These accounts started in the late nineteenth century. Some wrote about the golden covering of the main temple, some mentioned the distribution of *kadaprasad* among the visitors, some documented the religious greatness of the place, and some were surprised that there was no harassment by *pandas* at a place of pilgrimage. Not all of them returned with a smiling face. Take the case of Krishnakumar Mitra, who visited Amritsar in 1878 and was astonished by the idol worship around the gurdwara. He firmly believed that Sikhism abjured idolatry.[81] Later under the impact of the Singh Sabha movement, idolatry and the ascendancy of the Brahmins in the vicinity of the Golden Temple were ruthlessly eliminated. This set his mind at rest and his confidence in the vitality of Sikhism was revived.

A number of gurdwaras redolent with the memory of Guru Nanak found their place in Bengali Sikh studies. Apart from two,[82] all of them were in undivided British Punjab. Guru Nanak was born in Talvandi village, later renamed Nanakana Sahib. According to folklore, gurdwaras sprang up where the child Nanak was born, had his childhood frolics, went to primary school, grazed cattle, etc. How these places looked, what role the Guru played in these areas, were not altogether unknown to Bengali writers.[83] The Panja Sahib gurdwara built in Hasan Abdal in district Rawalpindi west of Lahore also did receive attention. Folk tradition has it that here Guru Nanak stopped a falling rock with his palm. The Panja Sahib gurdwara was set up to commemorate it.[84]

[81] *Tattwakaumudi*, 16 Ashar 1800 Saka, p. 28 and 1 Ashwin 1800 Saka, pp. 86-7; Mitra, *Atmacharit*, p. 105. Earlier Debendranath Tagore in his autobiography spoke of the existence of images of Hindu gods and goddesses in the *parikarma* of the Golden Temple (1873). Coming after Mitra, Manomohan Chakrabarty, a disciple of Ashwinikumar Datta, mentioned the same thing (1886). Cf. Debendranath Tagore, *Atmajibani,* Calcutta reprint, 1962, p. 186; Manomohan Chakrabarty, 'Barishale Paitallish Bachhar', *Brahmabadi*, Ashar 1338 BS, pp. 66-8.

[82] One of the two was situated in Chittagong and the other was in Puri. According to Sikh sources, Guru Nanak visited both places during his eastern Indian *udasi.* Also see anonymous, 'Satyadaser Satprasanga: Nanak-Math', *Dharmabandhu*, Phalgun 1294 BS, pp. 251-5; Tripuracharan Choudhury, 'Chattale Sikh Mandir', *Bharatbarsha*, Baisakh 1323 BS, pp. 717-24. Dissident Sikhs also had gurdwaras of their own. We get relevant information from Jaladhar Sen's 'Gurudwar', *Sahitya,* Sraban 1301 BS, pp. 275-87.

[83] Basantakumar Chatterjee, 'Nankana Saheb', *Bharatbarsha*, Ashar 1334 BS, pp. 94-7. Supra, p. 134.

[84] Anonymous, 'Panj Saheb', *Bamabodhini Patrika*, Bhadra 1300 BS, pp. 138-42. About Bengalis in the vicinity of Rawalpindi, see Jnanendramohan Das, *Banger Bahire Bangali—Uttar Bharat*, pp. 436-7.

Sikhs regard these gurdwaras with great respect. In the British days, government offices, schools, hospitals, railway stations and the like grew up in different parts of Punjab and many educated Bengalis found employment there. They became familiar not merely with the big cities but also with folk tradition and legends connected with the Sikh Gurus in the local environs.

XII

Sikh Gurus not only resisted political tyranny. Some of them were great poets and lyricists. Their *banis* are considered an integral part of the Sikh milieu, especially the religious life of the Sikhs. The first five and last two Gurus wrote in metrical form. They did not miss the attention of Bengali authors.

Sikh faithfuls begin the day remembering the *Japji Sahib*. There the formless God is worshipped in poetic language. The Sikh sacred text *Adi Granth* begins with the *Japji* and scholars have read in it the essence of the Sikh faith. *Japji* is regarded in Punjabi literature as a great poetic vision. Rammohun Roy, Debendranath Tagore, Akshaykumar Datta and other prominent personalities of the Brahmo Samaj introduced Bengali readers of the nineteenth century to portions of the *Japji*.

But the credit for printing the full-length *Japji* goes to a non-Brahmo, who had lived in Punjab—Sashibhusan Mukherjee.[85] The preface has a conservative and critical tone but he did not hesitate to say that Guru Nanak had 'served nectar in his mother tongue for the delectation of the common man'. In his opinion, *Japji* is a book dear to all communities. But the founder of Sikhism, he said, did not adopt any particular method in writing it. While translating, Mukherjee began by printing a part of the original Punjabi in Bengali script. At the foot of it is the Bengali translation coupled with brief notes. For the benefit of the Bengali reader, he Hindiized the Punjabi version, leading to a few discrepancies. Also, since he used colloquial Punjabi, the written Punjabi text did not reach Bengali readers.

At the beginning of the twentieth century, the *Japji Sahib* first appeared in book form in Bengali (1900).[86] The translator and

[85] Sashibhushan Mukherjee, 'Japji', *Nabajiban*, Magh 1295 BS, pp. 262-72; Phalgun 1295 BS, pp. 328-43, 397-414. For his conservative Hindu bias, see his 'Sikh Dharma', *Aryabartya*, Baisakh 1317 BS, pp. 10-19.

[86] Lalbehari Singh Khatri, *Japji Saheb*, Berhampore 1307 BS. The book was written primarily for the Sikhs of Bengal and Assam.

publisher was Lalbehari Singh Khatri who was a Nanakpanthi Sikh. He hailed from Bhagalpur in Bihar. Those Sikhs who lived permanently in eastern India did not know Punjabi and could not read the *Japji*. Lalbehari considered it his religious duty to translate it to relieve their frustration. It was printed in bold letters so that the local Sikhs could read it. But as Bengali was not the translator's mother tongue, some Hindi and Persian words generally unknown to Bengali readers crept in, creating confusion and slackening the pace of the language.

In the next few years, the *Japji* was translated a number of times.[87] Chronologically, the translation by Asutosh Deb in *Sahitya-Samhita* was the first. He wrote a very brief preface and then printed the whole of *Japji* in Punjabi along with the Bengali translation. But the liberties he took with joint letters and words create the impression that he overstepped his mark as a translator. Besides, while translating, he missed some significant features of Sikhism. One wonders why he did not acknowledge his debt to Sashibhusan Mukherjee in writing the foreword.

In the pre-Independence period, three more editions of the *Japji* appeared in Bengali. The first was written by Abinashchandra Majumdar of the Lahore Brahmo Samaj,[88] the second by a Muzaffarpur lawyer, Jnanendramohan Datta and the third by Jatindramohan Chatterjee who was converted to Sikhism in old age. Among these three, the one by Abinashchandra Majumdar is perhaps the most valuable. In his preface, he has warned readers against the drawbacks of his translation. He had lived in Punjab for years and had absorbed the local culture. His translation and comments take us to the inner world of Sikhism. *SikhGuru Nanaker Jiban-Dharma o Japji* by Rai Bahadur Jnanendramohan Datta is another interesting addition to Sikh studies in Bengali. His translation of the *Japji* does not give us an insight into the Sikh mind. But his comments are simple and his language restrained. His

[87] Asutosh Deb, 'Japji', *Sahitya-Samhita*, Ashar-Sraban 1309 BS, pp. 137-74; Bhadra-Ashwin 1309 BS, pp. 257-73. There was some general discussion of Guru Nanak's message in the same periodical in Agrahayan 1317 BS, with observations on *Japji Sahib*.

[88] Abinashchandra Majumdar, *Guru Nankkrita Japji*, Calcutta 1325 BS. About Abinashchandra Majumdar, see Jnanendramohan Das, *Banger Bahire Bangali—Uttar Bharat*, p. 416; *Prabasi*, Magh 1332 BS, pp. 574-5. Abinashchandra had also translated a few *sabads* of Guru Tegh Bahadur. See *Uttara*, Ashwin 1332 BS, pp. 43-9; Kartik 1332 BS, pp. 98-100; Magh 1332 BS, pp. 299-302; Phalgun 1332 BS, pp. 362-7.

observations add up to a brief account of the philosophy of Guru Nanak, conveyed to a Bengali readership. In the case of Jatindramohan, however, emotionalism has taken precedence over logic.[89] According to him, the *Japji* is the gem of all *shastras* and should be called *Gana Gita*. Perhaps his recent conversion partly explains this hyperbole.[90]

Bengali readers were not totally in the dark about *Sukhmani Sahib* of the fifth Guru Arjandev. It was not so popular as the *Japji*. At the beginning of the twentieth century Satyapendra Mullick translated parts of it. Some of the chapters were translated in verse and published in *Bharati* (Paush 1308 BS) and later in *Sudha* (Phalgun 1308 BS). But in neither did he reproduce the original text of the work. And as the translation did not follow the order of the original, appreciation was marred. In the pre-Independence period, two more translations of *Sukhmani Sahib* appeared. They were by two disciples of Bijaykrishna Goswami—Jnanendramohan Datta and Kiranchand Darvesh.[91] Jnanendramohan's translation came out first. In his short preface, he described *Sukhmani Sahib* as a limitless sea of happiness and tranquillity and urged Bengali readers to enjoy its essence. The book also had the original Punjabi text and comments and so won much acclaim. Kiranchand Darvesh did painstaking work but did not prove so popular.

In the period under review, not much elaborate discussion was made of *Adi Granth* and *Dasam Padshah ka Granth*. The reason may lie in the sheer size of both the books. A few stray articles on *Adi Granth*

[89] Jatindramohan Chatterjee, *Japji Athaba Nanak Gita*, Calcutta 1353 BS, pp. 32, 37, 43. He made further contributions to the translation of other Sikh religious texts but these were all published after Independence. See the author's 'Jatindramohan Chatterjee: A Forgotten Scholar of Sikh Studies', *Studies in Sikhism and Comparative Religion*, October 1990, pp. 85-9.

[90] Three more translations in Bengali in poetic form can be mentioned. Anonymous, *Upasansar*, Dhamrai 1319 BS. The translator had called the *Japji* a valuable text but has explained it with the eyes of a devotee. The disciples of Bijaykrishna Goswami—Kiranchand Darvesh (1915) and Satishchandra Mukherjee (1935)—wrote the other two. In the interest of poetry, both deviated a little from the original. Besides, they interpolated their own ideas.

[91] In his preface to *Sukhmani*, Banaras 1945, Darvesh writes that he started his translation in 1917 but could not finish it on schedule.

come to our notice[92] but it is hard to tell why the writing of the tenth Guru did not evoke that much Bengali interest. May be it was because there was no unifying thread running through the book. Akshaykumar Datta made a brief mention of *Dasam Padshah ka Granth* but in the nineteenth century writers were reticent about it. In his appendices, Tinkari Banerjee provided a brief note on the different Guru's works in his *Guru Gobinda Singha* (1918). But after his researches for three decades he unhesitatingly asserted that *Chaupayan Chautrish Abtaran Knia*, *Mehedi Mir* and *Isti Charitra* which form part of *Dasam Padshah ka Granth* were not written by the Guru. Later, Kartikchandra Mitra and Debendranath Mitra echoed what Tinkari Banerjee wrote. Jatindramohan Chatterjee made some significant contribution in the field but all that was written and published after Independence. The epoch-making translations of *Adi Granth* by Haranchandra Chakladar marked an important addition in this field. A disciple of Bijayakrishna Goswami, Haranchandra taught anthropology and ancient Indian history at the University of Calcutta. He devoted more than four decades to translating different portions of the Sikh sacred texts. His critical notes and lucid exposition of the intricate Sikh philosophy projecting it in the broader Indian religious perspective gave Bengali Sikh studies a significant dimension never attained before. But these were not completed before 1947 and the bulk of it still remains in manuscripts.[93]

XIII

The vast mass of literary source material dealing with the Guru period represents the varied and complex response of the Bengali mind to the history and culture, religion and literature of the Sikhs. They illustrate the pioneering role of the Bengali Brahmos in popularizing the message of the Sikh Panth in this part of India. The process began with Raja Rammohun Roy and it persisted throughout the nineteenth century. They brought out some of the finest biographies of Guru Nanak and their scholarship in this field still deserves plaudits. The Brahmo lukewarmness about the later Sikh

[92] Dinendrakumar Roy, 'Sikhdharmagrantha o Dharmaniti', *Bharati*, Chaitra 1301 BS, pp.707-17; Panchanan Ganguli, 'Granthasaheb', *Upasana*, Bhadra 1336 BS, pp. 85-93; Anil Chandra Banerjee, 'Adigrantha', *Prabasi*, 1352 BS, pp. 140-2.

[93] For a detailed discussion, see the author's 'Sikh Sacred Literature', *Studies in Sikhism and Comparative Religion*, October 1986, pp. 101-8.

tradition, particularly the political developments associated with the milieu and message of the Khalsa, only goes to show that their interest was not all embracing, but partial and fragmented. This arena of Sikh studies, however, did not remain long unilluminated. A few Hindu nationalists and Sanatani authors enriched it. They provided a significant perspective to the Bengali understanding of Sikhism. Actually the development of a militant nationalist movement offered an additional stimulus to these authors. The Bengali literary world was so enthralled by the spirit of martyrdom and self-sacrifice of the Sikhs that Guru Gobind Singh with his Khalsa came to dominate Sikh studies through the last two decades of the nineteenth century. The early twentieth century politics of Swadeshi offered cumulative support to this genre of history writing. Again the Bengali appreciation was not always characterized by a spirit of universal admiration for the Panth. For example, Guru Gobind Singh was not only accused of 'radicalizing' the message of Guru Nanak, even 'diluting' it for his short-term needs in the name of resisting the Mughals. Tagore's criticism of the last Sikh Guru, as we have already seen, gave rise to bitter debates in Punjab. Its repercussions were soon heard in the city of Calcutta continuing even in the post-Independence decades. But Rabindranath's denunciation of the message of the Khalsa (1909) does not represent his final assessment of the Sikh Panth. It underwent a significant change in the later years of his life.[94] The evolution in Tagore's attitude towards Sikhism over a period of five decades (1882-1935) underlines how a creative artist brought diversity to the Sikh studies of the period.

Thus, Sikh studies of the Guru period in Bengali were marked by several trends of conflicting political aspirations and religious beliefs. People from different walks of life with different attitudes participated in the exercise. They depicted the Sikh Gurus from different vantage points. Monotheism and anti-idolatry as represented by Guru Nanak are seen side by side with Guru Nanak as the defender of Hinduism, not to mention Guru Nanak, the preacher of Islam. And such a combination does not appear invalidated by contradiction. Similarly, the tenth Guru is shown as renouncing all, a *sannyasi* and a patriot. On the other hand, some brand him a 'failure'. Our experience does not end here. The Bengali pursuit of Sikhism has tried to represent Guru Gobind Singh in the garb of Hinduism seeking Hindu-Muslim unity in the midst of communal

[94] Infra, pp. 182-3.

frenzy and ill feeling. Attempts have been made to project the Sikh Gurus in a Bengali framework. Such projections gave Sikh studies in Bengali interesting but strange diversities.

The writers also differed in the selection of their sources. From the beginning, primary Punjabi literary evidence was freely accessible. Brahmo biographers like Akshaykumar, Mahendranath and Krishnakumar experimented with the *Janamsakhi* sources in the nineteenth century. Another characteristic of Sikh studies in Bengali is its interface with the sources available in the English language. Different interpretations have been presented over the century drawing on writers like Malcolm, M'Gregor, Wilson, Cunningham and Macauliffe. It was the essayist Akshaykumar Datta who first sought the help of British writers. In his essay Forster, Prinsep, Malcolm, M'Gregor and Wilson were mentioned but what is common knowledge is that he found himself in agreement with Wilson. Rabindranath himself admitted that his poem 'Sesh Siksha' was largely derived from Cunningham's study. Then came Krishnakumar Mitra, Rajanikanta Gupta, Saratkumar Roy and others. They collected materials from different sources and then polishing them up through deletion and adaptation sought to develop a critical tradition of historical research. But many Bengali writers did not refer to their sources. Their narration often strayed from the critical path of analysis and branched off into a world of imagination. They also made factual errors, but the playwright Samaddar perhaps remains unsurpassed. The errors in his work are many and bizarre. The most notable among them is the old emperor Aurangzeb expressing 'regrets' to Guru Gobind Singh for his 'misdeeds'. Not one historian has so far corroborated the episode. Between the distortion of sources in the writing of Samaddar and the critical methodology and the wealth of information in the Brahmo writings, there is a yawning gap. They represent the two extreme points of Sikh studies in Bengali.

CHAPTER V

Bengali 2

DURING THE DAYS of Punjab crisis (1980s), a significant political slogan raised by the *khadkus* was: *Raj karega Khalsa*—'The Khalsa shall rule'.[1] Many of them whole-heartedly believed that the Sikhs would soon win political freedom and establish their dominance in the region. In other words, there would once again be the Khalsa Raj in Punjab. Their dream has not come true due to various reasons. To many of us, the Sikh political aspirations may have seemed evanescent and unreal like the thinning mist of the morning. But to a student of eighteenth century Punjab history, the demand may not appear to be anything new. The political belief has been running silent but deep and without a break for over last 300 years of the Sikh Panth. After Independence (1947), this political assertion followed two distinct trends—one underlined the fulfilment of Sikh political struggle in the emergence of a free India,[2] while the other continued to look forward to the creation of a separate Sikh State (Khalistan) outside the territorial limits of the Indian Union.[3]

[1] The above is in the *Tanakhah-Nama* of Bhai Nandlal (1633-1715), a close associate of Guru Gobind Singh, and it constitutes a part of the Sikh daily prayer. The *Tanakhah-Nama* is a valuable piece of eighteenth century Sikh religious literature. It also refers to many Khalsa *rahit maryadas*. See McLeod, *Historical Dictionary of Sikhism*, p. 151; idem, *Who is a Sikh?*, p. 50.

[2] According to Ganda Singh, the 'old aspirations of the Sikhs have come to be fulfilled in the establishment of the people's Raj', 'the Sovereign Democratic Republic of India'. Gopal Singh, *A History of the Sikh People*, New Delhi 1979, p. 745.

[3] A group of Sikhs (including many Sikh expatriates from the United States of America, Canada and the United Kingdom) raised a political demand for the creation of Khalistan outside the framework of the Indian Constitution. For a critical discussion on the different aspects of Punjab crisis (1980s), see Amrik Singh (ed.), *Punjab in Indian Politics: Issues and Trends*, New Delhi 1985. In recent years there have been attempts to resurrect sympathy for the Khalistan movement through Internet access. Cf. Asit Jolly, 'Cyber Khalsa', *The Asian Age*, 13 September 1998.

I

According to many Sikh faithfuls, as the age of the Gurus was drawing to a close in the early eighteenth century and Sikhs had continued their war of resistance under Banda Bahadur against the Mughals, the above battle-cry was almost on every Sikh soldier's mouth. In the assertion there is a directive to preserve religion and society for posterity, so believe the Sikhs. That is why Sikh resistance of eighteenth century never lost its vitality. Once or twice the Sikhs had to retreat from their goal temporarily but they did not surrender to the Mughal or the Afghan persecutions, maintains the famous Sikh historian Harbans Singh. Another feature of this period of Sikh history is their steadfast faith in the uninterrupted tradition of martyrdom and its permanent impact on subsequent community life.

Banda Bahadur spearheaded this phase of the Sikh resistance movement. Rabindranath in his article, 'Sikh-Swadhinata', drew our attention to the Sikh tradition of martyrdom under Banda Bahadur. It appeared in *Balak* (Ashwin-Kartik 1292 BS). Here Tagore gives an account of how Banda Bahadur achieved quick success, defeated the Mughals and established Sikh supremacy in some parts of Punjab. The Mughals, however, soon recovered lost ground. Along with 740 followers, the Sikh hero was captured in Gurdaspur fort and he was brought to Delhi as a prisoner in great humiliation. Later they were mercilessly killed. It is all based on Cunningham.[4] But Rabindranath, departing from Cunningham, presented a picture of the contemporary frame of mind: 'It was Gobinda's mission to save his people from the persecution of foreigners. Banda Bahadur took on the same task.'

Tagore was brought up in the midst of nationalist fervour and was aware of the 'agony of enslavement'. So, while looking back on past dependence, he was reminded of the 'subjection' of the Sikhs in Punjab. The 'exploiters' were 'Muslims' (not Mughals) who in his eyes were 'torturing foreigners'. A young Rabindranath wrote the article in 1885. Yet the Census of 1881 showed that the Muslims in Punjab formed a majority. How can the sons of the soil who represent the majority be called 'foreigners'? Can the conflict

[4] To what extent young Rabindranath followed Cunningham can be seen if one compares 'Sikh-Swadhinata', *Rabindra Rachanabali*, vol. XV, p. 509 and Cunningham's *A History of the Sikhs*, p. 86.

between Banda Bahadur and the Mughals be regarded as a confrontation between 'foreigners' (Muslims) and 'Indians' (Sikhs)? Contemporary historical writings provide interesting information about Banda Bahadur's followers, many of whom were not necessarily Sikhs.[5] Rabindranath's essay did not refer to them. It did not even have the poetic imagination that went into 'Bandibir' in later years. It is also hard to tell how much of it satisfied its young readers. 'Sikh-Swadhinata' is, however, an index of Tagore's one-time closeness to *Hindutva*. This Tagore is not the same as the one who took quite a different position in many of his later writings on the history of the Sikhs. Still it stands out as perhaps the first extensive account in Bengali of the exploits of Banda Bahadur.[6]

The poem 'Bandibir' (1899) has almost immortalized Banda Bahadur in Bengali imagination. Written more than a hundred years ago, it is in the nature of a ballad. In Bengali Sikh studies of the post-Guru period, it was perhaps the most popular and widely discussed poem. It falls into two parts. In the first half, the 'new-born Sikh people' are found locked in a bloody battle with the Mughals, their spirit kindled by the message of the Gurus. The Sikhs seem to have been carrying on the struggle under the leadership of Banda Bahadur. But the first half gives no indication of that. The second half revolves round Banda Bahadur. Here we find the Sikh hero in the fortress of Gurdaspur, vanquished and in chains. In the earlier part, Rabindranath had relegated the leadership question to the background perhaps to suggest that it was a spontaneous popular uprising.

[5] For example, Banda Bahadur's movement had the support of the lower classes including Hindus and Muslims. Cf. William Irvine, *Later Mughals, 1707-20*, vol. I, Calcutta n.d., pp. 96, 98. But later on many merchants and traders of northern India who were mostly Hindu Khatris as well as the *madad-i-maash* holders who were generally all Muslims helped the Mughals in suppressing Banda Bahadur with an iron hand. For details, see Alam, *The Crisis of Empire in Mughal North India: Awadh and the Punjab*, pp. 145-55.

[6] Even before Tagore, Rajnarayan Bhattacharya had briefly mentioned Banda Bahadur (1846). Similarly, Rajanikanta Gupta also spoke of Banda Bahadur in his lecture on the Sikhs at City College, Calcutta (1883). The word 'Bandhu' appearing at a point of his lecture could be a corruption of Banda Bahadur. See *Panjabetihas*, pp. 76-7; *Sikh*, p. 10. But Tagore was the lone Bengali littérateur who referred to Banda Bahadur's martyrdom on different occasions. Tagore's 'Sikh-Swadhinata' has the first reference.

The poet's sympathies were almost always with the Sikhs. He makes it clear how 'fearless' and 'determined' they were to defend their religion and challenge the oppressor. It is hard to find in the literature of eastern India a parallel to the deep regard with which the martyrdom of the Sikhs is valorized here. The rich language going with a choice of poetic words opened before the reader the door to a dream world of Sikh sacrifice and heroism. Dry facts of history are sometimes relegated to the background when Tagore depicts the Mughal-Sikh contest in his masterly style. It seems to be particularly true in the second part of the poem where the last days of Banda Bahadur with his son are described.

It has been said already that Rabindranath's 'Sikh-Swadhinata' was based on the writing of Cunningham. After a gap of more than a decade, the poet became better acquainted with Sikh history and wrote 'Bandibir'. Cunningham gave a brief but grave account of the whole episode relying mostly on Malcolm's reference to historian Ghulam Husain's *Siyar al-Mutakhirin*. The British administrator-historian (Cunningham) devoted around three sentences to the death of Banda Bahadur's son and added three more to narrate the killing of Banda Bahadur's followers. He wrote that the Sikh hero killed his son with his own hands but the poet probed the likely reactions of the father's heart. Tagore realized that much was left unsaid in Cunningham's work. So the poet had to rely on his imagination.[7] He first tried to appreciate what the sources tell us and then sought to fill the void created by lack of historical evidence with his poetic vision. Tagore strove to present the anguish of a father at the loss of his flesh and blood. In the poem father and son pray passionately for the continued success of the Sikh Panth before the son's death. Written sources do not testify to that. But what is there in his scheme of history to stop the poetic flight of fancy?

At this stage Cunningham no longer deeply influences the poet. Obviously Rabindranath had followed him up to a point and then fallen back on his imagination to carry his message to the readers. It

[7] This incident recurs in Sikh oral history tradition. It suggests that whenever a Sikh was asked to embrace Islam by the Mughals, he refused to give up his religion and was consequently sentenced to death. The long list includes Guru Tegh Bahadur, *Sahebzadas* and Sikh heroes like Banda Bahadur, Taru Singh, Mani Singh and others. Many Bengali authors as well as British administrator-historians had referred to these episodes. Rabindranath seems to have been familiar with the tradition. It helped him reconstruct the last act of Banda Bahadur's life. Tagore once more referred to it in the early 1930s. Infra, pp. 182-3.

is hard to tell where the poetic fancy takes off. With this larger vision, Rabindranath tried to get to his perception of history and that is why he could bring his poetic imagination so close to it. The historian attached to facts may raise eyebrows at the imagined dialogue between Banda Bahadur and his son. But the poet based his work on some uncharted areas of history and gave them an added dimension, which moved the readers. It is the historian who initially showed him the way.

The tolerance that Rabindranath had for Banda Bahadur was not always shared by other Bengali authors. The four writers who subsequently made a relatively detailed analysis of Banda Bahadur's political role assumed a more critical attitude. The writings fall into two categories. First, where Banda Bahadur's role against the background of the evolution of Sikh history came under discussion. Second, those writings, which were confined to the life of Banda Bahadur. Here only those writers representing the first category would be considered. They were Dinendrakumar Roy, regular contributor to *Bharati*, and Saratkumar Roy, author of *SikhGuru o Sikhjati*.[8]

Neither of them was prepared to accept Banda Bahadur as a pure Sikh. But nowhere have they defined a 'true Sikh'. It seems that by a pure Sikh they meant Sikhs who sported the five Ks and the turban. According to them, Banda Bahadur belonged to the Bairagi order who were generally devoid of these symbols. In the post-Guru period, he was nonpareil for his valiant leadership. However, for the fact that Banda's military success was short-lived, he himself was responsible, they say. Banda was a skilful and enterprising man but Tat Khalsas and other Sikhs did not welcome his 'anti-religious' heroism and his effort to 'change' Sikhism on the lines of Hinduism. Besides, he lacked the magnanimity of his master—Guru Gobind Singh. Finally, his military policy was retaliatory and it generated deep hatred in the minds of the people of the occupied territories, hastening his downfall and tragic end.

The two other pieces devoted to Banda Bahadur do not expose him to such severe criticism. The first is by Basantakumar Banerjee of

[8] Dinendrakumar Roy, 'Sikh Sampradayer Adhahpatan', *Bharati*, Phalgun 1302 BS, pp. 617-18; Saratkumar Roy, *SikhGuru o Sikhjati*, pp. 58-60.

Chandannagar known for his aggressive Hindu nationalist viewpoint.[9] He wrote: 'Banda Bahadur's achievement in Indian history may not have been altogether glorious but it was far from insignificant. He gave up his life for the Sikhs but did not receive the honour he deserved. Sikhs do not hold him in genuine respect. That does not matter. He was a great man and did great things.'[10]

In support of his evaluation, he quoted in a footnote from the first volume of M'Gregor's *History of the Sikhs*. But he offers no reason for thinking that the Sikhs had no genuine respect for Banda. Perhaps the writer's Hindu bias can partially explain it. The article is called 'Bairagi Banda'. The author was probably under the impression that Banda Bahadur's outlook, which was initially moulded by the Hindu concept of renunciation, was in conflict with the Sikh philosophy of 'denunciation of renunciation'. Basantakumar shows that Banda Bahadur's aim was to avenge the wrongs done by the Mughals in the days of the tenth Guru. He did whatever he thought necessary to carry out the Guru's instructions and to put down the wrongdoers. 'He did all this with the spirit of a recluse.' It is true that later his differences with the Tat Khalsa Sikhs widened. But Basantakumar tried to trace the causes of discord to the different life-missions of the two, i.e. the Bairagis and the Tat Khalsas. He probably thought that the philosophy of renunciation advocated by Hinduism and the worldly attitude of the Sikhs could not co-exist and that led to the conflict between them. On the other hand, in all that Banda Bahadur did he was motivated by his loyalty to the Guru. It was for him that he gave up his earlier Bairagi lifestyle, shifted his area of activity from Nander in Maharashtra to Punjab and began a struggle for the Sikhs. Banerjee was all praise for Banda Bahadur even as he held the Sikhs primarily responsible for their differences with him.

Bhupendralal Datta published the last article on Banda Bahadur after a long interval in the periodical *Udayan* (1934).[11] He had long been sympathetic towards the contemporary national movement and the essay also made no secret of his bias in favour of armed struggle against state oppression and tyranny. His discussion was not confined

[9] Supra, pp. 158-60.

[10] Basantakumar Banerjee, 'Bairagi Banda', *Swadeshi*, Chaitra 1313 BS, p. 203.

[11] Bhupendralal Datta, 'Banda ki Sachcha Padshah?' *Udayan*, Paush 1341 BS, pp. 1129-37.

to the struggle between the Sikhs and the Mughals. Some other relevant and significant points were raised while reviewing Banda Bahadur's role. Did the Sikhs really recognize him as their Guru? To what extent was his movement mass based? What was the nature of his leadership towards the end? It is also necessary to mention the skill with which the author passed on from one point to another.

The essay begins with the great enthusiasm and ebullience with which Banda Bahadur's advent was welcomed by the Sikhs in Punjab. The writer accords him the honour and status of a Guru, denied to him by contemporary sources. The author had no difficulty in grasping the fact that the Sikh rebellion led by Banda enabled deprived peasants and the downtrodden of the society to rise against the oppressive Mughal administration. The author wrote: 'In a short span of time, he commanded an army of forty thousand men. Not all of them were Sikhs. The entire Sikh community including women and children was not so large. Non-Brahmins and lower caste people from the Hindu community as well as Jats gathered under the banner of the Sikh Guru and made a bid to assert their authority.' Datta argued that Banda Bahadur achieved success in the initial phase of the movement from the grass roots support which he mustered in Punjab. He captured Sarhind and set up his own administration there. But his destructive activities and his antipathy towards Muslims later on helped the Mughal offensive to suppress the movement ruthlessly. It also appears from the essay that Banda Bahadur's movement fell into two parts. He was virtually invincible in the first phase when he established his sway over the Sarhind region, where he built the Lohgarh fort. Afterwards, during the reign of the new Mughal emperor, Farrukhsiyar (1713-19), the Mughals launched a vigorous counter-offensive strong enough to break the back of Sikh resistance under Banda Bahadur.

The author describes the last days of Banda Bahadur in detail. He raises the question whether Banda Bahadur could be called a *Sachcha Padshah* in view of his early military success and the deep respect and support of the people that he received; he leaves it at that. However, in his fulsome sympathy for Banda Bahadur, he glorifies him to an extent never matched by any Sikh historian.[12] Banda Bahadur's leadership was timely but the writer never hinted at how

[12] Khushwant Singh, however, described him as *padsah*. See his *A History of the Sikhs*, vol. I, New Delhi reprint, 1997, p. 107. See also Irvine, *Later Mughals, 1707-20*, vol. I, p. 95.

he was responsible for the subsequent fragmentation of the Sikh community.

In his old age Tagore had yet another occasion to refer to the tradition of martyrdom of the days of Banda Bahadur. Here his focus was not on Banda Bahadur but on one of his followers, the young Nehal Singh. In his collection of poems 'Shesh Saptak', he visualized a young enchained Sikh hero, imprisoned by the Mughals while fighting under Banda Bahadur's besieged army in the Lohgarh fort in Gurdaspur district. Rabindranath does not cite any source.[13] Shortly before coming to write it, he had spent some time in Lahore talking to important Sikh leaders (1935), who expressed pain and anguish over one of Tagore's earlier writings on the last Sikh Guru. Tagore's dialogue with them, however, brought an amicable end to it.[14] After his return, Rabindranath wrote the poem. His recent impression about the Sikhs might have prompted him to write the poem on a theme of Sikh history after nearly three decades. It carried the message of sacrifice and martyrdom to a new dimension.

As in 'Bandibir', the story of the siege of Lohgarh fort constitutes the background of the poem. But Tagore added to it many interesting details missing in his earlier poems. We, thus, find how some of the Mughal military officials 'have planned to starve the handful of besieged Sikhs fighting under Banda Bahadur; all communications between the fort and the world outside have been snapped; the besieged soldiers are reduced to eating powdered bark and branches

[13] *Rabindra Rachanabali*, vol. III, Calcutta 1983, pp. 194-6. The central theme of the poem seems to be largely based on Irvine's account outlining Banda Bahadur's last days. Cf. *Later Mughals, 1707-20*, vol. I, p. 318. After his return from Lahore (1935), when Tagore was contemplating of writing another poem on the history of the Sikhs, Jadunath Sarkar might have enriched his understanding of the Sikh martyrdom tradition. On matters relating to Sikh history, Rabindranath's closeness to Sarkar may be pushed back to 1911, when Tagore's introductory note to Saratkumar Roy's *SikhGuru o Sikhjati* was translated by Jadunath. It was later on published in *Modern Review*, sparking off a bitter debate. Incidentally, Sarkar also edited both the volumes of Irvine's *Later Mughals*. For a further description of the scene of martyrdom, also see Harbans Singh, *The Heritage of the Sikhs*, New Delhi 1994, pp. 110-11.

[14] *Akali Patrika*, 15, 17 and 19 February 1935; *Amrita Bazar Patrika*, 19 February 1935; *Forward*, 21 February 1935; *Ananda Bazar Patrika*, 18, 20 and 22 February 1935; Prabhatkumar Mukherjee, *Rabindrajibani o Rabindrasahitya Prabesak*, vol. III, Calcutta 1397 BS, pp. 4-15.

of trees and raw meat'. Finally, the fort fell in the hands of the Mughals and the besieged Sikh soldiers met their end shouting 'Victory to the Guru'. The poet then turns to an evocation of the young Sikh hero Nehal Singh in chains: 'His is a fresh, serene countenance lit up by an inner light; it is as if some divine sculptor has carved out his eighteen-year-old body; he stands like a young cypress, straight but lissome and an exuberant vitality overflows his body and mind. With his hands bound, he is brought to the court of the victors. The executioner is ready with his sword.' At that moment, a letter reaches there ordering his release and pardon because he is not a 'Sikh' and he 'has been forced by the Sikhs to join them'. 'The young man's face is flushed in shame and grief; he cries, "I do not care for my life in exchange for falsehood, in truth is my final liberation, I am a Sikh".' The poet narrates the episode in a stark prose rhythm, highlighting the youthful vitality of Nehal Singh in sharp contrast to the 'destruction in the offing' and 'his unflickering adherence to Truth, which is the cardinal meaning of his faith'.[15]

The poem does not project the same old Tagore of 1909 fulminating against Sikh militarism and its road to 'naked aggrandizement'. Here he is once again a votary of the Sikh tradition of martyrdom. It perhaps makes the brief interlude of 1909 almost a closed chapter. The poem offers an opportunity of retracing Tagore's return to Sikh studies. Rabindranath had perhaps before him a role model for the Sikhs. Instead of becoming mere soldiers in the army, he expected, they would carry the spirit of divine truth and toleration as well as the message of love and sacrifice spread by the Sikh Gurus. Tagore hoped that the Sikhs would bear up against all pain and torture to uphold the higher ideals of humanity. He perhaps believed that there lay the message of all religions, Sikhism in particular. The sufferings of the non-violent Akali *satyagrahis* of Jaito and Nankana Sahib in the 1920s might have reconfirmed his faith about the Sikhs of history. They perhaps inspired him to go back to the days of the Sikh struggle of the eighteenth century. That also offered him an opportunity of valorizing once again the tradition of Sikh martyrdom and carrying it to a new height.

[15] Amalendu Bose, 'Tagore on the Sikhs', in Harbans Singh (ed.), *Perspectives on Guru Nanak*, Patiala 1990, p. 518. I have used Bose's English rendering of a portion of Tagore's poem. For a contemporary reference to the episode, see J.S. Grewal and Irfan Habib (eds.), *Sikh History from Persian Sources*, New Delhi 2001, pp. 158-9.

II

After Banda Bahadur's death, the Sikh struggle was temporarily without a front-ranking leader. Harassed by the Mughal attacks, we are told, the Sikhs then concentrated on defence. Martyrdom, however, continued unabated. These deeds accomplished in the early eighteenth century were often retold in the next century, and were, thus, kept alive in Sikh oral tradition.[16] Writings by the faithfuls whose narration depended on memory were liable to exaggeration, but they gave later historians an insight into their perception of the tradition of martyrdom. Many of these accounts of martyrdom reappear in Sikh studies in Bengali. Drawing on secondary sources in English, they discussed the sacrifices of Mani Singh (1673-1738), Mehtab Singh (? -1745), Hakikat Rai (1724-42), Taru Singh (? - 1743), etc., the writers repeatedly stressing the fact that they died under the 'oppressive machinery' of the Mughals to preserve the spirit of Sikhism. These were mostly written in the first half of the twentieth century at a time when anti-British feeling ran high. But there was also a communal angle in installing the Muslims in place of the British.

Chronologically, Bhai Mani Singh was the first of these martyrs. In her extremely popular compilation of biographies, *Sikher Balidan* (1905), Kumudini Bose[17] was perhaps the first to recall the martyrdom of Mani Singh. His life has been briefly related in one of the chapters of that small book. But the writer projected the characteristics of the man in bold relief.[18] 'An honest and religious Sikh

[16] Here Sinha's views may be noted: 'The Sikh point is not recorded in any contemporary or even semi-contemporary work. The . . . . stories of their [Sikhs'] achievements were known; old men would relate these to young men and in congregational gatherings the deeds of the old heroes were no doubt recited. In this way, a traditional history of the Sikhs continued to exist, though it was transformed, transmuted, added to or altered according to the sweet will of the reciter. . . . Under such circumstances, parochial patriotism and jingoism no doubt coloured events and even made victories out of defeats. . . . [A] Sikh point of view of Sikh history . . . is absolutely necessary.' *Rise of the Sikh Power*, pp. 123-4. Also see McMullen, *Religious Beliefs and Practices of the Sikhs*, p. 114.

[17] Supra, p. 130.

[18] Kumudini Bose, *Sikher Balidan*, pp. 22-6. For a similar view, Basantakumar Banerjee, 'Mani Singha', *Bharati*, Magh 1315 BS, pp. 451-7. See also Sinha, *Rise of the Sikh Power*, p. 4; Gopal Singh, *A History of the Sikh People*, p. 369.

much given to caring for others, he won the hearts of most people. His influence prompted many to embrace Sikhism at a time when Mughal invasion had assumed ferocity, to the consternation of the Mughal governor of Punjab.' According to Sikh tradition, his conflict with the Mughals was precipitated by his inability to pay the promised paltry sum of Rs. 5000/- to the provincial treasury. And that led to his death sentence. Nevertheless, Mani Singh's martyrdom powerfully affected the Sikh psyche.[19] The writer projected the incident from the point of view of a twentieth century Bengali woman committed to inspire the youth at the time of the Partition of Bengal. It was also the writer's intention to make her readers aware of the oppression of the medieval state machinery that made it impossible even for 'a quiet, self-absorbed and religious person to live in peace'.

Another prominent Sikh martyr of the age was Mehtab Singh, who was mentioned by Basantakumar Banerjee in one of his pieces on the Sikh heroes of the eighteenth century. The life-sketch appeared in *Bharati* (Chaitra 1315 BS). In his endeavour to protect the Golden Temple, Mehtab Singh was found storming the imperial citadel and courting death at the hands of the Mughals. Basantakumar's links with the militant nationalist movement prompted him to focus on the intrepidity of Mehtab Singh. The whole account is presented in a dramatic style with Mehtab Singh at the centre of the stage. The speed with which he launched an offensive against the eighteenth century Mughal administration reminds the readers of the contemporary radical politics of the Bomb and the Boycott of early twentieth century Bengal. Banerjee's eighteenth century Sikhs did not hesitate to attack the enemy in defence of their home and religion. Basantakumar's political bias thus once again came in the open and it was identified with the hopes and aspirations of Mehtab Singh.

The third martyr recalled was Hakikat Rai. The three essays written about him were all published in the first decade of the twentieth century (1905-10).[20] Of the authors, two are already known to us—

[19] Gurtej Singh, 'Bhai Mani Singh in Historical Perspective', *Proceedings, Punjab History Conference*, Third Session, Patiala 1968, pp. 120-7.

[20] Kumudini Bose, 'Hakikat Rai', *Sikher Balidan*, pp. 27-30; Basantakumar Banerjee, 'Hakikat Rai', *Aitihasik Chitra*, Baisakh 1316 BS, pp. 26-33; Bipinbehari Chakrabarty, 'Hakikat Rai', *Bharati*, Ashar 1317 BS, pp. 185-7.

Kumudini Bose and Basantakumar Banerjee. The third writer was Bipinbehari Chakrabarty with his only contribution ever to Bengali Sikh studies. All the three writers go into ecstasy over Hakikat Rai's martyrdom. But there are great disparities in the three accounts of the incident.

We may begin with the two better known and familiar writers. Kumudini Bose and Basantakumar Banerjee differ over Hakikat Rai's year of birth—there is a gap of more than 50 years.[21] Bose refers to Hakikat Rai as a devout Sikh, but says nothing about which group he belonged to. The second writer does not consider the Sikh community as a monolith. Taking into account the different sects, he describes Hakikat Rai as a Sikh Khatriya (Khatri?). It seems Hakikat was not a Khalsa of Guru Gobind Singh and the writer seems to hint at this deviation.

The problem takes a new turn with our third writer. Chakrabarty probably gathered a part of his information from Latif's *Lahore* and wrote the short biography.[22] He suggests that information on Hakikat Rai can be obtained from a village ballad written by a Punjabi poet called Aggar. What is surprising in his essay is that he calls Hakikat Rai a Hindu and not even a Khatri Sikh. When these brief sketches were being written, a conflict raged about the dividing line between Hindus and Sikhs, causing considerable political uneasiness in Punjab,[23] but not affecting Bengali Sikh studies. In this

[21] These differences in the writings of Kumudini Bose and Basantakumar Banerjee strike the reader. Again, both of them were reticent about their sources. It appears that Kumudini was not correct about Hakikat Rai's year of birth and one wonders why the same error recurs in the different editions of *Sikher Balidan*.

[22] Bipinbehari Chakrabarty did not mention his sources, either. It seems he got some information from S.M. Latif's *Lahore—Its History, Architectural Remains and Antiquities,* Lahore 1892. For the source of the anecdote, see Sant Singh Sekhon and Kartar Singh Duggal, *A History of Punjabi Literature,* New Delhi 1992, p. 93.

[23] One may get an impression of the embittered Hindu-Sikh relationship in Punjab from the following examples. A few Punjabi Hindu authors (e.g. Bhai Parmanand, Santram and others writing in Hindi) suggested that Banda Bahadur was a world-renouncing (Bairagi) Hindu and they emphatically claimed that Hindus and Sikhs belonged to the same religious tradition. Bairagi Banda was generally projected as a martyr of their (Hindu) community. It is also argued by many that on hearing about the growing valour of the Keshadhari Sikhs, they increasingly invested Hakikat Rai with a Sehajdhari/Hindu identity. On the other hand, Ganda Singh's Banda is a member of the Khalsa order with usual symbols and ideals. Again in the first half of the twentieth century, a section of Punjabi (Hindu) authors could not make up their mind as to what roles to assign to the different sub-sects in defining Sikhism. Also

part of India, Hindu and Sikh were considered almost synonymous words. All Bengali writers were not equally interested in discerning the exact line of demarcation between a Hindu and a Sikh then fiercely debated in Punjab. Since Hinduism was making great strides in eastern India, Bengali Hindu writers and readers hardly faced any serious dissent in incorporating the Sikhs within the fold of Hinduism.

The martyr who was best known to the Bengali readership was perhaps Bhai Taru Singh, immortalized by Tagore as Toru Singh in his poem 'Prarthanateeta Dan' (1899).[24] It is a sixteen-line poem where through dialogue, he showed how Taru Singh prepared for martyrdom. The poet said it with an economy of words. In his account, Tagore did not indicate where Taru Singh was first imprisoned nor did he deal with many other allied and important issues. But in no way could this omission belittle the significance of the poem, with Tagore stressing Taru Singh's silent self-sacrifice in defence of his religion, and how he spurned the 'cruel-mercy' of the Mughal power. That was the focus of the poem. The poem also presents two conflicting forces—the Mughal state terror on one side and a common man's strength of character and natural dignity on the other side asserting itself in the ultimate gesture of defiance. Naturally, in the clash between the two, Rabindranath was in sympathy with the weak, oppressed and ordinary folk. Taru Singh belonged to the second group. In a very limited number of words, Rabindranath presented a character full of human dignity—that of a martyr standing against state oppression and tyranny.

Rabindranath wrote about Taru Singh's preparation for martyrdom in a brief and poignant style. But Kumudini Bose and Basanta-

---

see *Punjab Advocate* (Mianwali) and *Akhbar-i-Am* (Lahore) of February 1911, *Selections from the Punjab Native Newspapers Report*, 1911, p. 159; Narang, *Transformation of Sikhism*, pp. 57-9. For the Punjabi Hindus' 'growing anxiety' in the period, see Indu Banga, 'Emergence of Hindu Consciousness in Colonial Punjab', in P.C. Chatterjee (ed.), *Self-Images: Identity and Nationality*, Shimla 1989, pp. 200-17.

[24] There are perhaps two minor factual errors in Rabindranath's poem. According to him, the Pathans imprisoned Taru Singh. But it was the Turani governor, Abdus Samad Khan who took him prisoner. Turani is not synonymous with Pathan. Secondly, instead of Suhridganj as suggested by Tagore, the place came to be known as Sahidganj in Lahore.

kumar Banerjee related the incident on a broader canvas.[25] Both writers spoke about how he looked after the Sikhs with compassion and love. He 'offered food to travellers in his home which became a place of pilgrimage for hundreds of Sikhs'. The Mughals looked upon him as 'a rebel, robber and rogue', even as one committing 'treason'. He was arrested and given an option either to embrace Islam or to court death. Taru Singh accepted the second and refused to be converted. After prolonged torture, he was put to death. The authors had no doubt that Taru Singh's tragic death exacerbated relations between the Mughals and the Sikhs in the first half of the eighteenth century. These two essays, however, could not carry the message of martyrdom of Taru Singh to the level earlier attained by Tagore in his 'Prarthanateeta Dan'.

These sketches in poetry and prose invoking the eighteenth century Sikh martyrdom tradition no doubt bring us close to the contemporary Bengal militant politics since the days of Partition. These writings sometimes also carried a message of deep hatred against the Muslims. A section of the educated Bengali Hindu middle class psyche of the period moved in a vicious circle often dictated by communal considerations. It continued to gather strength from the rising tide of the separate electoral politics popularized by the Act of 1909.

III

Outside the pale of martyrdom, an important chapter of Sikh studies in the post-Guru era is that of the Lion of Punjab, Ranjit Singh. Colonial rule and servitude seemed to have produced a sense of humiliation that the writers sometimes tried to efface by projecting an exaggerated view of the political success of the maharaja. In the writings of many Hindu authors, there is a pronounced moral support for the Sikh monarch. Not that the maharaja was never criticized. The combination of praise and censure for the maharaja from these writers fascinated Bengali readers. These works fall into various categories. For convenience, we will begin with those aiming at historical evaluations of Ranjit Singh.

[25] Kumudini Bose, 'Toru Singha', *Sikher Balidan*, pp. 31-7; Basantakumar Banerjee, 'Toru Singha', *Bharati*, Phalgun 1315 BS, pp. 505-8. Basantakumar Banerjee also described the martyrdom of Subeg Singh in *Bharati*, Kartik 1315 BS, pp. 336-9.

The first full-length account of Ranjit Singh's reign was published (1861) within 12 years of the annexation of Punjab (1849). The writer was one of the textbook writers of the day and taught at the Hooghly Normal School. His name was Brahmamohan Mullick (1832-?).[26] The biographer is reticent about his source. By this time the book *Origin of the Sikh Power in the Punjab and Political Life of Maharaja Ranjit Singh* (1834) by Prinsep had received considerable attention. The influence of Prinsep is only too obvious in Mullick's study. In some places, the divisions into chapters and the sequence of subjects are straight out of Prinsep. Brahmamohan's work pleased the authorities and his study was prescribed for schools.

The book under discussion describes the political history of Punjab during the time of Ranjit Singh. It is in eight chapters. The first chapter begins with a brief reference to the Sikhs as they were at the time of their Gurus. This we do not come across in the volume of Prinsep.[27] The Sikh monarch, however, appears in the second chapter and here Mullick gradually comes closer to the British administrator-historian. The chapter talks about his birth, genealogy, accession and expansion of Ranjit's sway up to the west bank of the Ravi till 1804. The third chapter is relatively long and that is partially because it deals with the growth of Anglo-Sikh relations till 1809. The next chapter is concerned with the growing military strength of Ranjit Singh in north and west Punjab, with a detailed account of Ranjit Singh's victorics over Kashmir, Multan, Peshawar, and his struggle with the Afghans on the right bank of the Indus. The last chapter portrays the king as a conqueror and an administrator.

The writer does not have too high an opinion of Ranjit Singh. Here he seems to have followed in the footsteps of Prinsep. Like Prinsep, he has been quite enthusiastic about the maharaja's common sense, valour, memory and military talent. Following Prinsep, Brahmamohan also found the Sikh monarch cunning, selfish,

[26] Brahmamohan Mullick was a distinguished student of Hindu College. He began his career as a Deputy Inspector of Schools and earned considerable esteem for his work. In his writings he made no secret of his loyalty to British rule. See also Harimohan Mukherjee, *Bangabhashar Lekhak*, vol. I, Calcutta 1311 BS, pp. 696-7; Subalkumar Mitra (ed.), *Saral Bangla Abhidhan*, Calcutta 1923, p. 979; Bipinbehari Gupta, *Puratan Prasanga*, vol. II, Calcutta 1330 BS, p. 58.

[27] Brahmamohan Mullick, *Maharaja Ranjit Singher Jiban Brittanta*, Hooghly 1919 Bikrami, pp. 1-15. Earlier, Rajendralal Mitra briefly referred to the Sikh maharaja in his penny magazine *Bibidhartha Sangraha* (1852).

obsessed with sex and dissolute. In the opinion of Brahmamohan, 'seizing other people's kingdoms and plunder were the principal mission of the maharaja's life'.

Needless to say, Brahmamohan's ruthless assessment was not altogether based on any critical evaluation of the contemporary primary sources. Recent studies show that the kingdom was not farmed out among the rentiers as suggested by Mullick. Their powers of collecting rent were also limited. Besides, official policy sometimes bypassed the rentiers and gave encouragement direct to hard-working peasants to increase the area of their arable land. The maharaja often sent instructions to the *kardars* to keep a watch over the moneylenders so that they could not harass the cultivators. Such instances can be quoted from the history of the period. As Mullick was loyal to the colonial rule, he regarded Prinsep's book as gospel truth. Like Prinsep, he was often trenchant in his criticism of the Sikh monarch's activities. However, the Bengali authors of the late nineteenth and early twentieth centuries portrayed the virtues of the Sikh monarch in a different manner. Brahmamohan's writing showed his attachment to colonial rule on one hand and on the other, it betrayed his contempt for someone like the pre-colonial Ranjit Singh. He laid stress on the foibles of the Sikh monarch's character and his exploitative administration. Subsequently, when the nationalist authors attempted a changed evaluation of the maharaja, they gave him a role in the saga of national awakening, making Mullick's assessment look partial and faulty. They never referred to Brahmamohan in their writings, which does indicate his comparative lack of importance in the evolution of Bengali Sikh studies of the period.

Towards the end of the nineteenth century when national consciousness had achieved a distinct stage of development, Bengali Sikh studies characterized Ranjit Singh's rule as a memorable chapter of Indian history, providing cogent answers to the snipping of writers like Brahmamohan Mullick and British administrator-historians like Henry Prinsep. The authors got entangled in a debate with these writers in their attempt to depict Ranjit Singh as an ideal ruler. Their scheme of history drove them in a different direction.

One of the pathmakers was Bankimchandra the essayist. He did not discuss Ranjit Singh separately. Nor did he involve himself in Sikh studies for that matter. While looking for an answer to the question as to whether there was any 'national feeling' in India before British rule, he referred to the history of the Sikhs and wrote a short paragraph on the Khalsa military power under Ranjit Singh.[28] He was, however, silent on the vast range of Sikh history outside that period. Besides, Bankimchandra did not make a distinction between Hindus and Sikhs. According to him, Ranjit Singh with his magic powers tied the Hindus in a national bond. It 'enabled Hindu acquisition of a part of the territories belonging to the Pathans'. In his opinion, this bond of national unity was otherwise often missing among the Hindus. In this sense Ranjit Singh's reign represents a chapter of 'Hindu pride' in search of India's 'glorious past'. Bankimchandra's projection of the Khalsa Raj thus 'gave a rational ground for hope' to his readers. There is hardly any doubt that it sought to provide an answer to the contemporary 'experience of subjection' and 'looked forward to history for its roots of power'.[29]

The paragraph mentioned above shows that *Hindutva* dominated Bankim's treatment of the Sikh past. The same attitude can be seen in Rajanikanta Gupta's works. Rajanikanta was more intimately connected with Sikh studies and so his presentation occupied a larger space than Bankim's.[30] Gupta did not merely write about Ranjit Singh's military successes. He also referred to the Sikh monarch's 'strength of character, courage, patronage of learning and concern for his subjects'. But the emphasis was on his military achievements peaking with long, sanguinary battle with the Pathans on the north-west frontier. Prinsep wrote about the 'acts of cruelty' perpetrated by Ranjit Singh in winning these battles, but Rajanikanta had given them a go-by. He was effusive over the victory of Ranjit Singh and his Akali forces. On the other hand, the Pathans who had opposed Ranjit Singh's army there, were labelled as 'bigots', 'prone to rioting' and motivated by 'fires of religious animosity'. Rajanikanta thus not only identified himself with the victories of the Khalsa Raj but also made no secret of his hatred of its Muslim adversaries.[31]

[28] Bankimchandra Chatterjee, 'Bharat-Kalanka: Bharatbarsha Paradhin Kena', *Bibidha Prabandha* , vols. I-II, Calcutta reprint, 1346 BS, p. 144.

[29] Cf. Partha Chatterjee, 'Claims on the Past: The Genealogy of Modern Historiography in Bengal', in David Arnold and David Hardiman (eds.), *Subaltern Studies VIII: Writings on South Asian History and Society*, Delhi 1994, p. 3.

[30] Supra, pp. 133-4, 145. Rajanikanta Gupta's essay on Ranjit Singh was included in *Beermahima,* Calcutta 1292 BS, pp. 71-84.

[31] Gupta, *Beermahima*, p. 93. See also his *Sikh*, p. 23. For the implications of these anti-Muslim phrases, see Gyanendra Pandey, 'The Colonial Construction of

In the first half of the twentieth century, the children's writer Jogendranath Gupta (1883-1965) also described Ranjit Singh as a Hindu warrior. It was the sixth book in the three-anna series of national biographies meant for teenagers. Accordingly, it is not big in size and the language is lucid and attractive. He does not appear to have worked very hard to collect materials. He has, of course, said nothing about his sources. There is no doubt that he had read Rajanikanta's writings meticulously. He made the book all the more attractive to his readers with necessary quotes from Rabindranath's poems about the Sikhs.

In the first ten pages, the writer spoke of the militarization of the Sikhs as a 'reaction against Mughal tyranny' and thereafter proceeded to present the genealogy of Ranjit Singh. In his opinion, the Lion of Punjab was not a man who had jettisoned his idealism. On the contrary, he was inspired by the sacrifices performed by the Indian heroes of the past. The writer kept Ranjit Singh's image untarnished avoiding references to the foibles of his character. His Sikh hero had to fight since his childhood to establish himself and had quite early resolved to save his 'land from the Muslims' and 'set up a Hindu kingdom'. So the major battles he fought were with the Muslims. His successive victories were therefore 'a row of feathers in the Hindu cap'. They also constituted, as the author wrote, 'a glorious chapter' in Indian history.[32]

To Jogendranath, Sikh, Hindu and Indian nationalism were synonymous words. Ranjit Singh was not merely shorn of a separate Sikh identity. He assumed the mantle of an aggrandizing Hindu hero representing Indian nationalism. Having read the book, young readers would develop great contempt for the group which was anti-Ranjit Singh. The treaty of Amritsar (1809) created a major obstacle in extending his empire to the east of the Sutlej. That would not upset the readers so much. On the other hand, the 'bloody battles' with the Afghans that the Sikh monarch fought relentlessly in the north-west and the south-west would create an anti-Muslim feeling among his readership. Instead of highlighting the manifold British aggressive designs beyond the Sutlej, Jogendranath perhaps unwittingly deepened the communal divide. Incidentally, the monograph came

---

Communalism: British Writings on Banaras in the Nineteenth Century', in Ranajit Guha (ed.), *Subaltern Studies VI: Writings on South Asian History and Society,* Delhi 1989, p. 168.

[32] Jogendranath Gupta, *Ranjit Singha,* Calcutta 1330 BS, pp. 8, 14, 16, 17, 19.

out (1923) in the wake of the Non-cooperation Movement when the forces of communalism had once again been dominating the national politics. The biographer no doubt responded to their demands.

IV

Sikh studies in Bengali did not just stop at showering effusive praise on Ranjit Singh for his role as 'an epoch-making Hindu hero', some of them looked at Ranjit Singh from a different angle. First, we will mention two essays, both of them virtually translations from the writings of two British administrator-historians. Second, we will try to assess the section on Ranjit Singh in the total corpus of Sikh studies in Bengali done by Saratkumar Roy of Santiniketan.

The first essayist is Dinendrakumar Roy, whose article appeared in the periodical *Janmabhumi* more than a hundred years ago. It does not focus on the Sikh maharaja but highlights the other high and mighty heroes holding responsible positions at his Khalsa darbar. Dinendrakumar's writing can be divided into two unequal halves. The essay is of eleven pages. In the first two pages he has recounted the political success of the maharaja. His discussion is based on material garnered from Lepel Griffin's *Ranjit Singh*. Griffin had listed about fifteen courtiers of various ranks, viz., Fakir Azizuddin, Jamadar Khushal Singh, Raja Tej Singh, Diwan Dinanath, Bhai Ram Singh, Sardar Lehna Singh, etc. Dinendranath dittoed it.[33]

Dinendrakumar Roy commanded respect in the evolution of Sikh studies in Bengali. He collected necessary materials with a spirit of dedication and put forward his views on a number of areas of Sikh studies quite forcefully. However, the imitation of Griffin in the article under review raises a few questions. We should remember that the essay in *Janmabhumi* marked Dinendrakumar's debut in Sikh studies. The first effort was not as brilliant and powerful as his later essays and biographical sketches. To present interesting facts about the Sikhs to readers in his mother tongue, he did not hesitate to borrow them from a British administrator-historian. That was probably his objective at the beginning. But never again did he resort to such blind imitation.

33 For a comparative study, see Dinendrakumar Roy, 'Ranjit Singher Darbar', *Janmabhumi*, Phalgun 1301 BS, pp. 135-8; Griffin, *Ranjit Singh*, pp. 117-31.

Another instance of such blind imitation can be seen in *Aitihasik Chitra* (1311 BS). The writer was Bodhisattwa Sen. His name does not come up again in Bengali Sikh studies. He tried to spell out the relation between Ranjit Singh and the British and in doing so, unhesitatingly borrowed materials from the recently published book, Thorburn's *The Punjab in Peace and War* (1904). He mentioned the author's name in a footnote but not the name of the book.[34] No Bengali writer considered him a trustworthy guide for interpreting Anglo-Sikh relations under Ranjit Singh. Thorburn wrote his chapter on Ranjit Singh in a light vein, with a lot of drama thrown in, and allowed many bazaar gossips to creep in. It would appear that Bodhisattwa Sen was not very familiar with the source materials dealing with the reign of Ranjit Singh and in his ignorance, attached undue importance to Thorburn's recently published volume.

The treaty of Amritsar (1809) was the foundation-stone of the relations between the British and the Sikh darbar. Long before Thorburn published his book, authorities like Prinsep and Cunningham had discussed the subject. Our writer passed them by and used Thorburn as his only source, and many important issues relevant to the subject were left out. Irrelevancies came in which do not admit of rational explanation. One such example is the long description of the funeral rites after Ranjit Singh's death. The writer does not explain why he has put it in. May be, it is because Thorburn's book had just come out and to market his essay in a hurry, Sen crammed in the juicy anecdotes, even if irrelevant. But the information we get about Ranjit Singh and the British via Thorburn from 'Ranjit Singha o Ingraj' does not throw light on the subject and it diverts us from the main theme.

Saratkumar Roy's portrayal of Ranjit Singh took up almost one-third of his monograph, *SikhGuru o Sikhjati*.[35] The book is by and large indicative of the author's familiarity with the sources in English. Roy did not hesitate to call the period 'a glorious chapter in Sikh history'. He said that though Ranjit Singh was, strictly speaking, an illiterate, who derived a wealth of knowledge in a hard way from the

[34] Bodhisattwa Sen, 'Ranjit Singha o Ingraj', *Aitihasik Chitra*, Ashwin 1311 BS, pp. 8-11; Kartik 1311 BS, pp. 135-8; Agrahayan 1311 BS, pp. 184-7; Paush 1311 BS, pp. 215-22; S.S. Thorburn, *The Punjab in Peace and War*, New Delhi reprint, 1985, pp. 1-25.

[35] Saratkumar Roy's book is 165 pages, the Sikh maharaja takes up 56 pages.

school of nature and equipped himself to preside over a vast empire. The strength of his character, farsightedness and ability to size up fellow human beings made him the natural leader of the Sikhs.

Saratkumar picked out three areas of the Sikh monarch's life history to evaluate his achievements. First, he relates Ranjit's accession to the throne and conquests that put an end to the internal dissensions of the *misls* age. Besides, the writ of the Lahore darbar ran over the territory stretching from the Sutlej on the east to Attock on the west. As a result, the Sikhs for the first time had the distinction of establishing a vast, independent state. He discussed Ranjit Singh's triumph over the Afghans but he neither glorified it nor belittled it by relating it in any way to the greatness of *Hindutva*. Secondly, Saratkumar examined the Sikh maharaja's military reforms with adequate importance. The writer felt that Ranjit's role was tailored to suit contemporary needs and demands. Lastly, while explaining Ranjit Singh's friendly relations with the British, the author never thought that the treaty of Amritsar signalled a final victory or defeat for the Sikhs. He did not consider the question important. But the chapter leaves one in no doubt that in the eyes of the author, the Anglo-Sikh amity was dictated by shrewd political considerations on both sides.

Saratkumar's evaluation of Ranjit Singh was based on a more solid ground of fact and was couched in more articulate language than the writings of the others. A Hindu bias or a proneness to hero-worshipping did not cloud his vision. On the other hand, the Lion of Punjab's moral foibles did not make him condemn the entire Sikh community as Brahmamohan Mullick had done, nor did he marginalize them to keep the maharaja's image unsullied, as did Jogendranath Gupta. Saratkumar tried to present Ranjit Singh with his warts and all.

V

Another category of writings generally represented Ranjit Singh as an imbodiment of debased humanity. This is the impression conveyed by a body of writing that includes a short paragraph of a longer essay or sections of texts where the Sikh monarch is briefly mentioned in the context of other developments of medieval Indian history. Generally speaking, the writers did not find anything good or praiseworthy in the personality of the maharaja. They made trenchant criticism not merely of the Sikh monarch's policy of annexation but also of his moral failings. He was often accused of oppressing the Muslims of his kingdom. Here we will first refer to Rabindranath's critical remarks. Then we will put together significant extracts from the writings of Bengali Muslims available in different periodicals.

As mentioned earlier, Rabindranath did not write any independent essay on Ranjit Singh. The references are somewhat oblique and can be found in comparisons with Shivaji or Guru Gobind Singh. In the essay under discussion the tenth Guru has been put in the dock (1909), with the poet showering the entire blame for the all-round decline of the Sikh community on the tenth Guru and then pointing an accusing finger at the maharaja:

> By fair means or foul Ranjit Singha formed a well-knit Sikh community only to further his own selfish designs. He did not engender in them [Sikhs] any great feeling which could hold them together after his death. . . . His love of pleasure was boundless. However, he achieved success. . . . But what did he leave behind for the Sikhs? Disunity, distrust and indiscipline.[36]

But despite all this criticism, he apparently spared him from one accusation for the time being : 'A word of praise for him. Nothing could prevent him from achieving what he wanted. In one respect he controlled his indomitable ambition. He did not cross the crimson line, which demarcated the British empire.'

Rabindranath's critical remarks need to be tested in the light of other sources of history. While reviewing the issue, it is necessary to refer to two other related points. First, before recording these bitter observations, he had made a brief reference to Ranjit Singh in his 'Sikh-Swadhinata' (1885), where the poet perhaps deliberately reserved his judgements about the maharaja's reign. But as the political backdrop changed, so did Rabindranath's attitude to Ranjit Singh. Second, Rabindranath's harsh comments have been with us for over 90 years. His strong observations (1909) about the tenth Guru raised a bitter controversy. At that time nobody reviewed

[36] Tagore, 'Shivaji o Guru Gobinda Singha', *Rabindra Rachanabali*, vol. XV, pp. 525-7. Tagore's observations had a deep impact on Sikh studies in the city of Calcutta. Sinha seems to have unconsciously followed them while writing the history of Ranjit Singh. According to him, the Sikh monarch was 'a supreme example of an intellect without a conscience. He . . . did not breathe into the hearts of his people any noble sentiment that would have held them together after his death.' *Ranjit Singh*, p. 190.

seriously his digs at Ranjit Singh. Should we continue to accept the poet's censure of the maharaja?

Apparently, silence may mean endorsement. But the tenth Guru was the actual target of the poet's tirades. Perhaps scholars have been too preoccupied with the refutation of these criticisms to take cognizance of the incidental attack on Ranjit Singh. Besides, the observations that the poet made about the maharaja's loose morals cannot altogether be dismissed as untrue. But there is a need to re-examine the other part of the statement. Did the maharaja wholly build up the Khalsa Raj 'by hook or by crook' and maintain the same with his 'irresistible cunning'? A few recent studies on the reign of Ranjit Singh show that the Khalsa state apparatus drew wide support and endorsement from the Sikhs, Hindus and Muslims of Punjab.[37] They also highlight the administrative patronage behind improvement in agriculture, development of trade, expansion of commercial network and rapid urbanization in the *manjha* area. British administrator-historians hardly showed any serious interest in identifying these areas of economic development. The severe criticism levelled by Lepel Griffin against Ranjit Singh might have exercised an indirect influence on Tagore's assessment.[38]

Occasional references to the maharaja in the *Dobhasi Bangla* generally convey an unsympathetic and hostile attitude to Ranjit Singh in the nineteenth century.[39] From the third decade of the nineteenth century

[37] For the popular support towards the maharaja's rule, see J.S. Grewal, *The Reign of Maharaja Ranjit Singh: Structure of Power, Economy and Society,* Patiala 1981; Indu Banga, 'The Ruling Class in the Kingdom of Lahore', *Journal of Regional History*, Annual Number 1982, p. 23.

[38] For Lepel Griffin's harsh comments about the Sikh monarch, see *Ranjit Singh*, pp. 91-5, 219. But Tagore did not hold Lepel Griffin in high esteem. Cf. his essay written in 1299 BS, 'Sir Lepel Griffin', *Rabindra Rachanabali,* vol. XIII, pp. 291-2. Tagore, however, wrote these bitter words about Ranjit Singh in his introduction to Saratkumar Roy's book *SikhGuru o Sikhjati* (1909). Roy extensively used Griffin's *Ranjit Singh*. Perhaps it might have partly contributed to the formulation of Tagore's views regarding the Sikh monarch. Further, in the same essay (1909) Tagore was extremely bitter about the Sikh military tradition in general. Here he criticized Guru Gobind Singh as well as Ranjit Singh. But Tagore's observations in the essay, as we have already seen, are not all based on critical analysis of historical evidence. Supra, pp. 151-2.

[39] Kaji Abdul Mannan comments on the subject: 'Muhammad Enamul Haq wrote his book, *Muslim Bangla Sahitya* in 1957. In this book he observes: "Dobhasi Bangla or Musalmani Bangla is a creation of the British period. It was the dialect of little

Ranjit Singh's aggressive policy in the north-west led to a long-drawn struggle with the Pathans. At the same time, the Wahabi Movement under the leadership of Syed Ahmad Barelvi hit Punjab and exacerbated Sikh-Pathan relations. The Wahabis had numerous complaints against the Sikhs. So they wanted to tackle their enemy as sternly as they could.[40] To strengthen their *jihad* against the Sikhs, the Wahabis reached out to their fellow-religionists in eastern India and mobilized funds as well as crusaders. The Farazi movement was on in Bengal under Titu Mir (1782-1831), and Muslim peasants of Bengal extended their help and sympathy to the anti-Sikh Wahabis faraway in Punjab. But in 1831, at the battle of Balakote, Syed Ahmad was defeated and slain, bringing Wahabi hostilities to the Sikh State in Punjab to a halt. But even after the signal defeat on the battleground, Bengali Muslims did not forget the idealism of the Wahabi Movement. The following quote shows how ardent was their desire to fight with the Sikhs in the world of imagination:

> If Allah desires, brother, I will go to Lahore,
> Carry on a *jihad* against the Sikhs there,
> If I win, I will be *gazi* and if I lose, a *sahid*,
> I will die but God is imperishable.[41]

These lines suggest the intensity of the anti-Sikh feeling of the

---

educated or illiterate Muslims of lower Bengal who were influenced by the Ohabi movement. . . . Titumir (1831) and Dudhu Mia (1847) were residents of this area. Their movement for religious reform, called the Ohabi and Faraeyegi movements respectively, influenced this area. . . . The continued Hindu hostility to Muslims especially in lower Bengal filled their language with more and more Persian and Urdu words. This language gained popularity through Ohabi and Faraeyegi movements and a good deal of religious literature was produced in it".' *The Emergence and Development of Dobhashi Literature in Bengal upto 1855 A.D.*, Dacca 1974, p. 154; Sukumar Sen, *Islami Bangla,*Calcutta 1400 BS, pp. 148-200.

[40] For a detailed discussion, see Anisuzzaman, *Muslim Manas o Bangla Sahitya,* Dhaka 1378 BS, pp. 44 -7.

[41] It is a *puthi payar* Abul Mansur Ahmed used to recite on his way to his village school at Dhanikhola. His elder brother (known as *Gajisaheb*) went into *jihad* against the Sikhs in his late teens. Dhanikhola was at that time a centre of the Wahabi Movement. Their house was a small gym. The Mansurs learnt from 'their patrons in childhood that Lahore was an area to the far west of Hindusthan'. And 'Sikhs were the enemies of Allah. They were even worse than Hindus were. The English believed in God, they worshipped the prophet Jesus. Not the Sikhs'. Abul Mansur Ahmed, *Amar Dekha Rajnitir Panchas Bachhar,* Dhaka 1967, p. 7. About Abul Mansur Ahmed, see Murshid, *The Sacred and the Secular: Bengal Muslim Discourses* 1871- 77, pp. 124, 131, 139.

Wahabis in Bengal towards the second half of the nineteenth century.[42] What surprises us is that while the military conflict between the Pathans and Sikhs partly stimulated the composition of these anti-Sikh couplets, Rajanikanta Gupta and Jogendranath Gupta in their Sikh studies regarded the same bloody conflict as a 'glorious chapter' of 'Hindu achievements'. It only goes to show how diametrically opposed were a section of Bengali Hindus and Bengali Muslims in their understanding of the history of the Sikhs. A significant area of Sikh studies in Bengali was thus dominated by religious sectarianism. It can also be mentioned that communal feelings had made a deep foray into Sikh studies by the last quarter of the nineteenth century and its impact continued even in the first half of the next century.

From the beginning of the twentieth century, Bengali Muslim politics increasingly leaned on the colonial government for protection against the Hindu dominance and distanced itself from the national movement led by the Indian National Congress.[43] Simultaneously, Muslim writings on medieval Indian history in Bengali also took a different stance from the works produced by Bengali Hindus. The fiction, plays, etc., written by Hindu Bengalis about the reign of Ranjit Singh often showed great magnanimity about his failings. As a result, the monarch came to influence the Bengali Hindu mind powerfully as a 'generous', 'fair-minded', 'patriotic person'. But the image did not carry any credibility with educated Bengali Muslim authors, who perceived the maharaja as 'a naked aggressor' and 'an epitome of religious intolerance'. Some of them welcomed the British as they had 'protected Muslims from the hands of Maratha marauders and Sikh demons'.[44] Here is an extract, which is an instance of the Bengali Muslim writers' view of Ranjit Singh:

In the province of Punjab in north-western India, in the middle of the three Hindu states of Patiala, Nabha and Jhind, a Muslim principality was formed with eighty-six villages in the middle of the fifteenth century. It is known as the state of Malerkotla. In the nineteenth century, Ranjit Singh, blind of

[42] About Syed Ahmad Barelvi's allegations against the Sikhs, see Amalendu De, *Bangali Budhhijibi o Bichhinnatabad,* Calcutta 1987, p. 17.

[43] On Bengal Muslim politics of the time, see Chandiprasad Sarkar, *The Bengali Muslims: A Study of their Politicisation 1912-29*, Calcutta 1991.

[44] 'Islam Pracharak', Sraban-Bhadra 1310 BS, quoted in Wakil Ahmed, *Unish Shataker Bangali Musalmaner Chinta-Chetanar Dhara*, vol. I, Dhaka 1983, p. 452.

one eye, tried hard to liquidate the Muslim state. But thanks to God almighty, all his efforts were in vain.[45]

Here is another instance:

Prompted by political self-interest, Shivaji, Sambhaji, Shahji and especially Ranjit Singh of Punjab formed a Hindu confederacy to devastate mosques, castles and *majhars*. Compared with that, the demolition of temples by Mahmud, Aurangzeb and Tipu Sultan was insignificant.[46]

Neither of the paragraphs conveys anything praiseworthy about Ranjit Singh. The Sikh monarch also provoked bitter comments for various other reasons. He was accused of treating Sultan Shah Shuja of Afghanistan very shabbily and appropriating the Kohinoor from him. In the territories occupied by him, it is alleged that he did not allow his Muslim subjects full freedom to perform daily prayers. Perhaps that is partly why the defeat of the Khalsa in the Sikh wars and the annexation of Punjab by the British relieved these writers of much of their anxiety. Incidentally, it may be noted that Bengali Muslim authors' aversion to Ranjit Singh goes hand in hand with their enthusiasm for Guru Nanak. These two distinct trends of their perception about two separate chapters of Sikh history underline how their reactions were dictated by certain specific and immediate needs of the community. A significant portion of this literature was no doubt a result of their 'search for an identity' since the last quarter of the nineteenth century. The Muslim articulation was no doubt a complex response to the aggressive Hindu nationalism of the period and it 'concentrated more on polemics than on satisfying the needs of literary taste'.[47] It was quite varied and sometimes conflicting in character, reflecting the fragmented nature of their social consciousness under colonial rule.

VI

Two novels and a play were written about the reign of Ranjit Singh, giving Sikh studies in Bengali yet another distinction. The first of these creative efforts was made in the 1890s. By the time Sikh studies

[45] Abdul Hakim Khan, 'Malerkotla Rajya', *Masik Mohammadi*, Ashwin 1339 BS, pp, 841-2.

[46] Eslambadi, 'Musalman Amaley Hindur Adhikar', *Al-Eslam*, Kartik 1322 BS, p. 393.

[47] Mohammad Shah, *In Search of an Identity: Bengali Muslims 1880-1940*, Calcutta 1996, pp. 53-4.

in eastern India had made considerable progress. The play, which came last, was written and staged towards the closing phase of the nationalist movement when Calcutta was scarred by riots in the 1940s. Fifty years, thus, separate the first novel from the play. The ethos and the environs were naturally shown differently.

Chronologically, the first place goes to the celebrated writer and dramatist Manomohan Bose (1831-1912), who was the author of *Duleen*,[48] a novel set in the reign of Ranjit Singh. When Manomohan started writing the novel, Bankimchandra was at the peak of his fame. It is possible that the great master influenced Manomohan. Manomohan's distinction lies in the fact that unlike other novelists of the time, he did not choose the more popular Rajput and Maratha histories as his backdrop. Instead he brought to his readers a glimpse of the world of the Sikhs under Ranjit Singh. He thus initiated his journey:

> This is the main objective. . . . The immensely powerful Ranjit Singha was to all intents and purposes the last independent king of India. . . . I intended to focus on his highly talented achievements, his administration, courtly and social codes of conduct. At the same time I sought to point out why his empire did not last, why his death meant its eclipse, what were the systematic drawbacks. . . . I have. . . . praised the good aspects but that has not blinded me to the shortcomings.[49]

Manomohan has thus claimed to be 'objective' while following the format and using the materials of Henry Lawrence's novel, *Adventures of an Officer in the Punjaub*.[50] Manomohan's pro-

[48] For the life of Manomohan Bose, see Brajendranath Banerjee, *Sahitya-Sadhak Charitmala*, vol. IV, No. 51, Calcutta 1352 BS, pp. 5-64. Sunil Das (ed.), *Manomohan Boser Aprakasita Diary*, Calcutta 1981, also provides valuable details. The novel appeared in book form in 1891, after being serialized in two periodicals, *Madhyastha* and *Gan o Galpa*. First, the novel was titled *Duleener Ashcharya Jiban*, but later on it was slightly altered and brought out in the present form (1891). Cf. Subodh Choudhury, *Kabi o Natyakar Manomohan Bose*, Calcutta 1983, pp. 172-3.

[49] Manomohan Bose, *Duleen Athaba Ranjit Singha Sankranta Aitihasik Nabanyas*, Calcutta 1813 Saka, pp. 423- 4.

[50] H.M.L. Lawrence, *Adventures of an Officer in the Punjaub*, vols. I-II, Patiala reprint, 1970. Lawrence observed the politics of Punjab from close quarters. So his writing is packed with experience. Manomohan Bose followed Lawrence's first volume so closely that the novel almost became an adaptation. That does not apply to the second volume.

tagonist, Duleen, is an efficient, honest and responsible official who served under Ranjit Singh in the Kangra region of Punjab. Many European military experts held responsible positions at the Lahore darbar. Duleen was described as one of them but there is no evidence to prove that such a man really existed. Manomohan selected the name himself but the character primarily emerged out of the pages of Lawrence's novel. A substantial part of the activities of the hero at the Lahore darbar seem to be based on Lawrence's account. It is only on his joining a responsible post at Kangra fort that Duleen's personal life comes into prominence and there the writer allows his imagination to come into full play.

In the novel, the author has tried to provide an intimate profile of the Sikh political structure. The envy and rivalry among the top brass at the Lahore darbar, betrayal caused by a handful of silver, quick changes in political allegiance, the rapid spread of corruption in the central judiciary, planned attacks on the high officials posted in remote provinces are cited as some of the factors that enfeebled the Sikh polity. At the same time the Sikh monarch's strength of character, acute perception and ability to take prompt decisions made him eligible for assessment by a different yardstick. But the author also takes note of the maharaja's inability to appoint competent ministers and officials and his indifference to putting down their insolence and assertiveness. A lot of other interesting things come into the novel, viz., how the maharaja issued *parwanas,* the importance of Dhyan Singh in Sikh politics, the great abhorrence of the Pathans for Sikh political authority, etc. These are not recorded in any other work about the Sikh monarch in Bengali.

To what extent Manomohan Bose can take credit for furnishing all these data himself is open to question. Much of it is borrowed from Henry Lawrence. But by translating a significant portion of it, Manomohan earned the gratitude of contemporary Bengalis. Where he bypassed Lawrence and tried to correlate the changes in the political world with the mystery of the human mind, he came a cropper. But in the last one hundred pages of the novel that he wrote on his own, the substance and structure of the novel differ significantly from what Lawrence had to offer. In this part of the novel Manomohan quite often moves away from Lawrence's account. In the process Punjab recedes so far to the background that one is no longer sure if it is still a historical novel about Ranjit Singh. But it is its bold departure from the beaten track of Rajput and Maratha history that gives *Duleen* a special place.

Duleen does not throw much light on the broader canvas of Sikh history beyond the assortments of political information that Manomohan Bose conveyed. The social edifice built around the maharaja, the relations between the people who lived close to the royal authority, their religious prejudices and social mores are portrayed in the novel 'Sikh Samrat o Satir Shap'[51] by Kaliprasanna Chatterjee (1863-1919).[52] Kaliprasanna had been brought up in Punjab since childhood. He was for a long time connected with the newspaper world there, its movements for educational developments and religious reforms. He could thus have a closer view of the Sikhs of the Lahore darbar. So some of the characters that were close or not so close to the Sikh monarch emerge as large as life in his novel. The magnanimity of maharaja Ranjit Singh, the simplicity of prince Sher Singh,[53] the prince's confidence in his second wife Kamala, the limitless scorn of maharani Zinda (Jindan of history) for her daughter-in-law (Kamala), Kamala's regard for her father-in-law (Ranjit Singh) are conveyed in the novel.

The dramatis personae in Kaliprasanna's novel were not all historical characters. In the fiction, Kaliprasanna exercises his imagination to bring history, folklore and popular memory together to an extent that blurs the distinction between these. The central character is Ranjit Singh but the story unfolds with the maharaja's eldest son Sher Singh and his love for Kamala whom he marries; the hard-hearted youngest queen Zinda can never take kindly to the marriage. Jealousy and anger drive her to harm Kamala as best as she can. She is so consumed with anger that she throws Kamala's newborn son out of the palace. Kamala commits suicide, but not before putting a curse on the family saying that all will be lost in one generation.

[51] The novel 'Sikh Samrat o Satir Shap' was serialized in *Parichay* from Jyaistha to Agrahayan in 1364 BS, but never published as a book. It is difficult to say when exactly the novel was written. With no clues provided by the author, one can only conjecture that it was written in the early years of the twentieth century.

[52] Nemaisadhan Bose has given an outline of how closely Kaliprasanna Chatterjee was connected with events in Punjab. See, S.P. Sen (ed.), *Dictionary of National Biography*, vol. I, Calcutta 1967, pp. 276-7.

[53] It is surprising that one so knowledgeable about Punjab as Kaliprasanna describes Sher Singh as Ranjit Singh's eldest son. Kharak Singh, his eldest son, has been described by contemporary writers as mentally unbalanced, an addict, and devoid of judgement. Kaliprasanna, however, recreates him—of course as Sher Singh—as personification of kindness and compassion, a man of fine taste and lofty vision. Sher Singh was actually the name of Ranjit Singh's second son.

The novel closes with these words of imprecation. The writer suggests that in the gradual rise of Ranjit Singh's empire lay the seeds of its decline. Such an oral tradition about the fall of the Sikh kingdom had long been in circulation in Punjab. The writer lifts it to a dramatic and tragic dimension by putting these words of legend in the mouth of imaginary character, Kamala.

The social praxis of the contemporary Sikh Punjab has very often escaped the attention of Bengali writers. It is here that the novelist Kaliprasanna stands apart from the other Bengali writings. With his knowledge and experience of Punjabi social milieu, he could convey traces of it to his readership. Both Manomohan and Kaliprasanna narrated the story of the Khalsa Raj almost as eyewitnesses, but they were strikingly different in their points of view, and in their choice and handling of experiences and materials. Kaliprasanna did not view Punjab through the eyes of a foreigner, as did Manomohan relying on Henry Lawrence. They suggest the presence of two closely related streams of Sikh studies trying to reconstruct the Khalsa Raj from their own perspectives. There is hardly any doubt that the Sikhs as depicted by Kaliprasanna stand closer to history, but the projection via foreign writers *a la* Manomohan perhaps matches the conventional Bengali notions about the Sikhs.

From Kaliprasanna's writing, one can have a feel of the connections between the Sikhs and Hindus in Punjab. It also suggests that there were manifold tensions within the Sikh Community. In terms of the social background and economic means of its members, the Sikh Community in Punjab was far from being homogenous. Kaliprasanna could speak without hesitation about the widespread casteism in the Sikh society of the period.[54] At weddings, the high-

[54] Malcolm was perhaps the first to write elaborately about the caste system among the Sikhs in his *Sketch of the Sikhs; A Singular Nation, Who Inhabit the Provinces of the Penjab, Situated Between the Rivers Jumna and Indus,* London 1812. In the post-Independence years, Indera P. Singh also spoke of the separate gurdwaras for the Mazhabi Sikhs at the village level. Cf. 'A Sikh Village', in Milton Singer (ed.), *Traditional India: Structure and Change*, Philadelphia 1959, pp. 273-97. Many researchers report that in countries beyond India, the Ramgarhias often built separate gurdwaras of their own. For a further discussion on the point, see Sewa Singh Kalsi, *The Evolution of a Sikh Community in Britain: Religious and Social Change among the Sikhs of Leeds and Bradford,* Leeds 1992. In recent times, McLeod has also referred to the prevalence of caste in Sikhism. See *Evolution of the Sikh Community*, pp. 83-94; *Historical Dictionary of Sikhism*, p. 59. But many contemporary Sikh authors maintain that there is nothing like Hindu caste system among the Sikhs. Jagjit Singh, 'The Caste System and the Sikhs', in Jasbir Singh Mann and Harbans Singh Saraon (eds.), *Advanced Studies in Sikhism,* Chandigarh 1989, pp. 278-300.

born Sikhs (Kaliprasanna's 'Brahmin Sikhs', for instance) followed predominantly Hindu customs and rituals but the Jat peasants merely went round the *Adi Granth* and performed *Anand Karaj*. The novelist shows how much of a follower of Hindu customs Ranjit Singh was though he was a Sikh. The novel also records how at the Naulakhsha temple inside the Lahore palace, hundreds of Brahmins and Sikhs read the hymns of Goddess Chandi as well as the *sabads* from the *Adi Granth*. It appears from the novel that during the period, Hindus and Sikhs got very close to one another and established a relationship of mutual give and take at different levels of society. To what extent the Sikhs lost or enriched their distinct identity as a result is a question that Kaliprasanna has tackled from his own religious conviction.

Like many educated Hindus in Punjab, Kaliprasanna was close to the Arya Samaj Movement of Swami Dayanand. He did not, therefore, want to draw a dividing line between Hindus and Sikhs. In his eyes, Ranjit Singh was the 'last glorious sun of the Hindus'. So his maharaja had equal respect for Hindu and Sikh religious practices. The monarch used to visit several places of pilgrimage for the Sikhs. But he did not give Hardwar a miss, either. He used to take a dip in the Ganga there and drink the sacred water; he worshipped the *Akalpurakh* and the *Salgram* with equal reverence. Kaliprasanna consequently was perhaps not very enthusiastic about the separate Sikh identity question of the time. He, however, gave a wide range of information about the Sikh social world during the reign of Ranjit Singh and that gives him a distinct place in Bengali Sikh studies.

A four-act play was written hailing Ranjit Singh's conquests and bid to unify the Sikhs who had split themselves into innumerable political units in the closing years of the eighteenth century. The playwright was none other than the famous actor and director, Mahendranath Gupta (1910-84).[55] His play *Punjab-Keshari Ranjit Singha* was first staged at Star Theatre, Calcutta, towards the end of July 1940 and ran to a packed house for two and half months.[56] So far Bengali studies in Sikh history had been confined to books and periodicals. It was now made accessible to the general public in a big way.

[55] For an introduction to Mahendranath Gupta's writings, see Sukumar Sen, *Bangla Sahityer Itihas*, vol. IV, Calcutta 1971, p. 275.

[56] Mahendranath Gupta, *Punjab-Keshari Ranjit Singha*, Calcutta 1941. After minor changes, it was staged again in 1943.

The play portrays Ranjit Singh as a great patriot and an ideal human being. It is not difficult to understand that the objective of the dramatist was to draw attention to the cause of Indian independence. Beyond it, he identified himself with the agonies of the upper caste Bengali Hindu middle class feeling beleaguered in the face of the communal politics of the 1940s. The dramatist, however, could offer some solace and confidence to his community in its hour of political isolation. Mahendranath's *Punjab-Keshari,* thus, conveyed a sense of the contemporary regional political sentiments and aspirations. That partly explains why the play was such a hit.

Although a Sikh leader, Gupta's Ranjit Singh sought unification in his kingdom to such an extent that not merely Hindus and Muslims but also the English traders and French soldiers would be bound together in ties of friendship and cooperation! The high-pitched patriotism gave the play the quality of a Bengali *jatra*. To cater to the ordinary viewer, music and dance, political intrigue, instances of extreme sacrifice for the country, humour in the mouths of comic roles were some of the ingredients thrown in. The playwright was a student of history, but in the drama the historical framework was rather loosely put up. He took liberties with the sequence of events throwing dates and years to the winds; what is more he put words in the mouths of historical characters which would often be missing in the contemporary recorded sources. The dialogue had echoes of the unfulfilled dreams and aspirations of the contemporary Hindu Bengalis.

The playwright devoted the main plot to Ranjit Singh's attempt at building up an independent Sikh State stretching from the Sutlej to Peshawar. The audience was treated to a major happy ending. To make it a success on stage, Gupta deviates from recorded sources at will, and does not show much concern for the chronological continuity of history, organization of facts buttressed by logic, the unfolding of the historical characters, etc. The dramatist uses a few historical names, some events associated with them and then falls back on fancy and imagination to relate the development of events. He did not care to verify the information he put in his play and presented it as gospel truth. For example, there is nothing in history about the heir apparent Kharak Singh's revolt which occupies an important place in the playwright's scheme of history. Again, Shah Shuja did not present the Kohinoor to the Sikh monarch as a token of friendship. Ranjit Singh acquired it through relentless psychological pressure and persecution.[57] Thirdly, we find the Bhangi *misl* chief Sahib Singh who had actually died in 1811 on the stage even after the annexation of Multan (1816). Fourthly, General Mokham Chand could not have been alive when the battle of Naushera was fought with the Afghans.[58] He had died in 1814. But the dramatist describes him as the 'greatest friend who had won the battle of Naushera'. Fifthly, in the play Ranjit Singh had imprisoned his mother Raj Kaur to symbolize the 'enslavement of motherhood in a country in fetters'. Contemporary sources, however, ascribe her imprisonment to moral lapses and her propensity to intrigue.[59] Finally, it is debatable whether Ranjit Singh and Jindan were such flawless characters as presented by Mahendranath Gupta.

The play tried to take Sikh studies in Bengali to the wider Hindu urban middle class world, seriously challenged by the loss of its political power in the provincial politics since the 1930s. The ravages of war and communal strife threatened even the city of Calcutta, its most important seat of power. It looked forward to 'a deeply conservative world view of an embattled elite, determined to pay whatever price it had to in order to cling to power and privilege'.[60] Mahendranath's *Punjab-Keshari Ranjit Singha* sought to give it an illusive taste of power and promised to nurture its wounded ego in the imaginary world of history. Its great commercial success led the dramatist to stage it again three years later. The audience lapped it up again. They expected to see an ideal, patriotic Sikh (i.e. Hindu) king and they got what they wanted.

[57] Griffin in his *Ranjit Singh* (pp. 100-2) shows what humiliation and torture Ranjit Singh inflicted on Shah Shuja to wrest the Kohinoor from him. But Mahendranath Gupta was silent on the point.

[58] For the relevant information on Mokham Chand, see Griffin, *The Panjab Chiefs*, pp. 555-6.

[59] Griffin, *Ranjit Singh*, p. 106.

[60] Joya Chatterjee, *Bengal Divided: Hindu Communalism and Partition, 1932-47*, New Delhi 1996, p. 267. The Sikhs of Calcutta initially objected strongly to the staging of Mahendranath Gupta's play, *Punjab-Keshari Ranjit Singha*. After some time, the Sikhs made such a fuss that the play was on the verge of being taken off the stage. At last, negotiations with them led to a settlement enabling the play to be staged again. Debnarayan Gupta, a senior playwright of the Calcutta stage, furnished the above information in an interview (29 June 1991). The play has been severely criticized by Somendrachandra Nandi in *Aitihasik Natak Samalochana*, Calcutta 1981, pp. 610-15.

VII

Following the death of Ranjit Singh (1839), a state of deep political uncertainty and turbulence became manifest in the Khalsa darbar. The government in Lahore also ceased to be competent to rule and confrontation with the East India Company became inevitable (1845). There were frequent bloodbaths at Lahore during the period. A few descendants of Ranjit Singh and his courtiers and ministers even lost their heads. Historians can guess how insecure the common man's life had become. But in their works the nameless commoners are not treated separately. Fortunately, Bengali Sikh studies deal with the varied experiences of some of these men and women. In the present section, we will refer to three short stories that describe how insecure life and property had become despite Khalsa governance. The author of the stories was Nagendranath Gupta (1862-1940) who was for sometime with *The Tribune*.[61] He had spent many years in Lahore. Like Kaliprasanna, he was well acquainted with the prominent spots in the city, like Anarkali bazaar, Takshali darwaza, Mori darwaza, Dabri bazaar, etc. His style lacked the earthy smell of Punjabi unlike Kaliprasanna's, and it offered an exaggerated view of political disorder along the lines laid down by a number of British authorities on the eve of the First Sikh War. They projected a grim picture of the law and order situation prevailing in and around Lahore and sought to build up a moral defence for immediate British intervention. Gupta seems to have depended primarily on these sources and hence his projection of the political scene of the trans-Sutlej territories was full of uncertainty and fluid. The author seems to provide a simple answer to the complex question prevailing in and around the Lahore darbar. Why did the Sikh power collapse so quickly after the death of Ranjit Singh? From Nagendranath's point

[61] Even today it is a highly respected and widely circulated English daily published from Chandigarh. It was first brought out from Lahore. Nagendranath Gupta began his career as a schoolteacher (1878) and for sometime served *The Tribune* editorial desk in Lahore. Gupta depended on the accounts of English authorities about the First Sikh War. In his autobiography, he describes personalities of his times and makes some interesting comments about his own literary pursuit. See his *Reflections and Reminiscences*, pp. 141-205. He wrote three short stories based on Sikh history. Two of them—'Jamal Jalil' and 'Suraj Kaur' appear in *Nagendra Granthabali*, vol. I, Calcutta 1925, pp. 159-68, 189-98, while the third one, 'Teja Singha' was published in *Prabasi*, Ashar 1311 BS, pp. 142-51. For contemporary and semi-contemporary English writings, on Sikh history, see G. Khurana, *British Historiography on the Sikh Power in Punjab*, New Delhi 1985.

of view, it was all the fault of the Khalsa Raj. But he failed to take note of the aggressive role of the English Company in this regard. His attempt to reconstruct history from the secondary British sources, however, did not prevent him from making an effective use of his imaginative power and other relevant oral traditions of the region.

The first story, 'Teja Singha' appeared in the literary monthly *Prabasi.* Its hero Teja Singh was an able official under Ranjit Singh. Later when the Khalsa darbar had hit rock-bottom, he tried to hang on to the fading sense of values and build a bridge between the past and present with honesty and self-assurance. The maharaja was alive at the beginning of the story but in the latter half he was dead. The writer argued that the maharaja in his lifetime had planted the seeds of disloyalty and selfishness among his subjects and after his death these grew into a massive tree.

While there was 'decline' all around, the tall, 27-year-old Sikh youth Teja Singh burst upon the scene like 'a flash of light'. Some literary critics may consider him an exception in the post-Ranjit Singh political ambience. Gupta has not presented him as a pacifist leader like Lehna Singh Majithia, who is reported to have told the Khalsa soldiery not to go to war with the British. But 'in the prevailing atmosphere of conspiracy, nobody heeded his warning'. Teja Singh wanted to reverse the tide of events and had to pay the price with his life.

Finally, when he found the war with the English inevitable, he did not turn a 'traitor' like Tej Singh or Gulab Singh. He was a 'repository of faith and confidence.' Cunningham had written about the great enthusiasm and excitement caused in the Khalsa army during the First Sikh War. Teja Singh in Nagendranath's tale shared the ebullience. His encouraging leadership was stated to have inspired the Sikh soldiers and caused deep anxiety in the minds of the 'treacherous' Khalsa leaders. The 'traitors' hired an assassin to put an end to the life of Teja Singh. He died. His death virtually signified the collapse of the 'noble Khalsa idealism' and precipitated the subsequent defeat of the Sikhs.

Almost a similar message is conveyed in the story called 'Jamal Jalil'. It is written in a lighter vein than 'Teja Singha' and no important politicians of the Sikh darbar are present in it. But there is some indication of how the women of the royal family with 'evil designs' got their 'favourites' appointed to important posts in the Khalsa administration and were anxious to establish their sway over it. The background is of course the post-Ranjit Singh era. Such 'unholy' influence steadily asserted itself after the maharaja's demise and the administration becamc like a rudderless boat.

Lachmi Kaur, very close to maharani Meera, is an important character. There may be grave doubts about how authentic the Sikh names are. Meera was probably maharani Jindan. In certain areas, the control of Meera over the Khalsa administration bears resemblance to that of Jindan. The story is named after the two junior associates of Fakir Nuruddin, youngest brother of Fakir Azizuddin who played an important role in the Lahore politics of the 1840s. If the story has to be fitted into a framework of historical dates, the time span of 'Jamal-Jalil' is roughly around the mid-1840s when political intrigues dictated by 'petty selfish designs' often dominated Sikh polity. Erosion of the Khalsa authority was held to be primarily responsible for it. Nagendranath may have left gaps in the description of events, but he also tried to describe the bustling life of Lahore, shopping at Anarkali bazaar, how ladies emerged from their privacy and strolled down highways, how some of them were even abducted and sent into hideouts away from public gaze, etc. With all this Gupta sought to draw attention to the 'chronic administrative laxity' of the period.

The third and last 'Suraj Kaur', is about a beauty who operated from the interior of her home and had a hand in Lahore's politics of secret assassination of the period, but was killed in the end by an assassin herself. All the imagined characters are from the Sikh community. They are all involved in the 'game'. Here we do not find any person from the darbar, army, or royal family directly connected with it. Nagendranath, however, tried to indicate how the 'darbar politics of Lahore extended beyond the court and engaged men and women of some other quarters in the game of murder'. One wonders how for 'a handful of silver', people can kill a lover, a political adversary or a member of the royal family with 'a bright future'. Such people as a group have occasionally been discussed by historians but not individually. Nagendranath blended history with oral tradition and constructed imaginary characters like Mangal Singh, Sundar Singh, Hari Singh, Prem Dei and Suraj Kaur. They were different from one another not only in appearance, dress and lifestyle, their tastes differed too, and so did the apparent aims of their lives. The story is ten pages long, drawing a number of distinctive Sikh characters wittingly or unwittingly into 'a circle of invisible murder', beginning with the death of Hari Singh and climaxing with the murder of Suraj Kaur.

The author located his story faraway from the nerve-centre of politics, viz., the Lahore darbar in the Lahore fort. He left out people in the higher stratum of Sikh society and focused on the varied groups of people who lived in the shadow of death on the eve of the First Sikh War. There is no reference to brisk shopping in the Anarkali bazaar or Dabri bazaar as in 'Jamal Jalil'. There is no idealist young man like Teja Singh who could retain his integrity unimpaired in myriad misadventures. 'Here everybody is anxious to save his bacon, nobody stirred out of home without a weapon, nobody trusted the next man, everybody was scared, there was murder lurking everywhere, everyone was going round in a circle of darkness; if some one laid a trap, he was entrapped himself.'

The author suggests that long before the fall of the Sikh political power (1849), the Khalsa had forfeited its moral right to rule. If that was the scene at Lahore, the centre of the kingdom, the state of affairs in the extremes, the north-western and south-western regions, is not hard to imagine. Some such information was recorded in the writings of British administrator-historians, accounts of foreign travellers and journalists or the secret documents of the political agents in Lahore. Nagendranath had perhaps read a few of them and then made considerable use of his imagination. His story is ultimately a product of his creative vision.

VIII

Nagendranath Gupta did not write about the personalities who occupied the centre of the Sikh political stage in the post-Ranjit Singh period. But others were not silent about them. Many wrote about maharani Jindan, mixing praise with criticism. The Sikh queen was perhaps one of the most controversial figures of the period.

In the middle of the nineteenth century, at the time of the First Sikh War (1845-6), a section of the educated Bengalis became quite enthusiastic about the Sikh politics of Punjab. Rajnarayan

Bhattacharya (1817-50?) sifted through a lot of material and wrote *Panjabetihas* (1846), recording the history of Punjab from ancient times to the British governor-general's visit there (1846).[62] Towards the end of the book, two separate paragraphs are devoted to a brief evaluation of Jindan's intimacy with her Prime Minister, Lal Singh and its repercussions in Punjab politics. It was perhaps the first significant discussion of maharani Jindan in Bengali. Not a word of praise was there about the queen. Questions have been raised about whether Jindan was a legal wife of Ranjit Singh and whether Duleep Singh was their legitimate issue. Bhattacharya was unsparing in his criticism of the Sikh queen's moral laxity. Here he also made no secret of his gender bias. In the light of analysis and assessment in subsequent times, his conclusions may seem one-sided. Presented only with her moral lapses, the queen appeared as an ignominious character to the Bengali readers.

One can assume a few possible reasons for Bhattacharya's assessment. When he wrote *Panjabetihas*, the Anglo-Indian press in Calcutta in unison held the Khalsa darbar responsible for starting the First Sikh War. Rajnarayan got his materials from these sources and severely berated the Sikhs. Besides, Indian nationalism had not yet made its mark in Bengali Sikh studies. The qualities in Jindan praised later were not noticed at the time. For that we have to wait for another three decades.

It was left to the nationalist writer Rajanikanta Gupta to attempt the first revaluation of maharani Jindan (1883).[63] In the early days of Indian national consciousness, he criticized British administrator-historians in several works. In his opinion, they wrote to serve their own political interest. Needless to say, Gupta was doing almost the same thing from another end. It was with this attitude that Rajanikanta reviewed the role of the Sikh queen. His analysis falls into two

[62] Cf. Bhattacharya, *Panjabetihas*. He came from the village Majira in Burdwan district. In the preface to his book, the writer has provided relevant information about the historical source materials he had used. *Panjabetihas* has special importance in Bengali historical studies. See Bimalaprasad Mukherjee, 'History', in Jagannath Chakrabarty (ed.), *Studies in Bengal Renaissance,* Calcutta 1977, p. 366; Haranchandra Rakshit, 'Banglar Lekhak', *Janmabhumi*, Kartik 1307 BS, pp. 110-20. The book was printed three times in a very short space of time. For a partial evaluation, also see J. Long, 'A Descriptive Catalogue of Bengali Books', cited in Dineshchandra Sen, *Bangabhasa o Sahitya,* vol. II, Calcutta reprint, 1986, p. 775.

[63] Rajanikanta Gupta, 'Jindan', *Bharat-Kahini*, Calcutta 1883, pp. 70-85.

parts, viz., to sketch out her role in Sikh politics with sympathy and to refute in strong language the allegations levelled against her. Rajanikanta tried to depict Jindan as 'a rare and great personality' in Sikh politics. He felt that the British administrator-historians would not have maligned her if she had remained inactive behind the *purdah*. She had gradually assumed an important part in the contemporary politics before she was worsted by British intrigue and exiled (1847). Rajanikanta had very little doubt that her exile had a serious impact on Sikh politics.[64] He was not uncritical about Jindan's moral foibles and admitted that she had a special feeling for Lal Singh. However, without castigating her for that, the author wanted her to be considered with 'forgiveness and tolerance'. He realized that the British administrator-historians would not give the queen her due recognition and felt the need for the writing of Indian history from 'an Indian standpoint'. Gupta's sense of 'national pride' led him to believe that if reliance was placed only on the writings of Britishers, the whole of Indian past would be defiled like the character of maharani Jindan. What he wished to convey was that it was not possible for foreign writers to fathom the spirit of Sikh history. He therefore considered 'the study of national history untrammelled by foreign influence' to be one of the main objects in historical studies.[65]

[64] Jindan's exile from Punjab produced a strong anti-British feeling among the Sikhs. Many historians argue that it hastened the Second Sikh War. Rajanikanta Gupta was one of them. See his *Sipahi Juddher Itihas*, vol. I, Calcutta 1886, p. 17. But the British administrator-historians put the blame on Jindan for her exile. According to them, the queen caused great embarrassment to the newly introduced British administrative machinery in Punjab. British officials charged her with conspiracy. See Charles Gough and Arthur D. Innes, *The Sikhs and the Sikh Wars*, Patiala reprint, 1970, pp. 155-6. But ten years after the event, this argument had few takers even in Bengal, as the following quotation bears out: 'The British repaid their gratitude [after the Mutiny] to the Sikhs in ample measure. Lord Dalhousie exiled the queen from the palace and imprisoned her in the hellhole of Sheikhpuri [Sheikhupura]. She was not allowed even to see her maids. General Moslyn said to her, "Her Majesty, if you wish to see your son, climb into this carriage, I have come to take you to the palace." The queen readily obliged out of her affection for her son, but Moslyn took her to Chunar fort and imprisoned her there. . . .' 'Sambad Bhaskar', 29 January 1857, cited in Benoy Ghosh, *Samayikpatre Banglar Samajchitra*, vol. III, Calcutta 1964, p. 373. It no doubt leaves out many significant factors leading to her exit from Punjab. But it indicates how enthusiastic the Bengali press was about the queen.

[65] Rajanikanta Gupta, 'Bharater Itihas Adhyayan', *Bharat-Kahini*, pp. 7-8. See also Chatterjee, *The Nation and its Fragments* (pp. 76-7) for why this need for writing nationalist histories was felt in the late nineteenth century. For the contemporary English attitude about Jindan's relations with Lal Singh, see Carmichael Smyth, *A History of the Reigning Family of Lahore*, Patiala reprint, 1970, pp. 163-4.

Rajanikanta presents Jindan as an embodiment of a somewhat inarticulate protest. He wrote the piece a few years before the establishment of the Indian National Congress. A decade elapsed and the character of the national movement underwent a rapid change. The language of protest became strident. To what extent did the spirit of the age influence Bengali Sikh studies? A poem by an anonymous writer, 'Sikhganer Prati Maharani Jindaner Ukti' (Stirring call of Maharani Jindan to the Sikhs) conjures up how the Sikh queen urged her people to drive the British out of Punjab at the time of the First Sikh War. Towards the end the poet claims that the queen's appeal had unified the Sikhs to fight the British, filling the English with concern and leading them to remove the queen from the palace and incarcerate her in the Sheikhupura fort.

History confirms that the queen was imprisoned in the Sheikhupura fort. But the historians ascribe it to other factors. The poet did major brushwork to project the queen as 'an innocent victim' of 'British designs'. There was no reference to her moral lapses in the poem. On the other hand, she was lionized as a figure of protest. In the past Rajnarayan Bhattacharya, however, had said nothing of the sort. Rajanikanta gave a definite indication but did not go very far. The poem under discussion contains bitter reflections on British rule recorded in the speeches of the contemporary national leaders. The Sikh queen did not fight in a deadly battle like the queen of Jhansi. But the poem perhaps for the first time in Bengali Sikh studies portrayed a rebellious woman.[66] It is noteworthy that it appeared in *Bamabodhini Patrika*, organ of educated Brahmo women. The author offers to Bengali readers a new gender orientation.[67]

[66] *Bamabodhini Patrika*, Jyaistha 1298 BS, pp. 49-51. For the regenerating role of the *Bamabodhini Patrika* in the late nineteenth and early twentieth centuries Bengal, see Ghulam Murshid, *Sankocher Bihbalata: Adhunikatar Abhighate Bangaramanir Pratikriya, 1849-1905*, Dhaka 1985, pp. 197-204.

[67] Apart from Jindan, some other Sikh women figured in Bengali Sikh studies. These essays were published towards the end of our period or beyond it. They highlight the courageous role of three Sikh women in contemporary Sikh politics. Here we may refer to three articles by Amiya Bose, 'Sikh Ramani—Chandkaur', *Bangashri*, Magh 1354 BS, pp. 145-7; 'Sikh Ramani—Sadakaur', *Bharatbarsa*, Bhadra 1354 BS, pp. 239-41; 'Rani Sahebkaur Sikh Ramani', *Bangashri*, Baisakh 1355 BS, pp. 419-20. See also, Basantakumar Banerjee, 'Sikhramani', *Prabartak*, Agrahayan 1330 BS, pp. 698-701. The last essay, is of a more general nature, provides an outline of the fighting role played by Sikh womenfolk of the eighteenth century. In this sense it differs from Bose's articles which highlight three different Sikh women in three separate essays.

A fair part of maharani Jindan's life revolved round the two Sikh wars. Historians find her directly involved with the first war and indirectly with the second. The first began when she was at the centre of Sikh politics. Many allege that she had incited the Khalsa army to open hostilities with the British. Later the East India Company accused her of conspiracy, removed her from power and imprisoned her at the Sheikhupura fort in Gujranwala district. Several scholars have suggested that the Second Sikh War was hastened by a complex set of circumstances that followed from the maharani's fall from power, and imprisonment, a conclusion upheld by many Bengali authors on the subject.

The pioneer in this direction was Barodakanta Mitra (? - 1933?). His famous *Sikhjuddher Itihas o Maharaja Duleep Singha* (1893) portrays Jindan as a combination of strength and weakness as seen in the light of the Sikh wars.[68] He expressed great admiration for the Sikh queen's strength of character and ability to provide effective leadership at a critical moment of Sikh history. The author refused to accept the allegation against Jindan that she had incited the Khalsa against the East India Company in the First Sikh War. On the contrary, he showered praise on her for keeping up the moral and organizational cohesion of her army like Elizabeth I of England. Barodakanta dismissed the charges of immorality against her as bazaar gossip. But the writer complained that after the end of the First Sikh War, the queen could not appreciate the British effort to restore law and order in Punjab. The hurdles she put up compelled the British to imprison her at the Sheikhupura fort.

One has to read between the lines to see the two elements in Barodakanta's evaluation of maharani Jindan. While on the one

[68] In Bengali Sikh studies, Barodakanta Mitra is perhaps the first author to classify his source materials under three heads, viz., (1) different categories of printed official documents and other primary sources, (2) secondary materials of significance, (3) contemporary Indian and foreign newspapers and miscellaneous periodicals. The official documents relate to the causes of the Second Sikh War, and the state of affairs at the Lahore darbar on the eve of the conflict (1845). The list of secondary sources includes around thirty books published between 1831 and 1890, including works by Prinsep, Cunningham, Bell, Ross, Thackwell, etc. To narrate the last days of Duleep Singh's life, he relied on newspapers like *Moscow News*, *Times*, *Englishman*, etc. But there was no mention of *The Tribune* in the list. Perhaps no writer in this field after Barodakanta made such extensive use of newspapers. Swarnakumari Devi, editor of the literary periodical *Bharati*, reviewed the book with deep respect and appreciation. Cf. *Bharati*, Jyaistha 1301, pp. 127-8.

hand, he rejected the charge that she egged the Khalsa on against the British, on the other hand he absolved the British resident of any responsibility and held the queen solely responsible for her imprisonment. Unlike many of his predecessors, he would neither praise Jindan nor criticize her one hundred per cent. There lies the difference between their evaluations of Jindan.[69]

IX

Roughly in the middle of the nineteenth century the East India Company defeated the Sikhs in two successive wars and annexed Punjab. Bengali interest in the Sikh wars extended beyond the activities of Jindan. What were the historical causes of the wars? What was the course of the wars? Was there really a conspiracy on the battlefield? In what circumstances were the Sikhs compelled to sign a peace treaty with the British? These were some of the questions that disturbed the Bengali mind. Undoubtedly, the most important and valuable book on the history of the Sikh wars was Barodakanta Mitra's *Sikhjuddher Itihas o Maharaja Duleep Singha*. But Rajnarayan Bhattacharya's *Panjabetihas* had earlier thrown some light on the First Sikh War and therefore deserves to be discussed first.[70]

Panjabetihas earned considerable popularity among the Bengali readership because it was published shortly after the end of the First Sikh War. The book gives a detailed account of the events, which led up to the war. The author held the Khalsa darbar entirely responsible for beginning the war after violating the treaty with the British. According to his version, following the assassination of Prime Minister Jawahir Singh (September 1845), the Khalsa army took control of the Lahore darbar and spread a jingoistic hysteria, that drove the Sikh generals to cross the Sutlej and attack the English (December 1845). The British had no alternative but to declare war. The Khalsa was defeated for its inept leadership and indiscipline.This reading of history underlines Bhattacharya's closeness to the writings

[69] For an evaluation of Barodakanta Mitra's studies in Sikh history, see the author's 'Maharaja Duleep Singh in the Eyes of Non-Sikhs: A Survey of Indian Historical Tradition', in Prithipal Singh Kapur (ed.), *Maharaja Duleep Singh*, Amritsar 1995, pp. 77-8.

[70] Supra, pp. 211-12.

of Smyth and M'Gregor and his distance from the world of Cunningham.

The author saw the defeat of the Khalsa as an expression of 'divine will'. The way Rajnarayan rang down the curtain on the First Sikh War did not leave any scope for critical assessment. His book is rooted in a conservative attitude, reducing the war to a conflict between 'justice' and 'injustice' and the ultimate triumph of 'justice'. In his opinion, the Indians should appreciate the significance of 'divine justice'. The historian in a sense represented the spirit of his age, a period marked by a swell of loyalty towards the East India Company. His study also shows that the author had no first-hand knowledge of the documentary sources that could have given him a better insight into the history of the war. He seems to have been more anxious to write his book in a hurry to capture the market and so relied on secondary sources. He gauged the great curiosity in the Bengali mind directly after the First Sikh War, especially about the future of the Sikh State. He wanted to cash in on it.

About 50 years after the publication of *Panjabetihas*, Barodakanta Mitra wrote *Sikhjudhher Itihas o Maharaja Duleep Singha*.[71] The tragic end of Duleep Singh (1891) in France might have prompted him to write the book. The writer begins with an account of the line of weak Sikh kings during the post-Ranjit Singh period and a general evaluation of them. He would not credit any of them with the exception of prince Nao Nihal Singh, with any administrative ability. Barodakanta underscored the moral degeneration of the Sikh leaders at the Khalsa darbar (1839-45), but found that despite the all-round decline, the army had retained its loyalty and disciplined conduct.

As for the causes of the First Sikh War, the author cites the following: (1) the growing British power east of the Sutlej, (2) the appointment of Major Broadfoot as the commanding officer with his hawkishness, and (3) the excitement in the Khalsa army over his aggrandizing policy.[72] While narrating the course of the war, he does not overemphasize Prime Minister Lal Singh's mischievous designs at the battle of Mudki (December 1845). On the contrary, he highlighted the great self-sacrifice of the old Shyam Singh Attariwala

[71] Supra, pp. 215-16.

[72] Mitra, *Sikhjudhher Itihas o Maharaja Duleep Singha*, pp. 56-9, 65-6. Here Mitra seems to have relied on Cunningham, *A History of the Sikhs*, pp. 250-6 and Smyth, *A History of the Reigning Family of Lahore*, pp. xix-xxvi.

at the battle of Sobraon (February 1846). His heroism has been compared to that of Leonidas at Thermopylae, a point perhaps borrowed from Rajanikanta Gupta's *Sikh*.

Barodakanta describes elaborately the political arrangement subsequent to the First Sikh War with due seriousness and highlights the 'constructive role' of the British Resident. Here he makes no secret of his bias in favour of Henry Lawrence's measures for pacifying the Sikh aristocracy. But in the same breath he cites Lord Dalhousie's aggressive policy as an important cause of the Second Sikh War. In his opinion, the deliberate procrastination of the East India Company in suppressing the revolt at Multan (1847) further complicated the political situation of the region and disaffection spread in different parts of Punjab, paving the way for the commencement of hostilities (1848). The way Lord Dalhousie removed the minor Duleep Singh from the throne and annexed Punjab seemed 'a total betrayal of British political ethic'.

There is hardly any doubt that Barodakanta sought to provide a new direction in his analysis of the Sikh wars. Avoiding extremities, he took into account some of the wider issues of the war and argued that these were an outcome of numerous factors long at work. A hundred years have elapsed since he wrote, but nobody has so far succeeded in producing another information-packed work like his on the subject in Bengali. What makes him equally memorable is his accumulation of footnotes to establish himself as a historian dedicated to factual substantiation.[73]

The last notable work on the Sikh wars was *Sikh-Itihas*, published during the anti-Partition movement and reflecting the anti-English sentiment of the times. Its chief architect was Durgadas Lahiri (1855-1932).[74] The Bangabasi group of publications in Calcutta had

[73] His appreciation of British rule strikingly differs from that of Rajnarayan and reminds us of the spirit of the moderate Congress politics of his age. Subsequently a number of articles were written about the Sikh wars and Duleep Singh based on Barodakanta's *Sikhjudhher Itihas o Maharaja Duleep Singha*. A few of them were published in different issues of *Aitihasik Chitra*. Cf. Sureschandra Majumdar, 'Maharaja Duleep Singher Parinam', *Aitihasik Chitra*, Baisakh 1316 BS, pp. 46-8; Jyaistha 1316 BS, pp. 49-62. In Hindi, Nandkumardev Sharma made no secret of his debt to Barodakanta in his *Punjab Haran aur Maharaja Duleep Singh*, Calcutta 1979 Bikrami.

[74] For a biographical sketch of and introduction to the literary career of Durgadas Lahiri, see *Sahitya o Samskriti*, Sraban 1375 BS, p. 338. Lahiri was widely respected for his world history in several volumes.

meanwhile initiated a lot of thinking and action in that direction.[75] It was on their initiative that Durgadas Lahiri supervised the translation into Bengali of Cunningham's *A History of the Sikhs*. He also edited the translation and added a long essay on the Second Sikh War, which was not in Cunningham's book. The entire volume ran into 740 pages. The section on the Second Sikh War written by Lahiri ran to 61 pages. Our discussion primarily concerns Lahiri's own contribution because it significantly differs from many of the earlier writings on the Sikh wars.

The writer had divided the piece into five roughly equal chapters.[76] In the first chapter, he analyses the causes of the Multan revolt (1847) and observes the indirect influence of 'an intolerant' British administration behind it. He has a strong feeling that the British Resident, Frederic Currie had done financial harm to Diwan Mulraj and driven him to revolt. The battle of Multan is featured in the third chapter, that analyses the war plans of both sides but centres on Mulraj's defeat, the occupation of Multan by the British and the trial and exile of Mulraj. The fourth chapter throws light on the battle of Chillianwala where Lahiri was convinced that the Britishers were defeated. The fifth and last chapter describes the battle of Gujrat. According to him, the British had to deploy troops and weapons to an extent unparalleled in the past to win the battle. But in his opinion it almost became 'a pyrrhic victory' for the English.

Durgadas Lahiri's study demonstrated deep admiration for Cunningham's writings on the Sikhs. In his editorial notes, he hailed Cunningham as the chief spokesman of the oppressed Sikh people.

[75] The Bangabasi group enriched Bengali literature in many ways in the late nineteenth and early twentieth centuries. See Nirmal Kumar Das (ed.), *Jogeshchandra Rachanabali,* Calcutta 1976. For recent discussions on the subject, see Amiya Sen, *Hindu Revivalism in Bengal, 1872-1905: Some Essays on Interpretation,* Delhi 1993, pp. 236-8. See also, anonymous (Amritalal Chakrabarty), *Sikh-Juddha,* Calcutta 1894.

[76] Pramathanath Sanyal took up the job of translating Cunningham's *A History of the Sikhs* into Bengali. Durgadas Lahiri added the chapters on the Second Sikh War. The Bangabasi press published the whole book in 1314 BS under the title, *Sikh-Itihas*. The Bengali version of Cunningham's book, like the English original, was promptly banned. See S.S. Bal, 'The first edition of J.D. Cunningham's *A History of the Sikhs*', *Proceedings, Punjab History Conference*, Eleventh Session, Patiala 1976, pp. 58-9. During these years the same group also brought out a Hindi version of Cunningham's *A History of the Sikhs*. In 1987 the Bengali version of the book was reprinted with a new foreword. But the foreword does not provide the historical backdrop of the Second Sikh War.

One would certainly be missing the enthusiasm for Cunningham in the writings of Barodakanta,who was sometimes critical because Cunningham did not carry his study forward beyond the First Sikh War. Another important aspect of Lahiri's attitude was his respect for the bold Sikh resistance against the English. Their defeat in the wars left him with a sense of deep remorse. Rajnarayan was pleased with the establishment of British administration; Lahiri was mortified by it. The agony and enthusiasm of contemporary nationalism manifested themselves in equal measure in Lahiri's writings. He also targeted the British governance of the time which he did not hold in any high regard. That sets him apart from Barodakanta. Lahiri regarded British rule as an engine of oppression, not so Barodakanta. The two writers typified two different traditions. Barodakanta belonged to the age of moderate Congress politics committed to constitutional ways and held English rule in great esteem. Durgadas, on the other hand, breathed the air of the politics of Swadeshi, Boycott, and the Bomb. Unlike Barodakanta, he was, therefore, pronouncedly anti-British.

X

Sikh studies in Bengali often set the past and historical inquiry aside to bring contemporary events into the focus. In the fourth decade of the nineteenth century when Ranjit Singh was ill, Calcutta newspapers carried the news as well as of the comings and goings of his emissaries. When the Sikh wars started in the next decade, there were reactions in the city again. Calcutta was the hub of British political activity and so more news was available here than in other Indian cities. The news, which appeared in English newspapers, was rehashed in Bengali papers and periodicals. Improvement in printing, expansion of means of communication, the growing size of the Bengali middle class, etc., gave Calcutta an edge in this regard. News from Punjab and about the Sikhs found place in the Bengali press in Calcutta from the middle of the nineteenth century. They stimulated the imagination of poet Iswarchandra Gupta (1812-59),[77] whose poems on the Sikh wars we shall now take up for review.

[77] For a biography of Iswarchandra Gupta, see Brajendranath Banerjee (ed.), *Sahitya-Sadhak Charitmala*, vol. I, No. 10, Calcutta 1350 BS, pp. 1-62. About the importance of *Sambad Prabhakar* in nineteenth century Bengali journalism, see Benoy Ghosh (ed.), *Samayikpatre Banglar Samajchitra*, vol. I, Calcutta 1962, pp. 1-45.

Iswarchandra Gupta wrote six poems during and at the end of these wars in *Sambad Prabhakar*, which he edited. He not only criticized the Sikhs for crossing the Sutlej and attacking the British but even called their effort 'sheer audacity'. Gupta was immensely popular for his sarcastic and delightful style of writing evident in these poems. He did not see a trace of bravery in the Khalsa troops locked in battles with the Company's army. When at last the vanquished Sikhs returned to Lahore, they looked comic to the poet. No other Bengali writer before and after made the Sikhs appear so ridiculous. He did not keep the reason a secret. The poems called 'Sikh Sangram', 'Dwitiya Sikhjuddha', and 'Juddher Jai' end with tributes to the British Raj.[78] The poet expressed not a word of sympathy for the Khalsa's defeat. On the contrary, he thanked God for the victory of the rulers and urged the people to stand united and seek protection under the umbrella of British royal favour.

However, his wisecracks about the battles of the Khalsa soldiers and his steadfast loyalty to the British rulers are not all that Gupta had to offer in his poems. Gupta expressed deep remorse over the decimation of the Punjabi people and the deposition of the minor, Duleep Singh, and found the annexation of Punjab after the war quite 'unethical'. He appealed to the good sense of the British 'with folded hands' to spare the kingdom of Duleep Singh, and begged the 'mercy' of British imperial authority so that the 'injustice' was not prolonged and the British image remained unsullied.[79] The poems, rooted in the greatest veneration for the Raj, show how effectively Gupta utilized his poetic talent in the field of journalism. A lot of other poems must have been written about the Sikh wars but it is doubtful if they were so appealing.[80] The poet showered a great deal of abuse on the Sikh leaders and made fun of their war efforts in a style that has virtually remained unsurpassed even today. But amid such sharp sarcasm and irony, his pain at the dethroning of the minor Duleep Singh is not difficult to see. With all his loyalty, Gupta could foresee the British line of action in Punjab, but could only hope that

[78] For these poems, see *Iswarchandra Gupter Rachanabali*, vols. I-II, pp. 103-10.

[79] The same attitude was expressed in the contemporary *Sambad Bhaskar*, a fortnightly newspaper. See its editorials of 23 March 1849 and 15 November 1849 and *Sambad Prabhakar*, 11 April 1849.

[80] 'The Sikh War Song', for example, reveals a different mindset about the Sikh wars. On the subject, see Mrinalkanti Chanda, *History of the English Press in Bengal,* Calcutta, 1987, p. xxvi.

ethical and moral considerations would humanize it to a considerable extent.

In the mid-nineteenth century, the poet Gupta drew contemporary events within the ambit of Sikh studies. In the 1920s, the Akalis started the movement for gurdwara reform that gave Sikh studies in Bengali a contemporaneous dimension. Several newspapers and periodicals chose to write not just about the Akali *satyagrahis* but also related the reactions of Bengalis and Sikhs in Calcutta. During the period two leading monthlies, *Prabasi* and *Bharatbarsha,* featuring important news items about India and abroad, were by and large sympathetic to the national movement. Hence, they published reports on the Akali *satyagrahis* involved in the gurdwara reform movement along with their photographs, something not so common in contemporary Oriya and Assamese publications. Nationalist newspapers highlighted the Nankana massacre as well as its repetition at Guru-ka-Bagh. On the second occasion, *Prabasi* attacked the official policy of repression in the strongest terms and extended full support to the Akali agitators.

But the most articulate support to the Akali movement came from the newborn daily *Ananda Bazar Patrika*, founded on the first of Baisakh 1329 BS (15 April 1922). The memory of the Nankana massacre of the Akalis still rankled. At least on fifty occasions in 1922,[81] the *Patrika* offered in-depth evaluation of different aspects of the movement and a photo feature and three valuable editorial comments. Two trends are evident in the pages of the newspaper in 1922: (1) all sympathy and support to the Akali agitators and (2) severe criticism of the repressive policy of the government. The police torture of Akali demonstrators, their trial, the consequent reaction among the Sikhs in cities in and out of Punjab, the joining of retired soldiers and the Nirmala sect, the unrest among the Sikh soldiers in the Indian army, the presence of the senior Akali leaders at the Gaya Congress session—all these issues are covered in the *Ananda Bazar Patrika* throughout the year. Sometimes these news items are said to have been received on the wire and sometimes from other newspaper sources. Though sympathetic to the Akalis, the newspaper would from time to time publish official handouts against

[81] The first news item on the Akalis appeared in *Ananda Bazar Patrika* this year (1922) on 6 Baisakh (20 April) and the last one on 6 Paush (21 December).

them. No less important than the news were the editorial comments. The following editorial of the *Patrika* would bring out the extent of the Akali support in faraway Calcutta:

> For the last two months the Sikhs at Guru-ka-Bagh have been suffering all kinds of torture and imprisonment. . . . It is hard to tell how long the state of affairs will continue and what will be its outcome in the near future. On one side are the army and the baton-wielding police to protect law and order, on the other there is truth, justice, and the non-violent Akali agitator fighting for his religion. It is unprecedented in world history. . . . [In] these days of moral decline, the example of self-sacrifice, which the Sikhs have set, should fill all humanity with pride.

Later on, mass support for the Akalis came from various corners. One such issue was the Nabha affair. The maharaja of Nabha, Ripudaman Singh, abdicated (1923), in the face of growing animosity with the local level British administration. This sudden political development at Nabha led Akali *satyagrahis* to a miliant stance. The All-India Congress leadership championed the cause of the Akalis. It popularized the Akali movement in the princely states and the events there came to deeply influence national life. The Akalis hailed the Nabha maharaja as their national leader and spread the message that he was a victim of British conspiracy. *Ananda Bazar Patrika* published such news occasionally in a highly emotion-charged language and tried to mobilize support for the Akalis in Calcutta. When the Akalis appealed to the nation at large to observe 9 September 1923 as 'Nabha Protest Day',[82] many Sikh and non-Sikh residents of Calcutta expressed widespread support and came out in the streets. Once again in 1928, they arranged *diwans* inside the gurdwaras to protest against British terrorization. National leaders like Subhas Chandra Bose were invited to speak there. In response to the call to boycott the Simon Commission, the Sikhs did not put their buses and taxis on the road on the day of the strike. Similar incidents were reported during the days of the Civil Disobedience Movement and even afterwards.[83] It will be no exaggeration to say that since the early 1920s, the Sikhs in Calcutta

[82] *Ananda Bazar Patrika*, 9 September 1923.

[83] Anonymous, 'Kalikatae Sikh Michhil', *Masik Basumati*, Baisakh 1330 BS, pp. 198-204; Tanika Sarkar, *Bengal 1928-34: The Politics of Protest,* Delhi 1987, pp. 16, 36, 95; Ranjit Kumar Roy, 'Simon Commission Boycott 1928: A Study of Sikh Participation in Urban Politics of Calcutta', *The Sikh Review*, August 1991, pp. 46-53. For Subhas Chandra Bose's close political understanding with the Sikhs of Calcutta and elsewhere, see Subhas Chandra Bose, *The Indian Struggle, 1920-34,*

maintained close links with the local Congress leadership in the national movement. One must recognize the primary role of the Akali movement in bringing about this Sikh-Bengali political understanding.

XI

Sikh studies of the post-Guru period offer an interesting view of the Bengali mind of the period. A significant number of pre-Independence writers in Bengali found the unbroken tradition of martyrdom of the Sikhs worth remembering. It began with Banda Bahadur and stretched to the days of the Akali movement and even beyond. Some of the Sikh women too, drew their attention. The discussion and debate over queen Jindan is an instance in point. Rajanikanta Gupta started the debate in the late nineteenth century and the growing anti-British sentiment also enriched the process of historical enquiry.

Seveal interesting novels, plays and short stories were written about Ranjit Singh and the period that followed him. The spectacular political triumph of Ranjit Singh and the failure of his successors inspired Bengali creativity. One or two plays were written about the tenth Guru but they flopped. The post-Guru period is no doubt richer in this respect.

In the Sikh studies of the post-Guru period, there is, however, a tendency to bypass the contemporary Punjabi literary sources. There was no writer who used Punjabi literature as materials of history like Bhai Mahendranath, Krishnakumar, Ritendranath, Abinashchandra or Sashibhusan. Kaliprasanna Chatterjee is a shining exception. But though he infrequently used spoken Punjabi while writing about everyday life in the novel, he was silent about the relevant Punjabi sources dealing with the Khalsa Raj. At the time, many were content to flip through easily available secondary sources in English.

Calcutta 1948, pp. 225-7; Hemendra DasGupta, *Subhaschandra,* Calcutta 1946, pp. 106-11, 126-8; Nalinikishore Guha, *Bangalae Biplabbad,* Calcutta 1976, pp. 312-13; Bhagat Ram Talwar, *The Talwars of Pathan Land and Subhas Chandra's Great Escape,* New Delhi 1976, pp. 59-61, 252-7; Sucheta Mahajan, 'British Policy, Nationalist Strategy and Popular National Upsurge, 1945-6', in Amit Kumar Gupta (ed.), *Myth and Reality: The Struggle for Freedom in India, 1945-7,* New Delhi 1987, pp. 72-3; Leonard A. Gordon, *Brothers Against the Raj,* New Delhi 1990, pp. 244-5. I am indebted to Girishchandra Maiti for drawing attention to some of these sources on Subhas Chandra Bose and his intimate political link with the Sikhs.

There can be thus no two opinions about the fact that in Bengali studies of the post-Guru period, Punjabi literary evidence lost much of its importance. But mention should also be made of the development of Sikh studies in the second decade of the twentieth century at the postgraduate level of the University of Calcutta. Outside Punjab, Calcutta University was the only institution which brought Sikh studies into an academic framework. So far Bengali Sikh studies had been predominantly confined to the vernacular. University research was more committed to the critical use of historical sources and documentation and was carried out in English, reaching a serious readership with a consequent qualitative change in its methodology and understanding of the past.

Along with that came about the political understanding between the Sikhs and Bengalis on certain issues of the national struggle. The Sikhs of Calcutta joined the national movement, and the Punjabi newspaper *Deshdarpan* published from the Kavi Press in south Calcutta also attached increasing importance to local news from the 1940s. There were new Sikh settlements and new gurdwaras in south Calcutta—all these underlined the growing faith and confidence of the local Sikhs towards the city. The Sikh taxi driver in Calcutta became an institution symbolizing the Bengali Hindu's reliance on Sikh prowess.[84] The positive Bengali attitude to the Sikh sardars more or less continued in the post-Independence years. Punjab tragedy of the 1980s and the Khalistani demand for a Sikh homeland outside the Indian constitutional framework no doubt led to a few temporary flutters here and there. But the Sikhs are not generally regarded as a community that may disturb the peace of the region. Perhaps its legacy is still there in the early years of the new century.[85]

[84] It may be partly due to the active participation of a section of Calcutta Sikhs in favour of Bengali Hindus against the Muslims during communal riots of 1946. Cf. Suranjan Das, *Communal Riots in Bengal, 1905-47,* Delhi 1991, pp. 91, 167, 182. For a caricature of the contemporary Bengali Hindu psyche about Sikh prowess, see Pramathanath Bisi's 'Sikh', *Pranabir Nikristha Galpa,* Calcutta n.d., pp. 78-85. For an interesting discussion on the Sikh taxi drivers of Calcutta and Bengali confidence about them, see *The Telegraph*, 31 July 1994.

[85] Suchitra Bhattarcharya's novelette *Parabash,*Calcutta 1985, is a significant attempt to appreciate the Calcutta Sikhs' trauma following the Operation Blue Star.

CHAPTER VI

Conclusion

SIKH STUDIES in the three eastern Indian languages represent an attempt by non-Sikhs living beyond Punjab to understand and communicate the message of Sikhism. The authors came from various walks of life, spoke separate languages, belonged to different political traditions and varied religious beliefs. They generally wrote on their own initiative and interpreted the Panthic history for the people of the area stretching from Berhampore on the coast of Orissa to Dibrugarh in the Assam valley. Their participation brought a multivalence to Sikhism, which was often missing in the writings of many Punjabi authors of the same period. They enriched the modern Indian literary tradition and set a novel example of mobilization through the vernacular printing press. Much of it was an indirect legacy of the dispersal of the British administrative network around the major urban centres and the Indian response to it. Of these three languages, Sikh studies in Bengali steadily surpassed the others in depth and extent as well as in variety and quality.

I

The dominant trend in these writings was a reconstruction of the history of the Sikh Gurus. The Brahmos of the city of Calcutta were the first to review the life and mission of Guru Nanak. They were primarily concerned with Sikhism's message of monotheism and social protest. These issues received serious attention in the biographies of the founder of the Sikh Panth. The Bengali Brahmos critically analysed their sources, often consulted Punjabi texts and came up with some outstanding studies of the first Sikh Guru. They inspired their Brahmo counterparts of Orissa and tried to stimulate almost similar enquiries in Cuttack and Balasore. Assamese achievements in the field were comparatively less significant maybe from the limited success of Brahmoism in the region.

With the emasculation of the Brahmo movement in the late

nineteenth century, the interest that Brahmos had shown in Sikhism also waned, leading in its turn to a significant change in the course of Sikh studies. The Brahmo withdrawal left the door wide open for Hindu nationalist and Sanatani authors to step into the arena. The contemporary political scene, which had long been animated by Hindu militant ideology, favoured the publication of biographies of the Sikh Gurus with a marked Hindu flavour. From Guru Nanak, the monotheist and anti-idolater of the Brahmo model, attention steadily shifted to Guru Gobind Singh, the defender of Hinduism against political oppression and religious injustice. The last Sikh master was extolled together with other medieval Hindu heroes like Prithviraj Chauhan, Rana Pratap and Chhatrapati Shivaji for resisting Muslim tyranny and domination. In other accounts the Sikh Guru was projected either as a puranic hero envisaging sweeping political transformation or as a conservative Hindu high priest eschewing social change through his institution of the Khalsa. The Brahmo biographies of Guru Nanak needed to be revised. Instead Guru Nanak was placed within the context of medieval reformers like Ramananda and Chaitanya seeking to save the Sanatan Hindu religion from many of its existing maladies. It was emphasized that the Sikh Guru had no plan of setting up a separate religion from that of the Hindus. Even the accounts of self-sacrifice of the fifth and the ninth Sikh Gurus were systematically exploited for reinforcing the growing Hindu orientation to Sikhism of the region.

Reconstruction of the post-Guru phase of Sikh history continued to be animated by an almost identical imagery. It sought to highlight the executions of Banda Bahadur, Bhai Taru Singh, Bhai Mani Singh and others, who came to be included in the Hindu martyrology and the reconstructed versions of their tragic denouements were embellished with modern phraseology. These accounts were expected to be remembered by the succeeding generations for the defence of their own religion. Ranjit Singh's reign also received a distinct Hindu colouring. The Sikh monarch was depicted with many interesting Hindu insignia even in the school textbooks and theatrical performances. He was hailed as the last independent Indian sovereign restoring Hindu military might after a gap of nearly seven hundred years of Muslim rule. The Maharaja was not, however, spared for his failings and deviations from the Hindu way of life.

The bulk of such studies was often articulated in the language of communal ideology. Both Hindus and Muslims contributed to the process, though the writings of the latter were few in number and these remained scattered and fragmentary. In view of the overwhelming preponderance of Hindu authors of different shades, Sikh studies in eastern India virtually remained a Hindu territory where the Muslims had an occasional entry. With the exception of a small group of Brahmos, these authors were generally unconcerned about, if not oblivious of, the contemporary Sikh search for a separate communal identity in Punjab. On certain important issues, perhaps the eastern Indian Sikh studies had been closer to the hopes and aspirations of the Punjabi Hindus. Its dominant assimilationist rhetoric, when it identified itself with Hindu majoritarian invasiveness in the post-Independence decades, was destined to give rise to many complex political repercussions in the politics of Punjab during the last quarter of the twentieth century.

II

The Sikh past gradually became an important vehicle of nationalism, providing a kind of legacy to the Indians' fight for freedom from British rule in its different phases since the late nineteenth century. With the evolution of anti-British sentiment and the spread of popular support for the Swadeshi agitation, the politics of the extremists and the upsurge of the twentieth century mass mobilization, many looked back to the history of the Sikhs with considerable pride and enthusiasm. While outlining its history of 500 years, the authors did not generally conceal their fascination for the martyrdom of the Sikh Gurus, the Khalsa's readiness to fight for its political freedom, the sufferings of the non-violent Akali *satyagrahis* and many other similar accounts of sacrifices. Sometimes, these were steeped in the language of open defiance and provided an ideology of righteous resistance to British rule. In many eastern Indian homes, it carried the message that the Sikhs had earlier suffered untold tragedies in defence of their political honour and human dignity against state despotism. These need to be remembered while negotiating with the Britishers. Authors resurrected many such episodes in a style and manner calculated to raise the political barometer of the region. Readers were not always ready to recapitulate them as mere poetic rhetoric or dramatic excitement. Instead they seemed to carry a kernel of truth from the sources of history and hence needed to be read, remembered and retold for invigorating the Indians' resistance to British rule.

However, all did not speak in the same voice and style. Nor did everyone envisage an immediate end of British rule in India. In the beginning, Sikh studies flourished in the midst of the politics of loyalty. Its early manifestations surfaced shortly after the annexation of Punjab. One of the exponents earnestly appealed to the colonial masters to give a second thought to their policy of deposition of the young Sikh prince Duleep Singh from his ancestral possessions. It was even suggested that this could tarnish the fair image of the British in India. The muted voice of appeal conveyed a sense of ambivalence even in the loyalists' appreciation of British rule in the country. There was, however, nothing to suggest that it led to any significant modification in their attitude towards the colonial administration. Nor did it usher in an era of violent protest, for which we have to wait for another quarter of a century. Even after the rise of militant nationalism in the twentieth century, the support for the English did not altogether evaporate. It continued to pour in occasionally from Assam (Lakshminath Bezbarua), Orissa (Sivaprasad Das) and Bengal (Tinkari Banerjee), underlining the blessings of British rule. Again there were others who upheld anti-British sentiments at the regional level. They had also subtle differences among them regarding methods to be followed for resisting the British. Sikh studies thus remained a composite area of intellectual activity seeking to accommodate diverse, sometimes mutually conflicting, political aspirations and the role models within a well-defined literary ambit.

III

The history of the Sikhs was again intimately associated with the process of reconstruction of the past in the three eastern Indian languages. Bengali Brahmos, who represented the upper echelon of the Western educated middle class, pioneered the process. Their critical response to the different categories of sources as well as their rigorous methodology gave history writing a big push at the beginning. They had generally been aware of the *Janamsakhis* though all of them did not use them with equal expertise and competence in the biography of the first Sikh Guru. A few of these writings were highly acclaimed and are still recalled in important academic discussions. On the other hand, the Brahmos of Orissa were not seriously concerned about primary sources on Sikh history, usually borrowing information from their Bengali counterparts. Their writings on Guru Nanak thus did not reach the height and maturity attained by the Bengali Brahmos of the same period.

In Bengal, many authors continued to refer to Punjabi primary sources even after the Brahmos had left the scene. A revised edition of Guru Gobind Singh's biography, based on *Suraj Prakash,* was brought out in the early decades of the twentieth century. It, however, lacked much of the Brahmo sophistication in the treatment of primary sources. Later on, translations of the sacred Sikh texts like the *Japji* and the *Sukhmani* came to be published from time to time, but they missed the sensibility evident in the works of Haranchandra Chakladar.[1] These were mostly brought out in the post-Independence decades. Chakladar's style and interpretation of the intricate Sikh philosophy gave his works an expansive height never attained before by any author of the region. But the *Adi Granth* as well as *Dasam Padshah ki Granth* continued to elude the vernacular readers primarily because of their voluminous size.

Sikh studies in the region also reveal a close knowledge of the works of British administrator-historians. The initial contact occurred at an early phase of British rule, but the dependence did not diminish even in the first half of the twentieth century. In fact it grew stronger. In some cases, the Indian authors displayed a tendency to uncritically accept the interpretations of these British authors in their entirety. Cunningham decidedly exercised the most powerful influence on the Bengali researchers on Sikhism. He was projected as a beacon heralding Sikh liberty. On the other hand, authors like Rajanikanta Gupta did not hesitate to criticize some of these British sources as biased and malicious.[2] The growing anti-British sentiments no doubt played a significant role in this regard. It was also alleged that, in the interest of their imperial concern in India, British administrators had made a travesty of the Sikh political tradition. They therefore sought to project an alternative model of the Sikh past 'not distorted by foreign interpreters'.

In the midst of these conflicting views, a critical trend of historical research steadily evolved, which often reviewed the English authors after processing them through the litmus test of the author's own perception. An outstanding work of the genre is Barodakanta Mitra's *Sikh Juddher Itihas o Maharaja Duleep Singha,* remarkable for its wealth of material and the writer's logical clarity in pursuing his historian's craft.[3] In his quest for the Sikh past, he was also the first to add a series of footnotes and a long and separate bibliography

[1] Supra, p. 172.
[2] Supra, p. 213.
[3] Supra, pp. 217-18.

emphasizing the need that history should be documentary and critical. The significant step forward in Bengali Sikh studies was generally missing in the Assamese writings of the period. In spite of their long tradition of *Buranji* writings since the medieval days, the Sikh past did not achieve a criticality in Assam. On the contrary, many front ranking authors devoted much of their artistic talent and energy to creative writings highlighting the varied roles of the Sikh soldiers in Assam. These no doubt reserved for them a distinct place in the evolution of Sikh studies in eastern India. But it may be argued whether these works could altogether compensate for the absence of an analytical historical tradition on the Sikhs in Assamese. In Oriya, however, Sivaprasad Das showed some modest initiative in the same direction. If his critical and sober assessment of Guru Gobind Singh was an explicit response to Tagore's unsympathetic utterances about the last Sikh Guru, it definitely represents an important step forward in the early twentieth century Oriya historiography. Chintamani Acharya also tried to enrich the mother tongue, but his efforts were generally marked by plagiarism and therefore often lacked originality.

IV

The local social milieu and cultural experience occasionally imparted a regional flavour to Sikhism in the three eastern Indian languages. Instead of marginalizing local specificities and stimulating certain interesting readjustments in the reception and transmission of the message of the Sikh Panth in this part of the country, they highlighted the plurality and fragmentation within the local Sikh tradition. Thus, we have the Guru Nanak of the Oriya folk memories, which is strikingly different from the Guru Nanak of the Gaudiya (Bengali) Vaishnava perceptions.[4] Again the dichotomy has been traced to the *malita, sadhukatha* and other categories of Assamese sources. These raw materials furnish a revised version of the Sikh military activity not widely known in Punjab. Noted Assamese littérateurs could carve out two dissimilar personalities like Kumedan Singh, the foreign mercenary plundering Assam, and Chaitanya Singh, the patriot who died in defence of Assamese liberty.[5] These interesting images are not exact replicas of the Sikhs of Punjab. They do not always refer to the external symbols of Sikhism and maintain silence

[4] Supra, pp. 75-6, 140.
[5] Supra, pp. 51, 55-63, 67-8.

about the *rahit maryadas*. On the contrary, they offer an opportunity of recasting Sikh traditions within the broader Indian parameters. The significant reorientation of the Sikh ethos perhaps points to its comparative plasticity outside its place of origin. It may not fit in well with the much-articulated definition of Sikhism. But, in view of the long history of Sikh diaspora within India and outside, we could not altogether ignore these heterogeneous Sikh images as mere aberrations for emphasizing 'cultural pluralism' and representing 'a shared identity'.

There is yet another side to the issue. Apart from rich oral traditions and literary sources, the region is populated by a few distinct categories of 'hyphenated' Sikhs whose history may be pushed back to more than two hundred years. The Assamese-Sikhs are traditionally agricultural and live in rural areas, but the Agraharis (also called Patnaiyas or Bihari-Sikhs) are predominantly associated with the various retail trades and are domiciled in and around the city of Calcutta. These two communities constitute less than 1 per cent of the regional population and have very little experience of Punjab and Punjabi language. They do not represent homogeneous groups.[6] Generally speaking, these men have taken local brides and through them incorporated regional lifestyle, value system, rituals, dress and other parameters of localism. Of the five Ks, they are particular about their *kesh*; otherwise they can hardly be distinguished from the rest of the local population. Many of them have never been to the *parikarma* of the Harimandir Sahib at Amritsar and try to maintain a safe distance from their Punjabi-speaking brethren at the social level. They celebrate *gurpurabs*, etc., in their distinct local style and sometimes declare themselves to be Sikh-Hindu, Sanatani Hindu or simply Hindu.

The Sikh diaspora is often bracketed with the so-called 'hybridity'[7] in different parts of the world. To any outsider these Assamese-Sikhs and Bihari-Sikhs (Agraharis) perhaps belong to this category. It may, however, be debated whether the process of

[6] This is particularly true regarding their earlier marriage system. Those who were economically well off and comparatively highly placed in society used to give away their daughters in marriage to bridegrooms in distant places like Patna, Katiahar, Purnia and Sasaram. The impression is based on my personal interviews with Dhyan Singh, President, Assamese Sikh Association, Guwahati (23 April 1994) and Manmouji Singh, President, Chhoti Sikh Sangat, Calcutta (5-6 March 1997).

[7] I have borrowed it form Salman Rushdie's *The Satanic Verse* cited in Karen, op. cit., p. 217.

indigenization of immigrant communities whereby they gradually incorporate some of the mores of the neighbourhood and in course of time, claim the status of the sons of the soil, can be categorized as such. Their syncretic face as well as their gradual 'convergence with and assimilation to the local milieu' can hardly be missed by any student of Sikh history.[8] They perhaps need our greater attention due to their new identity articulation and the growth of a community consciousness in the land where their predecessors had come to settle in the past.

The regional Sikh world no doubt differs significantly from the one which may be called the 'Great Tradition' of Sikhism prevailing in Punjab. Authors of the eastern Indian Sikh studies were particularly keen in recording the message of the latter, and while doing so, they virtually lost the significance of the former. They never asked themselves about how, when and who transmitted the message of Sikhism in this part of India. The local Sikh milieu, its tenets and traditions, its fight for a distinct identity on certain arenas of social life, as well as its syncretic face in relations to the wider host community almost remain an uncharted domain in their writings. Rajanikanta Bardoloi's pen might have rehabilitated the Assemese-Sikhs to a world of honour and prestige. But the local Sikh life with its inner ramifications and aspirations did not find adequate reflections in the eastern Indian writings. With the exception of Phula Singh Chhetri of Assam, these people of mixed ethnic origin also do not occupy any dominant position in the field of Sikh studies. Perhaps, the authors of eastern India were not aware of these indigenous Sikhs as a separate ethnic group from the Sikhs of Punjab. Even today in the city of Calcutta, the Punjabi-speaking Sikhs do not always regard them as *pucca* Sikhs and try to keep them at an arm's length. The local Sikhs also do not have any meaningful social interaction with their Punjabi-speaking counterparts on equal terms largely because of poorer economic position and weaker muscle power. A similar form of tension and rivalry around the issue of Sikh identity dominates the Assamese-Sikh world. This arena of Sikhism, however, stands distinct and apart from the world of Sikh diaspora

[8] Cf. Asim Roy, *The Islamic Syncretistic Tradition in Bengal*, New Delhi reprint, n.d., pp.4-7. This process of interaction between Sikhism and the different local cultural and social traditions in places faraway from Punjab but within India offers an interting area of enquiry. I intend to review a few of these issues in the next volume of my present work.

in the countries of the West facing the challenges of the twenty-first century. These perhaps represent two separate but complementary faces of the contemporary Sikh world and the former cannot be meaningful and significant without a proper understanding of the latter.

V

A survey of these studies suggests that the bulk of it came from different categories of authors other than professional historians, and in the form of poems, short stories, fiction, plays, biographies, travelogues, essays, etc. There is hardly any doubt that some of the writers were not generally aware of the critical perspective of history writing and their narration often drifted into the world of imagination. These writings contained many factual inaccuracies and provided an imaginary history underlining 'a new claim to their past'. Their readers, who did not care to check the authenticity of their accounts, would not regard them as fantasies built on distortion of facts. The authors perhaps did not find it even mandatory to put their sources under a scanner before selecting them for any use.

Such histories, however, offered their authors an interesting channel for ventilating dormant love and hatred towards their friends and enemies.[9] In some cases it provided 'a limitless horizon' to bring the opponents to their knees, recant their fault and even seek pardon for their lifelong misdeeds! Such accounts may evoke protest from men who were their target of criticism and attack, but these would receive simultaneous support and appreciation from their 'own' people. In the eyes of their authors, history was not necessarily restricted to the critical academic world. On the contrary, it could be carried beyond the narrow limits of school textbooks and academic curriculum. These might be placed side by side with the other varieties of literary endeavour beyond the limits of archive-based history. Hence its wider appeal and readership among common people seemed to be more important to them than its analytical methodology dictated by strict adherence to facts and chronological sequence. In other words, like other intellectual activities, it was an endeavour of remembering the past in response to many of their contemporary pressing needs. It again offered 'a

[9] Supra, pp. 154-6, 205-7.

perennial source of power to the subject nation in defining its national goal' as well as its 'means of attainment'.[10]

Perhaps these values inherent in the historical writings on the Sikhs endeared the authors to their wider readership. It also managed to build up an impersonal link between the writers and their distant clientele who were not necessarily known to each other before. It not only facilitated the development of a metropolis-mufasil network over a vast tract of territory, but also provided an interesting re-orientation to Sikh history and religion through the eastern Indian languages. Its vernacularized reading of the different phases of Sikh history underlines its distinctiveness and suggests that these accounts in Indian regional writings could offer more plural choices to scholars in documenting the Sikh past. The folk image of the Oriya Nanak thus differs significantly from the portrait of a tolerant Guru Nanak found begging in a faraway land in the company of a woman of evil repute. They also stand almost poles apart from the widely respected and serious countenance of the Brahmo Guru Nanak often tormented by family ties. Similarly, the futile bid to project Guru Gobind Singh in a human garb on the Calcutta public stage or the contrasting role models of Kumedan Singh and Chaitanya Singh in the Assam valley deserve special consideration. These represent interesting attempts to introduce Sikh studies to the wider Indian regional literary world. It may open new doors to Sikh studies and add unexpected variations there.

VI

Sikh studies gradually broke fresh grounds in Bengal and steadily transcended the regional limits to attain a new height and respectability. The century-long search in Bengali for the Sikhs of history provided it with the necessary background. The Sikh past became an integral part of the professional teaching and critical research at the postgraduate level, stimulating publication of significant research works on Sikh history and religion in English. Some of these are still read, translated and quoted in serious academic discussions.

A modest beginning was made in the College Street campus of the University of Calcutta in the first quarter of the last century. At the request of the then Vice-Chancellor, Indubhusan Banerjee of the

[10] Chatterjee, *The Nation and its Fragments*, p. 91.

History Department took up teaching and research of Sikh history and religion.[11] Meanwhile Jadunath Sarkar had brought out a significant portion of his research on the reign of Aurangzeb, with brief references to the Sikhs of history.[12] But there was no serious effort to take note of relevant Punjabi sources for the reconstruction of the Sikh past. On the other hand, the postgraduate department of History of Calcutta University ensured, for the first time, a perennial channel of interaction with younger students in the classrooms as well as fellow scholars from other academic disciplines. In the way new people, new sources, images and ideas continued to enrich Sikh studies.

To Indubhusan Banerjee goes the credit of providing a distinct shape to Sikh studies at the University of Calcutta. In his magnum opus, *Evolution of the Khalsa* in two volumes, he points to how the peaceful sect gradually turned into a 'military order' under the force of circumstances. Banerjee, however, had no doubt that the Khalsa underlined 'a new ideology' and took note of various 'psychological and social-anthropological factors' which had so long remained beyond the arena of regional Sikh studies. More recent scholarship may criticize him for his 'blindness to the significance' of the *banis* of Guru Nanak, but his pioneering study of the role of the Jats in the 'transformation of the initially peaceful Sikh community into Guru Gobind Singh's Khalsa' makes it an important work even today.[13]

If Banerjee had studied the evolution of the Sikh Panth under its ten Gurus (1469-1708), the political history of another 123 years (1716-1839) was enlivened in the works of Narendra Krishna Sinha of the same department. Contemporary national sentiments were reflected in both of his works—*Ranjit Singh* (1933) and *Rise of the Sikh Power* (1936). He found the eighteenth century Sikh movement 'a nation up in arms against its enemies, struggling for independence'. He did not agree with Sarkar that these people were mere 'plunderers' and 'brigands'. On the contrary, Sinha euphorically

[11] For a brief introduction to Indubhusan Banerjee's teaching and research in the University of Calcutta, see Pramathanath Banerjee et al. (eds.), *Hundred Years of the University of Calcutta*, Calcutta 1957, pp. 336, 385; A.C. Banerjee, 'Indubhusan Banerjee', in Fauja Singh (ed.), *Historians and Historiography of the Sikhs*, pp. 239-58.

[12] J.N. Sarkar, *A History of Aurangzib*, vol. III, Calcutta 1928; A.C. Banerjee, *Guru Nanak to Guru Gobind Singh*, New Delhi 1978, p. 195.

[13] For a critical assessment of Indubhusan Banerjee's contributions, see the relevant essays by A.C. Banerjee and J.S. Grewal in Fauja Singh (ed.), *Historians and Historiography of the Sikhs*, pp. 239-63.

elevated them to the status of a 'national militia' fighting for the defence of their religion and liberty. He found Ranjit Singh 'a man of destiny' providing definite political shape to what had been envisioned by Guru Gobind Singh more than a century ago. His emotional exuberance about Sikh political greatness may prompt a section of his critics to bracket him with the older tradition of Hindu nationalist historiography. But nowhere in his writings did Sinha equate the Sikhs with the Hindus.

But Sikh studies were not always restricted to the teaching and researches of the History Department of the University of Calcutta. Teachers from other branches of social sciences came forward and enriched it in the post-Independence years. In the 1960s, for example, Suniti Kumar Chatterji and Niharranjan Ray were invited to deliver lectures by the two universities of Punjab.[14] Chatterji briefly talked on the tenth Guru. Ray, however, sought to underline why the 'discipline of sociology of religion' was required for a meaningful understanding of the message and milieu of the Sikh Gurus. He not only pointed out the syncretic tradition of Sikhism, but also tried to draw attention to the area of its distinctiveness. His lectures represent a significant attempt by a non-Sikh scholar to appreciate the philosophy of Sikhism in the wider perspective of medieval Indian religious tradition. The process continued afterwards. Anil Chandra Banerjee's research from the days of his association with the University of Calcutta in the early 1940s to his elevation to the Guru Nanak Chair, Jadavpur University in the early 1970s is another interesting pointer in that direction. He provided accounts of the Sikh Panth from the birth of Guru Nanak to the fall of the Khalsa Raj in five separate volumes published between 1949 to 1985.[15] His scholarly studies imparted dignity to the Guru Nanak Chair, which he held for a couple of years in the 1970s.

VII

The development of teaching and research on Sikhism strictly according to the norms and needs of the postgraduate academic

[14] Suniti Kumar Chatterji, *Guru Gobind Singh (1666-1708)*, Chandigarh 1967; Niharranjan Roy, *The Sikh Gurus and the Sikh Society*, New Delhi 1975.

[15] *Anglo-Sikh Relations*, Calcutta 1949; *Guru Nanak and His Times*, Patiala 1984; *From Guru Nanak to Guru Gobind Singh*, New Delhi 1978; *The Sikh Gurus and the Sikh Religion*, New Delhi 1983 and *The Khalsa Raj*, New Delhi 1985.

schedule have had a deep impact on the evolution of Sikh studies in regional languages. Paradoxically, its induction at the university level coincided with a gradual decline of Sikh studies in Bengali language. The process was well on its way around the third decade of the twentieth century. Already the rise of Gandhi had led to a significant change in the Indian scene, stimulating numerous literary works underlining the 'contemporary political milieu'. The reconstruction of the past came to take a back seat in the imagination of these authors. Instead, a large-scale mass mobilization, attuned to the contemporary political situation, figured prominently in their writings. Their heroes did not emerge from the pages of history, but represented ordinary folk of the contemporary rural or urban society. The significant shift in the literary direction caused an erosion of much of the early Bengali admiration and enthusiasm for the Sikhs of history. It is reflected in the number of publications dealing with the Sikh past since the 1920s. From then onwards, contemporary developments in Sikh politics led by the Akalis have received increasing attention rather than its glorious heritage.[16]

The gradual introduction of the university-centric Sikh studies enforcing a rigorous methodology as well as a vigorous scrutiny of the sources led to its further differentiation from the existing tradition. The older tradition of Sikh studies continued to prevail beyond the limits of the academic discipline, but it lost much of its earlier credibility in the process. There was hardly any constructive dialogue between these two complementary wings, which might have had an enriching influence on both of them. The new genre of Sikh studies spearheaded by university teachers possibly did not hold a very high opinion even about the significant works of the late nineteenth and early twentieth centuries. With one or two exceptions, these older vernacular sources were generally more remembered in rejection than in inclusion in the bibliographies. The persistent search of academicians for a more definitive and critical methodology often led to marginalization of their non-professional predecessors.

In the post-Independence years, the new scholarship steadily entered into the wider space demarcated as 'national' and 'mainstream'. The authors did not have to wait long for their 'warm' acceptance among the Sikh scholars of Punjab. Their writings generally fitted in well with the dominant tradition of Sikh studies at the all-India level.

[16] Supra, pp. 222-4.

Except for a few ripples of dissent or differences here and there, the scholars universally depended on the *Janamsakhis* for the reconstruction of Guru Nanak's life and mission. Neither did they debate on whether there was a major break in the early Sikh tradition or whether there should be a search for 'contemporary and near-contemporary evidence' to know all that had happened on the day of the Baisakhi of 1699.[17] Similarly, the Sikh oral tradition of martrydom was never seriously brought under a scanner.[18] On the contrary, they generally approved of those sources which had been 'nurtured in the Sikh tradition' and sought to reconstruct the Sikh past on the basis of 'information from such sources'.

The appreciation of the 'traditional' Sikh point of view brought the university-centric Sikh studies of Calcutta closer to the Sikh world in the post-Independence decades. With the tragedies of Partition (1947) in the background, it became an important cultural adhesive for bringing Punjab and West Bengal on a common platform and it was found relevant for building a 'powerful united India' in the post-colonial period. The academic exercise, often seeking uniformity and symmetry in different areas of Sikh studies, was expected to become a significant part of the larger national colloquium of the period. It was focused as a cementing process and engrafted into the womb of the Indian nation state system. The so-called 'national conscience' that evolved in the name of 'modern' 'scientific' Sikh studies often discouraged any form of plurality or dissent in the message of Sikhism. A few of those issues which had figured prominently in the three eastern Indian vernacular sources since the late nineteenth century were increasingly neglected in the new university-centric Sikh studies. Those profiles of the 'other' Sikhs dominating the eastern Indian vernaculars were increasingly cast aside. Perhaps, these were identified as 'unhistorical', 'communal', and 'archaic' images, which had no 'documentary' confirmation in the Sikh tradition. In the name of 'rationalizing' it to the new academic needs, the vernacular-based Sikh studies were generally ignored and silenced. Common human sentiments like joy and sorrow, pity and hatred, humour and satire, which often figured in heroic verses, picturesque poetry and historical romance only evoked cold reception. The tendency to identify the

[17] Cf. J.S. Grewal, 'The Khalsa of Guru Gobind Singh', *From Guru Nanak to Maharaja Ranjit Singh*, Amritsar 1982, pp. 86-7; Hew McLeod, *Sikhism*, p. xxiii.

[18] For a recent debate on this issue, see Louis E. Fenech, *Martyrdom in the Sikh Tradition: Playing the 'Game of Love'*, New Delhi 2000.

vernacular Sikh studies with an inferior level of scholarship almost became an approved norm of academic dialogue of the period. It was generally pushed aside and segregated to a world of silence and indifference. This 'disciplining' of the Sikh past is likely to deprive it of its intimate eastern Indian roots. Through this denial, it would not only be missing much of its rich non-Punjabi vernacular heritage conveying the 'virtues of ethnic and linguistic diversities', but also be turning its face from the Indian regional and plural cultural traditions.

Glossary

Adi Granth	- Sikh sacred text, also called the *Guru Granth Sahib*
Adwaita Vedanta	- non-duality; the school of Hindu philosophy postulating the monism of Sankaracharya
Agrahayan (also Aghan)	- eighth month of the year (from mid-November to mid-December)
Akali	- a follower of the timeless one, i.e. God; also meaning those Sikhs who spearheaded the gurdwara reform movement in the 1920s
Akalpurakh	- the timeless one, God
Alakh Niranjan	- ineffable one, God
amrit	- the nectar of immortality
Amritdhari	- those Sikhs who have taken *amrit*; an initiated member of the Khalsa
Anand Karaj	- Sikh marriage ceremony
Ashar (also Ahar)	- third month of the year (from mid-June to mid-July)
Ashwin (also Ahin)	- sixth month of the year (from mid-September to mid-October)
avatar	- incarnation of a deity, usually Vishnu
Bairagi	- a Hindu mendicant who roams about the country and practices certain austerities
Baisakh (also Bahag)	- first month of the year (from mid-April to mid-May)
bani	- utterance; works of the Gurus and the *bhagats* recorded in the *Adi Granth*
Bangal	- a foreigner, an outsider
Bangla Sal (BS)	- Bengali Year, add 593/594 for Christian Era equivalent
barkandaz	- a mercenary
Bhadra (also Bhada)	- fifth month of the year (from mid-August to mid-September)
bhadralok	- gentle-folk
bhagat	- an exponent of *bhakti*, also a Sant poet whose works appear in the *Adi Granth*
bhakti	- belief in, and adoration of, a personal God
Buranji	- history, also history of the Ahoms written in Assamese

Chaitra (also Chat) - twelfth and last month of the year (from mid-March to mid-April)

choga - a long loose dress generally used by a *fakir* or *darvish*

darbar - court

darvish - a Muslim mendicant

dharamsala - an inn; a place of worship; earlier name used for a gurdwara

dera - a camp; a temporary or permanent residential establishment

diwan - a congregational, religious meeting

Dobhasi Bangla - Bengali language with a high mixture of Urdu and Persian words

fakir - a Muslim ascetic

gurdwara - a place of Sikh worship

Guru - a spiritual preceptor, usually a person but sometimes understood as the inner voice of God

Guru-gaddi - hereditary seat of authority vested in Sikh Gurus

Gurumahasay - a teacher, also a village school master

hathyoga - '*yoga* of force'–the kind of *yoga* practiced by Nath *yogis*

Hindutva - Hinduness

Jyaistha - second month of the year (from mid-May to mid-June)

Janamsakhi - biographical literature on Guru Nanak written from the perspective of devout Sikhs

jatha - a group, also used for Akali volunteers during their struggle for gurdwara reform in the 1920s

jatra - traditional Bengali open air opera

jihad - holy war, Muslim equivalent of a crusade

kaba - the most exalted place of Islamic worship in Mecca

kadaprasad - sacramental food dispensed in gurdwaras

kalmah - Muslim confession of faith

Kaliyuga - the fourth and last of the cosmic era; the age of degeneracy

kardar - a revenue official

karmayogi - a person who seeks spiritual merit through selfless performance of worldly responsibility

Kartik (also Kati) - seventh month of the year (from mid-October to mid-November)

Keshdhari	-	a Sikh with unshorn hair, one of the marks of Sikh identity
khadku	-	a Sikh militant
Khatri	-	a mercantile caste, particularly important in Punjab
khara sauda	-	a good bargain, honest trading
kirat karna	-	earning bread by honest means
madad-i-maash	-	a category of religious land grant
Magh	-	tenth month of the year (from mid-January to mid-February)
mahant	-	head of a monastery or other similar religious institutions
majhar	-	Muslim shrine
malita	-	a continuous descriptive poem
malwa	-	the name of that portion of eastern Punjab which includes Ferozepur, Patiala, Malerkotla, Bhatinda and Faridkote districts
manjha	-	the central portion of the Bari Doab, land lying between the Beas and Ravi
Masiha	-	Oriya Year, add 593/594 to Masiha dates for Christian Era equivalents
Mazhabi	-	a Sikh from the chuhra (sweeper) caste
misl	-	an armed group of Sikh horsemen during the middle and later decades of the eighteenth century
Mughalbandi	-	three coastal districts of Orissa, viz., Jaleswar, Bhadrak and Cuttack and a few adjoining areas directly administered by the Mughals
mulmantra	-	the 'root *mantra*', the 'Basic Credal Statement' with which begins the Sikh sacred text *Adi Granth*
Na Anka	-	on the ninth regnal year (usually associated with the Orissa famine of 1866)
Nanakpanthi	-	the followers of Guru Nanak who do not observe the discipline of the Khalsa
namaj	-	Muslim liturgical prayer
nirguna	-	without qualities or attributes
Nirmala	-	saffron robe-wearing Sikh itinerant preachers who carried the message of Sikhism beyond Punjab. Their teachings are generally Vedantic
panchali	-	it is a form of doggerel poetry, cited or sung, mostly religious in theme, usually performed before somewhat informal assemblies

panda	- a person whose services are generally requisitioned for offering prayers, etc., to God in any Hindu sacred place
panjpiare	- five beloved
parikarma	- the walking around a pool surrounding a gurdwara
parivar	- family
parwana	- official order
Paush (also Puh)	- ninth month of the year (from mid-December to mid-January)
payar	- Bengali metre
Phalgun *(*also Phagun*)*	- eleventh month of the year (from mid-February to mid-March)
pir	- Muslim religious leader
pucca	- true, real Sikh
Punthi Sahitya	- lit. a book of manuscript; in the nineteenth century the term came to be specially associated with a section of literature created by semi-literate Muslims in the mixture of Arabic, Bengali, Persian and Urdu
purdah	- seclusion of woman
rag	- melody
rahit maryada	- a code of belief and discipline which all Sikhs (Khalsa) vow to observe at the time of initiation
qazi	- a Muslim judge
sabad	- Word, Gurbani; hymns of Gurus
Sachcha Padshah	- God
sadhukatha	- a moral tale, a fable
sahibzadas	- sons of Guru Gobind Singh
sahid	- martyr
Saka	- all-India calender year calculated from 78/79 BC
Sakti	- Goddess of power—a deity of the Hindu pantheon
Salgram	- a kind of ammonite found in the bed of the river Gandak, prized as sacred stone on account of the spiral pattern in it, regarded as representative of Vishnu and worshipped by Hindus
Sambat (also Bikrami)	- all-India calendar year beginning from AD 57/58
Sanatani	- conservative
sangat	- congregration; group of devotees

sannyas	-	renunciation of worldly life
sardar	-	the chief of a *misl*; in modern usage the standard mode of address for all Keshdhari male Sikhs
sati	-	burning of wife on her deceased husband's funeral pyre
satyagraha	-	Gandhian technique of non-violent resistance
Sraban (also Saon)	-	the fourth month of the year (from mid-July to mid-August)
subedar	-	the head of a *suba* or province
suddhi	-	conversion to Hinduism, purification
takhat	-	a centre of Sikh worldly authority
tarpan	-	an important post-mortuary Hindu ritual
tamol-pan	-	a traditional Assamese courtesy of receiving an honoured guest with betel nut and betel-leaf
udasi	-	travels of Guru Nanak for preaching his message
ulema	-	a scholar in Islamic jurisprudence
Vadda Ghalluhara	-	great massacre of the Sikhs by the Abdali in 1762
WaheGuru	-	praise to the Guru, the modern Sikh name for God
vakil	-	an envoy or a deputy
zamindar	-	landlord

Bibliography

PRIMARY SOURCES

Assamese, Bengali, Hindi and Oriya

Acharya, Chintamani, 'Sikhjatir Sadhana', *Mukur,* Agrahayan 1320 Masiha, pp. 248-52; Baisakh 1321 Masiha, pp. 6-11; Ashar 1321 Masiha, pp. 159-63.

———,'Ajit Singha o Jhujhar Singha', *Utkal Sahitya,* Sraban 1322 Masiha, pp. 146-50.

———, *Itihas Prasanga,* Part I, Cuttack 1916.

Acharya, Rajendralal, 'SikhGuru Nanak', *Nabyabharat,* Ashar 1308 BS, pp. 126-32.

Acharya, Ramchandra, 'Bharatar Samarpriya Jatisakal', *Mukur,* Magh 1330 Masiha, pp. 38-9.

Akinchan, 'SriNanak-Charit', *Grihastha,* Ashar-Sraban 1318 BS, pp. 185-202.

Annonymous, 'Nanak', *Bangadarshan,* Ashar 1285 BS, pp. 106-12.

———, 'Dwitiya Sikh Yuddha', *Utkal Madhup,* Bhadra 1800 Saka, pp. 75-7; Ashwin 1800 Saka, pp. 88-90.

———, 'Guru Gobinda', *Bangadarshan,* Magh 1285 BS, pp. 433-43.

———, 'Guru Gobinda Singha', *Nalini,* Baisakh 1288 BS, pp. 1-6; Jyaistha 1288 BS, pp. 33-9.

———, 'Satyadaser Satprasanga: Nanak-Math', *Dharmabandhu,* Phalgun 1294 BS, pp. 251-5.

———, 'Sikhganer Prati Maharani Jindaner Ukti', *Bamabodhini Patrika,* Jyaistha 1298 BS, pp. 49-51.

———, 'Panj Saheb', *Bamabodhini Patrika,* Bhadra 1300 BS, pp. 138-42.

———, *Sikh-Juddha,* Calcutta 1894.

———, 'Amritsarer Subarnamandir', *Satsanga,* Baisakh 1302 BS, pp. 21-5.

———, 'Kada Prasad', *Sahitya Sevak,* Jyaistha 1303 BS, pp. 161-3.

———, 'Amritsarer Gurudarbar', *Purnima,* Kartik 1307 BS, pp. 239-42.

———, 'Prabasir Toka : Sikhar Patan', *Assam Bandhav,* Phagun-Chat 1316 BS, pp. 129-34.

———, *Upasanasar,* Dhamrai 1319 BS.

———, 'Guru Nanak', *Anjali,* Jyaistha 1320 BS, pp. 34-7.

———, 'Amaratwa Labh', *Assam Bandhav,* Phagun 1320 BS, pp. 25-6.

———, 'Kalikatae Sikh Michhil', *Masik Basumati,* Baisakh 1330 BS, pp. 198-204.

———, 'Sikh Parichaya', *Sanskara*, Nos. 7-8, 1928, pp. 1-41.
Agarwala, Jyotiprasad, 'Lovita', Satyendranath Sarma et al. (eds.), *Jyotiprasad Rachanabali*, Guwahati 1981, pp. 187-229.
Banerjee, Anil Chandra, 'AdiGrantha', *Prabasi*, Agrahayan 1352 BS, pp. 140-2.
———, 'Sikh', *Prabasi*, Paush 1350 BS, pp. 250-5.
Banerjee, Basantakumar, 'Bairagi Banda', *Swadeshi*, Chaitra 1313 BS, pp. 203-10.
———, 'Sikh-Sadhana', *Aitihasik Chitra*, Bhadra-Ashwin, 1315 BS, pp. 234-41; Kartik 1315 BS, pp. 306-18; Chaitra 1315 BS, pp. 540-50.
———, 'Sikh-Guru', *Swadeshi*, Agrahayan 1314 BS, pp. 26-38; Paush 1314 BS, pp. 61-8; Phalgun 1314 BS, pp. 141-6; Baisakh 1315 BS, pp. 221-9; Ashar 1315 BS, pp. 319-24; Sraban 1315 BS, 343-7; Bhadra 1315 BS, pp. 370-4; Kartik 1315 BS, pp. 450-5.
———, 'Singha-Sishu', *Aitihasik Chitra*, Sraban 1315 BS, pp. 159-74.
———, 'Ajit Singha o Jhujhar Singha', *Aitihasik Chitra*, Agrahayan 1315 BS, pp. 337-55.
———, 'Subeg Singha o Sabaj Singha', *Bharati*, Kartik 1315 BS, pp. 336-9.
———, 'Mani Singha', *Bharati*, Magh 1315 BS, pp. 451-7.
———, 'Toru Singha', *Bharati*, Phalgun 1315 BS, pp. 505-8.
———, 'Hakikat Rai', *Aitihasik Chitra*, Baisakh 1316 BS, pp. 26-33.
———, 'Mahatab Singha', *Bharati*, Chaitra 1315 BS, pp. 541-7.
———, *Guru Gobinda Singha*, Calcutta 1909.
———, 'Sikhramani', *Prabartak*, Agrahayan 1330 BS, pp. 698-701.
Banerjee, Tinkari, *Guru Gobinda Singha*, Calcutta 1918.
Bardoloi, Rajanikanta, *Dandua Droha*, Guwahati reprint, 1954.
———, *Manomoti*, Guwahati reprint, 1974.
Barua, Gunabhiram, *Anandaram Dhekiyal Phukanar Jiban Charitra*, Guwahati reprint, 1971.
———, *Asam Buranji*, Guwahati reprint, 1972.
Bezbarua, Lakshminath, 'Bidrohat Hindudharmar Unnati (3)', *Banhi*, Saon 1838 Saka, pp. 454-74.
———, 'Padumkuari', *Lakshminath Bezbarua Granthabali*, vol. I, Guwahati 1988, pp. 552-78.
Bhattacharya, Banamali, 'Australia Bhraman', *Avahan*, Bhada 1857 Saka, pp. 1249-53; Kati 1857 Saka, pp. 106-9.
Bhattacharya, Harichandra, 'Nanak', *Banhi*, Ahar 1854 Saka, pp. 138-40.
Bhattacharya, Rajnarayan, *Panjabetihas*, Calcutta 1846.
Bhattacharya, Suchitra, *Parabash*, Calcutta 1985.
Bhuyan, Nakulchandra, 'Chandrakanta Singha', Jatindranath Goswami (ed.), *Nakulchandra Bhuyan Rachana Samagra*, Guwahati 1996, pp. 64-113.
Bhuyan, Surya Kumar, *Barphukanar Geet*, Gauhati 1925.
———, *Lachit Barphukan*, Gauhati 1947.

Bisi, Pramathanath,'Sikh', *Pranabir Nikristha Galpa,* Calcutta n.d., pp. 78-85.
Bora, Mahendra, 'Samurai', *Asamiya Kabita Chayan,* Dibrugarh 1987, pp. 99-102.
Bora, Tarinicharan, 'Nanak', *Jonaki,* Magh 1812 Saka, pp. 129-31
Bose, Amiya, 'Sikh Ramani—Sadakaur', *Bharatbarsa,* Bhadra 1354 BS, pp. 239-41.
———, 'Sikh Ramani-Chandkaur', *Bangashri,* Magh 1354 BS, pp. 145-7.
———, 'Rani Sahebkaur–Sikh Ramani', *Bangashri,* Baisakh 1355 BS, pp. 419-20.
Bose, Haranath, *Guru Gobinda,* Calcutta 1909.
Bose (Mitra), Kumudini, *Sikher Balidan,* Calcutta 1905.
Bose, Mahendranath, *Nanak Prakash,* vols. I-II, Calcutta 1807-15 Saka.
Bose, Manomohan, *Duleen Athaba Ranjit Singha Sankranta Aitihasik Nabanyas,* Calcutta 1813 Saka.
Bose, Sashibhushan, 'Nanak', *Bhaktacharitmala,* Calcutta 1918, pp. 310-27.
Burman, Dineshchandra, *Sikher Atmahuti,* Calcutta n.d.
Chakrabarty, Bipinbehari, 'Hakikat Rai', *Bharati,* Ashar 1317 BS, pp. 185-7.
Chakrabarty, Kshitishchandra, *Nanak,* Calcutta 1323 BS.
Chakrabarty, Manomohan, 'Barishale Paitallish Bachhar', *Brahmabadi,* Ashar 1338 BS, pp. 66-8.
Chakrabarty, Satischandra (ed.), *Brahmasangeet,* Calcutta 1931.
Chatterjee, Bankimchandra, 'Bharat-Kalanka: Bharatbarsha Paradhin Kena', *Bibidha Prabandha,* vols. I-II, Calcutta 1346 BS, pp. 133-44.
Chatterjee, Basantakumar, 'Nankana Saheb', *Bharatbarsha,* Ashar 1334 BS, pp. 94-7.
Chatterjee, Jatindramohan, *Japji Athaba Nanak Gita,* Calcutta 1353 BS.
Chatterjee, Kaliprasanna, 'Sikh Samrat o Satir Shap', *Parichay,* Jyaistha 1346 BS, pp.458-66; Ashar 1346 BS, pp. 560-70; Sraban 1346 BS, pp. 38-40; Bhadra 1346 BS, pp. 114-27; Ashwin 1346 BS, pp. 242-9; Kartik 1346 BS, pp. 313-28; Agrahayan 1346 BS, pp. 426-33.
Chatterjee, Sitalakanta, 'Punjab Bhraman', *Bharati o Balak,* Bhadra 1293 BS, pp. 270-6.
Chhetri, Phula Singh, 'Fateh Singha aru Joyabar Singha, *Alochani,* Ahin 1836 Saka, pp. 442-9.
Chitradas, 'Sikh Birangana', *Banhi,* Kati 1856 Saka, p. 39.
Choudhury, Tripuracharan, 'Chattale Sikh Mandir', *Bharatbarsha,* Baisakh 1323 BS, pp. 717-24.
Das, Chandramani, *Nanak,* Cuttack 1940.
Das, Gopabandhu, *Gopabandhu Rachanabali,* vols. II, VI-VIII, Cuttack 1977-78.
Das, Kunjabehari, 'Mahabir Ranjit Singha', *Sahakar,* Sraban 1346 Masiha, pp. 304-5.

Das, Nabakishore, 'Guru Gobinda', *Utkal Sahitya,* Magh 1346 Masiha, pp. 411-12.

Das, Sivaprasad, *Beerakesari Shivaji,* Cuttack 1929.

———, *Guru Gobinda Singha*, Baripada 1929.

———, *Sikh Prakash*, Sambalpur 1935.

———, *Uchcha Prathamika Bharat Itihas*, Cuttack 1951.

———, *Am Deshar Bir*, Cuttack 1957.

DasGupta, Bipinbehari, 'Guru Nanaksaheb', *Bangashri,* Kartik 1348 BS, pp. 657-63; Agrahayan 1348 BS, pp. 822-8.

Datta, Akshaykumar, 'Nanakpanthi', *Tattwabodhini Patrika*, Chaitra 1772 Saka, pp. 176-83; Ashar 1773 Saka, pp. 48-52; Kartik 1773 Saka, pp. 99-102; Magh 1773 Saka, pp. 135-7; Phalgun 1773 Saka, pp. 154-6.

Datta, Bhupendralal, 'Banda ki Sachcha Padshah?', *Udayan,* Paush 1341 BS, pp. 1129-37.

Datta, Dhaniram, 'Guru Gobinda Singha', *Alochani,* Ashar 1832 Saka, pp. 257-60.

Datta, Jibendrakumar, 'Gurur Ahban', *Prabasi,* Agrahayan 1316 BS, pp. 655-66.

———, 'Wahe Guruji ki Fateh', *Nabyabharat,* Agrahayan 1328 BS, pp. 410-12.

Datta, Krishnabehari, 'Guru Nanak', *Janmabhumi,* Agrahayan 1317 BS, pp. 324-6.

Datta, Rameshchandra, 'Amritsar', *Mukul,* Ashar 1302 BS, pp. 10-11.

Deb, Asutosh, 'Japji', *Sahitya-Samhita,* Ashar-Sraban 1309 BS, pp. 137-74; Bhadra-Ashwin 1309 BS, pp. 257-73.

Deka, Mathuranath, *Nanak,* Guwahati n. d.

Eslambadi, 'Musalman Amaley Hindur Adhikar', *Al-Eslam,* Kartik 1322 BS, pp. 389-93.

Eslambadi, Ali Ahmed Ali, 'Guru Nanaker Islam Priti', *Gulistan,* Ashwin 1340 BS, pp. 344-6.

Ganguli, Panchanan, 'Granthasaheb', *Upasana,* Bhadra 1336 BS, pp. 85-93.

Ghosal, Niradbhusan, *Sikh Abhyudaya*, Balasore 1929.

Ghosh, Ajit Kumar (ed.), *Rammohun Rachanabali*, Calcutta 1973.

Ghosh, Amodini, 'Nanak', *Bharatbarsha,* Ashwin 1320 BS, pp. 822-3.

Gogoi, Sashikanta, 'Gurur Karane', *Milon,* Chat 1856 Saka, pp. 15-18.

Goswami, Mamoni Raisom, *Tej aru Dhulire Dhusarit Pristha*, Guwahati 1994.

Goswami, Nityananda, *Sri Sri SatGuru Nanakjir Agamani Gita ba Jagat Guru Parichay,* Calcutta 1328 BS.

Gupta, Amritalal, 'Patiala o Amritsar', *Bharat-Mahila,* Ashwin 1318 BS, pp. 166-70.

Gupta, Gangaprasad, *Sikhon ka Sahas,* Banaras 1908.

Gupta, Iswarchandra, *Iswarchandra Gupter Rachanabali*, vols. I-II, Calcutta 1327 BS.
Gupta, Jogendranath, *Ranjit Singha*, Calcutta 1330 BS.
———, *Guru Gobinda Singha*, Calcutta 1333 BS.
Gupta, Mahendranath, *Punjab-Keshari Ranjit Singha*, Calcutta 1941.
Gupta, Maithilisaran, *Gurukul*, Chirgaon 2004 Bikrami.
Gupta, Nagendranath, *Nagendra-Granthabali*, vol. I, Calcutta, 1325 BS, pp. 159-68, 189-98.
———, 'Teja Singha', *Prabasi*, Ashar 1311 BS, pp. 142-51.
Gupta, Niranjan, *Bhram Nibaran Arthat kya Sikh Hinduon ke Rakshak Hai ?*, Delhi 1918.
Gupta, Rajanikanta, *Prabandhakusum*, Calcutta 1879.
———, *Aryakirti*, Calcutta reprint, 1908.
———, *Sikh*, Calcutta 1883.
———, *Bharat-Kahini*, Calcutta 1883.
———, 'Tegh Bahadur o Gobinda Singha', *Karnadhar*, Sraban-Bhadra 1296 BS, pp. 213-16.
———, *Beermahima*, Calcutta 1292 BS.
———, *Sipahi Juddher Itihas*, vol. I, Calcutta 1886.
Gupta, Samarbijayi, 'Maharaj Ranjit Singha', *Jayanti*, Magh 1861 Saka, pp. 12-17.
Haq, Mozammel, 'Baba Nanak', *Al-Eslam*, Baisakh 1325 BS, pp. 1-14.
Kakati, Banikanta, 'SikhGuru Nanak aru Tegh Bahadurar Kamrup Bhraman', *Chetana*, Puh 1841 Saka, pp. 223-8.
———, *Purani Kamrupar Dharmar Dhara*, Gauhati 1955.
Kar, Gokulchandra, *Guru Gobinda Singha*, Cuttack 1981.
Kavyananda, Rakhaldas, *Guru Nanak*, Calcutta 1928.
Khan, Abdul Hakim, 'Malerkotla Rajya', *Masik Mohammadi*, Ashwin 1339 BS, pp. 840-2.
Khatri, Lalbehari Singh, *Japji Saheb*, Berhampore 1307 BS.
Lahiri, Durgadas (ed.), *Sikh-Itihas*, Calcutta 1905.
Mahapatra, Basudeb, 'Atmabali', *Satyabadi*, Mithun 1326 Masiha, pp. 87-95.
Mahapatra, Kedarnath, *Uchcha Prathamika Nutan Bharat Itihas*, Cuttack reprint, 1950.
Mahapatra, Niranjan and Tripathi, Baidyanath, *Am Itihas Gap*, vol. II, Cuttack 1951.
Mahata, Anand Kishore, *Jiwan Charitra Sri Guru Gobind Singhji*, Lahore 1971 Bikrami.
Majumdar, Abinashchandra, *Guru Nanakkrita Japji*, Calcutta 1325 BS.
———, 'Guru Tegh Bahadurer Jibani o Bani', *Uttara*, Ashwin 1332 BS, pp. 43-9; Kartik 1332 BS, pp. 98-100; Magh 1332 BS, pp. 299-302; Phalgun 1332 BS, pp. 362-7.
Majumdar, Bimanbehari, *Sikhjatir Itihas*, Calcutta 1929.

———, 'Akali Sikhdiger Itihas', *Bangabani*, Magh 1330 BS, pp. 756-63.
Majumdar, Sureschandra, 'Maharaja Duleep Singher Parinam', *Aitihasik Chitra*, Baisakh 1316 BS, pp. 46-8; Jyaistha 1316 BS, pp. 49-62.
Mishra, Lingaraj, *Guru Gobinda Singha*, Cuttack 1935.
Mishra, Radhamohan, *Sikhon ka Balidan*, Bankipur 1911.
Mishra, Sibnarayan (ed.), *Akali Darshan*, Kanpur, n.d.
Mitra, Barodakanta, *Sikhjuddher Itihas o Maharaja Duleep Singha*, Calcutta 1893.
Mitra, Debendranath, *Sikh Parichay*, Chandannagar, n.d.
Mitra, Kartikchandra, *SikhGuru*, Calcutta 1928.
Mitra, Krishnakumar, 'Nanak Charit', *Suprabhat*, Sraban 1316 BS, pp. 41-6; Bhadra 1316 BS, pp. 49-54; Ashwin 1316 BS, pp. 97-101; Kartik 1316 BS, pp. 145-8; Agrahayan 1316 BS, pp. 193-6; Paush 1316 BS, pp. 241-5; Magh 1316 BS, pp. 289-93; Phalgun 1316 BS, pp. 333-40; Chaitra 1316 BS, pp. 385-7; Baisakh 1317 BS, pp. 433-6; Jyaistha 1317 BS, pp. 481-5; Ashar 1317 BS, pp. 529-33.
———, *Atmacharit*, Calcutta reprint, 1381 BS.
Mukherjee, Sashibhushan, 'Japji', *Nabajiban*, Magh 1295 BS, pp. 262-72; Phalgun 1295 BS, pp. 328-43, 397-414.
———, 'Sikh Dharma', *Aryabartya*, Baisakh 1317 BS, pp. 10-19.
Mullick, Brahmamohan, *Maharaja Ranjit Singher Jiban Brittanta*, Hooghly 1919 Bikrami.
Nandi, Bipinbehari, *Sikh*, Calcutta 1909.
Neog, Maheswar (ed.), *Orunodoi*, Guwahati 1983.
Nirala, Suryakant Tripathi, 'Jago Phir Ekbar', *Nirala Rachanabali*, vol. I, New Delhi 1983, pp. 136-8.
Pande, Rameswar Prasad, *Balidan*, Ajmer, n.d.
Panigrahi, Saratchandra, *Guru Nanak: Jiban o Darshan*, Cuttack 1994.
Parmanand, Bhai, *Bir Bairagi*, Lahore, n.d.
Patnaik, Bankanidhi and Mohanti, Kunjabehari, 'Nanak', *Sadhucharit Mala*, Cuttack 1932, pp. 25-33.
Patnaik, Brundabanchandra, 'Guru Gobinda Singha', *Bharatgaurab*, Cuttack 1937, pp. 47-61.
Patnaik, Madanmohan, 'SikhGuru Gobinda Singha', *Utkal Sahitya*, Magh 1319 Masiha, pp. 278-7.
Patnaik, Padmacharan, 'Sikh Dharmar Sar Katha', *Utkal Sahitya*, Baisakh 1342 Masiha, pp. 30-4.
Prasad, Beni, *Guru Gobind Singh*, Banaras 1977 Bikrami.
Prasad, Jayasankar, 'Bir Balak', *Prasad Granthabali*, Part I, Allahabad 1985, pp. 223-5.
Prasad, Raja Siva, *Sikhon ka Uday aur Ast*, Lucknow 1888.
Prem, Jiban Lal, *Guru Gobind Singh*, Lahore reprint, 1942.
Rajkhowa, Sailadhar, 'Pashan Pratima', Majumala Das (ed.), *Sailadhar Rajkhowa Rachanabali*, Guwahati 1992, pp. 31-3.

Roy, Dinendrakumar, 'Ranjit Singher Darbar', *Janmabhumi*, Phalgun 1301 BS, pp. 134-44.

———, 'Sikhdharmagrantha o Dharmaniti', *Bharati*, Chaitra 1301 BS, pp. 707-13.

———, 'Sikh Sampradayer Adhahpatan', *Bharati*, Phalgun 1302 BS, pp. 612-19.

———, 'Nirmali o Akali', *Bharatbarsha*, Ashwin 1324 BS, pp. 574-9.

Roy, Mahendranath, 'Guru Nanaker Jiban-Charit', *Aryadarshan*, Chaitra 1287 BS, pp. 555-63.

Roy, Matilal, 'Akali', *Prabartak*, Kartik 1329 BS, pp. 625-9.

Roy, Sadhucharan, 'Guru Nanak o Duijana Brahman', *Utkal Sahitya*, Ashar 1304 Masiha, pp. 135-7.

Roy, Saratkumar, *SikhGuru O Sikhjati*, Calcutta 1909.

———, 'Nanak', *Bharater Sadhak*, Calcutta 1914, pp. 34-47.

Saha, Kunjalal, 'Amritsar', *Nabyabharat*, Chaitra 1317 BS, pp. 722-5.

Sahu, Lakhsminarayan, *Guru Gobinda Singha*, Cuttack n.d.

Samaddar, Jatindranath, *Sikher Katha*, Calcutta 1317 BS.

Sampurnanand, *Akalion ka Adarsh Satyagrah*, Banaras 1922.

Sanyal, Brajasundar, 'Sikh Swadhinata', *Bharati*, Sraban 1313 BS, pp. 336-58; Agrahayan 1313 BS, pp. 757-3; Chaitra 1313 BS, pp. 1164-86.

Sarkar, Binaykumar, *Aitihasik Prabandha*, Calcutta 1914.

Sarkar, Pramathanath, 'Guru Arjun Singha', *Abasar*, Ashwin-Kartik 1325 BS, pp. 77-82; Agrahayan 1315 BS, pp. 146-51.

Sen, Bodhisattwa, 'Ranjit Singha o Ingraj', *Aitihasik Chitra*, Nabaparyay, Ashwin 1311 BS, pp. 8-11; Kartik 1311 BS, pp. 135-8; Agrahayan 1311 BS, pp. 184-7; Paush 1311 BS, pp. 215-22.

Sen, Jaladhar, 'Gurudwar', *Sahitya*, Sraban 1301 BS, pp. 275-87.

Sen, Kshitimohan, 'SriGuruNanak Janmyotsab', *Prabasi*, Paush 1344 BS, pp. 359-62.

Sen, Surendranath (ed.), *Prachin Bangla Patra Sankalan*, Calcutta 1942.

Senapati, Fakirmohan, *Bharatbarshar Itihas*, vol. I, Cuttack 1869.

———, *Abasarbasare*, Cuttack 1935.

Sharma, Nandkumardev, *Sikhon ka Utthan aur Patan*, Banaras 1972 Bikrami.

———, *Punjab-Keshri Ranjit Singh*, Bombay 1977 Bikrami.

———, *Punjab Haran aur Maharaja Duleep Singh*, Calcutta 1979 Bikrami.

———, 'Bachchonka Atmotsargya', *Balbir Charitabali*, Calcutta 1924, pp. 69-80.

Sharma, Somdatta, *Bartaman Bharat*, Lahore 1930.

Singh Bhupen, *Guru Teghbahadur*, Guwahati 1985.

Singh, Jiban, 'Sikh aru Sikh Prabrajan', Naren Kalita (ed.), *Rahar Rahadai*, Jorhat 1980, pp. 85-99.

Singh, Vir (ed.), *Bhangu Ratan Singh Sahid Krit Prachin Panth Prakash*, New Delhi reprint, 1998.

Singha, Jyotiprasad, 'Sikhdiger Jatiya Kirti-Swarnamandir ba Gurudarbar,' *Sudha*, Phalgun 1308 BS, pp. 134-8.

Tagore, Debendranath, *Atmacharit*, Calcutta reprint, 1962.

Tagore, Rabindranath, *Rabindra Rachanabali*, vols. I-III, VII, XI, XII and XV, Calcutta 1980-94.

Tagore, Ritendranath, 'Saisabe Guru Nanak', *Punya*, Ashwin-Kartik 1307 BS, pp. 90-6; Jagannath Tirthe Guru Nanak o Jagannather Arati', Phalgun 1307 BS, pp. 271-8; 'Guru Nanak o Makkeswar Siva', Kartik 1310 BS, pp. 82-7; Agrahayan-Paush 1310 BS, pp. 169-78; Phalgun, 1310 BS, pp. 278-86; Chaitra 1310 BS, pp. 363-8; Baisakh-Jyaistha 1311 BS, pp. 472-5; 'Guru Nanak Abatar', Sraban 1311BS, pp. 492-5; 'Guru Nanak', Bhadra-Ashwin 1311 BS, p. 197, 'Guru Nanaker Vyabasaik Buddhi', Kartik 1311 BS, pp. 216-20; 'Guru Nanak o Vaidya Haridas', Magh 1311 BS, pp. 327-30; 'Guru Nanakar Upanayan', Paush 1312 BS, pp. 441-6.

Tarafdar, Asutosh, 'Nanakpanthi-Nanakshahi', *Bharatbarsha*, Phalgun 1325 BS, pp. 334-5.

———, 'Akali Nihang', *Bharatbarsha*, Chaitra 1325 BS, pp. 500-2.

Vivekananda, Swami, 'Hindudharmer Sadharan Bhitti', *Janma Satabarsha Smarane Swamijir Bani o Rachana*, vol. V, Calcutta 1369 BS, pp. 267-88.

English

Official and Semi-Official Publications and the Writings of Contemporary British Officials and Others

Allen, B.C., *Assam District Gazetteers: Goalpara* and *Nowgong*, Calcutta, 1905.

Calvert, H.H., *Wealth and Welfare of the Punjab*, Lahore 1922.

Campbell, James, *Political Trouble in India, 1907-17*, Calcutta reprint, 1973.

Cunningham, J.D., *A History of the Sikhs*, New Delhi reprint, 1985.

Gait, Edward, *A History of Assam*, Guwahati reprint, 1972.

Ghosh, Jamini Mohan, *Sannyasi and Fakir Raiders in Bengal*, Calcutta 1930.

Gough, Charles and Innes, Arthur D., *The Sikhs and the Sikh Wars*, Patiala reprint, 1970.

Griffin, Lepel H., *The Panjab Chiefs: Historical and Biographical Notices of the Principal Families in the Lahore Kingdom*, Lahore 1866.

Griffin, Lepel, *Ranjit Singh*, New Delhi reprint, 1967.

Index to the Debates of the Assam Legislative Assembly, No. I, Shillong 1938.

Irvine, William, *Later Mughals, 1707-20*, vol. I, Calcutta n.d.

Jackson, V. H. (ed.), *Journals of Francis Buchanan (afterwards Hamilton), Patna-Gaya Report, 1811-2*, Patna 1925.

Lacay, W.G. (ed.), *Census of India 1931*, Bihar and Orissa, Report, vol. VII, Part I, Patna 1933.

Lawrence, H.M.L., *Adventures of an Officer in the Punjaub*, vols. I-II, Patiala reprint, 1970.

List of Publications Proscribed in Bengal from 1920 to 1934, Calcutta 1934.

M'Gregor, W. L., *The History of the Sikhs*, vols. I-II, Patiala reprint, 1971.

Malcolm, John, *Sketch of the Sikhs; A Singular Nation, Who Inhabit the Provinces of the Penjab, Situated Between the Rivers Jumna and Indus*, London 1812.

Mills, A.J. Moffat, *Report on the Province of Assam*, Guwahati reprint, 1987.

Mullan, C.S. (ed.), *Census of India 1931*, Assam, Report, vol. III, Part I, Calcutta 1932.

O' Malley, L.S.S., 'The Agraharis of Sasaram', *Journal of Asiatic Society of Bengal*, vol. LXXI, Part III, 1904, pp. 35-43.

Oman, J.Campbell, *The Mystics, Ascetics and Saints of India*, London 1905.

Prinsep Henry T., *Origin of the Sikh Power in the Punjab and Political Life of Maharaja Ranjit Singh*, Patiala reprint, 1970.

Report of the Line System Committee, vol. I, Shillong 1938.

Robinson, W., *A Descriptive Account of Assam*, New Delhi reprint, 1975.

Selections from the Punjab Newspapers Report, 1911, Lahore 1912.

Sinha, Sukumar and Banerjee, Himadri (eds.), *West Bengal District Records*, New Series, *Bankura District: Letters Issued*, 1802-1869, Calcutta n.d.

Smyth, G. Carmichael, *A History of the Reigning Family of Lahore*, Patiala reprint, 1970.

Thorburn, S.S., *The Punjab in Peace and War*, New Delhi reprint, 1985.

Tirmizi, A.I. (ed.), *Calendar of Persian Correspondence, 1794-95*, vol. XI, New Delhi 1969.

Trumpp, Ernest, *The Adi Granth*, New Delhi reprint, 1989.

NEWSPAPERS

Ajir Batari	13 November 1993.
Akali Patrika	15, 17, 19 and 20 February 1935.
Amrita Bazar Patrika	19 February 1935.
Ananda Bazar Patrika	20 April to 21 December 1922.
	9 September 1923.
	18, 19, 20 and 22 February 1935.
Forward	21 February 1935.

Nabasambad	27 July and 10 October 1887.
Sadiniya Asamiya	17 August and 28 December 1930.
Samaj	13 November 1935.
Sambad Bhaskar	23 March 1849 and 15 November 1849.
Sambad Prabhakar	11 April 1849.
Satya Samachar	13 November 1935.
Sevak	15, 22 and 29 July 1885.
The Asian Age	13 September 1998.
The Khalsa Advocate	5 January 1907.
The Statesman	9 November 1997 and 2 April 2000.
The Telegraph	31 July 1994.
The Tribune	21 February 1935.
Utkal Sevak	15 December 1921.

INTERVIEWS

Bani Neogy, Calcutta, 5 July 1991.
Debnarayan Gupta, Calcutta, 29 June 1991.
Dhyan Singh, Guwahati, 23 April 1994.
Man Singh Grewal, Calcutta, 10 July 1996.
Manmouji Singh, Calcutta, 5-6 March 1997
Rup Singh Sandhu, Guwahati, 25 April 1994.

UNPUBLISHED THESES

Bora, Shila, 'A Study of the Student Movement in Assam since 1916 (1916-1947)', Gauhati University Ph.D. thesis, 1984.

Hussian, Amanal Tassaduk, 'The Burmese and the North-East India (1750-1852)', Dibrugarh University Ph.D. thesis, 1999.

Kaur, Gurpreet, 'An Attempt to Account for the Popularity of Bhai Bala Janamsakhi', Guru Nanak Dev University M. Phil thesis, 1982.

Kaur, Satpal, 'Journalism in the Punjab and the *Khalsa Samachar* (1899-1919)', Guru Nanak Dev University M. Phil thesis, 1985.

Medhi, Birinchi Kumar, 'The Assamese-Sikhs: A Study of their Social Relations in a Rural Setting', Gauhati University Ph.D. thesis, 1989.

Perrill, Jeffrey, 'Punjab Orientalism: The Anjuman-i-Punjab and Punjab University', University of Missourie-Columbia Ph.D. thesis, 1976.

Pradhan, Bijay Kumar, 'National Movement in Orissa (1920-36 A.D.)', Rabindra Bharati University Ph.D. thesis, 1997.

Sur, Shyamali, 'Bangalir Itihastattwer Bikash, 1870-1912', Jadavpur University Ph.D. thesis, 1980.

DICTIONARIES AND ENCYCLOPAEDIAS

Barua, Hemchandra, *Hema Kosha*, Guwahati reprint, 1992.
Burman, Sibnath, *Asamiya Jibani Abhidhan*, Guwahati 1992.
Dutta, Amaresh (ed.), *Encyclopaedia of Indian Literature*, vol.II, New Delhi 1989.
Dilgeer, H.S., *The Sikh Reference Book*, Amritsar 1997.
Ghosh, Saurindrakumar, *Sahitya Sebak Manjusha*, vol. II, Calcutta 1986.
Hastings, James (ed.), *Encyclopaedia of Religion and Ethics*, vol. XII, New York 1961.
Kohli, S.S., *A Conceptual Encyclopaedia of Guru Granth Sahib*, New Delhi 1992.
Lal, Mohan (ed.), *Encyclopaedia of Indian Literature*, vol. IV, New Delhi 1993.
McLeod, W.H., *Historical Dictionary of Sikhism*, Lanham 1995.
Mitra, Subal Kumar (ed.), *Saral Bangla Abhidhan*, Calcutta 1923.
Mukherjee, Harimohan, *Bangabhashar Lekhak*, vol. I, Calcutta 1311 BS.
Nabha, Bhai Kahn Singh, *Mahan Kosh*, Patiala reprint, 1990.
Sen, S.P. (ed.), *Dictionary of National Biography*, vol. I, Calcutta 1967.
Sharma, Sridhar Mahapatra, *Oriya Prakashan o Prasaranar Itihas*, Cuttack 1986.
Singh, Harbans (ed.), *Encyclopaedia of Sikhism*, vols. I-IV, Patiala 1992-98.
Sinha, Nirmal (ed.), *Freedom Movement in Bengal, 1813-1904, Who's Who*, Calcutta 1968.

SECONDARY SOURCES

ASSAMESE, BENGALI, HINDI, ORIYA AND PUNJABI

Adhikari, Gokulchandra, 'Utkal Madhup', *Bhanja Pradip*, Paush 1348 Masiha, pp. 10-14.
Ahmed, Abul Mansur, *Amar Dekha Rajnitir Panchas Bachhar*, Dhaka 1967.
Ahmed, Wakil, *Unish Sataker Bangali Musalmaner Chinta-Chetanar Dhara*, vol. I, Dhaka 1983.
Anisuzzaman, *Muslim Manas o Bangla Sahitya*, Dhaka 1378 BS.
Banerjee, Brajendranath, *Sahitya-Sadhak Charitmala*, vols. I, IV and VI, Calcutta 1350 BS-55 BS.
Banerjee, Himadri, 'Satabdir Sikh Sandhan (Guru Parba)', *Rabindra Bharati Patrika*, Chaitra 1401 BS-Jyaistha 1402 BS, pp. 1-60.
Bardoloi, Rajanikanta, 'Mor Sowarani', *Avahan*, Puh 1857 Saka, pp. 317-25.

Bargohain, Homen (ed.), *Bingsha Satabdir Asamiya Sahitya*, Dibrugarh 1987.

Barua, Prafulla Chandra, *Asamar Batari Kakat Eti Ruparekha, 1846-1947*, Guwahati 1993.

Baruah, Pralhadkumar, *Jyoti Manisha*, Dibrugarh 1993.

Bharali, Sailen, *Asamiya Sahityar Aitihasik Upanyas*, Guwahati 1895 Saka.

Bhattacharya, Harichandra, *Asamiya Natya Sahityar Jilingani*, Gauhati 1968.

Bhoumik, Haripada (ed.), *Sekaler Sambadpatre Kolkata*, vol. II, Calcutta 1988.

Bhuyan, Jogendranarayan, *Unabingsa Satikar Asam-Sambad*, Dibrugarh 1990.

Bora, Dhrubajyoti, 'Dr. Suryakumar Bhuyanar Aitihasik Abadan', *Deuka*, October-November 1995, pp. 10-14.

Bose, Haranath, 'Bhraman na Niryatan', *Natyamandir*, Paush 1317 BS, pp. 451-67.

Chakrabarty, Basanti, *Kumudini Bose Amader Ratandidi*, Calcutta 1351 BS.

Chaturvedi, Parasuram, *Uttar Bharat ki Sant Parampara*, Allahabad 2021 Bikrami.

Choudhury, Prasenjit, *Itihas Charcha*, Guwahati 1995.

Choudhury, Subodh, *Kabi o Natyakar Manomohan Bose*, Calcutta 1983.

Das, Bharatchandra, *Byakti Parichay*, vol. II, Barpeta 1979.

Das, Bhubanmohan, *Nijara Kabi Sailadhar Rajkhowa*, Jorhat 1995.

Das, Birbar, *Aitihasik Sivaprasad Das*, Bargarh 1978.

Das, Jagannathprasad, *Desha Kaal Patra*, Bhubaneswar 1997.

Das, Jnanendramohan, *Banger Bahire Bangali—Uttar Bharat*, Calcutta 1322 BS.

Das, Kunjabehari, 'Pandit Basudeb Mahapatra', *Nabarabi*, October 1972, pp. 102-10.

———, *Kabi o Kahani*, Cuttack 1984.

Das, Nirmal Kumar (ed.), *Jogeshchandra Rachanabali*, Calcutta 1976.

Das, Sunil (ed.), *Manomohan Boser Aprakasita Diary*, Calcutta 1981.

Das, Suryanarayan, *Utkalmani Gopabandhu Das*, Cuttack 1987.

DasGupta, Hemendra, *Subhaschandra*, Calcutta 1946.

Dash, Ganganendra Nath, *Oriya Bhasa-Suraksha Andolan*, Cuttack 1993.

De, Amalendu, *Bangali Budhhijibi o Bichhinnatabad*, Calcutta 1987.

Devi, Abanti, *Bhaktakabi Madhusudan Rao o Utkale Nabajug*, Calcutta 1370 BS.

Devi, Anurupa, *Bhudev Charit*, Calcutta 1330 BS.

Dhillon, Balwant Singh, *Pramukh Sikh te Sikh Panth*, Amritsar 1997.

Ghosh, Benoy (ed.), *Samayikpatre Banglar Samajchitra*, vols. I-III, Calcutta 1962-64.

Goswami, Prafulladatta, *Baro Mahar Tera Git*, New Delhi 1970.

Guha, Nalinikishore, *Bangalae Biplabbad*, Calcutta 1976.

Gupta, Bipinbehari, *Puratan Prasanga*, vol. II, Calcutta 1330 BS.

Hazarika, Atulchandra, *Manchalekha*, Guwahati 1967.

Islam, Mustafa Nurul, *Samayikpatre Jiban o Janamat*, Dhaka 1977.

Kar, Bauribandhu, *Nana Alochana*, Bhubaneswar 1994.

Kavi, Ashit, *Oriya Prabandha Sahityar Itihas*, Cuttack 1985.

Lekharu,Upendrachandra, *Asamiya Sahitya Sebak Rajanikanta Bardoloi*, Guwahati 1953.

Mahanta, Goswami Jayashri (ed.), *Smritigrantha: Gurudwara Mataji*, Guwahati 1990.

Mahanta, Prafullakumar, *Asamiya Madhyabitta Srenir Itihas*, Guwahati 1991.

Mahanti (Bharadwaj), Janakiballav, *Adhunik Oriya Sahitya*, Cuttack 1963.

———, 'Chalit Satabdire Oriya Jibani Sahitya', *Jhankar*, February 1971, pp. 1059-69.

Mahatab, Harekrushna, *Sadhanar Pathe*, Part I, Cuttack 1949.

Majumdar, Bimanbehari, *SriChaitanya Charitrer Upadan*, Calcutta 1959.

Majumdar, Ujjalkumar, *Kabir Adhyayan*, Calcutta 1994.

Medhi, Birinchi, K.,'Asamiya Sikhsakal-Punjabar Para Pragjyotishpuralai', *Natun Din*, Special Number, Autumn 1991, pp. 25-31.

Mishra, Binayak, *Adhunik Oriya Sahityar Itihas*, Aska 1968.

Mishra, Chandrasekhar, *Satyabadire Satabarsha*, Cuttack 1953.

Mishra, Krishnabehari and Pande, Ram Vyas (eds.), *Hindi Sahitya: Bangiya Bhumika*, Calcutta 1983.

Mishra, Sachidananda, 'Mogal Tamsar Rachanakal', *Jhankar*, January 1974, pp. 940-5.

Mishra, Shrinibas, *Adhunik Oriya Gadya Sahitya, 1811-1920*, Cuttack 1978.

Mishra, Shyamsundar, 'Jhanjirimangalar Ramlila: Ek Bismrita Lokanatyakala', *Ramcharita Kathamrit*, Cuttack 1993, pp. 22-5.

Mukherjee, Bimalendu, *Biplabtirtha Chandannagar*, Chandannagar 1994.

Mukherjee, Prabhatkumar, *Rabindrajibani o Rabindrasahitya Prabesak*, vol. III, Calcutta 1397 BS.

——— (ed.), *Geetabitan: Kalanukramik Suchi*, Calcutta 1399 BS.

Murshid, Ghulam, *Sankocher Bihbalata: Adhunikatar Abhighate Bangaramanir Pratikriya, 1849-1905*, Dhaka 1985.

Nandi, Somendrachandra, *Aitihasik Natak Samalochana*, Calcutta 1981.

Nath, Dambarudhar, *Asam Buranji*, Guwahati 1996.

Nath, Rajmohan, 'Kamakhyat Sikh Guru Teghbahadur', *Asam Sahitya Sabha Patrika*, Bahag-Saon 1897 Saka, pp. 10-13.

Nayak, Labanya, *Oriya Charit-Sahitya*, Cuttack 1988.

Pal, Prasantakumar, *Rabijibani, 1292-1309*, vol. III, Calcutta 1394 BS.

Patnaik, Pathani, *Jibani-Sahitya: Ek Adhyayan*, Bhubaneswar 1977.

Rajkhowa, Sailadhar, *Atitar Sowarani*, Dibrugarh 1969.

Rakshit, Haranchandra, 'Banglar Lekhak', *Janmabhuni*, Kartik 1307 BS, pp. 110-20.

Rath, Mrutyunjay, *Mrutyunjay Granthabali*, vol. I, Cuttack 1971.

Roy, Mahendranath, *Babu Akshaykumar Dattar Jiban-Brittanta*, Calcutta 1292 BS.

Samantaray, Natabar, *Adhunik Oriya Sahityar Bhittibhumi (1803-1920)*, Bhubaneswar 1981.

Sarma, Satyendranath, *Asamiya Natya-Sahitya*, Guwahati 1983.

Sen, Dineshchandra, *Bangabhasa o Sahitya*, Calcutta reprint, vols. I-II, 1986.

Sen, Kshitimohan, *Bharatiya Madhyajuger Sadhanar Dhara*, Calcutta reprint, 1965.

Sen, Prabodhchandra, *Bangalir Itihas-Sadhana*, Calcutta 1360 BS.

Sen, Sukumar, *Bangla Sahityer Itihas*, vol. IV, Calcutta 1971.

———, *Islami Bangla*, Calcutta 1400 BS.

Sharma, Ramvilas, *Bharatendu Yuga*, Agra 1956.

Singh, Kirpal, *Janamsakhi Parampara*, Patiala reprint, 1990.

Singh, Ramavtar, 'Purva Bharat mei Sikh-Parivar : Punarvas ki Adi-Katha', *SriGuru Gobind Singh Traya Satabdi Mahotsav*, Calcutta 1967, pp. 54-60.

Singh, Randhir, *Udasi Sikhan di Vithia*, Amritsar 1959.

Talukdar, Nanda, *Sambad Patrar Raud-Kachalit Asamiya Sahitya*, Gauhati 1975.

ENGLISH

Ahluwalia, Jasbir Singh, *University of California Lectures in Sikhism*, Patiala n.d.

Ahluwalia, M.L., 'Records Relating to the Land Grants in Bihar to Nanak Shahi Maths and Priests', *Proceedings*, *Punjab History Conference*, Seventeenth Session, Patiala 1982, pp. 103-8.

Ahmed, Rafiuddin, *The Bengal Muslims 1871-1906: A Quest for Identity*, Delhi 1981.

Ahmed, Sharifuddin, *Dacca: A Study in Urban History & Development*, London 1968.

Alam, Muzaffar, *The Crisis of Empire in Mughal North India: Awadh and the Punjab, 1707-48*, New Delhi 1986.

———,'Sikh Uprisings under Banda Bahadur, 1708-15', *The Panjab Past and Present*, April 1982, pp. 95-107.

Ali, A.N.M. Irshad and Medhi, Birinchi K., 'The Assamese-Sikhs: Profile of a Minuscule Community', in S.B. Roy and Asok K. Ghosh (eds.), *People of India: Bio-Cultural Dimensions—A Tribute to Dr. Kumar Suresh Singh*, Calcutta 1983, pp. 167-79.

Anderson, Benedict, *Imagined Communities : Reflections on the Origin and Spread of Nationalism*, London 1991.

Archer, J.C., *The Sikhs in relation to Hindus, Moslems, Christians, and Ahmadiyyas. A Study in Comparative Religion*, Princeton 1946.

Bal, S.S., *British Policy Towards the Punjab, 1844-9*, Calcutta 1971.

———, 'The First Edition of J.D. Cunningham's *A History of the Sikhs*', *Proceedings, Punjab History Conference*, Eleventh Session, Patiala 1976, pp. 58-69.

Banerjee, Anil Chandra, *The Eastern Frontier of British India, 1784-1826*, Calcutta 1946.

———, *Anglo-Sikh Relations*, Calcutta 1949.

———, *Guru Nanak and His Times*, Patiala 1984.

———, *Guru Nanak to Guru Gobind Singh*, New Delhi 1978.

———, *The Sikh Gurus and the Sikh Religion*, New Delhi 1983.

———, *The Khalsa Raj*, New Delhi 1985.

Banerjee, Himadri, 'Maharaja Ranjit Singh in Bengali Literature', *Journal of Sikh Studies*, February 1985, pp. 55-64.

———, 'Guru Gobind Singh in Bengali Writings', *The Panjab Past and Present*, October 1985 pp. 354-62.

———, 'Sikh-Itihas: A Supplement to Cunningham's History of the Sikhs in Bengali', *The Panjab Past and Present*, April 1986, pp. 188-94.

———, 'Sikh Sacred Literature', *Studies in Sikhism and Comparative Religion*, October 1986, pp. 101-8.

———, 'Jatindramohan Chatterjee: A Forgotten Scholar of Sikh Studies', *Studies in Sikhism and Comparative Religion*, October 1990, pp. 85-9.

———, 'Nandkumardev Sharma's Writings on the Sikhs', *Sikhs: Past and Present*, December 1991, pp. 16-24.

———, 'Non-Sikh Perception of Sikh History: Sikh History in Hindi Writings during Bharatendu Yuga', *Punjab Journal of Politics*, Annual Number 1991, pp. 71-81.

Banerjee, Indubhusan, *Evolution of the Khalsa*, vols. I-II, Calcutta, 1962-73.

Banerjee, Pramathanath et al. (eds.), *Hundred Years of the University of Calcutta*, Calcutta 1957.

Banerjee, Sumanta, *The Parlour and the Streets: Elite and Popular Culture in Nineteenth Century Calcutta*, Calcutta 1989.

Banga, Indu, 'The Ruling Class in the Kingdom of Lahore', *Journal of Regional History*, Annual Number 1982, pp. 14-23.

———, 'Social Structure, Religious Ideology and Political Articulation—The Sikhs of Punjab', Presidential Address, Modern Section, *Indian History Congress*, Forty-ninth Session, Dharwad 1988.

Barik, Radhakanta, 'Gopabandhu and the National Movement in Orissa', *Social Scientist*, May 1978, pp. 47-52.

Barpujari, H.K., 'Lacunae in the Study of the History of Assam', *Proceedings of the Indian History Congress*, Twenty-fifth Session, Allahabad 1965, pp. 169-70

———, Presidential Address, Modern Section, *Proceedings, Punjab History Conference*, Thirteenth Session, Patiala 1979, pp. 146-54.

———, 'North-East India: The Problems and Politics since 1947', General President's Address, *Indian History Congress*, Fifty-sixth Session, Calcutta 1995.

——— (ed.), *The Comprehensive History of Assam*, vols. II-V, Guwahati 1992-94.

Barrier, N. Gerald, *The Sikhs and their Literature*, Delhi 1971.

———, and Wallace, Paul, *The Punjab Press, 1880-1905*, East Lansing 1970.

Barua, Birinchi Kumar, *History of Assamese Literature*, New Delhi 1978.

Baruah, S.L., *Last Days of Ahom Monarchy: A History of Assam from 1769-1826*, New Delhi 1993.

Baruah, Sanjib, *India Against Itself: Assam and the Politics of Nationality*, New Delhi 2000.

Bayly, C.A., *Rulers, Townsmen and Bazaars: Northern Indian Society in the Age of British Expansion, 1770-1870*, Cambridge 1983.

Bhadra, Gautam, 'Two Frontier Uprisings in Mughal India', in Ranajit Guha (ed.), *Subaltern Studies II, Writings on South Asian History and Society*, Delhi 1986, pp. 43-59.

Bhuyan, Surya Kumar, *Anglo-Assamese Relations, 1771–1826*, Gauhati 1947.

Bhatia, Shyamala, *Social Change and Politics in Punjab, 1898-1910*, New Delhi 1987.

Bhattacharya , Jayanta Bhusan (ed.), *Studies in the History of the North-East India: Essays in Honour of Professor H.K. Barpujari*, Shillong 1986.

Borua, Profulla Chandra, *Assamese Proverbs*, Guwahati 1962.

Bose, Amalendu, 'Tagore on the Sikhs', in Harbans Singh (ed.), *Perspectives on Guru Nanak*, Patiala 1990, pp. 514-20.

Bose, Subhas Chandra, *The Indian Struggle, 1920-34*, Calcutta 1948.

Brass, Paul R., *Language, Religion and Politics in North India*, Cambridge 1974.

———, *The New Cambridge History of India*, vol. IV.1, *The Politics of India Since Independence*, Cambridge 1994.

———, *Ethnicity and Nationalism: Theory and Comparison*, New Delhi reprint, 1996.

Boulton, John, 'Nationalism and Tradition in Orissa, with Special Reference to the Works of Phakirmohana Senapati', in R.J. Moore (ed.), *Tradition and Politics in South Asia*, New Delhi 1979, pp. 228-60.

Chakrabarty, Jagannath (ed.), *Studies in Bengal Renaissance*, Calcutta 1977.

Chakrabarty, Hiren, *Political Protest in Bengal: Boycott and Terrorism 1905-1918*, Calcutta 1992.

Chhabra, G.S., *The Advanced Study in History of the Punjab*, vol. I, Jalandhar 1960.

Chanda, Mrinalkanti, *History of the English Press in Bengal*, Calcutta 1987.

Chandra, Bipan, *Nationalism and Colonialism in Modern India*, Delhi 1979.

Chandra, Sudhir, 'Communal Consciousness in Late 19th Century Hindi Literature', in Mushirul Hasan (ed.), *Communal and Pan-Islamic Trends in Colonial India*, New Delhi 1985, pp. 180-95.

———, *The Oppressive Present: Literature and Social Consciousness in Colonial India*, New Delhi 1992.

Chatterjee, Joya, *Bengal Divided: Hindu Communalism and Partition, 1932-47*, New Delhi 1996.

Chatterjee, P.C. (ed.), *Self-Images, Identity and Nationality*, Shimla 1989.

Chatterjee, Partha, *The Nation and its Fragments: Colonial and Postcolonial Histories*, Delhi 1994.

———, 'Claims on the Past: The Genealogy of Modern Historiography in Bengal', in David Arnold and David Hardiman (eds.), *Subaltern Studies VIII: Writings on South Asian History and Society*, Delhi 1994, pp. 1-49.

Chatterjee, Satikumar, 'Response of the Brahmo Samaj to the Message of Guru Nanak', in K.R. Srinivasa Iyengar (ed.), *Guru Nanak—A Homage*, New Delhi 1973, pp. 103-10.

Chatterji, Sunti Kumar, *The Origin and Development of the Bengali Language*, I, London reprint, 1970.

———, *Jayadeva*, New Delhi 1973.

Chatterjee, Suranjan, 'New Reflections on the Sannyasi, Fakir and Peasants War', *Economic and Political Weekly*, 28 January 1984, pp. 2-13.

Clark, T.W. (ed.), *The Novel in India*, London 1970.

Cohn, Bernard S., 'The Role of the Gossains in the Economy of Eighteenth and Nineteenth Century Upper India', *The Indian Economic and Social History Review*, December 1963-February 1964, pp. 175-82.

———, *An Anthropologist Among the Historians and Other Essays*, Delhi 1987.

Craine, Robert I. and Spangenburg, Bradford (eds.), *Language and Society in Modern India: Essays in Honour of Professor Robert O. Swan*, New Delhi 1981.

Das, Chittaranjan, *A Glimpse into Oriya Literature*, Bhubaneswar 1984.

Das, M.N. (ed.), *Sidelights on the History and Culture of Orissa*, Cuttack 1977.

Das, Sisir Kumar, *A History of Indian Literature 1800-1910: Western Impact: Indian Response*, New Delhi 1991.

———, *A History of Indian Literature 1911-56: Struggle for Freedom: Triumph and Tragedy*, New Delhi 1995.

Das, Sunil Kumar, *SriChaitanya and Guru Nanak*, Calcutta 1985.

Das, Suranjan, *Communal Riots in Bengal, 1905-47*, Delhi 1991.

DasGupta, R.K., 'Influence of Sikhism in Bengal', in Gurmukh Nihal Singh (ed.), *Guru Nanak: His Life, Time and Teachings*, New Delhi 1988, pp. 207-16.

DasGupta, Sashibhusan, *Obscure Religious Cults as Background of Bengali Literature*, Calcutta 1969.

Dash, A., *Saint Nanak*, Cuttack 1971.

Dash, G.N., 'Jagannatha and Oriya Nationalism', in Anncharlott Eshmann et al. (eds.), *The Cult of Jagannatha and the Regional Tradition of Orissa*, New Delhi 1978, pp. 359-74.

Dev, Amiya and Das, Sisir Kumar (eds.), *Comparative Literature: Theory and Practice*, Shimla 1969.

Devi, Bandita, *Some Aspects of British Administration in Orissa (1912-36)*, New Delhi 1992.

Dulai, Surjit and Helweg, Arthur (eds.), *Punjab in Perspective*, East Lansing 1991.

Eschmann, Anncharlott (ed.), *South Asian Digest of Regional Writings*, vol. III, Hidelburg 1974.

Farquhar, J.N., *Modern Religious Movements in India*, New Delhi reprint, 1977.

Fenech, Louis E., 'Martyrdom and the Sikh Tradition', *Journal of the American Oriental Society*, October-December 1997, pp. 623-42.

———, *Martyrdom in the Sikh Tradition: Playing the 'Game of Love'*, New Delhi 2000.

Fox, Richard G., 'Urban Class and Commercial Consciousness in Colonial Punjab: The Genesis of India's Intermediate Regime', *Modern Asian Studies*, July-September 1984, pp. 459-89.

———, *Lions of the Punjab: Culture in the Making*, Barkeley 1985.

Freitag, Sandria B. (ed.), *Culture and Power in Banaras: Community, Performance and Environment 1800-1980*, Delhi 1989.

Gill, M.S., 'Distribution of the Sikh Population in India', *The Sikh Review*, February 1999, pp. 68-71.

Gogoi, Lila, *The Buranjis: Historical Literature of Assam*, New Delhi 1986.

Gohain, Hiren, 'Origins of the Assamese Middle Class', *Social Scientist*, August 1973, pp. 11-26.

Gopal, Madan, *Dayal Singh Majithia*, New Delhi 1994.

Gordon, Leonard A., *Brothers Against the Raj*, New Delhi 1990.

Goswami, Prafulladatta, *Ballads and Tales of Assam: A Study of the Folklore of Assam*, Gauhati 1970.

Grewal, Kulwant Singh, *A Bibliography of References in Bengali to Guru Gobind Singh*, Patiala 1967.

Grewal, J.S., *Guru Nanak in History*, Chandigarh 1969.

———, *Medieval India: History and Historians*, Amritsar 1975.

———, *Guru Tegh Bahadur and the Persian Chroniclers*, Amritsar 1976.
———, *The Reign of Maharaja Ranjit Singh: Structure of Power, Economy and Society*, Patiala 1981.
———, *From Guru Nanak to Maharaja Ranjit Singh*, Amritsar 1982.
———, *The New Cambridge History of India*, II.3, *The Sikhs of the Punjab*, New Delhi 1990.
———, *Guru Nanak in Western Scholarship*, New Delhi 1992.
———, *Historical Perspectives on Sikh Identity*, Patiala 1997.
———, and Banga, Indu (eds.), *Civil and Military Affairs of Maharaja Ranjit Singh: A Study of 450 Orders in Persian*, Amritsar 1987.
———, *The Khalsa over 300 Years*, New Delhi 1999.
———, and Irfan Habib (eds.), *Sikh History from Persian Sources*, New Delhi 2001.
Guha, Amalendu, 'Impact of Bengal Renaissance on Assam: 1825-75', in Barun De (ed.), *Essays in Honour of Prof. S.C. Sarkar*, New Delhi 1971, pp. 462-76.
———, 'East Bengal Immigrants and Maulana Abdul Hamid Bhasani in Assam Politics 1928-47', *The Indian Economic and Social History Review*, October-December 1976, pp. 418-54.
———, *Planter-Raj to Swaraj—Freedom Movement and Electoral Politics in Assam, 1826-1947*, New Delhi 1979.
———, *The Decline of the Ahom Kingdom, 1765-1826*, Calcutta 1986.
———, 'Neo-Vaishnavism to Insurgency: Peasant Uprisings and the Crisis of Feudalim in Late-Eighteenth-Century Assam', in Asoke Mitra (ed.), *The Truth Unites: Essays in Tribute to Samar Sen*, Calcutta 1986, pp. 26-69.
Guha, Ranajit, *An Indian Historiography of India: A Nineteenth Century Agenda and its Implications*, Calcutta 1988.
——— (ed.), *Subaltern Studies VI, Writings on South Asian History and Society*, New Delhi 1992.
Gupta, Dipankar, *The Context of Ethnicity: Sikh Identity in a Comparative Perspective*, Delhi 1989.
Gupta, Nagendranath, *Reflections and Reminiscences*, Bombay 1946.
Habib, Irfan, *The Agrarian System of Mughal India, 1556-1707*, Bombay 1963.
———, *An Atlas of Mughal India*, Delhi 1986.
Hans, S.S., 'The *Gurbilas* in the Early Nineteenth Century', *Journal of Regional History*, Annual Number, 1981, pp. 43-56.
———, *B-40 Janamsakhi: Guru Baba Nanak Paintings*, Amritsar 1987.
———, *A Reconstruction of Sikh History from Sikh Literature*, Jalandhar 1988.
Hazarika, B.B., *Political Life in Assam During the Nineteenth Century*, Delhi 1987.
Hazarika, Sanjoy, *Rites of Passage: Border Crossings, Imagined Homelands, India's East and Bangladesh*, New Delhi 2000.

Hawley, John Stratton and Mann, Gurinder Singh (eds.), *Studying the Sikhs: Issues for North America*, Albany 1993.

Irvine, William, *Later Mughals, 1707-20*, vol. I, Calcutta n.d.

Jones, Kenneth W., *Arya Dharam: Hindu Consciousness in 19th-Century Punjab*, New Delhi 1976.

———, *The New Cambridge History of India*, vol. III.1, *Social-Religious Reform Movements in British India*, Cambridge 1989.

———, 'Ham Hindu Nahin—The Arya-Sikh Relation, 1877-1905', *The Panjab Past and Present*, October 1977, pp. 330-55.

——— (ed.), *Religious Controversy in British India: Dialogues in South Asian Languages*, Albany 1992.

Juergensmeyer, Mark and Barrier, N. Gerald (eds.), *Sikh Studies: Comparative Perspectives on a Changing Tradition*, Berkeley 1979.

Kalsi, Sewa Singh, *The Evolution of a Sikh Community in Britain: Religious and Social Change among the Sikhs of Leeds and Bradford*, Leeds 1992.

Kapur, A. Rajiv, *Sikh Separatism: The Politics of Faith*, London 1986.

Kapur, Prithipal Singh (ed.), *Maharaja Duleep Singh*, New Delhi 1995.

Kaviraj, Sudipta, *The Unhappy Consciousness: Bankimchandra Chattopadhyay and the Formation of Nationalist Discourse in India*, Delhi 1998.

Kejariwal, O.P., 'The North-East in Indian Historiography: The Need for a Corrective', *Proceedings of the North-East India History Association*, Seventh Session, Pasighat 1986, pp. 17-24.

Khan, Dominique-Sila, *Conversions and Shifting Identities: Ramdev Pir and Ismailis in Rajasthan*, New Delhi 1997, p. 236.

Khurana, G., *British Historiography on the Sikh Power in Punjab*, New Delhi 1985.

King, Christopher R., *One Language Two Scripts: Hindi Movement in Nineteenth Century North India*, Delhi 1994.

Kohli, Atul (ed.), *India's Democracy: An Analysis of Changing State-Society Relations*, Calcutta 1988.

Kolff, D.H.A., 'Sanayasi Trader-Soldiers', *The Indian Economic and Social History Review*, June-August 1970, pp. 213-18.

———, *Naukar, Rajput and Sepoy: The Ethnohistory of the Military Labour Market in Hindustan, 1450-1850*, Cambridge 1990.

Kopf, David, *The Brahmo Samaj and the Shaping of Modern Mind*, Princeton 1979.

Latif, S.M., *Lahore: Its History, Architectural Remains and Antiquities*, Lahore 1892.

———, *History of the Panjab*, Ludhiana reprint, 1989.

Lavan, Spencer, *Ahmadiya Movement: Past and Present*, Amritsar 1976.

Leonard, Karen Isaksen, *Making Ethnic Choices—California's Punjabi Mexican Americans*, Philadelphia 1992.

Lorenzen, David N., 'Warrior Ascetics in Indian History', *Journal of the American Oriental Society*, January-March 1978, pp. 61-75.

——— (ed.), *Bhakti Religions in Northern India: Community, Identity and Political Action*, Albany 1995.

Macauliffe, M.A., *The Sikh Religion*, vols. I-VI, New Delhi reprint, 1978.

Mahajan, Sucheta, 'British Policy, Nationalist Strategy and Popular National Upsurge, 1945-6', in Amit Kumar Gupta (ed.), *Myth and Reality: The Struggle for Freedom in India, 1945-47*, New Delhi 1987, pp. 54-98.

Mahtab, Harekrushna et al. (eds.), *History of Freedom Movement in Orissa (1857-1911)*, vol. II, Cuttack 1957.

Maitra, Sureshchandra (ed.), *Selections from Jnanannweshan*, Calcutta 1979.

Majumdar, Bimanbehari, *Militant Nationalism in India and its Socio-Religious Background*, Calcutta 1966.

———, 'Guru Nanak and His Contemporaries', in *Guru Nanak*, New Delhi 1969.

Mann, A.S., *Relation of the Sikh Community with Assam*, Calcutta n.d.

———, *Guru Tegh Bahadur and Assam Pradesh*, New Delhi n.d.

Mannan, Kaji Abdul, *The Emergence and Development of Dobhashi Literature in Bengal up to 1855 A.D.*, Dacca 1974.

Mansinha, Mayadhar, *History of Oriya Literature*, New Delhi 1962.

McGregor, R.S., 'Bengal and the Development of Hindi, 1850-1900', *South Asia Review*, Jannuary 1972, pp. 137-46.

McLane, J.R., *Land and Local Kinship in Eighteenth Century Bengal*, Cambridge 1993.

McLeod, W.H., *Guru Nanak and the Sikh Religion*, Delhi 1978.

———, *The Evolution of the Sikh Community*, Delhi 1975.

———, (ed.), *The B-40 Janam-sakhi*, Amritsar 1980.

———, *Early Sikh Tradition: A Study of the Janam-sakhis*, Oxford 1980.

———, *Who is a Sikh? The Problem of Sikh Identity*, Delhi 1989.

———, *Sikhism*, Harmondsworth 1997.

McMullen, Clarence O., *Religious Beliefs and Practices of the Sikhs in Rural Punjab*, New Delhi 1989.

Mishra, H.K., *Famines and Poverty in India*, New Delhi 1991.

Misra, Tilottoma, *Literature and Society in Assam: A Study of Assamese Renaissance, 1826-1926*, Delhi 1986.

Misra, Udyan (ed.), *Nation Building and Development in North East India*, Guwahati 1991.

———, 'Immigration and Identity Transformation in Assam', *Economic and Political Weekly*, 22 May 1999, pp. 1265-71.

———, *The Periphery Strikes Back: Challenges to the Nation-State in Assam and Nagaland*, Shimla 2000.

Mohanty, Nivedita, *Oriya Nationalism: Quest for a United Orissa*, New Delhi 1982.

Mohapatra, Bishnu N., 'Anti-Colonial Politics in Orissa, 1920-36: The

Power and Limits of Oriya Nationalism', *The Calcutta Historical Journal*, July-December 1975, pp. 139-76.

Mukherjee, P., *History of Orissa in the 19th Century*, Bhubaneswar 1964.

———, 'The Employment of the People of Orissa in the Government Service in the 19th Century', *The Orissa Historical Research Journal*, July 1959, pp. 110-17.

Murshid, Tazeen M., *The Sacred and the Secular: Bengal Muslim Discourses 1871-1977*, Calcutta 1995.

Nag, Sajal, *Roots of Ethnic Conflict: Nationality Question in North-East India*, New Delhi 1990.

Narang, Gokul Chand, *Transformation of Sikhism*, New Delhi 1960.

Oberoi, Harjot, *The Construction of Religious Boundaries: Culture, Identity and Diversity in the Sikh Tradition*, New Delhi 1994.

Oberoi, J.P.S., *Religion, Civil Society and the State*, New Delhi 1994.

O'Connell, Joseph T., 'The Word "Hindu" in Gaudiya Vaisnava Texts', *Journal of the American Oriental Society*, July-September 1973, pp. 340-4.

———, 'Vaisnava Perceptions of Muslims in Sixteenth Century Bengal', in Milton Israel and Narendra K. Wagle (eds.), *Islamic Society and Culture: Essays in Honour of Professor Aziz Ahmed*, New Delhi 1983, pp. 289-313.

———, et al. (eds.), *Sikh History and Religion in the Twentieth Century*, Toronto 1988.

Paniker, K. Ayyappa (ed.), *Medieval Indian Literature: An Anthology*, vol. I, *Survey and Selections*, New Delhi 1997.

Pannikar, K.M., *Culture, Ideology and Hegemony: Intellectual and Social Consciousness in Colonial India*, New Delhi 1995.

Pati, Biswamoy, *Resisting Domination: Peasants Tribals and the National Movement in Orissa 1920-47*, New Delhi 1993.

———, *Situating Social History: Orissa (1800-1997)*, New Delhi 2000.

Patra, Kishori Mohan, 'Growth of Social Consciousness in Orissa in the 19th Century', *Proceedings of Indian Historical Records Commission*, Fortieth Session, vol. XL, 1970, pp. 144-51.

———, *Orissa State Legislature and Freedom Struggle 1912-47*, New Delhi 1979.

———, 'Growth of National Consciousness and Freedom Movement in Orissa', *The Indian Historical Review*, July 1985-January 1986, pp. 317-27.

Pettigrew, Joyce, 'Achieving New Frontier: Rural Political Patterns and their Impact on the Sikh Independence Movement', *International Journal of Punjab Studies*, January-June 1995, pp. 89-101.

Philips, C.H. (ed.), *Historians of India, Pakistan and Ceylon*, London 1961.

Phukan, Girin, *Assam: Attitude to Federation*, New Delhi 1982.

Pinch, William R., *Peasants and Monks in British India*, New Delhi 1996.

Pradhan, Atul Chandra, *The Nationalist Movement in a Regional Setting, 1920-34, The Rise of Congress to Power in Orissa*, New Delhi, n.d.

Prakash, Ved, *The Sikhs in Bihar*, Patna 1981.

Purewal, Shinder, *Sikh Ethnonationalism and the Political Economy of Punjab*, New Delhi 2000.

Ray, Niharranjan (ed.), *Sikhism and Indian Society*, Simla 1967.

———, *The Sikh Gurus and the Sikh Society*, New Delhi 1975.

Raychaudhuri, Tapan, *Europe Reconsidered: Perceptions of the West in Nineteenth Century Bengal*, New Delhi 1988.

Roy, Anuradha, 'Foreign Tyrants or Foster Brothers? Muslims in the eyes of the Hindu Nationalists in Nineteenth Century Bengal', *The Calcutta Historical Journal*, January-June 1995, pp. 123-59.

Roy, Rajat Kanta, *Social Conflict and Political Unrest in Bengal, 1875-1927*, Delhi 1984.

Roy, Ranjit Kumar, 'Simon Commission Boycott 1928: A Study of Sikh Participation in Urban Politics of Calcutta', *The Sikh Review*, August 1991, pp. 46-53.

———, (ed.), *Retrieving Bengal's Past: Society and Culture in the Nineteenth and Twentieth Centuries*, Calcutta 1995.

Roy, Saratchandra, *The Mundas and their Country*, Calcutta 1912.

Sagar, S.S., 'A Study of Janamsakhi Scholarship', *Journal of Sikh Studies*, August 1987, pp. 47-58.

———, *Historical Analysis of Nanak Prakash*, Amritsar 1993.

———, and Tak, R.S., 'Departmental Notes: Guru Nanak in Cuttack', *Journal of Sikh Studies*, August 1974, pp. 127-44.

———, 'Departmental Notes: Guru Nanak's Visit to Jagan Nath Puri', *Journal of Sikh Studies*, August 1976, pp. 158-75.

———, 'Departmental Notes : Guru Nanak's visit to Bhadrak', *Journal of Sikh Studies*, February 1977, pp. 147-65.

Saikia. Nagen, *Background of Modern Assamese Literature*, Delhi 1988.

Samal, J.K., *A History of Modern Orissa*, Calcutta 1984.

Samiuddin, Abida (ed.), *The Punjab Violence: Challenge & Response*, New Delhi 1989.

Sarkar, Chandiprasad, *The Bengali Muslims: A Study of their Politicisation 1912-29*, Calcutta 1991.

Sarkar, Jadunnath, *History of Aurangzib*, vol. III, Calcutta 1928.

Sarkar, Sumit, *The Swadeshi Movement in Bengal 1903-8*, New Delhi 1973.

———, *Writing Social History*, New Delhi 1997.

Sarkar, Tanika, *Bengal 1928-1934: The Politics of Protest*, Delhi 1987.

Sarma, S.N., *The Neo-Vaisnavite Movement and the Sattra Institutions of Assam*, Guwahati reprint, 1999.

Sastri, Sibnath, *History of the Brahmo Samaj*, Calcutta reprint, 1974.

Schomer, Karine and McLeod, W.H. (eds.), *The Sants: Studies in a Devotional Tradition of India*, New Delhi 1987.

Sekhon, Sant Singh and Duggal, Kartar Singh, *A History of Punjabi Literature*, New Delhi 1992.

Sen, Amiya, *Hindu Revivalism in Bengal 1872-1905: Some Essays on Interpretation*, Delhi 1993.

Sengupta, Indira Chowdhury, *The Frail Hero and Virile History*, New Delhi 1997.

Sengupta, Jayanta, 'The Political Economy of Oriya Nationalism, 1900-36: Problems of Backwardness and the Financing of Provincial Autonomy', *The Calcutta Historical Journal*, July-December 1995, pp. 85-137.

Shah, Mohammad, *In Search of an Identity: Bengali Muslims 1880-1940*, Calcutta, 1996.

Singh, Amrik, *Punjab in Indian Politics: Issues and Trends*, New Delhi 1985.

Singh, Avtar, *Ethics of the Sikhs*, Patiala 1970.

Singh, Bhagat Lakshman, *Sikh Martyrs*, Ludhiana reprint, n.d.

———, *The Sikh and His New Critics*, Lahore 1918.

Singh, Daljeet and Singh, Kharak (eds.), *Sikhism: Its Philosophy and History*, Chandigarh 1997.

Singh, Dharam (ed.), *Secularism and Sikhism: Essays in Honour of Professor Harbans Singh*, New Delhi 1994.

Singh, Fauja (ed.), *Historians and Historiography of the Sikhs*, New Delhi 1978.

Singh, Ganda, *Life of Banda Singh Bahadur*, Amritsar 1935.

———, *A Bibliography of the Panjab*, Patiala 1966.

——— (ed.), *The Panjab Past and Present, Annual Number*, Patiala 1969.

——— (ed.), *Early European Accounts of the Sikhs*, New Delhi reprint, 1974.

Singh, Gopal, *A History of the Sikh People*, New Delhi 1979.

Singh, Gurtej, 'Image of the Sikh Panth in the Work of an Early Nineteenth Century Sikh Historian', *Proceedings of the Indian History Congress*, Twenty-ninth Session, Patiala 1967, pp. 393-9.

———, 'Bhai Mani Singh in Historical Perspective', *Proceedings, Punjab History Conference*, Third Session, Patiala 1968, pp. 120-7.

Singh, Harbans, *The Heritage of the Sikhs*, New Delhi, 1994.

———, 'All India Sikh Gurdwaras Bill—Its Background and the Main Features', *The Sikh Review*, September 1998, pp. 32-7.

———, and N. Gerald Barrier (eds.), *The Punjab Past and Present: Essays in Honour of Dr Ganda Singh*, Patiala 1976.

Singh, I.J., *The Sikh Way: A Pilgrim's Progress*, Guelph 2001.

Singh, Indera P., 'A Sikh Village', in Milton Singer (ed.), *Traditional India: Structure and Change*, Philadelphia 1959, pp. 273-97.

Singh, Jagjit, 'The Caste System and the Sikhs', in Jasbir Singh Mann and Harbans Singh Saraon (eds.), *Advanced Studies in Sikhism*, Chandigarh 1989, pp. 278-300.

Singh, Joginder, 'Resurgence in Sikh Journalism: Early Decades of the 20th Century', *Journal of Regional History*, Annual Number, 1982, pp. 99-116.

Singh, Khushwant, *A History of the Sikhs*, vols. I-II, New Delhi reprint, 1997.

———, *The Fall of the Kingdom of the Punjab*, New Delhi reprint, 1971.

Singh, Makhan (ed.), *Sikh Heritage in Paintings*, New Delhi 1995.

Singh, Mohinder, *The Akali Movement*, New Delhi 1978.

——— (ed.), *The Sikhs: Forms and Symbols*, New Delhi 2000.

Singh, Nikky-Guninder Kaur, *The Faminine Principle in the Sikh Vision of The Transcendent*, Cambridge 1993.

Singh, Nripinder, *The Sikh Moral Tradition*, New Delhi 1990.

Singh, Pashaura, *The Guru Granth Sahib: Canon, Meaning and Authority*, New Delhi 2000.

Singh, Pashaura and Barrier, N. Gerald (eds.), *Sikh Identity: Continuity and Change*, New Delhi 1999.

Singh, Puran, 'The Sikh and His New Critics: Our Viewpoint', *Puran Singh Studies*, January-April 1981, pp. 26-39.

Singh, Sangat, *The Sikhs in History*, New Delhi 1996.

Singh, Sukhdial, *Historical Analysis of Giani Gian Singh's Writings*, Jalandhar 1996.

Singh, Sulakhan, *Heterodoxy in the Sikh Tradition*, Jalandhar 1999.

Singh, Trilochan, *Guru Tegh Bahadur: Prophet and Martyr*, Delhi 1967.

Sinha, Narendra Krishna, *Rise of the Sikh Power*, Calcutta reprint, 1960.

———, *Ranjit Singh*, Calcutta reprint, 1975.

Southgate, Minoo S., 'Potrait of Alexander in Persian Alexander—Romances of the Islamic Era', *Journal of the American Oriental Society*, July-September 1979, pp. 278-84.

Talib, Gurbachan Singh, *Selections from the Holy Granth*, Delhi 1975.

Talwar, Bhagat Ram, *The Talwars of Pathan Land and Subhas Chandra's Great Escape*, New Delhi 1976.

Tripathi, Amales, *The Extremist Challenge—India between 1890 and 1910*, Calcutta 1967.

Tuteja, K.L., *Sikh Politics 1920-40*, Kurukshetra 1984.

———, 'Hindu Consciousness, Communalism and the Congress in Pre-Partition Punjab', Presidential Address, Modern Section, Fifty-eighth Session, *Indian History Congress*, Bangalore 1997.

Wilson, H.H., *Essays and Lectures on the Religious Sects of the Hindus*, London 1868.

Index